Models of Teaching

For my husband, Andrew, and our daughter, Joanna—my finest teachers.
Jeanine M. Dell'Olio

For Theresa—my wife and the true love of my life;
For Kelsey and Keenan—my children and my inspiration;
My deepest thanks and unceasing devotion.
Tony Donk

Models of Teaching

Connecting Student Learning With Standards

Jeanine M. Dell'Olio
Hope College

Tony Donk
Hope College

SAGE Publications
Thousand Oaks ■ London ■ New Delhi

For information:

Sage Publications, Inc.
2455 Teller Road
Thousand Oaks, California 91320
E-mail: order@sagepub.com

Sage Publications Ltd.
1 Oliver's Yard
55 City Road
London EC1Y 1SP
United Kingdom

Sage Publications India Pvt. Ltd.
B-42, Panchsheel Enclave
Post Box 4109
New Delhi 110 017 India

Printed in the United States of America

Library of Congress Cataloging-in-Publication Data

Dell'Olio, Jeanine M.
Models of teaching : connecting student learning with standards / Jeanine M. Dell'Olio, Tony Donk.
    p. cm.
Includes bibliographical references and index.
ISBN-13: 978-1-4129-1810-7 (pbk.)
1. Education—Standards. 2. Teaching—Methodology. I. Donk, Tony. II. Title.

LB3060.82.D45 2007
379.1'58—dc22   2006026253

This book is printed on acid-free paper.

07   08   09   10   11   10   9   8   7   6   5   4   3   2   1

Acquisitions Editor:	Diane McDaniel
Associate Editor	Elise Smith
Editorial Assistant:	Ashley Plummer
Production Editor:	Libby Larson
Copy Editor:	Bonnie Freeman
Typesetter:	C&M Digitals (P) Ltd.
Proofreader:	Caryne Brown
Indexer:	Maria Sosnowski
Cover Designer:	Brian Fishman
Marketing Manager:	Nichole Angress

Brief Contents

Detailed Contents

Preface

The No Child Left Behind Act of 2001 has changed the landscape of teacher education. Teachers are entering the profession in an age of accountability unlike any seen in the last several decades. High stakes testing is now the norm throughout the country. In response to this federal initiative, most states are organizing their curriculum using content standards and benchmarks in core academic subjects, and some are using state-developed or national standards for the arts, technology, and physical education as well. Many teacher education programs use state or professional society benchmarks as the point of departure for their students' lesson plans and unit assignments. We believe that beginning teachers should have a thorough understanding of the articulation of the curriculum and that we as a nation should have a firm grasp of what our elementary and secondary students know and are able to do. However, all reform movements have unforeseen consequences. Our concern is that in this move toward frequent standardized testing, educators will become overly reliant on traditional methods of teaching at the expense of providing learning experiences that develop students' critical and creative thinking.

Over the past 25 years, classroom teachers have seen the positive effects of using the multiple intelligences in instruction and assessment; furthermore, current brain research supports the value of learning experiences that promote divergent thinking, and common sense alone tells us that students need variety in the classroom. The purpose of this text is to introduce 10 classic and contemporary models of teaching that can address content standards and benchmarks and also provide interesting, meaningful, and intellectually stimulating learning experiences for PK–12 students. In addition to presenting each model, we will analyze each one as it relates to philosophies of curriculum and instruction, research on teaching, learning theories, technology in the classroom, and typical content standards and benchmarks. This text treats each of these topics in both conceptual and practical ways. Our goal is that you will have a multidimensional experience with each model of teaching presented in the text.

Organization of the Text

Part 1: What We Teach and Why

Part 1 of this text introduces the structure of content standards and benchmarks and illustrates the types of knowledge they include. State standards are examined, as well as national standards developed by the professional societies.

We also introduce Eisner and Vallance's five philosophies of curriculum and instruction in Part 1. We have used Eisner and Vallance's philosophies as described in *Conflicting Conceptions of Curriculum* (1974)—academic rationalism,

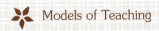

cognitive processing, curriculum as technology, self-actualization, and social reconstructionism—because we believe they provide an accessible framework for teachers. These five philosophies represent a wide range of educational beliefs, commitments, and practices.

Familiarity with these five philosophies will help promote your deliberation as you assess students' needs, plan for instruction, analyze and evaluate student learning, and later reflect on your own performance. The five philosophies will provide professional milestones against which you can analyze the changes in your own perspectives over time. Although you are a beginning teacher, it is not too early for you to begin exploring your assumptions about students, perspectives on curriculum, and beliefs about instruction. It is essential that you learn to analyze the professional practice of other teachers with curiosity and a willingness to learn without passing judgment.

Part 1 also provides an overview of both the formative and the summative assessment process and discusses how to incorporate student self-assessment in classrooms. Given the important role of assessment in guiding teaching and learning episodes, we have discussed it in the first part of this text to frame our discussion of the models of teaching. Other texts often deal with assessment as an ending point. We believe it is a starting point, as well as a feature of instruction that guides all classroom teaching and learning.

The three chapters in Part 1 establish both themes that will reappear throughout the text and scaffolding that will support your assimilation and accommodation of new concepts and perspectives.

Part 2: The Models of Teaching

Chapters 4 through 13 present 10 classic and contemporary models of teaching that can be implemented across the curriculum and across grade levels:

- Direct Instruction
- Concept Attainment
- The Inductive Model
- Reciprocal Teaching
- Question-Answer Relationship
- Jigsaw (in the context of cooperative learning structures)
- Role Playing
- Inquiry-Based Learning
- Synectics
- Advance Organizers

The steps or stages in each of these models help structure learning experiences designed to foster particular intellectual or social goals, but they are not inflexible. One major point we make in the text is that when teachers use the models of teaching, they should not let the models use *them*. The intention of this book is not to be prescriptive but rather to support your creativity as you design learning experiences. The ability to adapt a model of teaching to address student needs is essential for professional educators. This is especially true as teachers try to meet the varied demands of state benchmarks and the expectations of federal initiatives. Throughout the text, you will be reminded that professional teachers are deliberative in their planning (they think carefully about the choices they make) and reflective in their practice (they continually analyze the effects of those choices).

Our discussion of the models of teaching begins with Direct Instruction. We believe that as beginning teachers, you will have a deeper understanding and appreciation of models of teaching based on constructivist learning theory if you first understand the structure and strengths of traditional instruction based on behaviorist learning theory. We then discuss a variety of models that represent different roles for teachers and students (i.e., learner-centered instruction, etc.). One concern in methods courses is that many students do not observe in their field placements the variety of models of teaching that they are taught in class. We have developed two detailed case studies that provide you with an authentic experience of each model at the elementary and secondary levels.

The most difficult challenge facing teacher educators today is helping their students think like teachers, or in other words, helping them learn *from* their own teaching. This text will scaffold your preparation for instruction and post-lesson reflection. The various sections of the chapters about the models will help focus class discussions in several areas. When appropriate, case studies begin by describing how teachers have set up their classrooms prior to their lessons. The post-lesson reflections on each case study will provide opportunities for you to hear how veteran teachers analyze their practice. The observations these teachers make about their lessons will provide support for your analysis of your own teaching. You and your instructors may find that you analyze the progress of the case study lessons differently and identify alternate interpretations, follow-up lessons, or activities. We encourage this exploration.

The first case study and post-lesson reflection in each chapter in Part 2 are followed by a concise yet comprehensive explanation of the structure of each model of teaching. When appropriate, these sections begin with a discussion of special preparations needed for lessons that use the model. In some cases, a brief description of assessment applications follows. The second case study and post-lesson reflection provide a view of each model as it unfolds in a different subject and grade level. One of our goals in developing this text was to make each model accessible to you on the first reading. Toward this end, we have used a conversational tone throughout.

In the latter part of each of these chapters, we connect the teaching model with technology applications. In some cases, the model of teaching is used directly with technology, such as Inquiry-Based Learning with research via the Internet. In other cases, technology connections are described as follow-up lessons. Every model-curriculum-technology connection is presented in the context of the *National Educational Technology Standards for Students* (International Society for Technology in Education, 2000).

We have provided a brief summary of the background of each model, including pertinent information about its research base. While some of the models, such as Direct Instruction and Jigsaw, have been the subject of numerous studies over the years, others, such as the Inductive Model, have attracted far less educational

research. Regardless of their research base, we believe the value of the models chosen will be evident in their case studies and post-lesson reflections.

Each model is also related briefly to learning theories. Our assumption is that by the time you study curriculum and methods, you will have had a course in educational psychology. The discussion of curriculum and instruction relates each model of teaching to one or more of Eisner and Vallance's five categories. We have discussed each model as we interpret its relationship to theory and philosophy, but we realize that you and your instructors may view these connections somewhat differently. We see these differences as a valuable opportunity for in-class discussion or reflective essays.

The "Why Choose . . . ?" section provides questions that we hope will assist you in identifying when a particular model of teaching might be appropriate for your students. We have written the questions in these sections with reference to considerations of content or critical thinking skills. Our questions ask you to think carefully, not only about specific requirements of lessons or units but also about the cognitive or affective needs of your students.

The final section, "Putting It Together," provides exercises that ask you to apply your understanding of each model in a practical, classroom-based way. A good number of these exercises relate to the content standards and benchmarks in your state.

While specific content standards and benchmarks may differ somewhat from state to state, their substance and organization are likely to reveal more similarities than significant differences. For the purpose of consistency, we chose to quote the *Michigan Curriculum Framework* (Michigan Department of Education, 1996). We are assuming that your instructors will use the standards, benchmarks, and possibly grade-level expectations from your state. Differences between your standards and Michigan's may also inspire valuable class discussions.

Part 3: Developing Curriculum That Addresses Content Standards

Part 3 provides a working definition of curriculum development that can be used as a template for developing original instructional units:

> Curriculum development addresses what should be taught; to whom; when; organized in what fashion; using what strategies; what personnel; what resources; which assessments and evaluations; and includes a professional, student-centered rationale for each decision. (Passow, 1987, adapted by Dell'Olio, 1995)

Chapter 14 outlines this process for both single-subject and interdisciplinary curriculum design.

As part of its focus on curriculum development, Part 3 addresses the need for general education teachers to modify instruction for special-needs students. This section provides a perspective on classroom teachers' responsibilities and describes the process of collaborating with special educators. It also offers you a number of suggestions for modifying instruction for learning disabled students and modifying teacher language for native English speakers, techniques for working with English language learners, and ways of enriching the curriculum for gifted students.

We know that mastering different models of teaching will require a great deal of practice and patience—with yourself and with your students. As you explore these models throughout your career, you will continue to discover innovative ways to apply them across the curriculum.

Instructor's Resources CD

This CD offers the instructor a variety of resources that supplement the book material, including PowerPoint® lecture slides, Teaching Guide for the Standards-Based Lesson Plan Project, Teaching Guide for the Case Studies, Web resources, and more. Also included is a Test Bank, which consists of 20–30 multiple-choice questions with answers and page references, 10–15 true/false questions, as well as 10–15 short answer and 5–10 essay questions for each chapter. An electronic Test Bank is also available so that instructors can create, deliver, and customize tests and study guides using Brownstone's Diploma test bank software.

Web-Based Student Study Site

www.sagepub.com/delloliostudy

This Web-based student study site provides a variety of additional resources to enhance students' understanding of the book content and take their learning one step further. The site includes comprehensive study materials such as chapter objectives, flash cards, practice tests, and more. Also included are special features, such as the links to standards from U.S. States and associated activities, Learning from Journal Articles, Field Experience worksheets, Learning from Case Studies, and PRAXIS resources.

References

Eisner, E., & Vallance, E. (Eds.). (1974). *Conflicting conceptions of curriculum.* San Francisco: McCutchan.

International Society for Technology in Education. (2000). *National educational technology standards for students: Connecting curriculum and technology.* Washington DC: Author in collaboration with the U.S. Department of Education.

Michigan Department of Education. (1996). *Michigan curriculum framework.* Lansing: Author.

No Child Left Behind Act of 2001, Conference Report to Accompany H. R. 1, Report No. 107–334, House of Representatives, 107th Congress, 1st Session.

Passow, H. Class notes, fall 1987, Teachers College, Columbia University. Modified by J. M. Dell/Olio, fall 1995.

Acknowledgments

Our reviewers provided us with sustained support and thorough and relevant suggestions for strengthening each chapter of this text, and to them we are very grateful. The reviewers included Margaret Ferrara, University of Nevada at Reno; Kent Freeland, Morehead State University; D. John McIntyre, Southern Illinois University, Carbondale; Amany Saleh, Arkansas State University; and Marsha Zenanko, Jacksonville State University.

We would particularly like to thank Diane McDaniel at Sage for shepherding us through the writing, revising, and publication process of this text. Her interest and genuine enthusiasm for our work were edifying and very much appreciated. We are also grateful to Erica Carroll for her encouragement and unwavering attention to detail. We only wish we had her organizational skills.

part

What We Teach and Why

Part 1 will provide the framework for understanding the 10 models of teaching presented in this book. Concepts introduced in Part 1 will be discussed in Part 2 in the context of each model of teaching. Chapter 1 explains the standards-based reform movement and describes its effect on education in America. It also defines content standards and benchmarks, describes how they are developed, and illustrates the types of knowledge they include. In Chapter 2, you will be introduced to five distinct philosophies of curriculum and instruction. Each of these five philosophies answers the question What is the purpose of schools? in a different way. You may find your own beliefs about teaching and learning reflected in one or more of these five philosophies. Your personal philosophy of curriculum and instruction will become apparent in how you choose to address content standards

and benchmarks in your own classroom. Chapter 3 will provide an overview of current assessment practices—ways that teachers can see whether their students have understood the material required in the standards and benchmarks set for their grade levels.

Concepts introduced in Part 1 are essential to your understanding of the models of teaching presented in Part 2 and the process described in Part 3 for developing curriculum using content standards and benchmarks.

chapter 1

Working With Standards and Benchmarks

Perhaps the biggest question facing novice and veteran teachers alike is, What will I teach? After securing a new teaching position or shifting to a new grade level, all teachers must consider what content their students need to know, which skills they must develop, and at what level of proficiency they must be able to demonstrate those skills. For the high school biology teacher, the answer may seem obvious. However, on further examination, it becomes clear that the discipline of biology is deep and broad. The tenth-grade biology teacher must consider what students already know and at what level they can demonstrate their understandings and skills. Likewise, a kindergarten teacher needs to know what students bring to each teaching and learning situation across a broad spectrum of subjects and skills, as well as the levels and competencies that need to be targeted. These concerns have always loomed large in the daily work of teachers, and they continue to do so today as teachers, administrators, and others in the field of education look for guidance in implementing standards-based education.

To illustrate the issues and questions raised above, I (T. D.) will share an experience in my own early history as an educator. I was teaching fourth grade in my first elementary school setting. I did what many of my colleagues did: I used the textbooks adopted by the district to guide my instruction. I also reviewed the district report card so that I would know what categories and levels of performance needed to be reported to parents and students. After several days of poring over these documents, I was relatively satisfied that I understood the goals and aims for fourth-grade students in my school district. I then set my sights on what seemed to be the next logical step: deciding how to create learning experiences that would match my understanding of this curriculum. All seemed to be going relatively well until the day my fourth-grade teaching partner poked her head through the classroom door and asked me how our "bird projects" were coming since a local 4-H judge was scheduled to come in and rate them in a couple of weeks! After determining that her comments weren't the product of a cruel sense of humor, I began asking several questions: "What project?" "What judge?" "Is this required?" "Is it in the textbook for science?" After some time (and moments of panic) I discovered that students were to study local bird populations and build birdhouses as an annual project to be evaluated by a local 4-H official. The project was not listed in the textbook or even on the report card, but it was a requirement for all fourth-grade students. It seems that no one had remembered to tell me about it. My class did ultimately study the local bird population, and we managed to put together several birdhouses in assembly-line fashion, but I spent much of the rest of the year wondering what other content I was expected to cover that hadn't been fully explained to me.

As my story illustrates, new teachers and those new to a subject or grade level need guidance in determining what students need to know and be able to do, as well as expectations for proficiency levels. While teachers must also have models for how to develop appropriate teaching and learning opportunities, knowing what to teach and when are the essential first steps in the process. Teachers just entering the field, as well as those moving within a system, stand to benefit from the last several years of work in standards-based reform in education. In short, this major reform effort has sought to articulate what students need to know and be able to do in several disciplines and at all grade levels. In this chapter, we begin with a historical look at the roots of this movement and its current status and implications for classroom teachers. We will also discuss the types of standards and the terminology that have evolved from the movement and the ways they can serve as guideposts for classroom teachers considering both what to teach and how to promote levels of proficiency among their students. Along the way, we will also explore some of the issues raised about the development and use of various types of standards to guide instruction and assessment. Our goal in this chapter is not to teach you how to develop standards. Rather, our intention is to help you better understand where they come from and how you can and may be expected to use them in your work with students. Once you understand how to use standards and benchmarks to determine what to teach, the remainder of this book will help you determine models that best meet those teaching and learning goals.

The Standards-Based Reform Movement

While the call for higher standards and measures for accountability has a long history in American schooling, the current **standards-based reform movement** is a relatively young tradition. The release of the report *A Nation at Risk* in 1983 is often cited as the beginning of the movement (Kendall & Marzano, 2000, p. 1). This report denounced the state of education in the United States and called for major reforms. A variety of sources—governmental agencies, business groups, professional organizations focused on education, and schools—responded. In short, although sometimes wary of the substance and form of change, nearly all players seemed to agree that reforms designed to raise standards and accountability in the K–12 system of schools were necessary.

In their short outline of the history of the standards-based reform movement, Kendall and Marzano (2000) note several important events that led to the current standards and accountability system that governs schooling in the United States. Shortly after the report was issued, the National Council of Teachers of Mathematics (NCTM) began writing *Curriculum and Evaluation Standards for School Mathematics* (Kendall & Marzano, 2000, p. 2). This document represented an early attempt by a subject-centered professional organization to outline how the discipline of mathematics should be divided, as well as standards for those who teach mathematics at all levels of the K–12 system. The NCTM was among the first organizations to provide such a framework, and many other national professional organizations have followed suit in the past several years.

Another set of milestones noted by Kendall and Marzano (2000) included the meeting of President George H. W. Bush and the governors of all 50 states in Charlottesville, Virginia, in 1989. The result of that meeting was a call for new standards in five subjects covered in all schools: mathematics, history, geography, science, and English. In addition, the first President Bush used his 1990 State of the Union address to outline "National Goals for the Year 2000." This set of goals was further promoted when Congress established the National Education Goals Panel. At nearly the same time, the secretary of labor established the Secretary's Commission on Achieving Necessary Skills to consider the kinds of skills students would need to

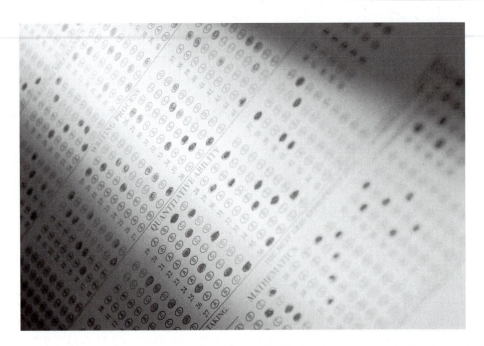

The standards-based reform movement has promoted high levels of accountability that include state-mandated assessments for K–12 students.

develop to ultimately and successfully enter the workforce. These efforts were advanced again when President Clinton signed the Goals 2000: Educate America First Act. This law called for standards at the national and state levels, as well as state assessment tools. It also added economics, civics, government, the arts, and foreign language to the list of subjects to be covered by standards (Kendall & Marzano, pp. 2–3).

In addition to the work being done at the national level, some states began to develop curriculum frameworks that outlined standards for school subjects taught within a state. Most notably, the state of California began in 1983 to develop a framework and set of content standards to be used in its public schools. President Clinton used his State of the Union address in 1997 to urge all states to not only develop high standards for all students but also establish a set of assessments for measuring reading proficiency in the fourth grade and mathematics proficiency in the eighth grade (Kendall & Marzano, 2000, pp. 2–5). By 1990, most states had adopted assessments to measure student achievement in a variety of subjects (Montgomery, Ranney, & Growe, 2003).

The convergence of efforts by national professional organizations, state educational agencies, business, and national governmental bodies is most recently reflected in the reauthorization of the **Elementary and Secondary Education Act**, commonly referred to as the **No Child Left Behind Act of 2001**. This act calls on each state to set standards for what all students "should know and learn" and to measure their achievement on an annual basis (No Child Left Behind Act of 2001 [Glossary]).

The No Child Left Behind Act places heavy emphasis on assessment of student achievement. Under *assessment*, the glossary for the No Child Left Behind Act states that

> Under *No Child Left Behind*, tests are aligned with academic standards. Beginning in the 2002–03 school year, schools must administer tests in each of three grade spans: grades 3–5, grades 6–9, and grades 10–12 in all schools. Beginning in the 2005–06 school year, tests must be administered every year in grades 3 through 8 in math and reading. Beginning in the 2007–08 school year, science achievement must also be tested.

The act also calls for publication of the results on an annual basis and **adequate yearly progress (AYP)**, which is defined as "An individual state's measure of yearly progress toward achieving state academic standards. 'Adequate Yearly Progress' is the minimum level of improvement that states, school districts and schools must achieve each year" (No Child Left Behind Act of 2001). Schools that do not make AYP can be sanctioned in a variety of ways.

In a relatively short span of time, standards-based reform has essentially become law (Resnick, Rothman, Slattery, & Vranek, 2004), and it has drawn both supporters and critics. While some oppose the mandates of *No Child Left Behind*, others embrace this act as a much needed reform of U.S. schools to both establish standards and ensure accountability at all levels. Our goal here is not to take a political stand on the legislation itself but rather to briefly examine some of the potential merits and limitations of the standards-based reform movement in general.

Proponents of the standards-based movement often argue that the development of standards makes the material to be learned and the level of proficiency to be attained transparent for all. Teachers are told what to teach but are free to select models of teaching that best allow them to meet the standards. In addition, clearly articulated standards allow parents and students to see the goals of schooling and measure progress toward those goals in various content areas. Proponents further argue that the increased accountability of testing based on the standards provides a feedback loop for teachers so that improvements can be made to curriculum and instruction. Others contend that clearly articulated standards will provide an opportunity to close the gap in educational achievement for traditionally marginalized students: poor and minority students (Cavazos, 2002; Riley, 2002; Paige, 2002; Cohen, 1996; Darling-Hammond, 1997; Ogawa, et al., 2003; all cited in Kirschner, 2004).

Critics of the standards-based movement have often worried about the tension between federal, state, and local control of schools. Some worry that state or national standards will, for all intents and purposes, eliminate the local control over school curriculums that has historically been the rule in this country. Others have worried that the high-stakes and mandated tests might not be well aligned with standards and curriculum, putting students at a disadvantage. Still others have concerns that weighty emphasis on a system of accountability that relies heavily on such testing may put poor and minority students at a disadvantage, given that these groups often do not fair well with such tools (Resnick et al., 2004).

While proponents and critics of the standards-based reform movement may each have valid points, only further research on the results of the movement and its elements can either support or eliminate their concerns. In the meantime, we believe that standards can and do allow all players in the educational system an opportunity to articulate and understand what it is that students need to know and be able to do. Standards, in and of themselves, need not prescribe what teachers must do to help students learn—although some believe that they should. All the models outlined in this text can be used by classroom teachers to reach the standards and benchmarks set for student learning. We believe that teachers should make professional choices about which models will help them, and more specifically their students, reach the standards that are set out for them.

One major issue with the use of standards must be addressed if standards are to be useful for the classroom teacher. Standards are developed at the state level, often-times on the basis of a variety of professional organizations' documents, and because no uniform system exists for articulating standards and benchmarks, their terminology may become a source of confusion.

In the section that follows, we will address standards and benchmarks, clarifying terms and demonstrating the use of each. We will also address a variety of issues that arise when standards are used to guide teaching and learning. Most teachers will be consumers, rather than developers, of standards and benchmarks as they determine which models of teaching and pedagogy to use to meet appropriate standards. Our goal is to help you become a well-informed consumer who can navigate the sometimes tricky waters of understanding content standards and benchmarks, as well as using them in the classroom.

State and Local Standards

Due in part to the requirements of the No Child Left Behind Act, each state has developed or reorganized a state-based **curriculum framework**. This document is designed to assist local districts and schools in aligning their own curriculums and assessments with state requirements (Kendall, Ryan, & Richardson, 2005). State-mandated proficiency tests are based on the contents of these documents, which typically consist of content standards and benchmarks for each subject taught in schools. In most districts, a curriculum director is designated to understand these documents and monitor them for periodic revisions. The curriculum director or a designated group within a local district often has the responsibility for ensuring that the local curriculum and assessment tools are aligned with the framework. Often teachers are part of this group and assist the curriculum director in selecting textbooks and other instructional materials for use in the local schools. This process may vary from one location to another as some states make textbook selections at the state level. It will be helpful to ask about the particulars of this process in your local school district.

As mentioned above, because states are charged with developing their own curriculum framework, there are variations in both the structures and terminology used (Neuman & Roskos, 2005). For example, some states list content standards and then provide benchmarks for a range of grades, such as kindergarten through second grade, while other states list benchmarks for each grade level. However, because of the requirement to do state-mandated annual assessments of all third- through eighth-grade students, states have begun to move toward a grade-level structure for most benchmarks as these provide a better guide for what will be assessed at each grade.

The terminology used in state curriculum frameworks continues to be a source of confusion. It is not uncommon to see the same level of standards described differently from state to state. For example, while some states use the term *content standard*, others use the term *goal*. In this chapter we will use the terms *content standard*, *benchmark*, *strand*, *performance standard*, and *lifelong-learning standard* to describe the contents of a curriculum framework developed at the state level, but we will also provide alternative terminology so that you can see how the level and type of standard being described matches that in your own location.

Content Standards

Over the last several years, as **content standards** have been developed, their form and substance have evolved, but their primary function has remained to divide a discipline into manageable parts. Kendall, Ryan, and Richardson (2005) provide a useful and current definition:

> A content standard is a description of what students should know and/or be able to do within a particular discipline. Content standards primarily serve to organize an academic subject domain through a manageable number (from 5–12) of generally stated goals for student learning. These statements help to clarify the broad goals within the discipline and provide a means for readers to navigate the standards documents when searching for specific content. (p. 1)

In some state curriculum frameworks, this same (or a very similar) level of organization may be referred to as a *goal, expectation*, or *learning result* (Kendall, Ryan, & Richardson, 2005, p. 2). To determine the label used in your location, refer to your own location's documents, which can usually be accessed through the Web site for your state's department of education.

For purposes of illustration, we have selected content standards listed in *Content Knowledge: A Compendium of Standards and Benchmarks for K–12 Education* (Kendall & Marzano, 2000) to show the structure of content standards that may be found in a typical state curriculum framework. For language arts, content standards might look like the following examples:

> Uses the general skills and strategies of the writing process. (p. 321)

> Gathers and uses information for research purposes. (p. 334)

Here are some examples of content standards for mathematics:

Uses a variety of strategies in the problem-solving process. (p. 47)

Understands and applies basic and advanced properties of the concept of geometry. (p. 56)

Each of the examples addresses a major segment of its subject and describes what students should know and be able to do. As is typical, these examples were developed on the basis of the divisions and standards articulated by organizations that represent current research and understanding of the subject. For example, the mathematics standards were based on work done by the NCTM, which illustrates another important aspect of content standards developed for state curriculum frameworks: They must incorporate current research and understanding in each subject area. Often, this research and understanding can be found in the standards developed by professional organizations that monitor, promote, guide, and conduct research on best practice in classroom settings.

Content standards are not designed to provide specific guidance at the classroom level. Rather, they are general statements with a broad level of specificity about the kinds of knowledge that can and should be promoted within each subject area. Kendall and Marzano (1995) classify knowledge into three types: procedural, declarative, and contextual. A brief examination of these types sheds light on how standards in general are developed, as well as how they are used specifically in the construction of content standards.

When content involves **procedural knowledge**, it often begins with "verbs, such as 'uses,' 'solves,' and 'predicts'" (Kendall & Marzano, 2000, p. 24). Procedural knowledge describes "skills and processes important to a given content area" (Kendall & Marzano, 1995, p. 11). Many school subjects include specific skills and processes that students must master in order to fully understand and use the content of the subject. For example, in mathematics it is important to be able to use a protractor to measure angles. In the language arts, a thesaurus may be needed to develop a written text. Such key words as *uses*, *solves*, and *predicts* can often help you determine when a standard is targeting procedural knowledge.

Oftentimes content is described as **declarative knowledge**. These types of standards frequently contain such phrases as "'understands that . . .' or 'knows that . . .'" (Kendall & Marzano, 2000, p. 24). Declarative knowledge can be thought of as knowledge "composed of the information important to a given content area" (Kendall & Marzano, 1995, p. 12). If you are teaching a high school anatomy course, it may be important for your students to know the names of the bones in the human body. If you are teaching a middle school English class, you may want your students to know the names for the various parts of speech, such as nouns, verbs, and adjectives. These examples illustrate information judged to be important to a full understanding of a subject.

Finally, content can also be described as **contextual knowledge**. This type of understanding includes "information and/or skills that have particular meaning because of the conditions that form part of their description" (Kendall & Marzano, 1995, p. 12). As its name implies, this type of knowledge is dependent on context. For example, knowing how to cut and paste paper involves procedural knowledge in the use of a pair of scissors and application of glue, but doing so in the context of creating a mosaic requires contextual knowledge. As a result, standards written to reflect the use of contextual knowledge also have language and phrasing that distinguish them. As explained by Kendall and Marzano, "Content that is contextual in nature also begins with verbs or verb phrases, but tends to look more like activities in that a particular skill is described in terms of the information or knowledge about or upon which the skill is applied" (2000, p. 24).

Although procedural, declarative, and contextual knowledge are reflected in content standards, this level of specificity is more commonly relegated to benchmarks (to be discussed in the next section). However, the development and articulation of content standards do reflect these three types of knowledge on a broad level, and an understanding of them is necessary for understanding the important functions and nature of content standards.

While content standards help educators see the various domains of a subject they are teaching, as well as the types of knowledge required to fully comprehend that subject, these standards can also be misused. The Council for Basic Education (1998) has listed and discussed a number of ways that standards can be misunderstood. We will address three of them here, using and expanding on the ideas the Council has articulated.

1. "Content standards determine the curriculum" (p. 4).

Local schools use content standards to determine their own curriculum. In most school districts, the curriculum director and teachers interpret the standards and then make decisions about pedagogy, assessment, and support materials, such as textbooks and other needed supplies. Content standards help local districts see the kind of coverage that is needed for each subject and what will likely be included on state-mandated assessments, but they do not dictate the nature or form of instruction. It is the responsibility of educators at the local level to make these determinations. Content standards are part of the curriculum framework. They are not intended to control how teachers reach learning goals and objectives.

2. "Content standards automatically exclude local content" (p. 6).

As part of a state curriculum framework, content standards outline the essentials of the content to be covered at local levels throughout the state. This does not preclude additions of local interest. For example, local historical events can easily be added to a curriculum even when they are not specifically attached to a content standard. Sometimes this can occur by using a specific event as an example and in this way connecting it to a content standard. At other times, the event may simply be viewed as an enrichment that is not specifically covered in the standards but is worthy of recognition due to its local significance. In any case, the content standards are meant to guide, not to constrain curriculum choices.

3. "Content standards by themselves will improve the system" (p. 6).

Content standards have true value only if they are used. When content standards reflect current research, theory, and best practice models, they can serve as important instruments. However, if they are neither understood nor used to guide curriculum choices, they are of little worth. As a result of the No Child Left Behind Act, few districts can afford to ignore their state's content standards because these standards are aligned with the mandated assessments of their students. Given the high-stakes nature of these assessment tools, attention to the standards is nearly assured. However, valuing the standards remains a decision to be made at the local level.

When viewed correctly, content standards provide general statements of what students should know and be able to do within specific school subjects. While they provide guidance at the local level, they do not contain the kind of specificity most teachers require for shaping classroom-based instructional decisions. Curriculum frameworks typically include a second level of standards to serve this function. These are often called benchmarks.

Benchmarks

Benchmarks help provide a more detailed understanding of content standards in state curriculum frameworks. They can be most easily thought of as components of a standard. As described by Yates (2004), a **benchmark** is "a specific statement of what all students should know and be able to do at a specified time in their schooling. Benchmarks are used to measure a student's progress toward meeting the standard" (p. 13). A set of benchmarks will typically help teachers structure learning goals and objectives for classroom-based instruction and will show teachers when students will be assessed on detailed components of a content standard.

Again, because curriculum frameworks are structured and worded at the state level, some of the terminology used to describe what we are calling benchmarks varies. Some documents refer to them as *indicators*, *learning expectations*, or *performance standards*—a term we will use differently in the next section of this chapter (Kendall, Ryan, & Richardson, 2005). Another potential source of confusion is the **grade level indicators** often attached to benchmarks in state documents, as well as in documents produced by some national organizations. As noted earlier in this chapter, in some of these documents, benchmarks are listed by grade ranges, such as elementary, later elementary, middle school, and high school. In other documents, benchmarks are listed by specific grade ranges: K–3, 4–6, 7–9, and 10–12. These ranges have been interpreted as a kind of time frame within which specific benchmarks need to be covered and mastered. However, with the mandated assessment component of the No Child Left Behind Act, which requires annual testing of students in

Grades 3–8, some states have moved to setting benchmarks for each grade rather than for a range of grades, which makes the targeting of instruction toward specific benchmarks more focused for each grade level.

For individual grades or a range of grades, benchmarks are designed to provide a breakdown of content standards into the more specific components of a subject. A few examples from *Content Knowledge: A Compendium of Standards and Benchmarks for K–12 Education* (Kendall & Marzano, 2000) illustrate the typical form and function of benchmarks. Content standards are followed by a sampling of appropriate benchmarks to illustrate how they represent a breakdown of the standard:

Content Standard: Uses the general skills and strategies of the writing process

Benchmarks:

1. Prewriting: Uses prewriting strategies to plan written work (e.g., discusses ideas with peers, draws pictures to generate ideas, writes key thoughts and questions, rehearses ideas, records reactions and observations) [Grades K–2]

2. Drafting and Revising: Uses strategies to draft and revise written work (e.g., rereads; rearranges words, sentences, and paragraphs to improve sequence to clarify meaning; varies sentence type; adds descriptive words and details; deletes extraneous information; incorporates suggestions from peers and teachers; sharpens the focus) [Grades K–2] (Kendall & Marzano, 2000, p. 321)

Content Standard: Uses a variety of strategies in the problem-solving process

1. Understands how to break a complex problem into simpler parts or use a similar problem type to solve a problem [Grades 6–8]

2. Understands that there is no one right way to solve mathematical problems but that different methods (e.g., working backward from a solution, using a similar problem type, identifying a pattern) have different advantages and disadvantages [Grades 6–8] (Kendall & Marzano, 2000, pp. 47–48)

It is important to note in these example benchmarks that, while they provide a more detailed and grade-range-specific breakdown of the components of the content standard, they are neither too narrow nor too broad. Indeed, this is a characteristic of a well-written benchmark. When benchmarks are written very narrowly, they risk being so specific that they can be accomplished with very little effort, perhaps even in a single lesson. When they are too broad, they may not provide enough specificity for educators who must translate them into a series of classroom-based learning experiences (Kendall, 2001). As described best by Kendall, Ryan, and Richardson (2005), "A benchmark should be specific enough that readers are clear about the instruction and learning it should entail, but not so narrow as to prescribe the day-to-day curriculum" (p. 2). Striking a balance between the narrow and the expansive is an important task for those who construct benchmarks and want them to be both understandable and usable.

A careful examination of the example benchmarks above also reveals the types of knowledge each promotes. For example, "Uses prewriting strategies to plan written work" is a procedural benchmark. Note that it begins with the key verb *uses* and lists skills and processes that are deemed important to the subject of writing: "draw pictures," "rehearse ideas," and so on. The mathematics benchmark "Understands how to break a complex problem into simpler parts or use a similar problem type to solve a problem" calls for contextual knowledge. Students must use their declarative and procedural knowledge to solve a problem that is set in a particular context. Finally, the benchmark "Understands that there is no one right way to solve mathematical problems but that different methods (e.g., working backward from a solution, using a similar problem type, identifying a pattern) have different advantages and disadvantages" calls for declarative knowledge. Note the key phrase *understands that* and how the benchmark describes information particular to the subject of mathematics. As you are beginning to understand the structure of benchmarks, we urge you to consult *Content Knowledge: A Compendium of Standards and Benchmarks for K–12 Education* (Kendall & Marzano, 2000) because it shows how each listed benchmark promotes one of the three types of knowledge. This resource can serve as a rich well of information for novice and experienced educators alike.

Although benchmarks can and do serve as valuable guides for classroom teachers, some caution is needed. When constructed well, a benchmark should be "a grade-appropriate or developmentally appropriate expression of knowledge or skill" (Kendall, 2001, p. 2). However, you must use your professional understanding of your students and their learning needs as a barometer to help you decide when, and even whether, your students are adequately prepared for the content or skills listed in a particular benchmark. Conversely, some students in your classroom will be beyond the benchmarks for your grade level. Consequently, we caution you to avoid using a list of benchmarks to develop sets of teaching and learning experiences without also considering the needs and skill levels of your learners. If students are not yet ready for some designated content or skills, even the best lessons will be in vain. On the other hand, if students have already mastered the content or skills designated for your grade or subject area, you risk boredom—at the very least. As you use benchmarks, bear in mind the words of Kendall (2001), who says that "because there is no definitive work available on what knowledge and skills should be addressed at each and every level, the work of grade placement of content is at best an 'educated guess,' at worst, an arbitrary assignment" (p. 17). Because standards and benchmarks are frequently designed by people with great expertise (and they may even represent a consensus of opinion within the field), they should be given very careful attention as you plan for your students' learning needs, but your own professional skill in determining what your students are and are not ready for is of equal importance.

Although content standards and benchmarks provide a helpful guide for educators at all levels, the sheer volume of some of these documents can make locating needed information laborious. As a result, many state curriculum frameworks include another level of descriptors, often referred to as topics or strands.

Topics or Strands

State curriculum framework documents are typically comprehensive and lengthy. Finding benchmarks or other needed information can become quite a feat—especially when they are listed on Web sites that require the viewer to scroll through several pages of documents. Recently, this became evident to me. In a lesson plan development assignment, I asked my own teacher education students to match their stated lesson objectives with the content standards and benchmarks listed in our state's framework. This task proved to be more difficult than I had imagined, and several students sought me out for assistance. Their frustration revolved around taking a subject, such as the language arts, and wading through several screens of content standards and benchmarks. It became clear to me that I had not done an adequate job of showing them another level of organization used in these documents: topic listings, also called strands.

A **topic** or **strand** can best be described as "a level of content organization that mediates between a standard and a benchmark. Under the geometry standard, for example, topics or strands might include Shapes and Figure, Lines & Angles, or Transformations/Motion Geometry" (Kendall, 2001, p. 3). In short, it may be easiest to think of topics or strands as subtopics used to organize a subject, with groups of benchmarks listed under each subtopic.

I helped my own students see how the subject of the language arts had been divided within the curriculum framework into its major categories: reading, writing, listening, speaking, viewing, and visually representing. Then, for a heading such as reading, several strands or topics were listed, with benchmarks after each one. For example, under a content standard listed in reading were several strands or topics, such as phonemic awareness, word study, narrative text, and informational text. Given this understanding of the organization of the standards document, my students were able to locate relevant benchmarks within specific subtopics rather than wading through all the benchmarks related to all the areas of the language arts. This level of organization is used in most subject listings in curriculum frameworks and can help make those documents far more user friendly.

Topics or strands will help you navigate your state's curriculum framework. Content standards and benchmarks will help you understand the domains of each subject, as well as providing a more detailed breakdown of what your students should know and be able to do at various levels. The question that educators must still address is one of proficiency levels. In short, how good is good enough? To address this issue, we turn next to developing an understanding of performance standards.

As teachers plan for instruction, they must carefully consider the performance standards articulated for each content area.

Performance Standards

Let's pretend for a moment that you are a middle school social studies teacher. You have consulted your district's document on the content to be taught in your course and have carefully designed a curriculum on the history of World War II. In addition, you have strategically aligned your curriculum with the content standards and benchmarks listed in your state's curriculum framework for your grade level. As you prepare to develop teaching and learning opportunities for your students, as well as appropriate assessments, several questions remain unanswered: How proficient will your students need to be with this material, and how will their proficiency be measured on the high-stakes, state-mandated assessment of the material? Will it be enough to plan so that your students will simply know the important dates and events in this period? Or will they need to compare and contrast these events with those surrounding present world events and political tensions? Addressing these questions is part of the role of performance standards.

As described by Yates (2004), "**Performance standards** state the level of mastery or competency at which students should know the standard" (p. 12).

Similarly, Kendall (2001) states that "a performance standard describes the levels of student performance in respect to the knowledge or skill described in a single benchmark or a set of closely related benchmarks. A performance standard might be described by means of a rubric or cut-score, or could even be expressed as a percentage correct of the test items designed to assess students on a particular benchmark" (p. 3). Performance standards articulate both how proficient students must be in relation to content standards and benchmarks and how their proficiency is to be reported.

Performance standards are typically developed using a **taxonomy**. Most familiar to many educators is the original Bloom's taxonomy (Bloom, 1956). It lists six levels of understanding concepts, beginning with knowledge (the lowest level), then comprehension, application, analysis, synthesis, and, at the highest level, evaluation. In many standards documents, performance standards are listed using verbs that match each level, such as list, summarize, apply, analyze, integrate, and assess (Kendall, Ryan, & Richardson, 2005). If your state documents use Bloom's taxonomy, knowing the required levels (and types of proficiency expected) for specific content standards and benchmarks will help you plan instruction. For example, if students need to "apply" information, you will need to move beyond a simple listing of dates and events (returning to our World War II example) and consider how students will need to use that information in other contexts.

Kendall, Ryan, and Richardson (2005) have argued that the hierarchal structure of Bloom's taxonomy does not reflect what is currently known about student learning, and they argue for an alternative taxonomy developed by Marzano.

Of most interest for the purpose of developing performance standards for classroom use . . . is a taxonomy of educational objectives designed by Marzano (2001). This taxonomy is consistent with recent research in cognitive science about the relative difficulty of mental tasks. Marzano notes that, with the complexity of a mental process or skill—such as performing long division—the more familiar one is with a process, the more quickly one executes it and the easier it becomes. Thus, mental processes and skills should not be ordered hierarchically in terms of their complexity. They can, however, be ordered in terms of levels of control—that is, some mental processes exercise control over other processes. (p. 5)

Marzano's taxonomy includes six levels—although Kendall, Ryan, and Richardson (2005) note that only the first four are used with any regularity in standards documents. They further suggest that each of the levels is ranked hierarchically based on levels of control and "the conscious awareness that is required to execute them" (p. 5), rather than a perceived complexity of the tasks themselves. The first four levels of Marzano's taxonomy are presented in Table 1.1.

Given that either Bloom's or Marzano's taxonomy or both may be used in your state's standards documents, we urge you to develop an understanding of the

| Table 1.1 | Marzano's Taxonomy: Levels 1–4 |

Level 1: Retrieval	Level 2: Comprehension	Level 3: Analysis	Level 4: Utilization
Recall	Synthesis	Matching	Decision making
Execution	Representation	Classifying	Problem solving
		Error analysis	Experimental inquiry
		Generalizing	Investigation
		Specifying	

SOURCE: Adapted from: Marzano (2001), in Kendall, Ryan, & Richardson (2005, pp. 6–7).

implications of each and an awareness of which one is used because it may have direct implications for the way you structure teaching and learning opportunities for your students. A more detailed explanation of the Marzano taxonomy can be found in Kendall, Ryan, and Richardson (2005).

As noted earlier, performance standards are often used to report the level of proficiency students have attained for stated standards and benchmarks. This information may also be presented to students' parents and guardians. It may be found on district report cards and the reports of student proficiency on state-mandated assessments. Table 1.2 lists the statements that accompanied the Parent Report on the State of Michigan's annual assessment of fourth graders in English Language Arts and Mathematics.

At several levels, then, performance standards can be helpful to classroom teachers and parents or guardians, as well as others involved in education. For the classroom teacher, performance standards provide assistance in determining the proficiency level at which students must demonstrate their mastery of content described in content standards and benchmarks. Performance standards also aid teachers in understanding how the information must be mastered, whether at the level of comprehension or analysis or some other level of a taxonomy of skills, thus helping teachers prepare appropriate classroom learning activities. Furthermore, the use of proficiency standards in reports on students' progress can supply parents and guardians with helpful information for planning supportive activities.

One more type of standard involves skills and processes that may not be subject specific but are nonetheless important for students to develop. They are often referred to as lifelong-learning standards.

Lifelong-Learning Standards

Some skills and processes are used in a variety of subject areas and even beyond the traditional subjects addressed in schools. For example, being a critical thinker

Table 1.2   Performance Level Descriptors

Level 1: Exceeded standards

The student's performance exceeds proficiency standards and indicates substantial understanding and application of key curriculum concepts defined for Michigan students.

Level 2: Met standards

The student's performance is proficient and indicates sufficient understanding and application of key curriculum concepts defined for Michigan students.

Level 3: Basic

The student's performance is not yet proficient, indicating a partial understanding and application of key curriculum concepts defined for Michigan students.

Level 4: Apprentice

The student's performance is not yet proficient and indicates minimal understanding and application of key curriculum concepts defined for Michigan students.

SOURCE: From the Michigan Educational Assessment Program, *Parent Report,* Fall 2005. Reprinted with permission of the Michigan Department of Education.

can be an important skill in such school subjects as history, reading, writing, or mathematics, but it is not confined to any one of these subjects. As a result, some state curriculum frameworks may have a separate category of standards related to these skills or processes.

Kendall (2001) defines a lifelong-learning standard as "a summary description regarding what students should know and/or be able to do across a variety of disciplines—for example, 'The student applies decision-making techniques'" (p. 4). He goes on to say that "lifelong-learning standards may address self-regulation, the ability to work with others, and critical thinking. Although they are 'content free' in description, this is because they are and can be applied to content across the curriculum" (p. 4).

Lifelong-learning standards may be included in a separate category in your state's curriculum framework. They may also be embedded into each of the subject area content standards and benchmarks. We mention them briefly here to alert you to them so that you can explore how your state has chosen to articulate and assess them.

Finally, as mentioned earlier, states often work closely with national professional organizations as they develop content standards and benchmarks. These organizations often represent researchers, university faculty, and classroom practitioners dedicated to conducting research and exploring theory, as well as learning from and influencing classroom-level instruction in particular subject areas. Although our intent is neither to promote individual organizations nor to provide a high level of detail on them, we believe that an awareness of their role is important as we consider the dynamics of working with content standards and benchmarks.

National Professional Organizations

Early on in the standards-based reform movement, various professional organizations established content standards within their own subject area. Among the first was the NCTM, which began writing content standards for mathematics curriculum and assessment in 1987 (Kendall & Marzano, 2000). In the ensuing years, several other subject-focused groups began writing or revising standards. This process has not been without controversy.

Some professional organizations believed that content standards should be written at a level of abstraction that would allow local interpretation. In short, they believed that specific content should be determined by states and local school districts rather than at the national level. Further complicating this situation, organizations often wrote standards using different formats, some focusing on skills and processes and others using a performance-based approach (Kendall & Marzano, 2000). Other organizations were criticized for producing standards with a political or ideological agenda (Glatthorn, 1998). In an attempt to bring coherence to the diversity of approaches used by these organizations, other groups dedicated their efforts to providing a synthesis of standards and benchmarks, drawing on those developed and used by states and professional organizations. One such example is the work done by the Mid-continent Research for Education and Learning organization.

The standards and benchmarks developed and promoted by various professional and national groups can be of great help to both local administrators and classroom teachers. In Table 1.3, we have supplied the names of many of these organizations and the Web sites that contain their standards documents. We urge you to explore these Web sites (as well as others you may discover) to familiarize yourself with the standards and benchmarks these organizations and agencies have developed or synthesized.

Table 1.3 Professional Organizations With Standards and Benchmarks for Subject-Matter Teachers

Subject	Organization	Web address
General resource	Mid-continent Research for Education and Learning	www.mcrel.org
Reading, literacy, and reading in the content areas	International Reading Association (IRA)	www.reading.org
	National Reading Conference (NRC)	www.nrconline.org
English	National Council of Teachers of English (NCTE)	www.ncte.org
Mathematics	National Council of Teachers of Mathematics (NCTM)	www.nctm.org
Social studies	National Council for the Social Studies (NCSS)	www.ncss.org
The sciences	National Association of Biology Teachers (NABT)	www.nabt.org
	National Science Teachers Association (NSTA)	www.nsta.org
	The National Academies Press (NAP)	www.nap.edu
	American Association of Physics Teachers (AAPT)	www.aapt.org
Foreign languages	American Council on the Teaching of Foreign Languages (ACTFL)	www.actfl.org
Music	National Association for Music Education (MENC)	www.menc.org
Physical education, health, and dance	American Alliance for Health, Physical Education, Recreation and Dance	www.aahperd.org
	National Association for Sports and Physical Education	www.aahperd.org/NASPE
The arts	National Art Education Standards	www.artteacherconnection.com (enter and click on National Standards
Technology	International Society for Technology in Education (National Educational Technology Standards for Students)	www.iste.org

SOURCE: Reprinted by permission of Richard J. Mezeske, Education Department, Hope College, Michigan.

Summary

Since the beginnings of the standards-based reform movement more than two decades ago, much work has been done to bring clarity to the question of what content teachers should address in their classroom-based instruction. As reported in a study by Kirschner (2004), classroom teachers can learn much about their own approaches to content studies, enhancing their "beliefs, knowledge, and practice" (p. 195), when they study and use the standards documents designed to guide their instruction and assessment practices. Despite ongoing debates over the need for consistency in standards documents and the use of mandated assessments based on them, curriculum frameworks that include well-designed content standards, benchmarks, topics, performance standards, and lifelong-learning standards can serve as powerful tools in your work as a teacher. Familiarizing yourself with them may even allow you to avoid your own version of a frantic assembly-line birdhouse-building session with your own students in the future!

In the models chapters in Part 2 of this book, we have used sample standards and benchmarks to illustrate how each of the models can aid you in reaching the standards and benchmarks set by your own state and local agencies. We urge you to consider how standards can be a vital component in helping you select models appropriate to your own learning goals and objectives for the students in your classroom.

Student Study Site

The Companion Web site for *Models of Teaching: Connecting Student Learning With Standards*

www.sagepub.com/delloliostudy

Visit the Web-based student study site to enhance your understanding of the book content and discover additional resources that will take your learning one step further. You can enhance your understanding by using the comprehensive Study Guide, which includes chapter learning objectives, flash cards, practice tests, and more. You'll find special features, such as the links to standards from U.S. States and associated activities, Learning from Journal Articles, Field Experience worksheets, Learning from Case Studies, and PRAXIS resources.

References

Bloom, B. S. (1956). *The taxonomy of educational objectives, handbook 1: Cognitive domain*. New York: Addison Wesley.

Council for Basic Education. (1998). *Standards for excellence in education: A guide for parents, teachers, and principals for evaluating and implementing standards for education*. Washington, DC: Author.

Glatthorn, A. (with Bragaw, D., Dawlons, K., & Parker, J.). (1998). *Performance assessment and standards-based curricula: The achievement cycle*. Larchmont, NY: Eye on Education.

Kendall, J. S. (2001). *A technical guide for revising or developing standards and benchmarks* (Report No. ED-01-CO-0006). Washington, DC: Office of Educational Research and Improvement. (ERIC Document Reproduction Service No. ED457198)

Kendall, J. S., & Marzano, R. J. (1995). *A report on the findings of phase I: The identification and articulation of content standards and benchmarks*. Paper presented at the annual meeting of the American Educational Research Association, San Francisco. (ERIC Document Reproduction Service No. ED383763)

Kendall, J. S., & Marzano, R. J. (2000). *Content knowledge: A compendium of standards and benchmarks for K–12 education*. Alexandria, VA: Association for Supervision and Curriculum Development.

Kendall, J. S., Richardson, A. T., & Ryan, S. E. (2005). *The systematic identification of performance standards*. Aurora, CO. Midcontinent Research for Education and Learning.

Kirschner, B. M. (2004). Working with curriculum standards to build a community of readers in a culture of non-readers. *Educational Horizons*, *82*(3),194–202.

Michigan Department of Education. (2005). *Parent report*. Lansing: Author.

Montgomery, P. S., Ranney, L., & Growe, R. (2003). *High-stakes tests versus high-quality education* (Report No. TM-035–318). Washington DC: Office of Educational Research and Improvement. (ERIC Document Reproduction Service No. ED481061)

Neuman, S. B., & Roskos, K. (2005). The state of pre-kindergarten standards. *Early Childhood Research Quarterly*, *20*, 125–145.

No Child Left Behind Act of 2001 (Glossary). Retrieved February 2, 2006, from www.ed.gov/print/nclb/index/az/glossary.html

Resnick, L. B., Rothman, R., Slattery, J. B., & Vranek, J. L. (2004). Benchmarking and alignment of standards and testing. *Educational Assessment*, *9*(1-2), 1–27.

Yates, S. (2004). *Constructive teaching through the deconstruction of standards*. Retrieved March 3, 2006, from www.ed.gov/teachers/how/tools/initiative/summerworkshop/yates/yates.pdf

chapter 2

Philosophies of Curriculum and Instruction

What is the purpose of schools? What should students be doing in school? What should teachers be doing? Not everyone will answer these questions in the same way. Our disparate beliefs about the purposes of schooling, our different assumptions about students and their potential, our favored approach to designing learning experiences, and our personal commitments as teachers to improving society will contribute to distinct and individual perspectives on our professional practice. These differences in thought, belief, and, ultimately, action can be seen in everything we do. Beliefs about educational issues drive decisions about our students and affect how we create our classroom environment. Our individual responses to these questions may be quite different from those of other teachers we know and respect. As professionals, we need a common vocabulary to name and share these perspectives with civility. In this chapter we will discuss categories and descriptors we can use as we talk about our different beliefs about the purposes of school.

Philosophies of Curriculum and Instruction

Various philosophies of curriculum and instruction, what we should teach and how we should teach, are described in *Conflicting Conceptions of the Curriculum*, by Eliot Eisner and Elizabeth Vallance. In their Introduction, they state that

> American education today, perhaps more than in the past, is studded with a variety of conflicting conceptions of the goals, content, and organization of curriculum. The complexity of educational thought is manifested not only in the diversity of papers presented in professional meetings and printed in professional journals; it is also apparent in debates, discussions, and controversies dramatizing school board and PTA meetings, and it is reflected and amplified by the involvement of the general public through mass media. (p. 1)

You may be surprised to find out that this was written in 1974, more than 30 years ago. We are still in the midst of such controversies regarding the "diversity" of ideas and the "complexity of educational thought" about teaching and learning. Perhaps this will always be the case in K–12 education. Ask one thought-provoking question about schooling in the United States, and you will receive as many opinions as there are people in the room. Consider these questions for a moment:

What is the purpose of schools?

Should the emphasis in schools be placed on developing literate, articulate, and opinionated citizens for our democratic society?

Should the main goal of schools in the United States be to produce skilled workers for business and industry?

Should the main concern of schools be to impart knowledge in the form of facts and formulas?

Should classrooms foster competition or collaboration among students?

Since human knowledge and understanding about the world multiply with such rapidity, should the focus of schools be on teaching students how to learn independently or helping them master an established curriculum?

Should our schools be places where self-knowledge and self-expression are the most valued outcomes?

Should our students be educated to follow rules or to reform rules? Accept the status quo or change it?

Can our schools accomplish all these goals? Only some? If so, which goals should we choose?

Your response to each of these questions says something about you personally as a citizen and professionally as a teacher. Your answers will also affect how you establish priorities and set goals for your students even though you will be given state content standards and benchmarks to address. As soon as you envision your own classroom, some ideas will take a back seat to others, and your distinct philosophy of teaching will begin to emerge.

Eisner and Vallance (1974) analyzed and described five philosophies of schooling that have "distinct conceptual biases" (p. 2) that render them substantively different from one another. If asked to characterize two exceptional but totally different teachers, you will find the vocabulary of these five philosophies valuable in your descriptions. Eisner and Vallance were not the first writers to categorize and label diverse views of schooling. However, they developed a multidimensional framework that delineates how the driving force of each philosophy—the assumptions, beliefs, and commitments that form their foundation—is embedded and manifested in almost every aspect of classroom life. Eisner and Vallance themselves stated that their particular organization of these ideas is only one way to regard diverse views and opinions about curriculum and instruction. However, their ideas are very accessible for new teachers as they begin to articulate and analyze their own perspectives on education.

The defining attributes of these five philosophies will be evident in the most important aspects of schooling—choice of content, lesson design, nature of students' involvement, teachers' roles, and choice and use of materials, among others. However, each one of the five philosophies addresses these aspects in different measure: each philosophy is focused on the developing students and their role in society, on the content of instruction, and on the processes of instruction, but each gives primary emphasis to a different aspect of schooling. You will see that all five philosophies present distinctive answers to the question, What is the purpose of schools?

Take a second look at the list of questions above and your answers to them. As you review the five philosophies of curriculum described below, consider your responses in light of the emphases of each philosophy.

Academic Rationalism

Of the five different philosophies of curriculum and instruction, **academic rationalism** is probably the most familiar to you. Academic rationalists are focused on the acquisition of content knowledge and the transmission of that knowledge to the young. In most cases, this philosophy excludes practical curriculums such as business education, home economics, industrial arts, driver's education, and work-study internships. The academic rationalist advocates that our greatest intellectual and aesthetic products, the finest ideas and ideals that humankind has produced over the centuries, should be the source of the K–12 and university curriculum.

These intellectual and aesthetic products have been described by scholars as the **canon**, or collection, of Western civilization. The canon consists of some of the finest exemplars of human thought and creativity throughout history. Disciplines across divisions of knowledge have contributed to the canon: the arts (music, theater, dance, and the visual arts), the humanities (literature, philosophy, religion, and history), the natural sciences (mathematics, biology, earth sciences, chemistry, and physics), and the social sciences (psychology, economics, political science, sociology, anthropology, and education). How was this canon of works initially determined?

When he was a student at Columbia University in 1921, noted educator Mortimer Adler took a course in Western civilization. His professor, John Erskine, had identified a collection of great books that were used as the curriculum in this course. As a professor himself, Adler was appointed to reconsider the titles on Erskine's list. Under the direction of Adler and John Maynard Hutchins, from the University of Chicago, scholars at the university reached a consensus in 1947 about an updated collection of classic writings across the disciplines. This collection of books, generally referred to as the Great Books series, was first published by the Encyclopaedia Britannica in 1952 (Hutchins, 1952). The Great Books have provided the curriculum for many institutions of higher learning for decades. Included in this collection were major works by Sophocles, Aristotle, Copernicus, Augustine, Aquinas, Dante, Shakespeare, Cervantes, Milton, Newton, Kant, Melville, Darwin, Marx, Tolstoy, and Freud, to name just a few. Originally, the set included 54 volumes. Great Ideas Today is a series of books that have been added annually to the Great Books collection to update the original set.

Academic rationalists believe that adults must be able to read, appreciate, analyze, and understand these "great productions of the human mind" (Hutchins, 1952, p. xiv). According to their beliefs, students' critical thinking skills will also be developed as they encounter the classics under the guidance of a skilled teacher. For example, students' analytical skills can be sharpened as they compare and contrast the plays of William Shakespeare and George Bernard Shaw. Curriculum developed from this canon exemplifies academic rationalism in practice.

Academic rationalism can be seen in secondary and elementary curriculums as well as at the college level. In 1984, Mortimer Adler pioneered the Paideia Schools, which focus on a classical liberal arts curriculum for K–12 students (Adler, 1983, 1984, 1998). **Paideia** means an education for broad cultural understanding. Currently the Paideia Schools have 50 school partnerships in 10 states (National Paideia Center, 2006). Adler proposed that the Paideia curriculum not be differentiated according to the perceived ability levels of students. He abandoned the idea of separate courses of study at the secondary level for college preparation and vocational tracks. The Paideia Program states that schools should teach the same curriculum to every student and not differentiate the curriculum to provide for student interest, perceived ability, or assumptions about society's need for particular knowledge or skills in the future. What is best for the most capable, Adler asserted, is best for all students.

This idea has continued to engender controversy among parents and educators because it raises the issue of uniformity versus specialization in K–12 curriculum. Should college preparatory courses of study be required of all students? Can it be expected that all students will be successful in such a course of study? Could this approach to the curriculum level the socioeconomic playing field for all students? Should alternative "tracks" of study at the high school level be available for those students who have not succeeded with this single academic curriculum? Our answers to these questions will reveal whether we believe that the purpose of school should be to provide a classical education for all students or to prepare some students as skilled workers for the new economy.

In 1987, E. D. Hirsch, Jr., published *Cultural Literacy: What Every American Needs to Know*. From an academic rationalist viewpoint, Hirsch explained why Americans should know factual information that he believes constitutes the core of humankind's common cultural heritage. According to Hirsch, this **cultural literacy** helps us thrive as members of contemporary modern culture because we have a solid understanding of the important ideas from our common past. Along with his rationale for the need for cultural literacy, Hirsch compiled a list of thousands of items culled not only from the traditional canon but also from modern culture. In Hirsch's view, without this core knowledge, individuals can neither appreciate nor understand the world in full measure. He believes that people lacking this core knowledge are illiterate and as disadvantaged as anyone unable to read in the conventional sense.

Some critics of American schooling believe the **progressive education** movement that began in the United States in the early 1900s moved K–12 curriculum away from this type of solid academic focus (Ravitch, 2000). Hirsch and his colleagues developed a Core Knowledge course of study to address what academic rationalists in the 1980s described as a watering down of the K–12 curriculum. The Core Knowledge K–8 curriculum is based in part on the classics and also on important concepts and information about contemporary life in a global society. This curriculum does not follow the traditional grade-level topics and sequencing of academic content. The "expanding horizons" approach to social studies common to most textbook series, in which students begin by studying their families, then their communities, their state, the nation, and then world topics, is dismantled in the Core Knowledge curriculum. Early elementary students study ancient cultures and literature typically presented in upper elementary grades. Although it has been criticized by some educators as not being developmentally appropriate for most elementary-age students, more than 400 schools in the United States have adopted this curriculum, and five international schools are Core Knowledge schools (Core Knowledge Foundation, 2006).

Critics of academic rationalism believe that this approach to teaching and learning underestimates the prior knowledge and experiences that students bring to the classroom. Some of the metaphors used to describe the academic rationalists' view of students have placed academic rationalism in a negative light. Earlier in this chapter, you read that one purpose of the academic curriculum is the transmission of culture in society from the elders to the young. **Transmission models of teaching** have been characterized disapprovingly as regarding students as empty vessels waiting to be filled with knowledge by the teacher. The banking metaphor has also been used negatively in the same way. Students are seen as empty and waiting for deposits of information. These metaphors describe academic rationalism as being disrespectful of students, their abilities, and their potential. Depending on your opinion of academic rationalism, you may regard its critics as either unfair or right on target. Another metaphor for academic rationalism with a less negative tone describes students as sponges ready to soak up learning found in texts and delivered by teachers. Advocates of academic rationalism believe that a challenging curriculum is highly respectful of students' intellectual abilities.

Given these views of students as receivers of knowledge rather than creators of new knowledge, it is easy to see why traditional forms of instruction are linked to academic rationalism. Traditional teachers generally lecture, provide direct instruction, or demonstrate a concept while students observe, listen, and take notes. Primary texts are preferred by academic rationalists over textbook syntheses of ideas in the humanities and social sciences. Memorization is expected in several disciplines. Assessment and evaluation measures advocated by the academic rationalist philosophy are traditional as well. Term papers and tests are typically used to assess and then evaluate student understanding and achievement.

However, Adler advocated the use in the Paideia Program of the Socratic—or **maieutic**—method of instruction in addition to traditional didactic instruction in K–12 classrooms. Rather than providing answers for students, the Socratic method poses a series of questions that prompt students' critical thinking about the topics being studied. Although his beliefs about the value of a classical curriculum are clearly those of an academic rationalist, Adler's preferred mode of instruction in several subjects is closely aligned with the cognitive processing philosophy, which you will read about in the next section.

What belongs in the canon of an undergraduate liberal arts education has been a topic of debate for decades. Some educators believe that the traditional K–12 curriculum championed by the academic rationalists and drawn from the traditional, Western-focused canon, is elitist. They mean that the canon reflects only the European male perspective on history, which they view as limited and exclusive. The traditional canon included no works from other cultures and no works written by women. Books from many cultures, including contributions of women from all over the world, are now part of many courses that examine the history of human civilization.

Advocates of the academic rationalist philosophy in curriculum and instruction would describe it as scholarly. Figures associated with academic rationalism, in addition to those already mentioned, include William Bennett, Allan Bloom, Wayne Booth, and Lynne Cheney.

Cognitive Processing

If you have ever designed, implemented, and analyzed an experiment in science or collected data for a project in social studies, you have firsthand experience of the

While the canon of the academic rationalist curriculum has broadened to include contributions from women and from traditions throughout the world, its focus on cultural literacy has remained.

cognitive processing philosophy of curriculum. The focus of **cognitive processing** is exercising and strengthening the "muscles" of the mind. If we say that the academic rationalist philosophy of curriculum is content driven, emphasizing *what* students learn, then the cognitive processing philosophy emphasizes the development of students' thinking abilities, or *how* students learn. Why did some educators advocate this shift in focus for K–12 instruction, and what does this philosophy look like in practice?

In 1957, during the Cold War, the Soviet Union launched *Sputnik*, the first satellite to orbit the earth. NASA was created by the United States in response to *Sputnik*, and the event also served as a catalyst for nationwide concern that U.S. school children were far behind their Eastern European counterparts in math and science achievement. Politicians found fault with the educational institutions in the United States for having failed to prepare students to work in the sciences and mathematics. In 1959, the National Science Foundation (NSF) funding for science education was increased from $5 million to $40 million to address what many believed was an issue of national defense. The NSF provided grants for scholars and scientists to develop innovative science and math education programs for K–12 schools. During the decade following the first *Sputnik* launch, many programs were developed to improve and invigorate science and math teaching.

You could say that cognitive processing as a distinct philosophy of education was launched in the 1960s as a result of nationwide reaction to *Sputnik* and scientists' dissatisfaction with the traditional pedagogy that dominated K–12 education at that time. The designers of these new programs believed that the purpose of schools should be to move beyond an emphasis entirely on content to one that teaches critical thinking skills to enrich students' problem-solving and decision-making abilities. Students needed to learn how to learn. This stance was an explicit criticism of the facts-and-formulas focus of the K–12 curriculum championed by academic rationalists. One argument against the traditional approach to curriculum and instruction was that since human knowledge increases with such alarming speed, to focus exclusively on academic content is to misuse students' valuable time in school. The advocates of the cognitive processing philosophy believe that students' energies are better spent on developing intellectual skills such as analysis, inference, induction, and evaluation, which apply directly to science and math and will also transfer to other disciplines.

Science education programs sponsored by the NSF after *Sputnik* focused on the development of students' cognitive skills and the application of the scientific method (see, e.g., *Elementary Science Study*, 1960; *Science: A Process Approach*, 1963; *Science Curriculum Improvement Study*, 1965). This major paradigm shift moved science education from an emphasis on teachers' deductive instructional methods to students' inductive learning experiences. Traditional deductive teaching in science begins with an explanation of a concept or scientific principle. After giving this explanation, the teacher works through an experiment that proves the principle while students observe the teacher's actions. Under the best possible circumstances, students are then given materials to replicate the experiment as demonstrated by the teacher. Performed correctly, students' experiments provide the same results as the teacher's demonstrations. Advocates of the cognitive processing philosophy believe that deductive teaching subverts authentic student learning. With deductive approaches, students are less likely to have the discovery moments that advocates of cognitive processing believe to be crucial to learning with understanding (Bruner, 1977). In this view, what students observe during a demonstration is not necessarily learned by those students if their minds are not actively engaged during the lesson. When they are given a passive role during lessons, students do not develop their own intellectual skills; they are not cognitively processing the experience at hand.

Furthermore, advocates of cognitive processing remind us that scientists themselves work in active ways to create new knowledge—they work inductively. **Inductive teaching models** have students work with concepts "from the inside out." In science instruction, rather than being given a scientific principle to observe through teacher demonstration or to prove through teacher-directed experimentation, students are presented with an engaging, meaningful question, one that scientists themselves would address. Through an inquiry process, most commonly the scientific method, students analyze the problem, generate hypotheses, choose from among those hypotheses, and sometimes design an experiment to test them. As the experiment progresses, students record findings, analyze their data, and then generate what scientific principles they believe are at work. In each stage of the process, students are developing cognitive skills as they make sense of the information gathered and the results generated. Students can induce principles of science through experience rather than absorb them passively in teacher-directed lessons. These experiences strengthen students' intellectual abilities as they do the work of scientists—or of historians, mathematicians, geographers, or sociologists.

Advocates of the cognitive processing approach suggest that once these intellectual skills have been introduced in the early elementary grades, they should continue to be developed through learning experiences in all subjects across the K–12 curriculum. Instructional units can be designed to emphasize specific critical thinking skills that will work in concert with academic content. For example, categorization, data analysis, and comparison and contrast might be the critical thinking skills emphasized in a second-grade unit on plants. These same skills, at a much more sophisticated level, can be emphasized in a ninth-grade world studies unit that examines political revolutions across different centuries.

Critical thinking skills can also be viewed as instructional objectives themselves as students learn to apply cognitive skills. For example, one objective in a second-grade life science unit might read, "The learner will predict the preferred diet of mealworms by hypothesizing, designing, performing, and analyzing a series of investigations." Students' learning what mealworms eat is of less significance in this lesson than having opportunities to design an experiment in response to a question, perform the experiment according to the design, and then analyze the efficacy of their investigations.

It is important to understand that inductive thinking skills are always used in learning in some way. However, students possess an individual repertoire of cognitive skills when they enter our classrooms. Traditional content organization and teaching methods do not necessarily engage cognitive abilities, nor do they cultivate these abilities with any deliberation. Too often, teacher-centered methods do not promote student thinking past basic levels of comprehension. Learning experiences can be designed to move students into the higher levels of critical thinking.

Unlike the academic rationalist view of learners as "empty vessels," cognitive processing's view is that learners at any age can produce knowledge, not just receive or replicate it. While traditional K–12 education focuses on the acquisition and re-creation of knowledge in the disciplines, the cognitive processing philosophy insists that only through significant experiences as problem solvers will students be able to create knowledge in the future. These beliefs are closely aligned with constructivist learning theory. In fact, you could say that the cognitive processing philosophy gives both structure and direction to constructivist learning theory as it applies to the classroom. Other figures associated with cognitive processing include Edward de Bono, Matthew Lipman, Maria Montessori, Jean Piaget, Robert Sternberg, and Hilda Taba.

Curriculum as Technology

Eisner and Vallance used the term *curriculum as technology* long before the advent of information technology and its effects on K–12 education. Technology as a philosophy of curriculum does not refer to using hardware, software, the Internet, Smart Board, or digital cameras in our teaching. The philosophy of **curriculum as**

technology means a technology of teaching, or a way to organize and deliver academic content. Rather than thinking of *technological* as meaning high tech, think systematic or incremental lesson and unit development and traditional instructional models. At some point in your K–12 education, you probably experienced curriculum organized in a technological way.

In the 1970s, some educational researchers wanted to determine "effective" teacher behaviors. Some specific teacher behaviors were found to be effective for some students in some particular contexts (Brophy, 1979; Rosenshine, 1979; Good, 1979; Good & Grouws 1979; Medley, 1979). In their desire to promote success for all students, researchers tried to identify instructional behaviors that were shared by all effective teachers. Much of the research done at this time resulted in a codification of these behaviors into a model of teaching generically termed *direct instruction*, which will be presented in detail in Chapter 4. This trend, also called *teacher effectiveness*, systematized how teachers were expected to behave in their classrooms and how they should be educated and evaluated in their preparation programs. This system was referred to as **competency-based teacher education**.

With this technological focus, academic content systematized what students learned and how they learned it. Academic goals crafted into discrete sequences of skills, systematized and prescribed lesson designs, and teacher behaviors were all expected to promote student learning. Nearly every subject in school was transformed into long-term **behavioral objectives** that would take students an extended period of time to master. These objectives were then broken down by the process of **task analysis** into short-term objectives that guided daily lessons. This organization of content was designed by individual states or by central administrative staff in local school districts. Traditional mathematics instruction, with its emphasis on step-by-step organization for computation and basic skill acquisition, is one example. In traditional mathematics instruction, a long-term objective is broken down into incremental steps. These steps are stated as measurable behavioral objectives and then are organized into a specific sequence of lessons in which skills build on one another, leading to the long-term objective. This type of content organization is sometimes referred to as *part-to-whole* curriculum and instruction. The sequence of lessons is called a **continuum**. For example, the standard multiplication algorithm may be the focus of a series of multiplication objectives for third and fourth graders. One long-term objective for computation in multiplication might be

357×493 The learner will multiply any two three-digit numbers, with regrouping in any column.

Given what she knows about the third- and fourth-grade math curriculum, a teacher may begin a continuum with this short-term objective:

20×3 The learner will multiply a multiple of 10 by a one-digit number to obtain a two-digit product.

Table 2.1	Multiplication Continuum

1.	20 × 3	The learner will multiply a multiple of 10 by a one-digit number to obtain a two-digit product.
2.	40 × 9	The learner will multiply a multiple of 10 by a one-digit number to obtain a three-digit product.
3.	23 × 3	The learner will multiply a two-digit number by a one-digit number, with no regrouping.
4.	37 × 2	The learner will multiply a two-digit number by a one-digit number, with regrouping in the ones column.
5.	46 × 8	The learner will multiply any two-digit number by any one-digit number, with regrouping in the ones and tens columns.
6.	323 × 2	The learner will multiply a three-digit number by a one-digit number, with no regrouping.
7.	445 × 2	The learner will multiply a three-digit number, with regrouping in the ones column.
8.	296 × 2	The learner will multiply a three-digit number by a one-digit number, with regrouping in the ones and tens columns.
9.	438 × 3	The learner will multiply any three-digit number by any one-digit number, with regrouping in any column.
10.	20 × 40	The learner will multiply two multiples of 10.
11.	21 × 13	The learner will multiply 2 two-digit numbers, with no regrouping.
12.	27 × 14	The learner will multiply 2 two-digit numbers, with regrouping in the ones column.
13.	29 × 56	The learner will multiply any 2 two-digit numbers, with regrouping in the ones and tens columns.
14.	300 × 80	The learner will multiply a multiple of 100 by a multiple of 10.
15.	112 × 25	The learner will multiply a three-digit number by a two-digit number, with regrouping in the ones column.
16.	133 × 46	The learner will multiply a three-digit number by a two-digit number, with regrouping in the ones and tens columns.
17.	357 × 493	The learner will multiply any 2 three-digit numbers, with regrouping in any column (long-term objective for this unit).

This objective will serve as the **entry-level skill** or **baseline skill** for this unit. The continuum will take students incrementally from the first objective on the continuum to the final, long-term objective. Each objective is slightly more advanced than the previous one. Table 2.1 shows an example of such a continuum.

A **pretest** can be written that uses examples of selected short-term objectives from the continuum to determine students' levels of competency as they begin each new unit. Given the class results of the pretest, the teacher may decide to work through the continuum of behavioral objectives using full-group instruction or to break the class into flexible skill-based groups for that unit. However the teacher chooses to organize the instruction, the class will move through the unit objectives in an orderly, "technological" manner.

Daily lessons are also designed in a sequential manner. Each lesson requires a task analysis to determine specific steps in solving the problems. The task analysis sequences these steps, and the teacher addresses each one directly. **Behaviorist learning theory** provides the foundation for this philosophy of curriculum (Skinner, 1968).

Given this content organization and the behavioral focus of daily lesson objectives, student learning is easy to measure. Assessments of this kind are neither difficult to design nor difficult to review. In the example given above, a parallel pretest and posttest can be developed to demonstrate student mastery at the beginning of the unit and at the end of the unit. It follows, then, that evaluation of student learning is also relatively easy because a percentage value can be applied to student work.

For many teachers, moving through a continuum at a regular pace is a priority because of the demands of standardized testing. All material must be covered to address all grade-level expectations for their state or district. However, in other districts, students must demonstrate competency in one skill before they move on to the next skill on the continuum. We call this approach **mastery learning**, and it is a hallmark of the technological philosophy. It does not complement any of the other four philosophies.

In the 1970s, this combination of a systematized, incremental approach to organizing content and teacher-directed instruction was pejoratively labeled a "**teacher-proof curriculum**." "Teacher-proofing" curriculum, texts, and teacher's manuals meant that teachers would be virtually unable to make mistakes in their instruction, curricular choices, assessment, and evaluation procedures. Teacher's manuals were published with "Say this" and "Do this" instructions. Some teachers applauded this standardization of materials and methods, while many other teachers and teacher educators were appalled at the development. Teachers who were pleased with this movement in education believed that it would lighten their work and provide a solid structure from which they could add to and embellish the curriculum. In their view, commercialized curriculums improved the likelihood that all students would have the same opportunities to learn. Students' education would not depend on teachers' skills, interests, and talents, or the lack thereof, but rather on the quality of books, teacher's manuals, and supplementary materials.

Other educators, however, believed that the very idea of teacher-proof curriculum and teacher's manuals belied the status of teaching as a profession. They believed that professionals did not require prewritten scripts to navigate their daily instructional responsibilities. Professionals must be able to develop ideas and materials to suit the needs of their real students, not someone else's generic conception of students at each grade level. Furthermore, they believed that competency-based teacher education contributed to the deprofessionalization of teaching by focusing on narrow, technical skills instead of creativity, originality, and spontaneity; in other words, competency-based teacher education promoted teaching as a science at the expense of teaching as an art.

In addition, some educators found that the technological approach to content organization and instruction rendered many students unable to see the forest for the trees. Many felt that the parts did not, in fact, lead to the whole when it came to student learning. It became evident to some teachers that this technological approach to teaching circumvented students' conceptual understanding. Attention to student mastery of computational skills, for example, did not necessarily result in student understanding of underlying concepts if the students' hands-on experiences were in any way shortchanged or compromised.

In the late 1980s, the technological perspective as a driving force in K–12 education began to wane in favor of constructivism—the learning theory that drives the cognitive processing philosophy. However, at the beginning of the 21st century, some commercialized academic programs, along with the textbook companies that publish their materials, are again designing teacher's manuals that support the technological approach in both curriculum organization and prescribed lesson delivery. In the last 15 years, some charter schools have advertised a "**back-to-basics**" curriculum and approach to instruction that imply a technological mind-set. Nationwide tutoring franchises that provide individualized courses of study for students organize their curriculum using the technological philosophy. Highly sequenced lesson objectives and mastery learning are fundamental principles often touted on brochures, television advertisements, and company Internet sites. As a result of the federally mandated restructuring of schools with consistently low test scores, some states are promoting, and even requiring, a reorganization of curriculum that uses technological principles of instruction as "research-based" effective teaching.

Several educational psychologists and writers influenced both the organization of content and the instructional design of the technologist philosophy. Studies in behaviorism had a great impact on educational thought during much of the 20th century. Nathaniel L. Gage (1978) and Robert Mager (1997) contributed to the literature on applying behaviorist principles to classroom practice through developing instructional objectives and designing lessons. In the 1970s, Madeline Hunter popularized her commercialized version of applied behaviorist learning, Theory Into Practice, through teacher education programs, seminars, and materials that were aligned with the technologist perspective.

Self-Actualization

As an integral part of your own philosophy of education, you may feel that students' opportunities to become well-rounded, fulfilled human beings should not take a backseat to the traditional focus of acquiring academic content knowledge in school. Many educators, both currently and in the past, share this view, which was driven by the humanist movement in psychology prevalent in the 1960s and 1970s. The academic rationalist, cognitive processing, and technology perspectives on curriculum address the **cognitive domain**—the intellectual components of human experience. Humanism, which drives the self-actualization philosophy of curriculum, relates to the **affective domain**, which refers to students' feelings, beliefs, attitudes, personal values systems, and levels of self-esteem. The **self-actualization** philosophy asserts that students will be equipped and motivated to be successful, self-directed learners if educators take into account the development of the affective domain.

Educating the whole child requires attention to the intellectual, emotional, and physical needs of students. Students' interests play an important role as teachers develop curriculum and choose models of teaching.

The self-actualization philosophy in practice can best be described as one that emphasizes the development of the whole child. Rather than a set academic curriculum, traditionally organized classroom, and teacher-centered instruction, this philosophy promotes establishing schools and classrooms as communities, providing students with a choice of activities and literature, and using nontraditional teaching methods. In the late 1960s and early 1970s, this approach was often referred to as the **open classroom** (Silberman, 1973). Even though much of the vocabulary of the self-actualization philosophy sounds rooted in an elementary context—teaching to the **whole child**, establishing a positive classroom climate, using student-centered instruction, implementing an open-classroom organization—the principles of self-actualization apply equally well across K–12 education. Let's look at the principles at work in a classroom setting that promotes students' self-actualization.

It is best to begin with those psychologists who were among the first to chart the landscape of the humanist movement. Carl Rogers developed **educational priorities** for schools in his book *Freedom to Learn* (1994). They are listed in Table 2.2. You will notice that none of these priorities mentions the acquisition of academic content knowledge explicitly. However, Rogers argued that academic learning experiences have a positive and powerful impact on students only when they occur under the conditions he describes. Rogers's educational priorities are not antithetical to traditionally conceived purposes of schooling, which focus on academic content knowledge. An academic focus can clearly coexist within the environment Rogers is advocating.

It is nevertheless equally clear that Rogers believed the nurturing of students' inner lives is a primary obligation of the schools. It is also interesting to notice that

Table 2.2	Carl Rogers's Educational Priorities

Establishing and maintaining a climate of trust in the classroom

Applying democratic principles to classroom decision making

Promoting students' positive self-esteem

Nurturing enthusiasm about intellectual and emotional learning processes

Promoting the concept of the individual as a lifelong learner

Nurturing the personal development of teachers

Helping students understand that "the good life" can be attained as a result of self-discovery and personal growth

SOURCE: Adapted from Rogers & Freiberg, 1994.

while neither the personal nor the professional development of teachers is mentioned explicitly as a priority in the academic rationalist, cognitive processing, or technological perspectives on curriculum, Rogers identifies teachers' development as an educational priority.

Many of Carl Rogers's ideas are shared by Abraham Maslow. Maslow introduced the idea of the **hierarchy of needs,** which individuals must have met if they are to become, in Maslow's own term, "self-actualized" human beings (1998). The seven needs are shown in Table 2.3. Maslow believed that learning can occur only when the four deficiency needs have been met.

Maslow believed that if students' physiological, safety, belonging, and esteem needs are not being met, it is unlikely that they will be able to attend to the intellectual and physical demands of schoolwork. Most states have helped address students' physiological needs by providing free and reduced-cost breakfast and lunch programs.

Maslow's other three deficiency needs are also addressed in the practices of the self-actualization philosophy of curriculum and instruction. Educators have long understood that students must experience schools and classrooms as safe places, free from threat. Learning cannot occur in a climate of fear and mistrust. Mistakes must be experienced and appreciated as an integral part of the learning process. The self-actualization philosophy sees this view as a required point of departure for classroom life. It also emphasizes students' need to feel that they play an important role in the classroom community. When students' opinions are respected and valued, the students experience themselves as contributing members of their society.

Maslow believed that when deficiency needs are met, individuals will be able to expend intellectual, emotional, and psychological energy in positive ways; in other words, their being needs can be developed. Maslow's being needs are clearly aligned with Rogers's educational priorities: opportunities to explore the world, develop aesthetic sensibilities, and realize one's potential. The personal rewards of meeting being needs motivate individuals throughout their lifetimes, and so the process of self-actualization is both self-generating and continuous.

Table 2.3   Abraham Maslow's Hierarchy of Needs

Being Needs

Self-actualizing needs	Finding and realizing one's potential
Aesthetic needs	Finding symmetry, order, and beauty
Cognitive needs	Knowing, understanding, exploring

Deficiency Needs

Esteem needs	Believing that we are inherently worthy and can contribute something to our society
Belongingness and love needs	Knowing those places in our world where we are comfortable and feel loved
Safety needs	A belief that we are in no danger
Physiological needs	For food, clothing, and shelter

SOURCE: Maslow, 1998.

The idea that students' individual choices should determine academic curriculum was a particular focus of another advocate of the self-actualization philosophy of curriculum. In 1921, Summerhill, a progressive residential school in England, was founded by A. S. Neill. Neill (1996) contended that children can identify their own interests and work continuously toward self-discovery if allowed the opportunity to do so. He believed that a structured, articulated curriculum is unnecessary if students are given the opportunity and encouragement to follow their individual interests and create their own courses of study. Summerhill School is still in existence. In the current climate of standards-based education and high-stakes accountability in the United States, it is unlikely that public school systems here will allow for Summerhill's level of student participation in determining curriculum.

Since the advent of the humanist movement in psychology in the 1960s, K–12 education has focused on the development of students' positive self-esteem. Rather than focusing on what students are unable to do, teachers are encouraged to acknowledge students' abilities and successes. However, there has been a backlash against what some have called the "curse of self-esteem" (Adler, J., et al., 1992). Some educators believe that when students are praised for their every effort, regardless of the quality of the work, they lose a true appreciation for the value of hard work and the significance of hard-won praise. This outcome is not the original intention of the humanist movement in psychology or the self-actualization philosophy of curriculum but rather the result of the way some educators have misinterpreted the philosophy in their practice.

The self-actualization philosophy of curriculum and instruction is illustrated by teaching practices that are aligned with the humanist movement in psychology. Instructional innovations that came of age in the 20th century to promote self-actualization goals are project work, cooperative learning, teaching to the multiple intelligences, differentiated curriculum, peer assessment, and self-evaluation. Other figures associated with self-actualization include Herbert Kohl and Philip Phenix.

Social Reconstructionism

Are you the first person in your immediate family to attend college? Historically, it has been true in many U.S. families that the first child to attend college becomes an educator. Education has always been the most direct route to upward social mobility and economic prosperity in the United States (Lortie, 2002). You could say that education has always "reconstructed" society in the United States. First-generation college students who become first-generation teachers have been a source of great pride for their families in the United States. Excellent teachers have come from every socioeconomic background; racial, ethnic, and cultural group; and religious affiliation. In the United States, many accomplished individuals in the professions and the arts had educators for parents.

That education has been a primary vehicle for social and economic mobility in the United States is no accident. In 1837, when he was first appointed secretary of the Massachusetts State Board of Education, Horace Mann advocated free public education as the right of all children in the United States, regardless of the circumstances of their birth. In the 1800s, disparate economic circumstances and the existence of private academies for children of the wealthy divided society. Horace Mann was the first educator in this country to make the case that only through an educated populace can the democratic ideal be realized. In the words of education historian Lawrence Cremin (1982), Horace Mann felt "the richest mines of Massachusetts were not deposits of gold and silver but rather the developed intellectual capabilities of its population" (p. 134).

Public education for all children and adolescents in the United States was the first instance of the use of education in a deliberate effort to change U.S. society. Following on this belief in the moral obligation of providing schooling for all U.S. citizens came the idea that curriculum and instruction can be designed to evoke significant changes in society (Cremin, 1982). This view of the purpose of schooling is called **social reconstructionism**. It is the view that society will be reconstructed as a result of the curriculums and instruction that are established, nurtured, and maintained in the schools.

Of the five philosophies of curriculum, social reconstructionism is the most explicitly political. One hallmark of this philosophy is the idea that teachers should be active agents for social change. Social reconstructionists believe that the purpose of education should be to help solve the problems of society. Teachers should raise the consciousness of students to help them move beyond the political status quo—beyond experiencing school as a place to replicate the existing society—and experience school instead as a place where society can be transformed. Teachers, curriculum, and instructional choices should propel students into political action. Racism and discrimination, poverty, violence, health issues, unemployment, homelessness, and pollution are all weighty social problems that the reconstructionists believe can be alleviated in part by a quality education for all U.S. students. For social reconstructionists, this means providing an education that heightens students' levels of awareness of the injustices in society.

Many school districts have had antibias curriculums, such as the World of Difference Institute's (Anti-Defamation League, 2006), in place for more than two decades. Since the Columbine school-shooting tragedy in 1999, school districts have developed curriculums that focus on the improvement of students' social and interpersonal relationships (DeRoche & Williams, 2001). Many school districts have service learning provisions at the middle and high school levels that require students to volunteer in programs such as soup kitchens, convalescent hospitals, or the Meals-on-Wheels program. It is not uncommon for elementary school children to participate in service learning projects as a regular feature of some instructional units in social studies (Duckenfield, 1992). Sex and drug education initiatives have become commonplace in U.S. schools, even though the substance of these programs varies widely and often engenders controversy among parents.

For social reconstructionists, teachers' instructional choices are actually part of the curriculum because they give students implicit information about their capabilities and their place in society. For example, a teacher's overreliance on traditional instruction may send a message to students that they are only to be receivers of knowledge in a passive relationship to learning. Explicit in the social reconstructionist philosophy is the value of authentic learning experiences and collaborative work among students and teachers. Hands-on, authentic, and group learning experiences allow students to interact with a variety of people and help them identify everyone's individual strengths and contributions to the group. It also provides them with a sense of their own power and efficacy in the world.

The social reconstructionist philosophy of curriculum requires no special materials or textbooks. Many teachers whose beliefs in these values drive their classroom practice have found creative ways to use traditional classroom materials in the service of reaching social reconstructionist goals. For example, sexism can be examined in the elementary grades using traditional basal readers from the 1950s and 1960s. At the middle school level, analytical thinking can be fostered by comparing and contrasting opposing views of a controversial subject, such as public school funding, that will have a direct effect on students and their families. At the high school level, positions about the best neighborhood for a halfway house for former drug abusers can be researched through newspaper and magazine articles, statistical databases found on the Internet, and student-designed telephone surveys. Textbooks at any level can be analyzed for bias in their narratives. Teachers who view themselves as social reconstructionists have also used the cities in which they live as primary source material for their curriculum. Museums, parks, businesses, government facilities, power plants, shopping centers, or places of worship have provided authentic contexts for learning experiences that challenge students' thinking about their roles in society.

Other figures associated with social reconstructionism include Michael Apple, Stanley Aronowitz, Paolo Friere, J. T. Gatto, Henry Giroux, Maxine Greene, Jonathan Kozol, Peter MacLaren, Deborah Meier, and Ned O'Gorman.

 # Summary

Various eras in education have favored some of the philosophies of curriculum over others. In the past few decades, they have been discussed in diverse writings about education and employed in the diverse ways classroom teachers do their work. Most educators, even though they may not employ the names used here, will agree that their beliefs, values, and practices are a combination of these five different philosophies in different measures. Some teachers identify strongly with a particular philosophy, and each decision they make in the classroom bespeaks that perspective. Most teachers consider themselves "informed eclectics" (Shulman, 1987). Informed eclectics see the strengths of each philosophy and borrow ideas in a deliberate way to develop their own professional practice. It is important to understand that teachers' belief systems affect the daily choices they make in their classrooms.

We do not teach in an intellectual or moral vacuum (Sarason, 1993). All educators, including the professors in your teacher education program, walk into classrooms with definite value systems in place. It is not possible to teach in a way that is completely objective and value free, and it is also undesirable. Reflective teachers think carefully about the decisions they make, and these professional choices always have public consequences. Your understanding of various perspectives on education will help you become aware of the choices you make among many possibilities each day. This will be true throughout your career as a teacher, and your attitudes, values, and beliefs may change over time. Continuing reflection about your students' learning and your own commitments as a teacher will help you analyze life in your classroom in greater depth and to your greater satisfaction.

Part 2 of this book describes 10 models of teaching that support student learning in different ways for different purposes. In addition to providing information and case studies that illustrate each model, each chapter briefly discusses a model in respect to theories of learning and the five philosophies of curriculum and instruction discussed in this chapter.

Student Study Site

The Companion Web site for *Models of Teaching: Connecting Student Learning With Standards*

www.sagepub.com/delloliostudy

Visit the Web-based student study site to enhance your understanding of the book content and discover additional resources that will take your learning one step further. You can enhance your understanding by using the comprehensive Study Guide, which includes chapter learning objectives, flash cards, practice tests, and more. You'll find special features, such as the links to standards from U.S. States and associated activities, Learning from Journal Articles, Field Experience worksheets, Learning from Case Studies, and PRAXIS resources.

Further Reading

Adler, M. (2000). *How to think about the great ideas: From the great books of Western civilization*. New York: Open Court.

Apple, M. (1996). *Cultural politics and education* (The John Dewey Lecture). New York: Teachers College Press.

Apple, M. (1999). *Official knowledge: Democratic education in a conservative age* (2nd ed.). New York: Routledge.

Apple, M. (2001). *Educating the "right" way: Markets, standards, God, and inequality*. New York: Routledge.

Apple, M. (2004). *Ideology and curriculum*. Oxford: Taylor & Francis.

Aronowitz, S. (1991). *Postmodern education: Politics, culture, and social criticism*. Minneapolis: University of Minnesota Press.

Bennett, W. (1993). *The book of virtues*. New York: Simon & Schuster.

Bloom, A. (1988). *The closing of the American mind*. New York: Simon & Schuster.

Bloom, B. S. (1956). *Taxonomy of educational objectives, handbook 1: Cognitive domain*. New York: Addison Wesley.

Booth, W. (2006). *The knowledge most worth knowing*. Berkeley: University of California Press.

Bruner, J. (1987). *Actual minds, possible worlds*. Cambridge, MA: Harvard UP.

Bruner, J. (2004). *Toward a theory of instruction*. Cambridge, MA: Belknap Press.

Cheney, L. (1989). *50 hours: A core curriculum for college students*. Washington, DC: National Endowment for the Humanities.

Cheney, L. (1990). *Tyrannical machines: A report on educational practices gone wrong and our best hopes for setting them right*. Washington, DC: National Endowment for the Humanities.

De Bono, E. (1973). *Lateral thinking: Creativity step by step*. New York: Harper.

De Bono, E. (1994). *De Bono's thinking course* (Rev. ed.). New York: Facts on File.

De Bono, E. (1999). *Six thinking hats*. New York: Back Bay Books.

Friere, P. (2000). *Pedagogy of the oppressed* (30th anniverssary ed.). London: Continuum International.

Gatto, J. T. (2002). *A different kind of teacher: Solving the crisis of American schools*. Berkeley, CA: Berkeley Hills Books.

Giroux, H. (1981). *Curriculum and instruction: Alternatives in education*. Berkeley, CA: McCutchan.

Giroux, H. (2003). *The abandoned generation: Democracy beyond the culture of fear*. New York: Palgrave Macmillan.

Giroux, H. (2005). *Schooling and the struggle for public life: Democracy's promise and education's challenge*. Boulder, CO: Paradigm Press.

Greene, M. (1988). *The dialectic of freedom*. New York: Teachers College Press.

Greene, M. (2000). *Releasing the imagination: Essays on education, the arts, and social change*. San Francisco: Jossey-Bass.

Hunter, M. (1982). *Mastery teaching*. El Segundo, CA: TIP Publications.

Hunter, R. (2004). *Madeline Hunter's Mastery teaching: Increasing instructional effectiveness in elementary and secondary schools*. Thousand Oaks, CA: Corwin.

Kohl, H. (1975). *The open classroom: A practical guide to a new way of teaching*. London: Methuen.

Kohl, H. (1987). *On teaching*. New York: Schocken.

Kohl, H. (1988). *Thirty-six children*. New York: Plume.

Kohl, H. (2004). *Stupidity and tears*. New York: New Press.

Kozol, J. (1992). *Savage inequalities: Children in America's schools*. New York: Harper Perennial.

Kozol, J. (2005). *The shame of the nation: The restoration of apartheid schooling in America*. New York: Crown.

Lipman, M. (1980). *Philosophy in the classroom*. Philadelphia: Temple University Press.

Lipman, M. (1982). *Harry Stottlemeier's discovery*. Montclair, NJ: Institute for the Advancement of Philosophy.

Lipman, M. (2003). *Thinking in the classroom* (2nd ed.). Cambridge: Cambridge University Press.

McLaren, P. (2002). *Life in schools: An introduction to critical pedagogy in the foundations of education*. Boston: Allyn & Bacon.

Meier, D. (2002). *The power of their ideas: Lessons from America from a small school in Harlem*. Boston: Beacon.

Montessori, M. (1988). *Montessori method*. New York: Schocken.

Pavlov, I. P. (2003). *Conditioned reflexes*. Mineola, NY: Dover.

Phenix, P. H. (1977). *Education and the common good: A moral philosophy of the classroom*. Westport, CT: Greenwood.

Sternberg, R. (1999). *Thinking styles*. Cambridge: Cambridge University Press.

Taba, H. (1967). *The teacher's handbook for elementary social studies.* Reading, MA: Addison Wesley.

References

Adler, J., Cohen, A. D., Houston, P., Manly, H., Wingert, P., & Wright, L. (1992, Feb. 17). The curse of self-esteem. *Newsweek,* 46–51.

Adler, M. (1983). *Paideia problems and possibilities*. New York: Macmillan.

Adler, M. (1984). *The Paideia program:* An educational syllabus. New York: Macmillan.

Adler, M. (1998). *The Paideia proposal:* An educational manifesto. New York: Touchstone.

Anti-Defamation League. World of Difference Institute. PK–12 curricula and teacher training. Retrieved June 8, 2006, from www.adl.org/education/edu_awod/default_awod.asp

Brophy, J. (1979). Teacher behavior and its effects. *Journal of Educational Psychology, 71,* 733–750.

Bruner, J. (1977). *The process of education*. Cambridge, MA: Harvard University Press.

Core Knowledge Foundation. (2006). *Core Knowledge K–8 schools*. Retrieved June 8, 2006, from www.coreknowledge.org

Cremin, L. (1982). *American education: The national experience, 1783–1876*. New York: Harper Colophon.

DeRoche, E. F., & Williams, M. M. (2001). *Character education*. Lanham, MD: Scarecrow.

Duckenfield, M. (1992). *Service learning: Meeting the needs of youth at-risk.* Washington, DC: National Drop-Out Prevention Center.

Eisner, E., & Vallance, E. (1974). *Conflicting conceptions of the curriculum*. Berkeley, CA: McCutchan.

Elementary science study. (1960). Cambridge, MA: Educational Development Center. Retrieved June 8, 2006, from www.coe.ufl.edu/esh/Projects/ess.htm

Gage, N. L. (1978). *The scientific basis of the art of teaching*. New York: Teachers College Press.

Good, T. (1979). Teacher effectiveness in the elementary school: What do we know about it now? *Journal of Teacher Education*, *30*, 52–64.

Good, T., & Grouws, D. (1979). The Missouri Mathematics Effectiveness Project: An experimental study in a fourth grade classroom. *Journal of Educational Psychology*, *71*, 355–372.

Hirsch, E. D., Jr. (1987). *Cultural literacy: What every American needs to know*. New York: Houghton Mifflin.

Hutchins, R. M. (1952). *The great conversation: The substance of a liberal education*. (Great Books of the Western World: Vol. 1). Chicago: Encyclopaedia Britannica.

Lortie. D. (2002). *Schoolteacher: A sociological study*. Chicago: University of Chicago Press.

Mager, R. (1997). *Preparing instructional objectives: A critical tool in the development of effective instruction* (3rd ed.). Atlanta, GA: Center for Effective Performance Press.

Maslow, A. (1998). *Toward a psychology of being* (3rd ed.). New York: Wiley.

Medley, D. (1979). The effectiveness of teachers. In P. Peterson & H. Walberg (Eds.), *Research on teaching: Concepts, findings, and implications* (pp. 11–27). Berkeley, CA: McCutchan.

National Paideia Center. The Paideia Schools. Retrieved June 8, 2006, from www.paideia.org

Neill, A. S. (1996). *Summerhill School: A new view of childhood* (Rev. ed.). New York: St. Martin's Griffin.

Piaget, J. (1977). *The essential Piaget*. New York: Basic Books.

Ravitch, D. (2000). *Left back: A century of failed school reforms*. New York: Simon & Schuster.

Rogers, C., & Freiberg, H. J. (1994). *Freedom to learn* (3rd ed.). New York: Prentice Hall.

Rosenshine, B. (1979). Content, time, and direct instruction. In P. Peterson & H. Walberg (Eds.), *Research on teaching: Concepts, findings, and implications* (pp. 28–56). Berkeley, CA: McCutchan.

Sarason, S. (1993). *The case for change: Rethinking the professional preparation of teachers*. San Francisco: Jossey-Bass.

Science: A process approach. (1963). University of Connecticut, Stamford.

Science curriculum improvement study. (1965). University of California, Berkeley.

Shulman, L. (1987). Knowledge and teaching: Foundations of the new reforms. *Harvard Educational Review*, *47*, 1–22.

Silberman, C. (1973). *The open classroom reader*. New York: Vintage.

Skinner, B. F. (1968). *The technology of teaching*. New York: Appleton-Century-Crofts.

chapter

The Role of Assessment

During a class session with a group of teacher candidates, I (T. D.) passed out samples of children's writing and asked them to "assess" the work. They did not hesitate and diligently began a process of marking errors in writing conventions, such as spelling, punctuation, and capitalization. In our ensuing conversation, they also discussed the content of each piece and rated the work on the basis of such characteristics as the use of interesting details and the complexity of ideas used in the writing. I then asked them to list their goals for future instruction with these young writers. This task proved to be more difficult. While they had little difficulty determining what was "wrong" with each piece of writing, using those same samples to identify instructional moves did not proceed as easily for them.

A number of explanations might shed light on the responses of this group of teacher candidates. For example, they may have relied on their own past experiences as K–12 students in similar scenarios, in which they completed a task and teachers graded their efforts, with little feedback or opportunity for remediation. As a result, perhaps they saw the role of teacher as assigning grades and finding "errors" in student work and had encountered few models for using the information to guide students. Or possibly they felt uncertain about what the goals of writing instruction for young children might be. Should they focus on mechanics, content, or both? What should students at this level know and be able to do? What could guide them as instructors? In short, my students may have had limited understanding of what I meant when I asked them to assess the writing samples and of the important role of assessment in guiding instruction.

In this chapter, we turn to the role of assessments in respect to content standards and benchmarks. We will define what an assessment is and how it guides instruction. First, consider the two brief scenarios that follow. As you do so, ask yourself how each teacher is using the assessment tool.

Two Approaches to Assessment

Scenario 1

Ms. Israels, a seventh-grade math teacher, has just completed a six-week unit on linear equations. The students in her class have had multiple opportunities to graph the domains and ranges of equations during both in-class lessons and homework assignments. Ms. Israels has carefully constructed a unit exam to test students on their understanding of these concepts. The students are given one class period to complete this examination. Afterward, Ms. Israels collects the exams and scores them based on correct or incorrect responses to each question. She also carefully considers the reasoning that is demonstrated by the work the students wrote down as they attempted to answer each question. The scores vary, but the students have individually and collectively shown proficiency in the concepts tested. Scores from the exam are recorded in Ms. Israels's grading program as percentages of correct responses. At the next class period, she returns the exams to the students and then tells them they will begin the next unit in their text on functions. The students open their books, and Ms. Israels begins the lesson.

Scenario 2

Mr. Calnin is a seventh-grade teacher in the same middle school. His students are also working with linear equations. Part way through this unit of instruction, he provides the students with a well-constructed quiz that attempts to measure what his students know about the concepts they have studied together. After his students have completed them, Mr. Calnin collects the quizzes and carefully considers the work that the students have done. Several students have made multiple errors and have clearly not demonstrated a proficient level of understanding of the concepts. As he reviews each of the quiz responses, Mr. Calnin looks at each student's work. When an error appears, Mr. Calnin tries to determine how the student was reasoning and makes notations in the margins of the student work of questions to ask the student. Mr. Calnin also considers how each student demonstrated understanding of the concepts throughout the past two weeks of instruction. He records both the student scores and the concepts he will reteach to individual students and to the class as a whole. During the next class period, he meets with students to go over their quizzes and gather further information about how they were reasoning as they worked on the quiz problems. He begins the next class by reteaching concepts that were misunderstood by several students in the class.

Both of these teachers were dedicated to teaching linear equations. Each considered the assessment tool to be an important way to determine what the students knew and were able to do with concepts that were taught. However, the teachers' use of the information gathered with the assessment tools differed. Ms. Israels used the exam to determine a summary grade for the unit of study, while Mr. Calnin viewed the quiz as a tool for deciding what to reteach. So what's the difference?

Working definitions of assessment vary; however, most educators recognize two forms of assessment: summative and formative. Ms. Israels's use of the examination demonstrated a **summative assessment**—a tool for determining a grade or summary. Her unit exam was primarily used to determine the level of proficiency with a concept at the end of a unit of study. Having determined that her students had a proficient understanding of linear equations, she decided to move on to the next concept in her plan of instruction. Mr. Calnin's use of the mathematics quiz illustrated a **formative assessment**—a tool for assessing the status of teaching and learning efforts while they are under way. He used the quiz to collect information on his students' developing understandings of linear equations and combined this information with data he gathered from students' daily work. Mr. Calnin also analyzed the reasoning his students were using on the quiz—taking notes and then adding more information from his subsequent conversations with the students. His goal was to discover what his students knew and were able to show about their understandings of linear equations. In short, his intention was to use this information to plan his next instructional steps—including reteaching concepts in which his students had not demonstrated proficiency.

Both summative and formative assessments are valuable tools for teachers. Assessing what students know and are able to do is required for such tasks as giving final grades, reporting to parents, helping students set learning goals, and planning for classroom learning opportunities. An examination or a quiz can be an effective assessment tool. What defines them is their use.

As you consider how to address content standards, benchmarks, and the teaching models outlined in this text, bear in mind that both summative and formative assessments are keys to success. They help us discover what students know and are able to do, and the content standards and benchmarks help us to chart goals and objectives for student learning. In this chapter, we will discuss the use of formative and summative assessments in more detail. We will consider the role that both teachers and learners play in the assessment process and how these instruments connect with content standards and benchmarks.

Summative Assessments

When many people think about assessment, their model is a grade on a report card, a unit test, a final exam, or the like. Most of us have encountered these types of

Many of us are familiar with summative assessments, such as a unit test in math, that report a grade at the conclusion of a unit of study. However, there are many types of summative assessments and many ways to record and present the information they yield.

assessment practices numerous times in our schooling experiences. Each is an attempt to summarize and make judgments about learning (Boston, 2002; O'Connor, 2002). Indeed, McTighe and O'Connor (2005) state that summative assessments "summarize what students have learned at the conclusion of an instructional segment. These assessments tend to be evaluative and teachers encapsulate and report assessments as a score or grade" (p. 11). This use of summative assessments plays important roles. It aids teachers in determining how the teaching and learning experiences they designed have improved students' understanding of course concepts, goals, and objectives. It also allows teachers to communicate this information to students and their caregivers. In addition, it can assist teachers and learners by providing a guide for future work: moving on to new or more advanced concepts or reteaching when goals and objectives have not been met at a proficient level.

Types of Summative Assessments

Examinations of various types (unit exams, final exams, etc.) tend to be the norm when it comes to summative assessments, especially in many middle and high school content area classrooms. In these settings, teachers often feel the pressure to report letter grades at the end of "marking periods," and many view tests as an efficient way to accomplish this task. When constructed fairly and reliably, to match learning goals and objectives, such exams can yield helpful information about what students know and are able to do. They may even have the added advantage of preparing students for the structure of state-mandated tests. However, reliance on these tools exclusively may put some students at a disadvantage because the tests may simply not be the best way for them to demonstrate their learning, nor do tests give a complete picture of learning. Think of it this way: If a written test on the rules of driving were the only thing that determined whether a 16-year-old was ready for a driver's license, would you be a comfortable passenger in that 16-year-old's vehicle? Or would you want the would-be driver to also demonstrate driving skills in a road test? The results of both tests would certainly provide a clearer picture of the driver's ability and produce a better decision about granting a license than would the result of either test alone.

Multiple types of summative assessments can and should be used because they may yield different and more comprehensive information as well as provide students with a variety of ways to demonstrate their learning (see Figure 3.1). In addition to tests and exams, these could include such tools as portfolios, performances, or final drafts of a paper or writing project (O'Connor, 2002). To illustrate this point, we will discuss two of these summative assessment tools: final drafts of writing and a performance of some type.

In many classrooms, whether students are writing narrative or expository texts, teachers typically require multiple drafts of a text, at various points of development, instead of the submission of only a final draft. Indeed, teachers recognize that the writing process includes cycles of prewriting, drafting, revising, and editing (a feature of many state content standards and benchmarks). As teachers apply writing goals and objectives consistent with this view of writing, they often engage with their students during the writing process, whether the text is a factual report or a short story. Rather than grading the various drafts that students produce, teachers use the

Figure 3.1	Common Types of Summative Assessments

1. Tests and exams	Written or oral assessments given at the end of a unit of study (used in all subject areas)
2. Portfolios	Collections of final works submitted (art projects, writing drafts, musical compositions, technical drawings, and other groupings of final works in various subject areas)
3. Final drafts	Completed versions of texts written (term papers or final drafts of stories, poems, or expository texts)
4. Mandated tests	Examinations dictated by district or state requirements
5. Performances	Presentation of a practiced skill or craft (vocal, instrumental, dramatic, and oratory)
6. Demonstrations	Exhibition of a final project (poster, replica, craft, experiment, or various other ways to show an object made or process completed)

drafts to determine what students know and are able to do and to guide students in areas of need. Teachers use the final draft for summative assessment because it demonstrates what the student has learned over the course of instruction.

Another option for summative assessment is a performance. It could involve a speech, demonstration, or artistic presentation. For example, students studying the American Revolution could demonstrate their learning by dramatizing a well-known character from that period and reporting on their character's life, developing and performing a play about the events of that time, using a PowerPoint presentation to demonstrate famous battlegrounds and the strategies used to win a battle, or even demonstrating some of the important arts and crafts of the period. The performance options are nearly limitless and allow students to use the multiple intelligences (Gardner, 1993) that best demonstrate that they have met the goals and objectives established for their learning.

The summative assessments used to evaluate and report student progress at the end of an instructional period need not be limited to one or two tools. In fact, we urge you to recognize the value of using a variety of assessment tools that will comprehensively reflect students' learning (McMillan, 2000). Emphasizing this holistic approach may be particularly important in light of recent and growing emphasis on high stakes testing in all states, in accordance with federal law. Students, parents, and teachers need to view mandated, high stakes summative assessment as part of a larger picture, not as the entire picture.

Mandated Summative Assessments—Benefits and Cautions

Over the past several years, much of the energy devoted at all levels of education and government to raising learning and performance standards in the nation's schools has focused on the role of assessment. Indeed, the focus is worldwide. For example, in England, students take annual national tests (SATS), and the results are used as a yardstick for the performance of the students and their schools. In the United States, we do not have a standardized national testing program for all students. Rather, recent federal law, such as the No Child Left Behind Act, mandates that each state have a testing program for all students that is based on the state's content standards and benchmarks in a variety of content areas. We believe that the thinking behind mandating these external and summative assessments provides reason for both caution and optimism.

Black and Wiliam (1998) discuss the emphasis on developing summative assessments in both England and the United States. They suggest that some consider the tests themselves to be the way to raise standards—in other words, they represent a carrot-and-stick approach to improving student performance—but that instead, educators should focus on teaching and learning in the classroom itself. Others might argue that using a mandated test forces schools and teachers to pay attention to the established content standards and benchmarks of their state because they know that a poor performance may result in consequences such as reorganization of the school. Our goal here is not to resolve these issues.

We believe that mandated state or nationally based assessments will be a part of the educational and political landscape in this country for the foreseeable future. Regardless of our opinions about them, we need to consider carefully how they can be used to provide helpful information for teachers, parents, and students.

State-mandated summative assessments should be seen as part of a total assessment program at the local and classroom level. Teachers and districts can combine the data from these tests with a variety of other measures to gauge the effectiveness of district-wide strategies and materials in promoting learning related to state content standards and benchmarks. Likewise, teachers can combine data from individual student results with their own assessments to develop goals and objectives for future instruction. In short, the information can be very helpful when viewed as one assessment tool among many.

In a similar vein, it is imperative to help parents and students understand the meaning of individual reports of mandated state summative assessments. I once had a student who had marked nearly every answer incorrectly on one section of a state assessment. His parents were understandably concerned about this report. However, as we met and reviewed the many classroom and district-based assessments of their son on material that was similar, it became clear that his performance on the state test did not accurately reflect his understanding. The results of these state-mandated assessments must be considered potentially helpful but not definitive in and of themselves. They are but "a snapshot of a student's performance on a given day" (Boston, 2002, p. 5).

One technical aspect of interpreting state- or district-mandated testing results for parents or other caregivers involves helping them understand the jargon often attached to such tests. Specifically, the results of tests are often reported with such terms as **standardized**, **norm referenced**, and **criterion referenced**. These terms can often be confusing to caregivers, making it difficult for them to interpret the results of the tests. Their definitions are provided in Figure 3.2. If the reporting function of such assessments is to have any value for parents and caregivers, we need to make sure that they understand what the results are telling them about their child's performance.

Figure 3.2   Assessment Terminology

Standardized test: This type of test has a specified procedure. Typically, teachers or other test administrators have a manual or other guide that stipulates exactly how the test must be administered, including timing, directions to be read, materials that can be used, and how the testing situation must be organized. Common examples of this type of test would include the SAT and ACT. Nearly all state-mandated tests are standardized. This ensures that all test takers receive the same directions and testing conditions (Zarrillo, 2007).

Norm-referenced test: This type of test allows for comparisons between the test taker and a sample of students—the "norm." Individual student scores can then be compared to those of others who took the test, and scores can be reported as percentiles. For example, a percentile score of 90 on a segment of a test would mean that the student scored better on that segment than 90% of those in the sampling group. The higher the percentile score, the better the student performed against the norm (Zarrillo, 2007).

Criterion-referenced test: These types of tests do not compare test takers to a norm. Rather, they are used to determine how well an individual performs on specified skills or understanding of particular content. Theoretically, all test takers can receive a perfect score on the test. Many teacher-constructed exams would fit this definition.

Summative Assessments and Classroom Learning Goals and Activities

As teachers consider learning goals, as well as teaching and learning activities, for their students, it has become a common practice to explicitly relate them to content standards, benchmarks, and grade-level content expectations. While teachers and school administrators may be familiar with these documents, it is less clear that students themselves always have a clear view of them or the learning goals and activities that result from them. It is worth exploring how these summative assessments and classroom learning goals and activities can intersect for students.

McTighe and O'Connor (2005) suggest that teachers "present summative . . . assessment tasks to students at the beginning of a new unit or course" (p. 12). The teacher can do this by merely describing what students will need to know and how they will need to demonstrate their understanding (pass a type of test, present a performance of some type, create a product, etc.). Among the merits that McTighe and O'Connor see in this approach is that "the summative assessments clarify the targeted standards and benchmarks for teachers and learners" (p. 12). Therefore, teachers must ensure that they have developed well-designed summative assessments that reflect the standards and benchmarks that will be used for the state assessment. In this way, both teachers and students have a clear view of the stated learning objectives and how they will be assessed (p. 12).

Presenting the summative assessment task to students at the beginning of a unit or course has an additional merit. McTighe and O'Connor (2005) note that doing so "provides a meaningful learning goal for students" (p. 12). Students are not only more focused on the goals that reflect the standards and benchmarks, but they can also see why they are doing certain activities and developing particular skills. A sports analogy illustrates this point. My son is a baseball fanatic. He goes to baseball clinics, where he is coached repeatedly on how to swing his bat. Why does he spend hours engaged in these activities? It is obvious. He wants to play the game well, and he sees the coaching sessions as helping him reach this goal. When students know in advance how their work in class may help them learn and perform well on the assessment, they see purpose in classroom teaching and learning activities. Figure 3.3 describes the way one teacher presented a summative assessment to a class at the beginning of a unit of study.

How can you assist your students at the intersection of mandated summative assessments and classroom learning goals and activities? Present the goals in a transparent manner at the beginning of a teaching and learning segment. Allow students to see what they are expected to know and be able to do so that in turn they can direct their attention to what will be assessed and see meaning in the activities designed to get them there.

Figure 3.3   Mr. VanderVelde's Introduction to a Study of Cells

Mr. VanderVelde has decided to introduce his unit on cells to his middle school biology students by explaining the state standard that this unit is based on. In this way, he hopes to help his students set a goal for their own learning, as well as prepare them for the way it will be assessed by the project he has designed and by the state-mandated test they will take in a few months. He begins by showing the students the specific standard they will be addressing, which has been written on a piece of chart paper: "All students will apply an understanding of cells to the functioning of multicellular organisms; and explain how cells grow, develop and reproduce" (Michigan Department of Education, 1996).

Mr. VanderVelde: Today we will be starting a new unit. This one will focus on cells. On the overhead, I've listed the state requirement for what you need to know and be able to do related to cells. (*He reads the standard.*) You might be wondering why I am telling you this. It is because I want you to know in advance where we are headed with this unit. As you know, you will be taking the state test in science soon, and this is one of the things you will be expected to understand. Think of this as our learning goal, something for all of us to work toward.

Mike: Okay. So what exactly will we be doing to get to this goal?

Mr. VanderVelde: I have a lot of things planned to help you learn about how cells grow, develop, and reproduce. By the end of this unit, each of you will construct a poster that shows the parts of a cell and how the cell does each of these things.

Kellia: What do we have to have on this poster and how are you going to grade it exactly?

Mr. VanderVelde: I have some posters here that students made for this project last year. I also have a grading rubric. (*He passes these out.*) What I would like you to do is read over the rubric first. (*He gives them time to do so.*) Now I want all of us to look at one of these posters and use the grading rubric to score it. After each of you has done that, we will talk about your scores for the poster and my expectations for your poster and what you will need to know.

Recording Summative Assessments in Relation to Content Standards and Benchmarks

While teachers and curriculum administrators spend many hours coordinating classroom materials and learning activities with content standards and benchmarks, the record of student efforts in these activities is often less well matched to goals. For example, teacher grade books or electronic programs often list percentage scores on tests or other summative assessments and then average those scores to determine grades. While this approach may be an efficient use of time, it yields little usable information about how student performance relates to specific goals based on content standards and objectives. Simply recording that a student earned an average of 90% on several assessments is insufficient if we want to determine the level of performance on specific goals and objectives. Which goals were achieved and which were not? Only a breakdown based on the content standards and benchmarks being addressed by the assessment tool can adequately answer these questions.

O'Connor (2002) suggests that "the most appropriate way to organize a grading plan would be to base it on individual standards or benchmarks" (p. 51). Whether using a grade book or an electronic grading program, teachers replace categories such as "unit test 1" with actual standards or benchmarks. Figure 3.4 provides an example of this type of grading plan. In this system, a summative assessment can be broken down into specific units that are coordinated with the standards and benchmarks that have been used to develop classroom teaching and learning segments. A student may achieve an overall score of 90% on the assessment, but the teacher can determine which specific goals and objectives were achieved at a satisfactory level, as well as target those that were not. For example, the student may have reached several objectives on the assessment with 100% accuracy but may not have demonstrated proficiency in respect to one objective. While the student's overall performance may be at the 90% level, recording performance as it aligns with objectives that are coordinated with standards and benchmarks allows the teacher to see and specifically target unsatisfactory understanding and performance.

Separating and recording performance on summative assessments that align with specific content standards and objectives has a number of advantages. One of these is your ability to quickly and visually see both how student performance matches the targeted content standards and benchmarks and how often you have provided learning and assessment activities that target them. In short, your grading program can become an informal bar graph. A visual inspection can easily reveal whether you have targeted all benchmarks adequately or focused students' attention on some benchmarks but not others. Not only are you able to see student proficiency; you are also able to balance instruction so that it targets all the required standards and benchmarks.

It is important to note that when you design a grading program that coordinates with standards and benchmarks, you must take care to provide sufficient opportunities to both develop and measure proficiency. Insufficient data may lead to misleading conclusions. For example, one of our children recently received a report card indicating that he had not reached proficiency with one stated objective. When we inquired about this, his teacher determined that the computerized grading program she was using had based that conclusion on one response on the only summative assessment used to measure this objective. Clearly, this is insufficient data on which to make a reliable determination. When coordinated carefully with standards and benchmarks, a grading program can be a very effective way to measure student performance, but you need multiple measures to assess accurately how well students are achieving the objectives.

One caution is worth remembering when you set up a record-keeping system. O'Connor (2002) points out that sometimes there are simply so many standards and benchmarks that record keeping becomes inefficient and time consuming. When you are faced with this situation, we urge you to combine similar standards and benchmarks and set up grading programs to reflect only those standards and benchmarks being addressed at the time. For example, many benchmarks may relate to a writing process like editing a final draft. Careful consolidation may allow you to put these

Figure 3.4   Grading Plan Based on Benchmarks

	Content Standard 3: Students investigate relationships such as equality, inequality, inverses, factors, and multiples and represent and compare very large and very small numbers.			
	Assessments and Scores			
Student name: _____	**Take-home exam** Oct. 22	**Group assessment** Oct. 25	**Unit test** Nov. 3	
Compare and order integers and rational numbers using relations of equality and inequality	+8/10	+10/10	+10/10	
Express numerical comparisons of ratios and rates	+5/5		+10/10	
Explain the meaning of powers and roots of numbers	+9/10	+9/10	+7/10	
Use calculators to compute powers and square roots		+5/5	+5/5	

SOURCE: Standards and benchmarks from Michigan Department of Education, 1996; chart adapted from O'Connor, 2002.

into one column or row for recording. In addition, some of these editing tasks may be developmental, and a category may begin with the tasks most pertinent for the students at that level, but it can be modified at a later time to reflect higher-level skills.

Using standards and benchmarks as the foundation for a grading program has one other important benefit. It allows for accurate and detailed reporting of what students know and are able to do. This becomes especially important when helping parents understand their child's performance. I can illustrate this point with an incident from my early days as a fifth-grade teacher. I had dutifully recorded percentages in my grade book for my students' mathematics assignments and unit exams. I reported these figures to parents at our parent-teacher conferences. However, at some point it occurred to me that if parents asked what a certain percentage suggested about the content their child had mastered, I was not prepared to tell them. My carefully documented grades were simply not detailed enough. Had my records been tied to the appropriate standards and objectives, I would have been far better prepared both to report to them in a comprehensive manner and to discuss future learning opportunities to attain proficiency or build mastery.

Summative assessments play an important role in determining student understanding and proficiency at the end of a unit of study. As they develop teaching and learning opportunities for the students in their classrooms, teachers must be conscious of the increasing emphasis on external summative assessments. Equally important are formative assessments, which guide teachers daily as they work to help students achieve the proficiency to be measured by summative assessments.

Formative Assessments

To distinguish formative assessments from summative assessments, it may be helpful to use a medical analogy. During an operation, a patient is constantly monitored for such things as pulse, respiration, and blood pressure. When the medical staff determines that one of these functions is not adequate, adjustments are made immediately to ensure a successful outcome. If measuring the outcome is the role of summative assessments, then monitoring the ongoing functions is the role of formative assessments. Formative assessments are continual, and they direct instruction. As teachers work with their students daily, they must constantly consider whether and how well students are mastering the content being addressed. Teachers observe, ask questions, clarify, listen to student explanations, and consider student performance on daily assignments and quizzes. The information they gather in this recurrent manner determines the direction of their instructional efforts—both immediate and future.

As described by Boston (2002), "Formative assessment is the diagnostic use of assessment to provide feedback to teachers and students over the course of instruction" (p. 1). Teachers need to gather and analyze information discovered through formative assessments, as well as share this information with students continually, so that common learning goals and objectives can be developed and achieved. Careful selection and use of multiple types of formative assessments are keys to achieving this outcome.

Figure 3.5 Common Types of Formative Assessments

Formal

1. Quiz: Brief written or oral assessment of ongoing areas of study (self-checking, teacher corrected, computer based, and oral)

2. Checklist: List of behaviors or skills related to learning objectives (used in all subject areas; can include demonstrated skills or tasks)

3. Homework: Independent opportunities to practice a skill or strategy (used in all subject areas)

4. Anecdotal record: Teacher's records and notes of observed demonstrations of student skill levels (used in all subject areas)

Informal

1. Questioning: Asking students to respond to questions or statements (oral or written; used in all subject areas)

2. Observation: Carefully monitoring student behaviors and responses (used in all subject areas)

Types of Formative Assessments

Formative assessments can and should be of two types: **formal** and **informal** (McTighe & O'Connor, 2005). Both can provide quick and efficient ways to "check the pulse" of student learning at any point in the teaching and learning process. When administered frequently, they can provide both the teacher and the student with valuable information on levels of mastery. They have the additional advantage of allowing for a change of course when current levels of understanding are inadequate or anticipated progress is not being achieved. They can also confirm that goals and objectives are being reached, allowing movement toward more advanced concepts or activities. Figure 3.5 outlines both types of formative assessment.

Assessments that are both formal and formative are varied. A weekly quiz or an observation checklist are common examples of this type of formative assessment. They are used by many teachers to gather information about student learning. For instance, a teacher can provide students with a self-checking quiz as an opportunity to see if a math concept, such as "borrowing" in simple two-digit subtraction problems, is being done accurately. The quiz provides both teacher and students with information that helps them determine whether the features of this operation should be reviewed, clarified, or expanded to three-digit problems—without waiting until a unit test and the potential for increased confusion for the learner. Similarly, a teacher can use a simple checklist to record observations as students demonstrate the strategies they use when they encounter an unknown word in a reading passage. For example, if a student uses only one strategy (skipping over the word), the teacher may record this and plan an opportunity to teach the student an additional strategy (using picture clues, for example).

Many other formal methods of formative assessment are routinely employed by teachers. Examples include checking the development of a student writing a draft and recording revision suggestions, having students develop a graphic organizer (such as a mind map), homework assignments, or any number of other content-specific status checks (O'Connor, 2002; Boston, 2002; McTighe & O'Connor, 2005). Each provides a feedback loop that can be used to organize future teaching and learning experiences.

Many informal methods of formative assessment are also frequently utilized at all levels and in all content areas (O'Connor, 2002; Boston, 2002; McTighe & O'Connor, 2005). These range from asking students questions when discussing a story or topic to carefully observing student behaviors and responses to set tasks. Attentive teachers use them as opportunities to analyze and adjust their teaching and other factors in the learning environment to facilitate student understanding.

When considering the use of formative assessments, variety is important. Indeed, McMillan (2000) argues that "good assessment uses multiple methods" (p. 5). A mix of both formal and informal types of formative assessment can provide a rounded and helpful understanding of student learning, as well as indicating how to adjust instruction when necessary.

The Role of Formative Assessment

The most important function of formative assessments is continual feedback to teachers and students. In this role, they are not part of the grading process (O'Connor, 2002). Rather, both teachers and students use them to make adjustments in their teaching and learning experiences. When used in this way, students are given the freedom to focus on their learning rather than just finding the right answers (Boston, 2002). I am reminded of a recent evening when my daughter was doing her algebra homework—an opportunity to practice graphing systems of equations. Her teacher had devoted considerable time to teaching and guiding the students through this process in class that day. However, as my daughter worked through one of the assigned problems, she became confused, and the example problems provided little assistance. After exhausting all her resources, she marked her area of confusion on the paper and went on to complete the assignment. The next day, she was able to ask her teacher about the problem, and her teacher was able to clarify the process while gaining insights into my daughter's mathematical reasoning. All were easily accomplished without the apprehension that often can accompany a graded assignment. Most important, learning resulted.

In lieu of evaluative grades, teachers use formative assessment to give and record feedback that is designed to improve performance (Boston, 2002). This kind of feedback can take many forms. In the illustration above, the teacher talked through the problem with my daughter and demonstrated the correct steps for graphing the equations. She may have also noted this in her own record-keeping system as a way to monitor progress. On other occasions, teachers may write comments on early drafts of student work, develop rubrics to help students monitor their own progress, have conferences with students about their work, or simply make suggestions for improvements. Whatever form it takes, the feedback itself is most important.

When students receive feedback that outlines their strengths and areas for growth in specific ways, learning improves (Black & Wiliam, 1998). This may be especially true for students who believe that they have little control over their ability to succeed. Low-achieving students often assume that their successes and failures in the learning environment are due to forces they cannot control—luck, the teacher, or even how they happen to be feeling at the moment (Ormrod, 2006). Formative assessments that provide useful feedback can aid them in understanding that they can exert more control over their learning. This understanding alone may increase effort and performance. Indeed, in his review of studies of assessment, Black and Wiliam (1998) argue that formative assessments help low-achieving students most and that their use with such students may help close the achievement gap between high- and low-performing students "while raising achievement overall" (p. 3).

With the important roles that formative assessments play in both teaching and learning experiences, as well as student achievement, a few words of caution are necessary. Formative assessment can work only in classrooms where teachers see knowledge as constructed and intelligence as flexible (Black & Wiliam, 1998). When teachers believe that understandings of concepts are uniquely crafted by the learner, based on the complex processes of assimilation and accommodation, they can use formative assessments to encourage the development of increasingly complex schema. Likewise, when teachers believe that aptitude can be influenced by guided learning opportunities, formative assessments can be an important tool in that process. However, if teachers assume that knowledge and intelligence are static—that students can learn only what they are handed and have only limited learning potential—those teachers will view formative assessments as having little useful value. We believe that evidence of the effectiveness of formative assessments to impact learning (Black & Wiliam, 1998) points to the utility of the former stance. Knowledge is constructed, intelligence is flexible, and formative assessments play an invaluable role in both.

Assessment and Issues of Quality

Although both summative and formative assessments play a significant role in teaching and learning, not all assessments are equal in design or use. This point is often made by teachers when they discuss the use of state-mandated summative assessments. It is not uncommon for teachers to complain that these assessments are poorly designed and lack alignment with teaching and learning or even with the state standards and benchmarks that guide instruction. This is of particular concern to educators because such assessments are used to evaluate the effectiveness of schools in high stakes ways. Whether summative or formative, all assessments must be designed and used with emphasis on quality and appropriate learning outcomes.

Whether the assessment is mandated by the state or the district or designed by the classroom teacher, an important issue is ensuring a match between what is taught and the assessment used to measure it (O'Connor, 2002; McTighe & O'Connor, 2005). Although this point may appear obvious, in practice disparities can and do occur. Take, for example, the case of an English teacher who understands that the district curriculum emphasizes and assesses writing. In response, the teacher places emphasis on such editing skills as the use of end punctuation and capitalization. This teacher may provide students with handouts that ask them to insert appropriate punctuation and capital letters in several sentences and with other, similarly focused activities. However, the district-level summative assessment used to evaluate writing focuses on students' ability to develop a constructed response to a particular set of readings. Although students must certainly pay attention to the use of punctuation in their written response, the assessment focuses on their facility in summarizing the information in the readings. As a result, the assessment does not measure what the teacher has emphasized, and the measured level of student achievement in writing will surely be impacted. This mismatch can and should be avoided by carefully aligning the information taught and the way students practice it in classroom learning situations with how it is presented on the assessment.

Another important consideration concerning assessments is the role of professional judgment and interpretation in the process (McMillan, 2000). On some state-mandated summative assessments, as well as assessments designed at the classroom level, proficiency may be measured using a multiple-choice test, while in other states or classrooms, to demonstrate proficiency in the same area, students may be required to perform a task and write out the results. Why do some assessments use one format while others elect to use a different one? Does each format equally measure proficiency? The answers lie in the professional judgment of educators at all levels of the educational system. Indeed, even the interpretation of the results from such different tools is a matter of professional judgment and interpretation. For example, it is common for state-mandated assessments to use such terms as *basic skills* and *functional level* to report the number of students who meet a certain level of proficiency, and these reports assume there is a common understanding of these terms. However, what is considered basic in one place may not be considered basic in another. Likewise, in the classroom, what determines a passing or failing performance can vary based on the judgment and interpretation of the individual teacher. Can we evolve a consensus on the most effective ways to design assessment tools and interpret their results? It is not likely that we can, nor is it our intention to suggest that a particular way is the best way. Rather, we believe it is important for teachers to always be aware that professional judgment and interpretation are consistently a factor when they consider the design and interpretation of their own assessment tools and those they are required to use.

A final consideration when using assessments is their efficiency and feasibility (McMillan, 2000). In our state a few years ago, several parents and high school educators complained to state legislators about the time consumed by the administration of the state-mandated high school proficiency tests. Their concern was that hours of time, which could have been dedicated to instruction, were instead being used for testing. This same concern can also be felt at the classroom level. Some districts require teachers to administer and report the results of various assessment tools at scheduled intervals, taking still more time away from learning opportunities. Of course, such concerns have merit, and care should be taken to avoid lengthy testing sessions when possible. Indeed, assessment works best when it can be done efficiently and in practical ways. We urge you to consider integrating assessment with instruction whenever possible, a particular virtue of formative assessment. Teachers observe, ask questions, and discuss with students—then record and analyze the resulting data. Summative assessments can also be integrated with classroom teaching at times. For example, earlier in this chapter I described my work with a group of

One way to promote the efficiency of assessments is to turn them into learning opportunities for other students—such as a performance or presentation.

fifth graders who were studying the Revolutionary War period. Each student studied the importance of a selected figure or event from the history of the period. The summative assessment was based on a performance that taught the class about what they had learned. (Some students became a famous character and told the class about their life, others created poems recounting their character's adventures, and one even told the story of the war using a PowerPoint presentation that included art and music from the period.) Their performances were summative assessments, and they provided beneficial learning opportunities for other students, who served as their audience. The process was both practical and an efficient use of time.

Facilitating Student Self-Assessment

In much of this chapter, we have relegated students primarily to the role of receivers in the assessment transaction. However, we believe that students can and should take an active role by conducting self-assessments that can be both summative and formative. In order to do so, students need to have a clear understanding of the criteria used for assessment and the ability to set appropriate goals based on the criteria.

Often in classroom settings, teachers set learning goals and the criteria for reaching them at varying levels of proficiency. Students may or may not know what is expected of them. When students do not have a clear understanding of expectations, they cannot be expected to reach them in an efficient manner. Often students simply lack models on which to base their own performance. Think of being handed a ball of modeling clay and told only to create "something." In some cases, this can encourage creative effort. In others, it can be a frustrating and unproductive experience—especially if you know that the final product will be evaluated in some way. Most often, students in your classroom will need and want to see models of varying levels of performance, as well as criteria for assessment (McTighe & O'Connor, 2005). Having these tools gives students the opportunity to more adequately assess their own efforts and accomplishments—in short, to self-assess.

The intention of showing students models is not to promote cookie cutter imitations of the original but rather to help students understand the criteria for a successful learning outcome. For example, I once taped student presentations in which they had to use a metaphor to illustrate how their life experience mirrored a particular theory of psychosocial development. With the students' permission, I showed a sampling of these tapes to students faced with the same assignment the next semester. I carefully selected examples that showed excellence in meeting various evaluative criteria, as well as some that did not. Before showing any of the videotapes, I distributed and briefly discussed a rubric that listed each of the criteria for assessment. Then we watched the first videotape, and students were asked to assess it using the criteria in the rubric. As each tape was shown and assessed, we discussed our ratings and the rationale for each one. Finally, with models and goals in mind, students were assigned the task of developing their own presentations. When they presented their work, it was clear that no one had imitated the tapes they viewed. Each presentation had the distinctive mark of its creator, and each clearly benefited from the work we had done with the established criteria. Finally, the students viewed a videotape of their own presentation and wrote a self-assessment paper based on the established criteria. This type of approach is supported by studies demonstrating that when learning objectives, criteria for assessment, and opportunities to reflect on performance are transparent, improvements in student performance are achieved (Boston, 2002).

This example also illustrates a more subtle, yet important, dimension of self-assessment. Students need to understand how various levels of quality measure up according to their teacher's criteria (Shepard, 2005). My students and I discussed examples of both excellence and developing proficiency. This allowed them to distinguish one from the other and set their goals. Without this component, students cannot effectively self-assess their efforts. For example, if one criterion is "speak fluently" but students do not see examples that demonstrate exceptional, proficient, and subpar levels of speaking, they cannot effectively set their sights on what constitutes excellence.

In many cases, as mentioned above, a rubric can help students understand established criteria. Figure 3.6 provides an example of a rubric. Rubrics are typically developed by the teacher and list individual components for assessment. Each component lists characteristics that illustrate each of four or more levels of performance, such as, *needs improvement*, *developing proficiency*, *proficient*, and *demonstrates excellence*. Well-developed rubrics allow students to clearly identify teacher expectations and set goals for their own level of performance. Indeed, in some instances, students themselves complete the rubrics as an exercise in self-assessment. The development of rubrics for particular kinds of assignments is complex and will not be addressed here, but several useful reference books on their construction are available.

Finally, students identified as effective learners are often those who are able to set and work toward their own goals (McTighe & O'Connor, 2005). Giving students a self-assessment role allows them to establish and enact the skills necessary for realistic goal setting. In this way, students become active agents in their own ongoing learning experiences.

Figure 3.6   Segment of a Writing Rubric

Indicators	Performance Levels			
	Excellent	**Proficient**	**Developing Proficiency**	**Needs Improvement**
Writing mechanics	All text is edited accurately, including capitalization, punctuation, and spelling.	Most text is edited accurately, including capitalization, punctuation, and spelling. Few errors.	Some text is edited accurately, including capitalization, punctuation, and spelling. Significant errors.	Few mechanics are edited accurately, including capitalization, punctuation, and spelling. Needs further editing.
Organization	All of the text is appropriately sequenced.	Most of the text is appropriately sequenced.	Some of the text is appropriately sequenced. Some segments need to be reorganized.	Text is not sequenced appropriately and needs further work.
Word choice	All technical terms are used accurately and appropriately throughout the text.	Most of the technical terms are used accurately and appropriately throughout the text.	Some of the technical terms are used accurately and appropriately throughout the text. Revision is required for clarity and appropriateness.	Few of the technical terms are used accurately and appropriately throughout the text. Revision is required for clarity and appropriateness.
Key:	**Excellent:** Completed goals in an exceptional manner. Went beyond requirements.			
	Proficient: Accomplished goals. Met all basic requirements.			
	Developing Proficiency: Met many goals with developing knowledge and skill.			
	Needs Improvement: Incomplete or demonstrated little effort toward meeting goals or both.			

Summary

All the models of teaching outlined in this text can benefit from summative and formative assessments based on content standards and benchmarks. Summative assessments are typically used at the end of a unit of instruction. They often include such tools as unit tests, portfolios of student work, final projects, and state-mandated assessment instruments. These tools are traditionally used to determine grades or report summary information in other ways. On the other hand, formative assessments are integrated with instruction and provide feedback that allows teaching and learning experiences to be modified as needed. In short, they guide instruction as it is occurring. Frequent quizzes, observation checklists, and questioning are common examples of formative assessments. What ultimately determines the role of any assessment is its use—to grade student work or to alter instruction. Both are necessary components of effective classroom teaching and learning opportunities.

In this chapter, we have explored the role of assessments, as well as their benefits and potential pitfalls. We have also looked at some of the connections between assessments and standards and benchmarks, as well as classroom learning goals and record keeping. We have stressed the need for alignment between the assessment tool and the teaching methods. We have also discussed the importance of quality in the assessment tool itself as well as its use as a measurement tool. Finally, the need for students to be active agents in the assessment process and to develop the capacity for self-assessment has been advocated.

Good assessment is an essential ingredient in the teaching and learning process. While it guides that process, it also evaluates its effectiveness. With or without external mandates, the importance of assessment cannot be emphasized enough. Without ways to determine whether teaching is having its desired impact or if adjustments need to be made, we can easily lose sight of our ultimate goal: student learning.

Student Study Site

The Companion Web site for *Models of Teaching: Connecting Student Learning With Standards*

www.sagepub.com/dellooliostudy

Visit the Web-based student study site to enhance your understanding of the book content and discover additional resources that will take your learning one step further. You can enhance your understanding by using the comprehensive Study Guide, which includes chapter learning objectives, flash cards, practice tests, and more. You'll find special features, such as the links to standards from U.S. States and associated activities, Learning from Journal Articles, Field Experience worksheets, Learning from Case Studies, and PRAXIS resources.

References

Black, P., & Wiliam, D. (1998). Inside the black box: Raising standards through class-room assessment. *Phi Delta Kappan, 80*(2), 139 ff. Retrieved September 10, 2006, from http://www.pdkintl.org/kappan/kbla9810.htm

Boston, C. (2002). The concept of formative assessment, *ERIC Digest,* 1–6. (ERIC Document Reproduction Service No. ED470206)

Gardner, H. (1993). *Multiple intelligences: The theory in practice*. New York: Basic Books.

McMillan, J. H. (2000). Basic assessment concepts for teachers and school administra-tors. Version of a paper presented at the American Educational Research Association, New Orleans, LA. *ERIC/AE Digest,* 1–7. (ERIC Document Reproduction Service No. ED447201)

McTighe, J., & O'Connor, K. (2005, November). Seven practices for effective learning. *Educational Leadership, 63,* 10–17.

Michigan Department of Education. (1996). *Michigan curriculum framework*. Lansing: Author.

O'Connor, K. (2002). *How to grade for learning: Linking grades to standards*. Glenview, IL: Pearson Education.

Ormrod, J. E. (2006). *Educational psychology: Developing learners*. Upper Saddle River, NJ: Pearson Education.

Shepard, L. A. (2005, November). Linking formative assessment to scaffolding. *Educational Leadership, 63,* 66–70.

Zarrillo, J. (2007). *Are you prepared to teach reading? A practical tool for self-assessment*. Upper Saddle River, NJ: Pearson Education.

part

The Models of Teaching

In Chapters 4–13 you will be introduced to 10 classic and contemporary models of instruction. Each of them is illustrated with two detailed case studies that demonstrate the introduction and application of the models in classroom settings. In short, you "listen in" as teachers and students explore content by means of each model. Examples of elementary and secondary applications are included to illustrate each model's appropriateness for all grade levels. Following these case studies, you will find post-lesson reflections that provide insights into the instructional moves these teachers considered as they planned each lesson and their opinions of the success of each lesson.

Each chapter also demonstrates how the models may be used to meet representative content standards and benchmarks. In addition, technology standards and performance indicators are discussed in relation to each model to assist you in their use in K–12 classroom settings. Special attention is given to the ways each model represents the philosophies of curriculum and instruction discussed in Chapter 2. Together, these features will help you see how the various models of teaching can breathe life into the standards, benchmarks, and performance indicators that articulate what your students must know and be able to do as a result of your work together.

chapter 4

Direct Instruction

When I (J. M. D.) began my teacher preparation program in the late 1970s, I was astonished to discover that elementary classrooms looked very different from the ones I remembered from the 1950s and 1960s. As I observed and participated in classrooms at various grade levels, I enjoyed watching many types of instruction, most of them models of teaching I had never seen before in a classroom. I also saw more familiar instruction. In time, however, it was clear to me that even in these conventional lessons, the teachers were doing some things that differed from the instruction of my childhood experience. In my methods course, I learned to understand and appreciate those differences.

Direct instruction, once described as **interactive teaching** (Stallings, 1975; Stallings, Cory, Fairweather, & Needles, 1978; Stallings, Needles, & Stayrook, 1979) and **active teaching** (Brophy & Good, 1986), is probably the model of teaching you are also most familiar with from your own K–12 school experiences. Direct instruction is the kind of teaching children usually mimic when they play school. Your knowledge of the characteristics of well-designed direct instruction will serve you well when you need to develop a traditional lesson. We also believe you will have a greater understanding and appreciation of hands-on, discovery models of teaching if you learn the components and structure of a strong direct instruction lesson. For this reason, our examination of the models of teaching begins with direct instruction. Recently, this model has also been referred to as **explicit teaching** (Coles, 2001; De La Paz & Graham, 2002; Gersten, Woodward, & Darch, 1986) and **instructivist teaching** (Kozioff, LaNunziata, & Cowardin, 2001); however, your cooperating teachers will most likely use *Direct Instruction* to describe their traditional lessons.

The specific format for Direct Instruction used in this chapter was first popularized by Madeline Hunter in the 1960s (Hunter, 1967a, 1967b, 1967c, 1967d, 1971, 1976, 1982, 1994). As you read the first case study, consider why Direct Instruction was also referred to as interactive teaching decades ago.

Case Study 4.1: Third Grade, Abbreviations in Addresses

Mrs. Newell teaches a traditional third-grade class in an urban neighborhood. Her students have been working with the writing process since first grade. They are conversant with the stages of the writing process and are quite independent, conferencing with one another and revising their own writing. The class wrote letters and addressed envelopes to their grandparents inviting them to the school's festival celebrating U.S. immigrant cultures past and present. As she was reviewing some of their work, Mrs. Newell recognized that a small group of the children needed a minilesson on writing abbreviations in addresses. It is included in the state's third-grade curriculum and will be assessed on the state's proficiency test.

She wants to teach this lesson quickly so that her students can return to polishing their writing pieces, so she has chosen the Direct Instruction model for planning and teaching this lesson. Here is her **long-term objective** for the minilesson for the letter-writing unit:

Using the standard five-part format, the learner will write friendly letters and thank-you letters and will address the accompanying envelopes using the correct abbreviations.

This is her **instructional objective**:

The learner will capitalize and write street and state abbreviations correctly when addressing envelopes.

These objectives reflect several content standards and elementary benchmarks in her state's language arts curriculum.

Mrs. Newell gives her class the signal for their attention, then asks for a small group of children to meet with her at the kidney-shaped table in the corner. They will need to come to the group ready to write.

Mrs. Newell: Raise your hand if you can tell us one way we use capital letters in our writing. I'll wait until everyone has an idea to share. Great! Everyone has a hand up. Sharon?

Sharon: At the beginning of each sentence.

Mrs. Newell: Exactly right. Another example? Greg?

Greg: For days of the week?

Mrs. Newell: Yes! When else do we use capitals? Nancy?

Nancy: We use them when we write the month of the year.

Mrs. Newell: Yes! Whisper to your neighbor one more time when we use capital letters in our writing. What else did you remember? Sally?

Sally: Barbara said our first and last names.

Mrs. Newell: Exactly right! If you were thinking that, you were correct also. Did any pair come up with ideas we haven't mentioned yet today? Andrew?

Andrew: We also use capital letters when we write the names of special places, like California.

Mrs. Newell: Excellent! Andrew reminded us of something we are going to be working on today—using capital letters in our addresses and using abbreviations in writing addresses. I noticed yesterday when you addressed your envelopes to your grandparents that most of you used the long way to write out street and city addresses. This was just fine to do. But today we are going to learn special abbreviations to use when we address envelopes. We will learn street address abbreviations and some state abbreviations that we use a lot.

We use abbreviations to shorten the words in the address we are going to write. This makes writing addresses faster. The post office also prefers that we use abbreviations on our mail, especially state name abbreviations.

Some abbreviations you already know are (*She writes these on the board*)

Mister → Mr.

Madam → Mrs.

Doctor → Dr.

September → Sept.

Monday → Mon.

Every abbreviation is a short form of the word it represents. Most abbreviations end with periods. Today we are going to learn the abbreviations for these words used in addresses:

street

avenue

boulevard

drive

court

Michigan

Ohio

Indiana

Do any of you live on a street that is called something else? Nick?

Nick: We live on Peach Tree Lane.

Mrs. Newell: Then let's add *lane* to our list. Do any of you have grandparents that live in another state besides Michigan, Ohio, or Indiana? Several hands! Lisa?

Lisa: My grandparents live in Florida. So do Ina's.

Mrs. Newell: How many of you have grandparents who live in Florida? (*Several hands are raised*.) Well, it looks like we should add Florida to our list of state names. (*She does so*.)

Later on in the school year, we will learn the abbreviations for many other states. Today we will focus on these abbreviations.

Let's begin. When we use words that name a special street, we need to begin by capitalizing the first letter of each word. Our school is on Hamilton Street. Let's practice with that. First I'll write Hamilton. Next, I'll write the abbreviation for street.

To form some abbreviations, you simply cut the word short, then add the period.

That is how we form abbreviations for these words. (*She models on a chart and "thinks out loud" as she writes*.) I first write a capital S, then I add a small t. The last thing I write is the period.

Hamilton St.

street → St.

(*Mrs. Newell works through a few more quick examples, again using "think alouds."*)

Which of you lives on Village Street? (*She writes this on the board without using the abbreviation*.) Charlie? Would you recopy the name of your street on the chart using the abbreviation? The rest of you think silently about what you would write if you were rewriting this street name. (*Charlie comes up to the chart and writes*.) Thumbs up if you would have written this abbreviation as Charlie has written it, thumbs down if you would change it, thumbs in the middle if you're not sure. Great job, Charlie! You wrote your street name perfectly. Add your house number in front of Village.

We also form the abbreviation for the word *avenue* by using the first few letters. (*She models on the board and thinks aloud as she writes*.) I write the name of the avenue first—Irvine Avenue—with what kind of letter? Everyone?

Group: Capital.

Mrs. Newell: Right. Capital **I**, Irvine (*She writes*). Next, I write the first three letters of the word *avenue* (*She writes*). Now I finish with a period.

> Irvine → Ave.
>
> Avenue → Ave.

Who remembers the letters used to abbreviate the word *street*? Gene?

Gene: S and T.

Mrs. Newell: Right. How do we write the letter S? Lee?

Lee: As a capital letter.

Mrs. Newell: Exactly. How do we end the abbreviation? Robin?

Robin: With a period.

Mrs. Newell: Yes! Let's use our sign language alphabet now. Show with your hands the three letters we use to write the abbreviation for the word avenue. (*They do so*.) Great. Looks like everyone remembered the signs for A, V, and E. How do we write the A? Amy?

Amy: With a capital.

Mrs. Newell: How do we end the abbreviation? Lauren?

Lauren: With a period.

Mrs. Newell: That's right. The abbreviations for the next two words do not use the first few letters. They are written differently. These abbreviations still begin with a capital letter and end with a period.

Court is abbreviated like this. First we write the name of the court. Let's practice with Brenda Court. Some of you live there. I write Brenda with a capital B. Next I write the abbreviation for court, which is capital C, small T. Thumbs up or down? Do I need a period at the end of the abbreviation? (*The children respond*.) Exactly right, I do need one.

> Brenda Court → Brenda Ct.

Mrs. Newell continues to directly teach the abbreviations for *road*, *boulevard*, *Michigan*, *Indiana*, *Ohio*, and *Florida* to the children. She illustrates how the abbreviations for states are now written with two capital letters and no periods.

She keeps the lesson fast paced, with many opportunities for student response. Frequently during the lesson, she reviews what has been taught quickly before she moves on to the next abbreviation. Mrs. Newell varies the students' response mode. Sometimes she allows for choral responses, sometimes for kinesthetic responses, such as the use of the sign language alphabet, and sometimes for thumbs up or thumbs down. She has also allowed the children to tell a neighbor how they would write an abbreviation she has asked for, and she has used competent student models to work on the board.

By now, Mrs. Newell is feeling confident that the group is ready to practice writing these abbreviations. She wants to supervise their practice before she brings this lesson to a close.

Mrs. Newell: I am going to ask you to write the abbreviations for each of the new words I write on the chart. In addition, you will need to write your own complete street address on your paper using the abbreviations we have learned.

When I dismiss you one at a time, you will need to take the envelopes you addressed yesterday from your writing folders. (*She writes*.)

1. Find envelopes

Then, you need to rewrite the street addresses and state names using the abbreviations we learned today.

1. Find envelopes
2. Use abbreviations

When you are done with that, you may put the envelopes back into your writing folders. You may choose to read your library book or write in your journals.

3. R.Y.L.B. or journals

What's the first thing you will do when you are dismissed? Connie?

Connie: Get our envelopes to our grandparents from our writing folders.

Mrs. Newell: Right! What will you do with the envelopes? Lisa?

Lisa: Change the addresses to use abbreviations.

Mrs. Newell: Yes. And what are your choices when you have put your envelopes back into your writing folders? Brandi?

Brandi: Journals or R.Y.L.B.

Mrs. Newell: Great. Here is your list.

Mrs. Newell erases the board and rewrites the words used during the lesson in a different order. As children rewrite these words using abbreviations, she checks their work. After they have also written their street addresses using abbreviations for the street and state, she dismisses them individually to work independently. Two students write the list of words using the correct abbreviations and remembering capital letters. However, when they write out their street addresses, they neglect to use capitals. Mrs. Newell spends a few extra minutes with these two children reviewing why it is important to remember to use capitals when they address envelopes. She gives them a few moments to correct their addresses, and then she dismisses them to find their envelopes.

Mrs. Newell now begins her conferencing time with a number of students who are already revising second drafts of their latest writing pieces. Ten minutes later, all the students in Mrs. Newell's class are either working independently on first or second drafts or peer conferencing quietly. She gathers her materials to prepare for students to read aloud to one another from their works in progress. A few minutes later, she gives the signal to gain the attention of the entire class.

Before she gives directions for moving to the rug for author sharing, she asks one of the students from the minilesson group to provide **closure** on the writing workshop time by stating what the lesson was about today and why it was important. Lisa tells the class that today they reviewed writing abbreviations in street addresses. She also says that they want to make sure to address envelopes correctly so that their letters are delivered.

Mrs. Newell asks which children have writing to share with the class before lunch.

Sally, Peter, and Chloe raise their hands. They are asked to bring their work to the rug area. The rest of the children are dismissed by shoe color to find a quiet seat on the rug. She brings the author chair to the front of the rug area and indicates that Chloe may have a seat and get ready to begin.

Case Study 4.1: Post-Lesson Reflection

Once the children are at lunch, Mrs. Newell collects the envelopes her students have addressed. She wants to assess quickly whether any further practice will be needed soon in using abbreviations in addresses. She is pleased to see that each envelope is addressed correctly. As she gathers her lunch and prepares to leave her classroom, she considers how the minilesson went and what needs to be done tomorrow during writing workshop.

Today during the review, students remembered many uses for capital letters: at the beginning of sentences, days and months of the year, names and places. The curriculum for third grade in Mrs. Newell's district expects students to also use capital letters for initials, at the beginning of quotations, and in titles of literary and other creative works. She will be reviewing student writing with an eye to assessing whether some of her students will require minilessons in these skills as well, or whether the entire class will need them.

Mrs. Newell notes that even though the Direct Instruction format she chose for this lesson is prescribed and predictable, it was effective for her objective today. By making the material relevant to her students' lives, as well as by keeping the lesson as fast-paced as possible, she was able to maintain the attention of the students in the small group. Frequent **checking for understanding** provided her with sufficient evidence that students grasped the concept and format of the abbreviations used in the lesson. Those frequent and varied checks for understanding also keep her students focused when she uses Direct Instruction for full-group lessons.

The brief **guided practice** given to students before they were dismissed provided Mrs. Newell with the chance to see which students needed some extra attention. The individualized dismissal from the group allowed students to proceed through the rest of the lesson time at their own rate.

The Stages of Direct Instruction

The following stages of Direct Instruction are presented in the classic order to help you understand and differentiate among them. Mrs. Newell's lesson followed this order; however, the Direct Instruction lessons you teach may vary the order. You may also find that you omit elements from time to time on the basis of the particular needs of your students and the content you want to teach. Professional teachers use the models of teaching, but they do not let these models use them. Consider the stages of Direct Instruction as chess pieces that have distinct "moves."

Focus Activity

Imagine that you are an energetic fourth grader, discouraged that your kickball team failed to beat your fiercest rival at recess. Recess is over, and it is time to line up to go back to class. Even though your team will have other chances on the field, you can taste the disappointment. Geography is right after recess, and although you generally enjoy this subject, your mind is still on your sorely felt defeat. Or you may be a junior in high school who has misplaced an expensive Palm Pilot, and you know that your parents will be angry if they find out. You are probably not ready to jump into a new topic in precalculus at the end of the day.

Teachers need to recognize that as we begin a new lesson or a new part of the school day, our students are not equally ready to begin with us. In addition to the varying degrees of prior knowledge that students bring to a lesson, they also come to the lesson with things on their minds such as a playground defeat, a misunderstanding with a friend, or wandering thoughts about what they might do after school. This is a natural part of life at school for most of us, isn't it?

Teachers cannot force students to shift their attention, but they can stack the deck by providing a **focus activity**. The purpose of this activity is to prepare students for new material at the beginning of a Direct Instruction lesson. Focus activities are short periods of two to three minutes to warm up the group. They may consist of a brief review of material covered earlier, a quick thinking game related to the subject to be taught, or something as simple as an engaging question to get students thinking. This motivating aspect of the focus activity is the reason some teachers refer to this part of the lesson as the "hook." The main point of the focus activity is to help students shift gears mentally from what happened prior to the lesson and to prepare them for attending to the new content.

Mrs. Newell wanted to expand her students' use of abbreviations when they wrote addresses. In her focus activity, she chose to review the use of capital letters by asking students what they already knew. She kept this activity fast paced and provided opportunities for the group to participate either individually or with a partner.

Stating the Objective and Providing the Rationale

After the focus activity, the teacher states the instructional objective to the students. The objective tells students what they will know or be able to do at the end of a lesson. The objective should be stated using vocabulary that is **developmentally appropriate** for the students. The teacher would describe a lesson to a colleague using professional vocabulary, but she would choose other words to describe that same lesson to a group of third graders. A similar objective would be stated differently still to a group of seventh graders.

In Direct Instruction, stating the objective is often paired with **providing the rationale** for the lesson. The rationale for a lesson tells the students why the content to be learned is important to their daily lives. It is not sufficient to tell students that lessons will be helpful on an upcoming test or important in a subsequent grade. Students need to see a lesson's meaning and relevance to their own lives. For example, Mrs. Newell explained that using abbreviations on envelopes is quicker for us and preferred by the postal service as well. It ensures that letters will be delivered. As with the objective, the rationale must be communicated in terms that students easily understand.

It is important in Direct Instruction to state the objective and rationale at the beginning of the lesson. This charts the course for the lesson and helps keep the teacher on track.

Providing this information to students early in the lesson is a feature of Direct Instruction, but not necessarily of all lesson designs. Other models of teaching delay the discussion of objectives, often until the end of the lesson, and for very good reasons. However, Direct Instruction defines explicitly at the beginning of each lesson what the performance expectations for the students will be and why they are important.

Presenting Content and Modeling

Presenting the content and **modeling** are generally interwoven so tightly in a traditional Direct Instruction lesson that it is difficult to say where one ends and the other begins. The content of a Direct Instruction lesson is what will be learned by the students: knowledge, skills, or procedures. Content can be presented by the teacher or given through a video, a reading selection, or technology such as a software program, CD-ROM, or Web site. Our discussion of content will focus on traditional teacher presentations. Modeling provides students with specific demonstrations of working with the content. The teacher explicitly demonstrates how the students can be successful in the lesson.

Content must be introduced clearly and systematically and explained in the context of students' everyday lives. As we discuss several ways of making the most of content presentation, consider how closely content presentation and modeling are joined together in Direct Instruction. Let's look first at providing clarity. The process of bread making can be explained to first graders or eighth graders in a clear fashion, but you would use less-sophisticated vocabulary with young children than you would with middle school students. Specific information about chemical interactions as a result of mixing ingredients in the right amounts and under the right conditions would be confusing to young children but highly appropriate for adolescents. The knowledge that certain ingredients allow bread dough to rise and bake into familiar loaves of bread will provide enough beginning understanding for young children. One aspect of clarity is determining how much information to give to students, then giving it in a precise manner.

Modeling should also provide verbal and visual cues for successfully mastering the objective. Sometimes a **think aloud** provides students with greater clarity in understanding a procedure for accomplishing a task. A think aloud is a kind of modeling in which teachers verbalize their thoughts and decisions as they carry out a task. For example, as a teacher demonstrates cutting out a construction paper square to serve as a math **manipulative** during the next lesson, she might "think out loud" in class, saying "I am cutting this square very carefully because we will be using it today to create fractional shapes. I need the sides of my square to be very neat. My smaller, fraction pieces should be accurate in size."

The demands of individual tasks will become apparent to you as you prepare think alouds for each lesson. In a handwriting lesson on the capital cursive F, for example, the teacher will write the letter on the board and simultaneously talk through the strokes needed to form the letter correctly. Next, the teacher may ask the students to write the letter in the air with their fingers (kinesthetic experience) or trace sandpaper letters using the same strokes in the same order (tactile experience) while the teacher models the letter formation a second time and repeats the think aloud. During the modeling stage of Direct Instruction, the teacher should make the content accessible to students in as many ways as possible.

Providing a systematic presentation of content is also essential for an effective Direct Instruction lesson. This is especially true if the content to be taught is sequential in nature, such as in teaching rules to games like bingo, Jeopardy, or softball. Procedural content in mathematics always needs to be presented sequentially. If your students have been working with manipulatives to learn the concept of single-digit multiplying, they may be ready to learn the partial-products technique for multiplication:

$$
\begin{array}{ccc}
\begin{array}{r} 46 \\ \times\, 7 \\ \hline \end{array} &
\begin{array}{l} 7 \times 40 = 280 \\ 7 \times 6\ \ = 42 \end{array} &
\begin{array}{r} 280 \\ +\ 42 \\ \hline 322 \end{array}
\end{array}
$$

What should be done first, second, third, and so on in computing the answer to this problem must be considered carefully by the teacher while she plans the lesson, not haphazardly attempted during the lesson. We need to break any procedure or way of thinking down into small steps. We call this process **task analysis**. Each separate step in using the algorithm must be presented with sufficient modeling and practice. When working with algorithms, the exact sequence of each step is crucial to the success and accuracy of the computation.

One way to aid clarity and ensure that you are presenting the content systematically is to list the steps in sequential order on the board, overhead, or chart paper as you model and think aloud. During the lesson, this type of modeling provides the visual learners in your class with an opportunity to access your words and actions after you have completed a step. The list provides a permanent record of what to do, and when, throughout the lesson. Many teachers prepare chart paper to be used during this visual think aloud so that they can keep the list handy for students' reference after the lesson is over. Other teachers have students record these steps in a math journal. The orchestration of doing, saying, and recording while you are modeling new content or reviewing previously learned content is one way to help students understand and successfully complete a task. When you use visual, auditory, kinesthetic, and tactile approaches (**V-A-K-T**), you unite the presentation of your content and modeling in a powerful way. You will see several examples of thinking aloud and multiple forms of modeling in the next case study.

It is important that teachers provide sufficient modeling of new tasks. You may want to use student models also. Allowing a capable student to model gives the class an opportunity to watch one of their own perform successfully. You will choose students to provide accurate modeling on the basis of their work in past lessons. You can also ask these students to think aloud while they do their work, which provides additional **rehearsal** time for the class as they begin to understand the content of your lesson.

Lessons that connect content with students' authentic life experiences are very motivating for students. Whenever possible as you work with new content or tasks in a Direct Instruction lesson, relate this content to your students' interests and everyday experiences. For example, younger students will need to use their multiplication skills as they plan for making and bringing birthday treats for their class. Older students may be motivated in a statistics lesson if it relates to computing athletes' performance averages. While providing the rationale for the lesson motivates students initially, content presentation and modeling give the teacher additional opportunities to connect new content to students' experiences.

Checking for Understanding

As you are teaching a Direct Instruction lesson, two types of feedback will help you decide whether students understand the material: what they say and what they do. In Direct Instruction, teachers check student understanding by asking specific questions and providing collective practice. In a well-crafted Direct Instruction lesson, teachers ask the entire class many questions that will reveal student understanding. Fast-paced questions at the knowledge and comprehension levels of Bloom's taxonomy are the most effective ones in a Direct Instruction lesson. If you

Cycles of content presentation, modeling, and checking for understanding indicate to teachers whether it is time to progress with the lesson.

have phrased these questions well, student answers will provide you with the immediate feedback you require. Your responses to their answers also provide students with a sense of their success.

The blanket question, Are there any questions? is seldom useful in a Direct Instruction lesson. Often students cannot readily articulate what questions they have. Students might also think they understand the content and have no need to ask questions. Invariably there will also be students who are able to articulate a question and are aware of their lack of understanding, but these students may be too embarrassed to speak up in class. If you ask specific questions to check for understanding, you can determine students' grasp of the content by the quality of their answers. Do you understand how to cut and paste a paragraph as you word-process? will not give you the feedback you need. What is our first step as we cut and paste? and How do we highlight our paragraph with the mouse? are examples of specific questions that check for understanding.

Just as Mrs. Newell modeled in the first case study, you can check student understanding by eliciting verbal responses—chorally, to a partner, or individually. Depending on the content of the lesson and the grade level of your students, you will "orchestrate" this in various ways. One typical choice is to ask for raised hands from the students who volunteer. It is wise to wait until a good number of students have raised their hands before calling on any one student. This **wait time** provides the class with a few quiet moments to process the question and arrive at an answer, something that students at all grade levels need. Beginning teachers have a tendency to call on the first hand raised in response to their questions, and this is understandable. Initially you will be relieved when you see that first hand. However, with experience and confidence, you will realize that those few moments of wait time are important. They will elicit greater full-class participation and help establish a reflective environment in your classroom. During this type of checking for understanding, some teachers will allow small groups to come up with an answer together and then share it with the full class.

When it is appropriate, choral responses are both effective as a learning tool and enjoyable. The students who have the correct answer rehearse the content. The students who are not yet sure of the answers benefit from hearing their peers recite correctly, and they do not feel singled out for not yet having the answers.

Many teachers utilize partner checks, such as "Turn to your neighbor and share one reason that wetlands need to be preserved." After a few moments, you can ask for their responses one at a time, asking for answers that differ from earlier responses: "Did another pair come up with a different idea?" This technique checks understanding for questions that have multiple answers. It also provides silent **positive reinforcement** for partners whose answers were identical or similar to the ones shared, even if they did not have the chance to offer their own ideas.

Silent **signaling** with gestures can also be used to answer questions. Younger students can be instructed to form letters or symbols with their fingers or hands (greater than, less than, equal to, for example), use the thumbs-up or thumbs-down sign, or use the sign language alphabet. Some teachers allow for "secret" gesture responses, such as "With your hand in front of your tummy, so that only I can see your answer, thumbs up for yes, thumbs down for no, and thumbs in the middle if you are not sure." For some students this is just plain fun; for others, it provides privacy when they are not sure of the answer. Clearly, student responses to your checking-for-understanding questions must be age appropriate. Secondary students respond best to straightforward questions and answers.

The other dimension of checking for understanding is to give collective practice that you will review before the lesson moves forward. This type of checking for understanding provides students with the opportunity to work with the new material directly. One example is to have them solve a math problem individually and review it aloud before you move on to the next example. You may want students to work in pairs as you check their understanding of new skills. This checking for understanding by doing should occur after ample teacher and student modeling. Once this scaffolding is in place, students should be ready to try the new skill directly. As you review this work aloud, you will know to what extent your students are able to apply what they have learned. You will also see what points need to be explained again or explained differently. As long as you continue to process student answers aloud, you are still in the checking-for-understanding stage of Direct Instruction and not yet into guided practice.

So far, we have discussed each of the elements of Direct Instruction as though there is a particular sequence to be followed. In some lessons, you may find that you use these elements in the order they have been presented in this chapter. However, most teachers intersperse their checking-for-understanding questions throughout their content presentation and modeling, as well as asking them after the skill has been demonstrated.

The cycle of content presentation, modeling, and then checking for understanding is one reason that Direct Instruction was once called interactive teaching. The continual teaching and checking for understanding during Direct Instruction provides students with small amounts of new material that will be assessed immediately by the teacher. This action, in turn, gives teachers an opportunity to reteach the content and provide additional modeling. Exactly how this cycle will play out in a classroom will depend on how well your students grasp the content or skill that is the focus of your lesson. Given time, you will think on your feet and adjust your actions as you progress through these cycles.

You will ask checking-for-understanding questions that address content knowledge you want students to understand and any skills or processes they need for success in the tasks assigned. You should also check their understanding of any routine tasks you will want them to accomplish after their **independent practice** has been completed. They might read, write in their journals, or complete any unfinished assignments. This procedure can help prevent the What do I do now? questions that arise when the teacher has not been specific enough with instructions. It will also buy you some uninterrupted time during students' guided practice to work with students who need reteaching.

Teachers' actions during the cycles of content presentation, modeling, and checking for understanding can be modified in many ways for special needs students and English language learners at all grade levels. Chapter 13 will provide examples of instructional modifications that can be included in your lesson plans.

Guided Practice

Earlier we mentioned two ways to assess your students' progress toward reaching mastery of a lesson objective: listening to what they say and observing what they do.

Checking for understanding addresses how students conceptualize and then verbalize their understanding. Checking for understanding also provides collective practice that will be reviewed in the full group before moving into individual practice periods. Guided practice is exactly that, practice that students do alone without the benefit of a partner and without the safety net of full-class review. You need to check each student's competence and reteach as needed before you allow them to finish tasks independently. Guided practice is your first opportunity to assess your students' individual understanding.

One way to provide guided practice before you dismiss students for independent seatwork is to give the class a few problems or questions to answer. These items must be structured in exactly the same way as the ones the students will solve in independent practice. For example, if you have prepared a handout of 10 math problems, you might choose to work with 3 of these problems during guided practice. Students can complete all 3 practice problems and then alert you when they are finished. As students raise their hands, stop by their work area to check their progress. If they have done each problem correctly, dismiss them one by one to complete the remaining work on their own. Another option is to have some students complete guided practice problems one at a time. Selected students may need more support, and you will want to check their work more frequently. The direction of your lesson and your knowledge of your students will tell you which of these options to choose.

During guided practice, the teacher assesses students' progress, analyzes errors, and addresses needs one-on-one. This is a very active and important stage of a Direct Instruction lesson. As you dismiss individual students to complete their assignment, you may find that a small group of students will benefit from a more structured reteaching of the skill. The last phase of guided practice provides time for you to review the content presentation and modeling section of your lesson, provide time for student think alouds again, recheck their understanding, and give additional practice. Again, you dismiss students one-by-one as they demonstrate the skill successfully.

The guided practice step in Direct Instruction gives teachers their first opportunity to assess what students can do on their own.

If someone is still having difficulty after reteaching, it is always appropriate to provide a review task or alternative assignment for that student to work on while other students are completing their independent practice. You may need to consider how best to reteach the material to that student later. You also may ask another student to peer-tutor (and excuse the student receiving tutoring from independent practice).

Independent Practice

Independent practice is an opportunity for students to practice skills independent of any monitoring by the teacher or help from another student. It is essential that students demonstrate mastery of the objective before being dismissed for independent practice. It is always more difficult to reteach skills that have been practiced incorrectly than to provide careful practice the first time around. This is another reason to monitor carefully during guided practice.

If you have prepared a handout with 10 math problems to serve as independent practice for your students, the first 3 might be used as guided practice problems and the last 7 as independent practice problems. Once the handout is completed, you will need to decide whether you want students to self-check their work or leave it for you to review. Many teachers choose to give homework on the same day that a skill has been introduced. Be very careful about this. You must be sure that your students understand their new material completely. If they practice a skill incorrectly at home, they will be reinforcing their errors, and it may be necessary to reteach that material.

Closure

Closure in a lesson is provided when the teacher is ready to begin the next lesson or activity in the school day and wants to "tie the bow" on the previous lesson. Closure brings any lesson to a satisfying finish both cognitively and aesthetically. In a Direct Instruction lesson, closure will occur after the independent practice period and before instructions are given for the next activity. The teacher will give the signal for attention and then ask for a quick review of what was learned during the lesson. While the teacher herself can provide this review, it is best for students to summarize or comment on what was accomplished during the lesson. Teachers can highlight students' **metacognitive** abilities by asking questions that not only reflect content concerns but also reinforce the value of the lesson: What did you learn in today's lesson that you did not know yesterday? Why is that learning important to you? Some teachers complete closure by previewing what will be happening in class the next day.

Teachers often complain that when parents ask their children what happened at school that day, the answer is invariably "Nothing." One way to address this situation directly is to inquire during closure, "If Mom asks you today what we did in math class, what will you answer?" Even when the teacher is not so forthright, closure provides a "rehearsal" for students to pull together what they learned during a class period.

Table 4.1   The Stages of Direct Instruction

Stage	Teacher Action	Students' Response	Notes
Focus activity	Presents quick (2–3 minutes) activity that engages students' interest and promotes students' thinking	Answer questions and participate in the activity	May involve review of yesterday's lesson or a related skill
State the objective	Describes in students' terms what they will be doing in today's lesson	Listen	Adjust vocabulary to suit particular group of students
Provide the rationale	Describes why the content from today's lesson is important and meaningful to students	Listen	Find current relevance—not "You'll need this next year"
Present content	Presents the content of the lesson sequentially	Listen and observe instruction	Prepare for clarity of instruction, systematically given
Model	Demonstrates skills and procedures, does think alouds	Observe	Consider using visual, auditory, kinesthetic, and tactile modeling
Check for understanding	Asks specific questions to assess student understanding of the content, procedure, or skill taught	Answer questions individually, chorally, verbally, and with signaling	Intersperse checking-for-understanding questions throughout content presentation and modeling sequence as needed
Provide guided practice	Provides and guides short practice period; dismisses individual students as they are ready for independent practice	Perform task or work with content individually while being monitored	Check individual students' work frequently to troubleshoot errors
Provide closure	"Ties the bow" on the lesson, reviews the importance of the content, may also preview what will happen tomorrow	Summarize or comment on the content of the lesson	Providing closure is most effective when students participate
Provide mass practice	Provides frequent opportunities to practice skill	Practice skill or work with content	Mass practice periods should immediately follow initial mastery of objective for the next few days to ensure overlearning
Ensure distributive practice	Provides brief, intermittent practice over the rest of the school year to keep skills fresh	Practice skill or work with content	Brief homework practice may serve this purpose

Mass and Distributed Practice

Students may master a skill during a Direct Instruction lesson, but that does not mean the skill has been learned for a lifetime. Skills must be practiced well beyond the demands of guided and independent practice. Students need a significant amount of practice in a short amount of time after they have learned new content so they can overlearn the material. This practice is called **mass practice**. **Overlearning** will occur when a student can perform a skill at the **automatic level**. Short opportunities to practice specific skills for several days in a row after the initial lesson will provide enough mass practice for a skill. Mass practice may be homework, in-class work, or center activities.

Even so, the teacher must provide practice in the skill from time to time throughout the school year to keep the skill alive in the students' repertoires. This is called **distributed practice**. Opportunities to practice skills once they have been mastered must be spread throughout the school year. Too frequently, teachers are dismayed that students lose a skill they performed well earlier in the school year. This situation generally occurs when content or skills have not been reinforced for some time. Every few weeks, a brief review of previously learned material will help students keep those skills alive. Both mass and distributive practice can occur in the context of an engaging activity, not just on a worksheet. A creative teacher can find ways to help keep students' skills up to speed by designing meaningful, authentic, and enjoyable tasks.

Case Study 4.2: Middle School, Improper Fractions and Mixed Numbers

Ms. Bernard teaches sixth-grade math in an urban middle school. One particular class has been struggling. She has often found that most of the students need to return to using manipulatives for some concepts. Lately they have been working with fraction manipulatives and diagrams in order to better understand equivalent mixed numbers and improper fractions, and she believes they are ready to rewrite improper fractions as mixed numbers without the use of manipulatives. Ms. Bernard has chosen Direct Instruction for this lesson as a follow-up to the group's successful fraction explorations. This is her long-term objective:

The learner will add, subtract, multiply, and divide any two mixed numbers with unlike denominators.

This is today's lesson objective:

The learner will write any improper fraction as a mixed number.

She has written this question on the board:

What is the difference between a mixed number and an improper fraction?

Ms. Bernard: Class! What have we been working on the last few days? Brian?

Brian: We worked with a partner with those fraction pieces.

Ms. Bernard: Right. What discoveries did you make? Sally?

Sally: There were two ways to write the same fractional amount. One had whole numbers and one was written just as a fraction.

Ms. Bernard: What did we call those two ways of writing the amount? Billy?

Billy: Well, both were fractions. But if the fraction was written with a whole number, you call it a mixed number, like 3 and ½.

Ms. Bernard: Billy, why did we say "mixed"?

Billy: Well, we wrote the amount using both a whole number and a regular fraction. We said there was a mixture in the way we wrote the amount. The number 3 and ½.

Ms. Bernard: Yes, and what did we call the other way to write the same amount? Linda?

Linda: An improper fraction because the numerator was a bigger number than the denominator. Three and ½ could also be written as 7 over 2.

Ms. Bernard: Today we are going to change improper fractions into mixed numbers without using the fraction shapes. It is much easier to compute the answer than to always rely on using manipulatives, and it saves a lot of time. You showed me yesterday that we can set aside the fraction shapes for a while.

I'll start with this example: $\frac{17}{4}$. (*She writes this problem on the board*.) I read that improper fraction as seventeen fourths. To turn it into a whole number, I need to divide. These steps will be familiar to you from whole-number division. I first divide the denominator, 4, into the numerator, 17. I ask myself how many groups of 4 I can find in 17, and I know the answer is 4. (*She writes this step on the board*.)

    1. Divide Numerator → Denominator.

Now, I write the 4 in the quotient space above the 17. I know that I need to write the 4 above the 7 in the number 17. Why is that? Jeff?

Jeff: Because you are dividing into 17 and not into 1.

Ms. Bernard: Yes. (*She writes this step on the board*.)

    1. Divide Numerator → Denominator.

    2. Write whole number in the Quotient space.

Now, I am going to multiply my number in the quotient by the divisor, 4×4, and record the answer below the 17. (*She writes the next two steps.*)

1. Divide Numerator → Denominator.

2. Write whole number in the Quotient space.

3. Multiply the Quotient by the Dividend.

4. Write the Product under the Dividend.

To finish, I subtract 16 from 17, which leaves me 1. I write the 1 as a Numerator next to 4 in the Quotient. (*She writes these two steps on the board.*)

1. Divide Numerator → Denominator.

2. Write whole number in the Quotient space.

3. Multiply the Quotient by the Dividend.

4. Write the Product under the Dividend.

5. Subtract.

6. Write the difference as a Numerator to the right of the Quotient.

My Divisor becomes a Denominator again under my new Numerator. (*She writes this on the board.*)

1. Divide Numerator → Denominator.

2. Write whole number in the Quotient space.

3. Multiply the Quotient by the Dividend.

4. Write the Product under the Dividend.

5. Subtract.

6. Write the difference as a Numerator to the right of the Quotient.

7. Write the Divisor as the Denominator.

Now I know that $\frac{17}{4}$, an improper fraction, is another way of saying $4\frac{1}{4}$, a mixed number. This procedure should be familiar to you from our work in division. I am going to work through another example, but faster this time. (*She talks through another problem.*)

Let's try another example, and I'll be asking you for the steps I should take. Let's look at this improper fraction: $\frac{39}{5}$. What do I do first? Sally?

Ms. Bernard structures a checking-for-understanding sequence in which individual students each provide one step in the sequence for turning $\frac{39}{5}$ into a mixed number. Sometimes students refer to the chart she created during her first example. Other students do not need this assistance. After this example, Ms. Bernard asks one of the students to provide a think aloud for the group as the student solves the last problem on the board. By now her students have seen this procedure modeled four times.

Ms. Bernard: (*showing a worksheet to the class*) This is your task for today. I am going to ask you to work alone on the first two problems. Please raise your hand when you have completed them, and I will check your answers. If your work is correct, you may finish the rest of the worksheet. When you are finished with the worksheet, where should you put it? Jeff?

Jeff: In our green class folder next to the aquarium.

Ms. Bernard: Yes. What do you need to do after you have put your work into the folder? Brian?

Brian: Take a math puzzle from the yellow pocket and our homework from the green pocket.

Ms. Bernard: Yes! Your homework is a review of work we have done this semester.

Ms. Bernard hands out the worksheet. Within a few minutes, most of the students have successfully completed their guided practice. She gives the go-ahead to finish their worksheets. She brings Billy and Tricia up to her table. They have both written the subtraction remainder as the denominator instead of the numerator in each of the solutions. Quickly, Ms. Bernard draws circles and fractional pieces on the board to represent the first example, and together they solve this problem using pictures. She refers them to the first problem they solved and asks them to compare their written answer to the one they just worked out on the board. With a startled "Oh!" Billy corrects his three answers. Ms. Bernard asks Tricia what she did when she first solved her problems. Tricia tells her that she switched the numerator and the denominator but now understands what to do next time. Before she lets them go back to their seats, Ms. Bernard asks them to work the fourth and fifth problems on the worksheet, just in case. Satisfied that they are ready for independent practice, she dismisses them both.

Within the next 10 minutes, it is clear that everyone in the class has completed the independent practice work and has taken the puzzle and their homework. Ms. Bernard gives the class signal, and the students become quiet. She thanks them for their diligence during the period. She asks someone to explain what they would say about class today if the principal stopped them in the hall. When the bell rings, Ms. Bernard dismisses her students.

Case Study 4.2: Post-Lesson Reflection ◆

Ms. Bernard was confident that this class was ready to move into computation work today. Their preparation with manipulatives and diagrams paid off, and few students had difficulties with the lesson. As she prepared for this class, Ms. Bernard decided on the examples she would use for modeling in advance, and she also drew clear diagrams to accompany each problem to be used in modeling and guided practice.

The effort she took in preparation was worthwhile when Billy and Tricia made their errors during the guided practice. By moving back to the use of diagrams as visual aids, they were able to self-correct their errors and move into independent practice. When the class meets tomorrow, Ms. Bernard will remember to ask them specific questions based on the errors they made today. During the opening part of her next lesson, she can briefly assess whether they remember today's procedure.

The next Direct Instruction lesson will be to write mixed numbers as improper fractions, the inverse of today's objective. With a more advanced group, Ms. Bernard might have chosen to combine the two skills. For this group, she felt it best to separate the two lessons.

After the students have been dismissed, Ms. Bernard briefly reviews the independent practice sheets placed in the green folder. At a glance, she can tell that each student met today's objective, and they are ready to move on.

Brief Background of Direct Instruction

If you are an advocate of teaching practices that are apparently more student centered than Direct Instruction, you may have been surprised to find that this model was once referred to as interactive teaching. Educational research was done in the 1970s to determine effective teaching behaviors. This research examined the practice of elementary teachers whose students consistently performed well on standardized tests (Brophy, 1979; Brophy & Evertson, 1974; Gage, 1978; Good, 1979; Rosenshine, 1979; Stallings, 1975). Keep in mind that these studies equated student success with achievement in math and reading skills, primarily at the knowledge and comprehension levels of Bloom's taxonomy.

Research illustrated that these effective teachers used similar elements in lesson presentation fairly consistently in their teaching. They behaved in particular ways during instruction, and these behaviors became the basic elements in what we now call Direct Instruction. Rather than telling and showing students new content to be learned and then assigning seatwork, the teachers observed in these studies asked many questions during lessons to check student understanding of the content or processes being taught. The teachers provided many opportunities for fast-paced student responses to these questions in a variety of ways. During instruction, correct answers were positively reinforced with statements like, "Exactly right!" Incorrect answers were dignified with the question redirected to elicit a correct student response. Reteaching occurred as needed during each lesson. Because of this continual interaction between the students and the teacher, Direct Instruction was considered much more interactive than traditional classroom teaching.

Many studies found that this particular pattern of instructional practices resulted in significant student achievement in basic reading and math skills. This pattern was generally referred to as Direct Instruction, even though specific formats of this lesson design have varied somewhat over time (Adams & Engelmann, 1996; Allington, 2002; Allington & Johnston, 2002; Becker & Carnine, 1980; Carnine, 1997; De La Paz & Graham, 2002; Din, 2000; Gage & Needles, 1989; Gardner et al., 1994; Medley, 1979; Peterson, 1979; Rosenshine, 1979; Scarcelli & Morgan, 1999; Simmons, Fuchs, Fuchs, Mathes, & Hodge, 1995; Ullmann & Krassner, 1966; Ulrich, Stachnik, & Mabry, 1970; Viadero, 2002; Wang, Haertel, & Walberg, 1993a, 1993b; Waxman & Walberg, 1999). These studies were not designed to analyze how various student characteristics might also affect achievement outcomes.

One consistent criticism of Direct Instruction has been that its emphasis on following steps in a rigid order results in cookie-cutter lessons. While effective Direct Instruction lessons do have certain characteristics in common, there is still a great deal of variability in how each specific lesson might be designed. Another misconception is that Direct Instruction makes all teachers appear to have the same teaching style. This is not the case at all. Distinctive personalities, clarity and intention throughout the lesson, genuine enthusiasm for the content, and individual pacing make Direct Instruction lessons unique to every teacher. As you review the research on Direct Instruction, pay close attention to the situations in which it has supported student learning. Keep in mind also that while many lessons in K–12 education can be taught using Direct Instruction, it is not uniformly appropriate for all students at all times.

Direct Instruction and Research on Teaching

Over the past 40 years, the Direct Instruction approach has been written about extensively in the literature on effective teaching (Anderson, Evertson, & Brophy, 1979; Brophy, 1999; Darch & Carnine, 1986; Gersten, Woodward, & Darch, 1986; Good & Grouws, 1979; Hunter, 1994; Medley, 1979; Paik, 2002; Peterson, 1979; Rosenshine, 1979, 1986, 1995). Studies have examined the efficacy of Direct Instruction for general and special education students not only in respect to reading and math but also regarding creativity, independence, and curiosity. Direct Instruction has been found to be particularly effective with elementary and secondary at-risk students academically; furthermore, it promotes self-esteem and positive social skills. In the past decade, Direct Instruction has been used to teach not only basic skills in reading and math but also chemistry, United States history, and literary classics.

In the 1970s, researchers also began looking at student characteristics as they related to achievement with Direct Instruction in traditional classrooms. Relative success depended on the desired cognitive or affective student outcomes, and a number of studies came up with contradictory findings. For example, Grapko (1972) found that low-performing students did better with Direct Instruction in basic skills. However, Bennett (1976) found that low-performing boys did better with nondirective, open approaches to basic skill instruction. Studies indicated that high-performing students with Direct Instruction in basic skills did well on standardized tests (Bennett, 1976; Ward & Barcher, 1975). Solomon and Kendall (1979), however, found that high-performing students with open approaches to instruction also did well.

When student characteristics and creativity were examined, findings were again contradictory. Solomon and Kendall (1979) found that low-performing students scored higher on paper-and-pencil measures of creativity with Direct Instruction, but high-performing students performed better on measures of creativity in open classrooms with less-traditional instruction. Ward and Barcher (1975) found no significant differences in low-performing students' creativity whether they were placed in traditional classrooms with Direct Instruction or in open classrooms, but high-performing students were seen to be more creative in Direct Instruction classrooms.

Affective outcomes were also studied in terms of student characteristics in both traditional classrooms with Direct Instruction and in open classroom settings. Direct Instruction has been used effectively in promoting positive self-esteem and social skills in students (Adams & Engelmann, 1996; Becker & Carnine, 1980; Binder & Watkins, 1990; Burke, 2002; Cashwell, Skinner, & Smith, 2001). Bennett (1976) found that students with strong self-concepts who were sociable and motivated achieved more in traditional classrooms. Students with negative self-concepts who were less sociable and less self-motivated were seen to achieve more in open classrooms. Anxiety also played a role in whether students achieved more in standardized test situations in either traditional or open classrooms. Students with low anxiety performed better on a mathematics test in traditional classrooms when they had experienced traditional instruction. Anxious students performed better in an open classroom setting (Papay, Costello, & Hedl, 1975).

Locus of control refers to the extent to which students feel they have control over their successes and failures in the classroom. Papay et al. (1975) found that students who received Direct Instruction in traditional classrooms and students who received less-traditional forms of instruction in open classrooms did not differ significantly in terms of locus of control. Wright and DuCette (1976) found that students who felt they had greater control over their school achievement (called *internals*) did better in open classrooms. However, students in this study who felt their efforts did not affect their achievement (called *externals*) performed about the same with either approach. Externals attributed their successes or failures to luck or other forces over which they had little control.

Direct Instruction has consistently been found effective for students at risk (Becker & Engelmann, 1978; Becker & Gersten, 1982; Bereiter & Engelmann, 1966; Darch, Gersten & Taylor, 1987; Dermody, 2001; Fazio, 2001; Meyer, 1984; Meyer, Gersten, & Gutkin, 1984; Mills, Cole, & Dale, 2002; and many others). Direct Instruction Follow Through was a longitudinal study of basic reading and math achievement of at-risk children from kindergarten through third grade. As a result of Direct Instruction, these students achieved higher test scores than their control group counterparts (Stallings, 1975). Additional studies evaluated these students in the fifth, sixth, and ninth grades (Becker & Gersten, 1982; Meyer, 1984; and Meyer, Gersten, & Gutkin, 1984), and the earlier findings were consistent with findings from the later studies.

Since the 1970s, Direct Instruction has been used almost exclusively in special education classrooms for teaching basic skills in reading and math. More recently, Direct Instruction has been found effective in teaching secondary chemistry to students with learning disabilities (Woodward & Noell, 1991), math (Kelly, Gersten, & Carnine, 1990), United States history (Carnine, Steeley, & Silbert, 1996), reading (Lovett et al., 1994), and literary classics (Dimino, Gersten, Carnine, & Blake, 1990). In these studies, instructors were focusing on concepts, relationships among ideas, and strategies, as opposed to basic skills. The model continues to be used for teaching basic reading skills, such as phonological awareness, to special education students, as it has been in the past (O'Connor, Notari-Syverson, & Vadasy, 1996; Torgesen & Davis, 1996). Current research on the continuing efficacy of Direct Instruction for students with special needs will be of particular interest to general education teachers who want to participate in inclusion programs (Butler, Miller, & Lee, 2001; Swanson, 1999, 2001; Troia & Graham, 2002) or modify instruction for students not formally identified as having special needs.

Other studies have pointed to the positive effects of Direct Instruction when coupled with cooperative learning and other experiential learning strategies in the classroom (Losardo & Bricker, 1994; Lovett et al., 1994). This instructional integration is routinely seen in classrooms across the country. Many teachers consider this practice appropriate in view of the diversity of students' instructional needs and the current focus on student collaboration. However, the growing emphasis on standardized test scores may place Direct Instruction "on the front burner" in U.S. classrooms.

When researchers have looked at all studies of Direct Instruction holistically, they have found that it has the edge on less traditional teaching when only student achievement outcomes are measured. When researchers have studied the achievement of specific groups of students, results have been mixed. However, we have seen over time that context is everything in the classroom. Teachers must deliberate over the needs of their students and decide which instructional method is the right one at the time.

In the past as well as today, Direct Instruction has not been without its critics. Many educators and teacher educators feel that the model constrains teachers' creativity. They believe its focus on mastery of prescribed behavioral objectives taught in a sequential manner places an unnecessary ceiling on student learning. However, most of today's teachers recognize that Direct Instruction is a beneficial model to have in their repertoires.

Direct Instruction and Learning Theory

Direct Instruction relates to the behaviorist and information processing learning theories as applied to the classroom. Two characteristics of Direct Instruction that relate specifically to behaviorism are positive reinforcement and lesson design (Hunter, 1994; Skinner, 1953).

B. F. Skinner believed that learning is a result of change in behavior (1953). The key concept of Skinner's work is reinforcement of behavior. Teachers' questions, behavioral expectations, and so on (stimuli) will produce a response from students: correct or incorrect answers to questions, appropriate or inappropriate behavior. The ways teachers respond to students' behaviors are said to be the consequences of those behaviors. Whether consequences are positive, negative, or neutral, they will have an effect on students' future behavior.

When teachers want students to repeat desirable behaviors, such as answering questions correctly or acting in socially appropriate ways, they will provide positive consequences, or reinforcement, for those behaviors. Examples of positive reinforcement are verbal praise, written comments, and good grades. It is important that teachers provide immediate reinforcement during lessons each time it is deserved.

Reinforcement can also be negative. In addition to working hard to enjoy teacher praise, students will work hard to avoid an unpleasant situation. For example, teachers inform students that any class work not finished during the period will be additional homework that night, and students will stay on task and finish their class work in a timely fashion to avoid that consequence.

Skinner (1968) and Markle (1969) organized aspects of behaviorism into principles for effective practice. Table 4.2 compares these principles and the Direct Instruction model.

Direct Instruction also relates to **information processing theory**. Information processing refers to how students receive, store, and retrieve information. As students receive sensory information during lessons, it becomes part of their **short-term memory**. Short-term memory is what students are able to focus on in a given moment and lasts from 20 to 30 seconds. They can use information in their short-term memories if they remain focused on it, and retrieval must be immediate (Anderson, 1990). Miller (1956) found that only five to nine items can be held in short-term memory at one time if those items are "chunked" into meaningful units. Numbers that we use each day, such as Social Security numbers and phone numbers, have been organized into chunks. In Direct Instruction lessons, teachers can make use of chunking during cycles of content presentation, modeling, and checking for understanding.

Table 4.2   Behaviorism and Direct Instruction

Behaviorism	Direct instruction
1. Information presented in small amounts	Task analysis, Content presentation
2. Many opportunities for immediate positive feedback	Checking for understanding
3. Use of question-answer format	Checking for understanding
4. Student responses required	Checking for understanding
5. Questions arranged by level of difficulty	Task analysis, Content presentation

To move information from short-term memory into **long-term memory**, students must use the information repeatedly. Guided, independent, mass, and distributed practice periods in Direct Instruction lessons perform that function. Once information is in long-term memory, it can remain there indefinitely, to be retrieved as needed (Anderson, 1990).

Using information processing theory, Robert Gagne identified nine instructional phases of learning that help students move information from reception through short-term memory and into long-term memory (Gagne & Driscoll, 1988). Table 4.3 shows how Gagne's steps align with the steps of information processing and Direct Instruction.

Direct Instruction and the Technologist Philosophy of Curriculum and Instruction

Direct Instruction also relates to the technologist philosophy of curriculum and instruction (Costa & Garmston, 1994; Eisner & Vallance, 1974). Remember that this philosophy refers to a "technology of instruction," a way to transmit knowledge and instruct skills in an efficient manner. The technologist approach to curriculum design is to develop a long-term objective that can be broken down into small component parts and daily instructional objectives. These objectives will be sequenced so that they build toward the long-term objective. This part-to-whole organization of content delineates the focus of each individual lesson, and the teacher's intent throughout each lesson is to ensure every student's mastery of the skill. Ms. Bernard's instructional objective was written very precisely and focused on one computational skill, renaming improper fractions as mixed numbers. She knew that a particular group of her students needed to have computational content broken down into small, manageable components.

The technologist philosophy is also apparent in the design of Direct Instruction lessons, in which lesson content is broken down into components that are analyzed into tasks and taught in a specific sequence of steps during content presentation and modeling. Because of this systematized structure of the model, many Direct Instruction lessons sound quite similar to the cases presented in this chapter, regardless of their content. Even if particular elements of the design are omitted from a lesson, most students experience Direct Instruction lessons in similar ways. Still, pacing and individual teacher style will contribute to variety and student interest in Direct Instruction lessons.

Technology and Direct Instruction

Direct Instruction is a straightforward way to teach skills in technology. In such lessons, Direct Instruction is the model of teaching, and technology itself is the content. Sometimes, exploration is integral to a learning experience that involves technology, such as when you want students to research a topic on the Internet or locate

Table 4.3   Gagne's Phases of Learning, Information Processing, and Direct Instruction

Gagne's Phases of Learning	Information Processing	Direct Instruction
1. Gain student attention	Reception	Focus activity
2. State the objective	Motivation	State the objective Provide the rationale
3. Recall prior knowledge	Retrieval	Focus activity
4. Present stimulus	Reception	Content presentation
5. Provide learning guidance	Explanations	Modeling
6. Provide feedback	Reinforcement	Checking for understanding
7. Elicit performance	Retrieval	Guided practice
8. Assess performance	Retrieval	Independent practice
9. Cue retrieval	Retrieval	Mass and distributive practice

SOURCE: Adapted from *The Conditions of Learning* by Robert M. Gagne. Copyright © 1965, 1970, 1977 by Holt, Rinehart & Winston, Inc.

a variety of appropriate Web sites for a class activity. However, the research skills students need to perform these tasks are most efficiently taught using Direct Instruction.

The International Society for Technology in Education (ISTE) is a global organization of educators who promote technology education at all levels of schooling. ISTE has long recognized that citizens in today's world need to be technologically literate. In the United States, the National Educational Technology (NET) Standards for Students were developed to describe what K–12 students should know about technology and be able to do with their technological skills. The organization has also developed the National Educational Technology Standards for Teachers. Many states have adopted both of these sets of standards to guide the technology education of their students and to codify the technology expectations they have of teachers. The NET Standards for Students are divided into six categories:

1. Basic Operations and Concepts
2. Social, Ethical, and Human Issues
3. Technology Productivity Tools
4. Technology Communication Tools
5. Technology Research Tools
6. Technology Problem-Solving Tools

Performance indicators at various grade levels (K–2, 3–5, 6–8, and 9–12) describe unit objectives in technology instruction that address one or more of these standards (International Society for Technology in Education, 2001). Classroom teachers, in collaboration with media specialists, can develop a sequential curriculum to promote student mastery of these indicators.

The original numbering of the performance indicators in *National Educational Technology Standards for Students: Connecting Curriculum and Technology* (International Society for Technology in Education, 2000) has been used in the examples below.* Only those performance indicators in each section containing material that can be taught using Direct Instruction are provided. Some of the performance indicators given below include components that relate to more than one standard. For example, at the Grades 3–5 level, Performance Indicator 5 combines the use of scanners (technology productivity tool) with multimedia authoring (technology communication tool). You will notice that the Grades K–2 and Grades 3–5 sections have several more examples showing where Direct Instruction can be used to teach technology skills than do the Grades 6–8 and Grades 9–12 levels. In the lower grades, students are learning the technology skills they will use in later levels. The operative verb in these early performance indicators is *use*, which places those tasks at the application level of Bloom's taxonomy. The higher levels of Bloom's taxonomy, analysis, synthesis, and evaluation, are represented in most of the performance indicators given at the Grades 6–8 and Grades 9–12 levels.

GRADES PK–2

NET Standard 1: Basic Operations and Concepts

Performance Indicator 1: Use input devices (e.g., mouse, keyboard, remote control) and output devices (e.g., monitor, printer) to successfully operate computers, VCRs, audiotapes, and other technology.

Direct Instruction Extension

Separate lessons can be taught for each of these input and output devices.

NET Standard 1: Basic Operations and Concepts

NET Standard 5: Technology Research Tools

Performance Indicator 4: Use developmentally appropriate multimedia resources (e.g., interactive books, educational software, elementary multimedia encyclopedias) to support learning.

Direct Instruction Extension

Separate lessons can be taught for each of these developmentally appropriate multimedia resources.

National Educational Technology Standards for Students: Connecting Curriculum and Technology by ISTE. Copyright © 2000 by International Society for Technology in Education (ISTE), 800–336–5191 (US & Canada) or 541–302–3777 (Int'l), iste@iste.org, www.iste.org. All rights reserved. Reproduced with permission of ISTE via Copyright Clearance Center. Reprint permission does not constitute endorsement by ISTE.

GRADES 3–5

NET Standard 3: Technology Productivity Tools

Performance Indicator 4: Use general purpose productivity tools and peripherals to support personal productivity, remediate skill deficits, and facilitate learning throughout the curriculum.

Direct Instruction Extension

Separate lessons can be taught for each of these developmentally appropriate productivity tools and peripherals.

NET Standard 3: Technology Productivity Tools

NET Standard 4: Technology Communication Tools

Performance Indicator 5: Use technology tools (e.g., multimedia authoring, presentations, Web tools, digital cameras, scanners) for individual and collaborative writing, communication, and publishing activities to create knowledge products for audiences inside and outside the classroom.

Direct Instruction Extension

Separate lessons can be taught for each of these technology productivity and technology communication tools listed.

GRADES 6–8

NET Standard 3: Technology Productivity Tools

NET Standard 5: Technology Research Tools

Performance Indicator 4: Use content-specific tools, software, and simulations (e.g., environmental probes, graphing calculators, exploratory environments, Web tools) to support learning and research.

Direct Instruction Extension

Separate lessons can be taught for each content-specific technology tool and category.

NET Standard 4: Technology Communication Tools

NET Standard 5: Technology Research Tools

NET Standard 6: Technology Problem-Solving Tools

Performance Indicator 6: Design, develop, publish, and present products (e.g., Web pages, videotapes using technology resources that demonstrate and communicate curriculum concepts to audiences inside and outside the classroom.)

Direct Instruction Extension

Separate lessons can be taught for each developmentally appropriate design, publish, and presentation product.

GRADES 9–12

NET Standard 3: Technology Productivity Tools

NET Standard 4: Technology Communication Tools

Performance Indicator 5: Use technology tools and resources for managing and communicating personal/professional information (e.g., finances, schedules, addresses, purchases, correspondence).

Direct Instruction Extension

Separate lessons can be taught for developmentally appropriate tools and resources to manage and communicate information.

Direct Instruction, Content Standards, and Benchmarks

Direct Instruction is best used across the curriculum when lesson content can be broken down into procedures or steps. When you use Direct Instruction, you can organize assessment using Bloom's knowledge, comprehension, and application levels. These levels are typically reflected in traditional assessments (e.g., multiple choice, true and false, fill in the blank, and short answer). However, Direct Instruction can also be used to teach cognitive processes explicitly (e.g., summarizing and predicting) and communication formats required by the analysis, synthesis, and evaluation levels of critical thinking (e.g., graphing, tables, essay format, and debate structure).

Below are some representative examples of content standards and benchmarks from the *Michigan Curriculum Framework*.* These content standards provide appropriate opportunities for teachers to use Direct Instruction to support student learning. The wording of standards and benchmarks for your state or school district may differ somewhat.

English Language Arts

CONTENT STANDARD 8: All students will use the characteristics of different types of texts, aesthetic elements, and mechanics—including text structure, figurative and descriptive language, spelling, punctuation, and grammar.

Elementary Benchmark: Identify and use mechanics that enhance and clarify understanding (conventional punctuation, capitalization, and spelling).

---

*Excerpts from the *Michigan Curriculum Framework* are reprinted with permission of the Michigan Department of Education.

Student mastery of this content requires clear and sufficient teacher modeling. The think aloud process is well suited for teaching these skills: using context clues, predicting, using subject-verb agreement, writing specific forms of poetry, and writing a well-structured and developed editorial.

The content standard and benchmark examples below illustrate concepts in social studies, math, and science that can be taught using Direct Instruction. In addition, inquiry processes in those core content areas (e.g., observing, predicting, and researching using multimedia) can be taught systematically using Direct Instruction.

Social Studies—Historical Perspective

CONTENT STANDARD 1: All students will sequence chronologically eras of American history in order to examine relationships and explain cause and effect.

Early Elementary Benchmark: Use analog and digital clocks to tell time.

Young children need explicit teaching when learning to tell time, especially with an analog clock.

Science—Use Scientific Knowledge From the Life Sciences in Real-World Contexts

CONTENT STANDARD 3: All students will apply an understanding of cells to the function of multicellular organisms; and explain how cells grow, develop, and reproduce.

High School Benchmark: Explain how multicellular organisms grow, based on how cells grow and reproduce.

Textbook reading alone is not sufficient for students to understand this material. Well-designed Direct Instruction using visual resources, perhaps in conjunction with technological resources, can support student learning of those benchmarks in science.

The math benchmarks below have been chosen specifically to demonstrate how Direct Instruction can be used throughout the grade levels as major concepts develop across one content standard.

Math—Patterns, Relationships, and Functions

CONTENT STANDARD 2: Students describe the relationships among variables, predict what will happen to one variable as another variable is changed, analyze natural variation and sources of variability, and compare patterns of change.

Elementary Benchmark: Use tables, charts, open sentences, and hands-on models to represent change and variability.

Middle School Benchmark: Represent variability or change by ordered pairs, tables, graphs, and equations.

High School Benchmark: Represent functions using symbolism such as matrices, vectors, and functional representation (f(x)).

Why Choose Direct Instruction?

Think about how you learn best and for what reasons. When I want to learn a particular cooking skill from my mother, I want her to show me that skill exactly as it needs to be done and then to critique my level of mastery as I practice doing it myself. In those moments, my needs are best served by Direct Instruction. If I want to create a new recipe, I want to experiment with the ingredients I like best without someone telling me how to go about the process. My preference in that moment will be trial and error, a playful approach to my creation. Earlier in this chapter, we considered the research on the efficacy of Direct Instruction. Under what circumstances would you use this model? Which content is best taught in a direct manner? Several considerations will help guide your decision to use Direct Instruction in your classroom:

1. Is the content of your lesson at the knowledge, comprehension, or application levels of Bloom's taxonomy of the cognitive domain?

2. If you are working with manipulatives or equipment, will Direct Instruction help you to teach the procedures for a math or science exploration clearly?

3. Are the students ready conceptually for teacher-driven instruction? If you are working on math computation, your students may be ready for Direct Instruction if they already have a solid, hands-on understanding of concepts embedded in the task.

4. Will Direct Instruction allow you to teach classroom management routines, rules, or game procedures in an efficient manner?

5. Must the content of a lesson be taught using small, sequential steps to ensure student achievement?

Summary

Over several decades, educational research has consistently shown Direct Instruction to be highly effective for teaching low-level reading and math skills. The model can also be used effectively to teach rules and procedures. Although Direct Instruction is generally used for objectives at the knowledge, comprehension, and application levels of the cognitive domain in Bloom's taxonomy, it can also be used to teach explicitly the cognitive processes required by analysis, synthesis, and evaluation.

The organization of a Direct Instruction lesson helps focus the teacher's attention on two things: first, the objective to be mastered, and second, the evolution of students' understanding throughout the lesson. Students are provided with sequenced content presentation and multiple ways to demonstrate what they can do. Lessons taught using Direct Instruction are easily assessed. The model is effective in mastery learning when students must achieve one instructional objective before moving on to the next.

Some teachers and teacher educators believe that Direct Instruction embodies the idea that teachers are the "keepers of the knowledge" in the classroom; what is to be learned must come only through them. Even if Direct Instruction does not resonate with your personal philosophy of teaching, it is important to remember that sometimes this model is highly appropriate, even in early childhood classrooms.

Putting It Together

1. Describe the advantages you see of using Direct Instruction in the elementary, middle, or high school classroom.

2. Review your state or district curriculum and, in two different subjects, find specific content that you might teach using Direct Instruction. Think carefully about the developmental needs of your students. Why is Direct Instruction the best choice for these lessons?

3. Choose a basic skill in math, writing, science, or social studies. Outline a Direct Instruction lesson, paying special attention to questions that check for understanding.

4. Describe a traditional lesson you have seen in a field placement class. Analyze the lesson, using the steps of Direct Instruction. Describe anything you would change about this lesson.

Student Study Site

The Companion Web site for *Models of Teaching: Connecting Student Learning With Standards*
www.sagepub.com/delloliostudy

Visit the Web-based student study site to enhance your understanding of the book content and discover additional resources that will take your learning one step further. You can enhance your understanding by using the comprehensive Study Guide, which includes chapter learning objectives, flash cards, practice tests, and more. You'll find special features, such as the links to standards from U.S. States and associated activities, Learning from Journal Articles, Field Experience worksheets, Learning from Case Studies, and PRAXIS resources.

References

Adams, G. L., & Engelmann, S. (1996). *Research on direct instruction: 25 years beyond DISTAR*. Seattle, WA: Educational Achievement Systems.

Allington, R. (2002). What I've learned about effective reading instruction from a decade of studying exemplary elementary classroom teachers. *Phi Delta Kappan*, *83*(10), 740–747.

Allington, R., & Johnston, P. H. (2002). What do we know about effective fourth grade teachers and their classrooms? In C. Roller (Ed.), *Learning to teach reading: Setting the research agenda* (pp. 50–65). Newark, DE: International Reading Association.

Anderson, J. R. (1990). *Cognitive psychology and its implications* (3rd ed.). New York: Freeman.

Anderson, L., Evertson, C., & Brophy, J. (1979). An experimental study in effective teaching in first grade reading groups. *Elementary School Journal*, *79*, 193–223.

Becker, W. C., & Carnine, D. W. (1980). Direct instruction: An effective approach to educational intervention with disadvantaged and low performing students. In Lahey & A. Kazdin (Eds.), *Advances in clinical child psychology, (Vol 3)*. New York: Plenum.

Becker, W. C., & Engelmann, S. E. (1978). *Analysis of achievement data on six cohorts of low-income children from twenty school districts in the University of Oregon Follow Through model* (Tech. Rep. 78–1). Eugene: University of Oregon Follow Through Project.

Becker, W. C., & Gersten, R. (1982). A follow-up of Follow Through: The later effects of the direct instruction model on children in fifth and sixth grades. *American Educational Research Journal*, *19*, 75–92.

Bennett, N. (1976). *Teaching styles and pupil progress*. Cambridge, MA: Harvard University Press.

Bereiter, C., & Engelmann, S. (1966). *Teaching disadvantaged children in the preschool*. Engelwood Cliffs, NJ: Prentice-Hall.

Binder, C., & Watkins, C. L. (1990). Precision teaching and direct instruction: Measurably superior instructional technology in schools. *Performance Improvement Quarterly*, *3*, 74–95.

Brophy, J. (1979). Teacher behavior and its effects. *Journal of Educational Psychology*, *71*, 733–750.

Brophy, J. (1999). *Teaching. Educational Practices Series–1*. Paris: UNESCO.

Brophy, J., & Evertson, C. (1974). *Process-product correlation in the Texas Teacher Effectiveness Study: Final report* (Research Report 74-4). Austin: University of Texas

Research and Development Center for Teacher Education. (ERIC Document Reproduction Service No. ED091394)

Brophy, J., & Good, T. (1986). Teacher behavior and student achievement. In M. Wittrock (Ed.), *Third handbook of research on teaching* (pp. 328–336). Chicago, IL: Rand McNally.

Burke, R. (2002). Social and emotional education in the classroom. *Kappa Delta Pi Record*, *38*(3), 108–111.

Butler, F. M., Miller, S. P., & Lee, K. (2001). Teaching mathematics to students with mild-to-moderate mental retardation: A review of the literature. *Mental Retardation*, *39*(1), 20–31.

Carnine, D. (1997). Bridging the research to practice gap. *Exceptional Children*, *63*(4), 513–521.

Carnine, D., Steeley, D., & Silbert, J. (1996). *Understanding U.S. history* (Vol. 2). Eugene: University of Oregon Press.

Cashwell, T. H., Skinner, C. H., & Smith, E. (2001). Increasing second grade students' reports of peers' prosocial behaviors via direct instruction, group reinforcement, and progress feedback: A replication and extension. *Education and Treatment of Children*, *24*(2), 161–175.

Coles, G. (2001). Reading taught to the tune of the "scientific" hickory stick. *Phi Delta Kappan*, *83*(3), 204–212.

Costa, A. L., & Garmston, R. J. (1994). *Cognitive coaching: A foundation for Renaissance schools*. Norwood, MA: Christopher-Gordon.

Darch, C., & Carnine, D. (1986). Teaching content area material to learning disabled students. *Exceptional Children*, *53*, 240–246.

Darch, C., Gersten, R., & Taylor, R. (1987). Evaluation of Williamsburg County Direct Instruction program: Factors leading to success in rural elementary programs. *Research in Rural Education*, *4*, 111–118.

De La Paz, S., & Graham, S. (2002). Explicitly teaching strategies, skills, and knowledge: Writing instruction in middle school classrooms. *Journal of Educational Psychology*, *94* (4), 687–698.

Dermody, M. N. (2001). Analysis of embedded skill lessons for literacy groups with inner-city Title I second grade students. *Reading Improvement*, *38*(1), 38–48.

Dimino, J., Gersten, R., Carnine, D., & Blake, G. (1990). Story grammar: An approach for promoting at-risk secondary students' comprehension of literature. *Elementary School Journal*, *91*(1), 19–32.

Din, F. S. (2000). Use direct instruction to improve reading skills quickly. *Rural Educator*, *21*(3), 1–14.

Eisner, E., & Vallance, E. (1974). *Conflicting conceptions of the curriculum*. Berkeley, CA: McCutchan.

Fazio, A. (2001). Excellence in teaching at-risk students. *Education*, *121*(4), 689–703.

Gage, N. (1978). *The scientific basis of the art of teaching*. New York: Teachers College Press.

Gage, N., & Needles, M. C. (1989). Process-product research on teaching. *Elementary School Journal*, *89*, 253–300.

Gagne, E. D., & Driscoll, M. P. (1988). *Essentials of learning for instruction* (2nd ed.). Englewood Cliffs, NJ: Prentice-Hall.

Gardner, R., Sainato, D. M., Cooper, J. O., Heron, T. E., Heward, W. L., Shelman, J. W., & Grossi, T. A. (1994). *Behavior analysis in education.* Pacific Grove, CA: Brooks/Cole.

Gersten, R., Woodward, J., & Darch, C. (1986). Direct instruction: A research-based approach to curriculum design and teaching. *Exceptional Children, 53,* 17–31.

Good, T. (1979). Teacher effectiveness in the elementary school: What we know about it now. *Journal of Teacher Education, 30,* 52–64.

Good, T. L., & Grouws, D. (1979). The Missouri Mathematics Effectiveness Project: An experimental study in fourth grade classrooms. *Journal of Educational Psychology, 71,* 355–372.

Grapko, M. P. (1972). *A comparison of open space and traditional classroom structures according to independence measures in children, teachers' awareness of children's personality variables and children's academic progress. Final report.* Toronto: Ontario Department of Education. (ERIC Document Reproduction Service No. ED088180)

Hunter, M. (1967a). *Motivation.* El Segundo, CA: TIP Publications.

Hunter, M. (1967b). *Reinforcement.* El Segundo, CA: TIP Publications.

Hunter, M. (1967c). *Retention.* El Segundo, CA: TIP Publications.

Hunter, M. (1967d). *Teach more—faster!* El Segundo, CA: TIP Publications.

Hunter, M. (1971). *Teach for transfer.* El Segundo, CA: TIP Publications.

Hunter, M. (1976). *Improved instruction.* El Segundo, CA: TIP Publications.

Hunter, M. (1982). *Mastery teaching.* El Segundo, CA: TIP Publications.

Hunter, M. (1994). *Enhancing teaching.* New York: Macmillan.

International Society for Technology in Education. (2000). *National educational technology standards for students: Connecting curriculum and technology.* Washington, DC: Author in collaboration with the U.S. Department of Education.

Kelly, B., Gersten, R., & Carnine, D. (1990). Student error patterns as a function of curricular design. *Journal of Learning Disabilities, 23*(1), 23–32.

Kozioff, M. A., LaNunziata, L., & Cowardin, J. (2001). Direct instruction: Its contributions to high school achievement. *High School Journal, 84*(2), 54–71.

Losardo, A., & Bricker, D. (1994). A comparison study: Activity-based intervention and direct instruction. *American Journal on Mental Retardation, 98*(6), 744–765.

Lovett, M. W., Borden, S. L., DeLuca, T., Lacerenza, L., Benson, N. J., & Brackstone, D. (1994). Treating the core deficits of developmental dyslexia: Evidence of transfer of learning after phonologically and strategy-based reading training programs. *Developmental Psychology, 30,* 805–822.

Markle, S. (1969). *Good frames and bad* (2nd ed.). New York: Wiley.

Medley, D. (1979). The effectiveness of teachers. In P. Peterson and H. Walberg (Eds.), *Research on teaching: Concepts, findings, and implications* (pp. 11–27). Berkeley, CA: McCutchan.

Meyer, L. (1984). Longitudinal academic effects of Direct Instruction Follow Through. *Elementary School Journal, 4,* 380–394.

Meyer, L., Gersten, R., & Gutkin, J. (1984). A Follow Through success story. *Elementary School Journal, 2,* 241–252.

Michigan Department of Education. (1996). *Michigan curriculum framework.* Lansing: Author.

Miller, G. A. (1956). The magical number seven, plus or minus two: Some limits on our capacity for processing information. *Psychological Review, 63,* 81–97.

Mills, P. E., Cole, K. N., & Dale, P. S. (2002). Early exposure to direct instruction and subsequent juvenile delinquency: A prospective examination. *Exceptional Children, 69*(1), 85–96.

North Central Regional Educational Laboratory. (2005). *NETS for Students: Achievement Rubric.* North Central Regional Educational Laboratory. Chicago: Learning Point Associates. www.ncrel.org/tech/nets/p-12rubric.pdf

O'Connor, R. E., Notari-Syverson, A., & Vadasy, P. F. (1996). Ladders to literacy: The effects of teacher-led phonological activities for kindergarten children with and without disabilities. *Exceptional Child, 63,* 117–130.

Paik, S. J. (2002). Ten strategies that improve learning. *Educational Horizons, 81*(2), 83–85.

Papay, J. P., Costello, R. J., & Hedl, J. (1975). Effects of trait and state anxiety on the performance of elementary school children in traditional and individualized multiage classrooms. *Journal of Educational Psychology, 67*(6), 840–846.

Peterson, P. (1979). Direct instruction reconsidered. In P. Peterson and H. Walberg (Eds.), *Research on teaching: Concepts, findings, and implications* (pp. 57–69). Berkeley, CA: McCutchan.

Rosenshine, B. (1979). Content, time, and direct instruction. In P. Peterson and H. Walberg (Eds.). *Research on teaching: Concepts, findings, and implications* (pp. 28–56). Berkeley, CA: McCutchan.

Rosenshine, B. (1986). Synthesis of research on explicit teaching. *Educational Leadership, 43,* 60–69.

Rosenshine, B. (1995). Advances in research on instruction. *Journal of Educational Research, 88*(5), 262–268.

Scarcelli, S. M., & Morgan, R. F. (1999). The efficacy of using a direct reading instruction approach in literacy-based classrooms. *Reading Improvement, 36*(4), 172–179.

Simmons, D. C., Fuchs, L. S., Fuchs, D., Mathes, P., & Hodge, P. (1994). Effects of explicit teaching and peer tutoring on the reading achievement of learning-disabled and low-performing students in regular classrooms. *Elementary School Journal, 95,* 387–408.

Skinner, B. F. (1953). *Science and human behavior.* New York: Macmillan.

Skinner, B. F. (1968). *The technology of teaching.* New York: Appleton-Century-Crofts.

Solomon, D., & Kendall, A. J. (1979). *Children in classrooms: An investigation of personality-environment interaction.* New York: Praeger.

Stallings, J. (1975). Implementation and child effects of teaching practices in Follow-Through classrooms. *Monographs of the Society for Research in Child Development, 40,* 7–8.

Stallings, J., Cory, R., Fairweather, J., & Needles, M. (1978). *A study of basic reading skills taught in secondary schools.* Menlo Park, CA: S.R.I. International.

Stallings, J., Needles, M., & Stayrook, M. (1979). *How to change the process of teaching basic reading skills in secondary schools: Phase II and phase III.* Menlo Park, CA: S.R.I. International.

Swanson, H. L. (1999). Instructional components that predict treatment outcomes for students with learning disabilities: Support for a combined strategy and direct instruction model. *Learning Disabilities, Research and Practice, 14,* 129–140.

Swanson, H. L. (2001). Searching for the best model for instructing students with learning disabilities. *Focus on Exceptional Children*, *34*(2), 1–15.

Torgesen, J. K., & Davis, C. (1996). Individual differences variables that respond to training in phonological awareness. *Journal of Experimental Child Psychology*, *63*, 1–21.

Troia, G. A., & Graham, S. (2002). The effectiveness of a highly explicit, teacher-directed strategy instruction routine: Changing the writing performance of students with learning disabilities. *Journal of Learning Disabilities*, *35*(4), 290–305.

Ullmann, L. P., & Krassner, L. (1966). *Case studies in behavior modification*. New York: Holt, Rinehart, & Winston.

Ulrich, R., Stachnik, T., & Mabry, J. (1970). *Control of human behavior* (Vol. 2). Glenview, IL: Scott, Foresman.

Viadero, D. (2002). Studies cite learning gains in direct instruction schools. *Education Week*, *21*(31), 15.

Wang, M. C., Haertel, G. D., & Walberg, H. J. (1993a). Toward a knowledge base for school learning. *Review of Educational Research*, *63*, 249–294.

Wang, M. C., Haertel, G. D., & Walberg, H. J. (1993b). What helps students learn? *Educational Leadership*, *51*(4), 74–79.

Ward, W. D. & Barcher, P. R. (1975). Reading achievement and creativity as related to open classroom experience. *Journal of Educational Psychology* 67, 683–691.

Waxman, H. C., & Walberg, H. J. (1999). *New directions for teaching practice and research*. Berkeley, CA: McCutchan.

Woodward, J., & Noell, J. (1991). Science instruction at the secondary level: Implications for students with learning disabilities. *Journal of Learning Disabilities*, *24*(5), 277–284.

Wright, R. J. & DuCette, J. P. (1976). *Locus of control and academic achievement in traditional and non-traditional settings*. Unpublished manuscript, Beaver College, Glenside, Pa., ERIC: ED123203.

chapter 5

Concept Attainment

How do we know that a koala is not really a bear? How do we know that a tomato is not a vegetable? Common misconceptions can be corrected once we are aware of the facts. Our sense of sight is often what we use to categorize objects in the world, but eyesight alone can be misleading. Once we know the attributes of vegetables, we know that tomatoes, which contain seeds, are actually fruits. Once we understand that baby koalas develop in their mother's pouch, we know that a koala is not a bear but a marsupial, like the kangaroo.

Categorization is an important critical thinking skill, and it demonstrates maturity of intelligence in young children. The **Concept Attainment** model of teaching provides a guided experience in exploring characteristics of items and their memberships in various categories. Concept Attainment is both flexible and versatile. Secondary teachers will find that Concept Attainment can be applied to most academic subjects, the arts, and some concepts in kinesiology. It has even been used successfully to help young children differentiate among the attributes of objects and ideas. It should come as no surprise that Concept Attainment lessons often introduce new vocabulary.

Concept Attainment developed in the 1960s from the research of Jerome Bruner, Jacqueline Goodnow, and George Austin (1959). Bruner (1961) was instrumental in helping teachers focus not only on content, or the "what" of teaching, but also on the "how" of learning. He created specific lesson designs with the express purpose of sharpening students' thinking, as well as helping them master academic content. In Bruner's Concept Attainment model, teachers work with students in indirect ways, facilitating cognitive growth though supported, engaging, and sustained inquiry.

The Concept Attainment model allows students to categorize items based on an analysis of their characteristics, or critical attributes. **Critical attributes** are the characteristics that define an object or idea and help explain what makes it unique. Critical attributes tell us what set an item belongs to. For example, mammals are vertebrates that bear live offspring that will be nursed by their mother. Rather than teaching the concept of mammals directly, teachers will present examples, called **exemplars,** of animals that belong together: Cat, dog, and monkey are all mammals, but snake, spider, and penguin are not. Successful Concept Attainment lessons will result in students' identifying a category, listing the critical attributes that belong to the category, and providing more exemplars of the category.

The structure of a Concept Attainment lesson engages students' critical thinking as soon as the lesson begins. In Concept Attainment lessons, students will be asked to observe, analyze, classify, develop hypotheses, verbalize their own ideas, and learn to analyze the ideas of others. As you read this case study, consider which learning theory and which philosophy of curriculum and instruction are exemplified by this model of teaching and why.

Case Study 5.1: Second Grade, Science

Mrs. Cook is a second-grade teacher in a rural elementary school. For the past several years, she worked as a special education teacher for her district, but she decided to return to general education this year. Mrs. Cook wanted to broaden her instructional repertoire, so recently she has been using the Concept Attainment model in her classroom. After several successful lessons, she is feeling confident about her understanding of the process. Students have told Mrs. Cook that they enjoy the "puzzle" quality of her "categories" lessons, which is what she named the Concept Attainment model for her second graders.

Mrs. Cook's students have been identifying and naming categories across the curriculum. Right now, her focus is on states of matter, one of the science benchmarks for the elementary grades. Yesterday this class learned the concept of solids in an informal, teacher-directed lesson. Most of Mrs. Cook's students had definite prior knowledge about the attributes of solids, and a few of them knew the term *solid*. However, she believes that many of these students have an incomplete understanding of the attributes of liquids. She hopes that today's Concept Attainment lesson will be an effective way for her students to describe liquids as another state of matter. Mrs. Cook has the following long-term objective for this science unit:

The learner will describe the critical attributes of solids, liquids, and gases and will provide examples of each state of matter.

Today's lesson has the following objective:

The learner will state two critical attributes of liquids—taking the shape of containers and taking up space.

Mrs. Cook's 22 second graders are seated in table formations with 4 or 5 students at each table. The class has just finished a "sponge activity" to pull them together and focus their attention after a rousing kickball game at recess. (Sponges "soak up" extra class time in quick but meaningful activities.) This particular sponge activity had them figure out the common characteristics of two objects. Mrs. Cook finishes the sponge activity and transitions into the lesson.

Mrs. Cook: This will be the last pair of objects before we move to our science lesson for today. What do a CD and a Frisbee have in common? (*Many hands are raised immediately*.)

Oh, this one was too easy! It seems almost everyone knows the answer—and so quickly. Since so many of you already have your hands raised, tell us what they have in common. (*She pauses*.)

Who will share what they decided? Marty?

Marty: They are both round.

Mrs. Cook: You're right.

Rolland: They are alike in another way, too. They are both flat, but the CD is flatter than the Frisbee.

Mrs. Cook: That's correct! We will be working with categories in this lesson. Who remembers what we call our guesses about the categories? Evelyn?

Evelyn: In science and social studies, we call them hypotheses. You sometimes call them our "thinking guesses."

Mrs. Cook: Yes, Evelyn. Second graders, I am going to ask you to work by yourself first today, and then you will work with a partner. Please remember to raise your hand when you have a guess. (*During recess she had written these headings on the board:* Yes, No, *and* Hypotheses.) As I write words in the *Yes* and *No* categories, think quietly about how they are different. (*She writes words on the board under each heading.*)

Yes	No	Hypotheses
orange soda pop	penny	

Remember that the first example in the *Yes* column has the attribute that we are looking for in today's lesson. The words in the *No* column do not. There is something about orange soda pop that you will not find in a penny. If you have an idea, keep it in your head for now. (*She pauses for just a moment.*)

I am going to add two new words to our lists—one under *Yes* and one under *No*. Our *Yes* word is apple juice. Our *No* word is cookie.

Yes	No	Hypotheses
orange soda pop	penny	
apple juice	cookie	

Wow! Several of you have ideas already! Shari, what do you think is the category that includes orange soda pop and apple juice?

Shari: They both have fruit in them. (*Mrs. Cook writes "have fruit" under the* Hypotheses *heading*.)

Yes	No	Hypotheses
orange soda pop	penny	
apple juice	cookie	have fruit

Mrs. Cook: Well, that is certainly true of apple juice, but that is not our category. Let me add one more set of *Yes* and *No* words to our lists—iced tea is a *Yes*, and a loaf of bread is a *No*.

Yes	No	Hypotheses
orange soda pop	penny	
apple juice	cookie	have fruit
iced tea	loaf of bread	

What do you think now? What do orange soda pop, apple juice, and iced tea have in common that a penny, a cookie, and loaf of bread do not? This time, turn to the person sitting next to you and talk this over. (*She pauses.*) How many of you have a new idea? So many hands! Ronnie, Margo, and Brian, tell me what you and your partners were thinking. Ronnie, you go first.

Ronnie: Eric and I thought they were all things to drink.

*Margo
and Brian:* So did we!

Mrs. Cook: Why do you think that is so? Marty, did you and your partner come up with the same idea?

Marty: Yes, we did. We drink those things at home and at school.

Sammie: No orange soda pop at school!

Mrs. Cook: We will add *things to drink* under our hypotheses heading, but we have not yet found our category.

Yes	No	Hypotheses
orange soda pop	penny	
apple juice	cookie	have fruit
iced tea	loaf of bread	things to drink

Now I am going to add some new words to our lists. Milk and corn oil are each a *Yes*. A scrambled egg and clouds are each a *No*. Look at our *Yes* list again carefully. Rebecca?

Yes	No	Hypotheses
orange soda pop	penny	
apple juice	cookie	have fruit
iced tea	loaf of bread	things to drink
milk	scrambled egg	
corn oil	clouds	

Rebecca: Well, we cannot drink corn oil, hut we can eat it. My mom fries chicken in oil on top of the stove.

Todd: My mom puts corn oil into her homemade salad dressing. We eat the salad. (*Mrs. Cook adds* things to eat *to the* Hypotheses *list.*)

Yes	No	Hypotheses
orange soda pop	penny	
apple juice	cookie	have fruit
iced tea	loaf of bread	things to drink
milk	scrambled egg	
corn oil	clouds	things to eat

Karyl: Yes, but *things to eat* can't be our *Yes* category because our *No* list has cookies, bread, and eggs.

Mrs. Cook: Nicole?

Nicole: Karyl is right, Rebecca. There are things to eat on our *Yes* list, like you said, but they are also on our *No* list.

Mrs. Cook: Another important observation. I am going to add two more items to the *Yes* list. Think about these carefully with your partner. Elmer's glue and lemon juice are each a *Yes*. A computer and a plastic pitcher are each a *No*. (She adds these to the list and waits.)

Yes	No	Hypotheses
orange soda pop	penny	
apple juice	cookie	have fruit
iced tea	loaf of bread	things to drink
milk	scrambled egg	
corn oil	clouds	things to eat
Elmer's glue	computer	
lemon juice	plastic pitcher	

Mrs. Cook: Sarah?

Sarah: All we could think of was that the list REALLY can't be things we can eat, now!

Mrs. Cook: Did any of you come up with a category for all the *Yes* list words? Isaac?

Isaac: Marty and I could only figure out that everything on the *Yes* list comes in a container. (*Mrs. Cook records this.*)

Yes	No	Hypotheses
orange soda pop	penny	
apple juice	cookie	have fruit
iced tea	loaf of bread	things to drink
milk	scrambled egg	
corn oil	clouds	things to eat
Elmer's glue	computer	come in a
lemon juice	plastic pitcher	container

Alex: Mrs. Cook, that is true of the *No* list also, isn't it?

Mrs. Cook: What do you all think about what Alex just pointed out? Jessie?

Jessie: He's OK about everything but the clouds on the *No* list, Mrs. Cook. Scrambled eggs don't come in a container, but we can put them in a container. But Mrs. Cook, I have another idea. I think that the *Yes* list is a list of things that are wet.

Mrs. Cook: What do you mean, Jessie?

Jessie: Well, Sally and I saw that you can spill everything on the *Yes* list, and they would be wet and have to be cleaned up right away. Everything on the *No* list could be spilled, but it wouldn't be hard to clean up.

Dorit: Not the clouds, though. Clouds can't be spilled.

Ahmad: Yeah, but things on the *No* list don't have to match, only things on the *Yes* list.

Mrs. Cook: Thanks for reminding us of that, Ahmad. (*She records* wet *in the* Hypotheses *list*.)

Yes	No	Hypotheses
orange soda pop	penny	
apple juice	cookie	have fruit
iced tea	loaf of bread	things to drink
milk	scrambled egg	
corn oil	clouds	things to eat
Elmer's glue	computer	come in a container
lemon juice	plastic pitcher	wet

Mrs. Cook: Sally?

Sally: I had to help my mom clean up corn oil she spilled on the floor when we were frying tortillas at home. It was hard to clean up because it was very slippery. Wet things have to be cleaned up by hand with a sponge or paper towel, not with a vacuum cleaner. The *Yes* list is full of wet things! Jessie and I were right!

Mrs. Cook: Yes, you were, Sally! Things that are wet have a special name. Yesterday, we talked about things that are hard. What did we call them, everyone?

Class: Solids!

Mrs. Cook: Solids. All the things on our *Yes* list today are things that are wet. We call those things *liquids*. What can we say about the list of liquids we already have on the board? Talk this over with your partner. (*She pauses.*) Tuan?

Tuan: Well, some wet things we can drink, but we can't drink them all!

Mrs. Cook: Anything else you noticed? Jensen?

Jensen: Richard and I said that you can pour them from a pitcher.

Priscilla: You can't pour corn oil from a pitcher.

Jensen: Well, you probably won't, but you COULD.

Next, Mrs. Cook will give the students the attributes of liquids. She first asks them to review the attributes of solids, learned in the lesson on states of matter.

Mrs. Cook: Boys and girls, in our last science lesson, we looked at one state of matter called *solid*. Who can remind us what a solid is? I'll wait a moment for everyone to think of the characteristics of solids. (*She pauses.*) Lizzie?

Lizzie: I remember that a solid has a shape of its own. It doesn't change its shape.

Mrs. Cook: Not even when it is placed into a container, Lizzie?

Lizzie: No.

Mrs. Cook: Right! What example did we use yesterday to talk about that? Shelby?

Shelby: One was marbles. If I put my marbles in a can, they rattle around in the can, but they still keep their marble shape.

Mrs. Cook: Yes, we did talk about marbles that way. I will write down the first attribute of solids again on the board.

Solids

1. Do not take the shape of their container

Mrs. Cook: There was one other characteristic of solids. Does anyone remember? Tyler?

Tyler: How much space something takes up.

Mrs. Cook: What did we call that, Ty?

Tyler: It's called volume, right?

Mrs. Cook: Yes, it's called volume. Let me add that characteristic of solids to the list.

1. Do not take the shape of their container

2. Definite volume—take up space

Well, liquids also have attributes, things about them that make them liquids. All liquids have these two attributes. I'll write these on the board. Number 1, liquids always take the shape of their containers. And number 2, liquids also have a definite volume. They always take up space.

Liquids

1. Do take the shape of their container

2. Definite volume—take up space

The water in a full glass has a greater volume than the water in a glass that is only half full. Think about the *Yes* exemplars on the board. Do they all have critical attributes 1 and 2 for liquids?

Class: Yes.

Mrs. Cook: I am going to call out other exemplars, and I am going to ask you to categorize each one as a *Yes* or a *No*. Water?

Class: Yes!

Brenna: That one was too easy!

Mrs. Cook: Soccer ball?

Class: No!

Mrs. Cook: Cup?

Class: No!

Mrs. Cook: Dish washing soap?

Class: Yes!

After calling out several more exemplars for the students to classify, Mrs. Cook decides the students are ready to generate their own exemplars. She asks them to think of as many different kinds of liquids as they can. The class comes up with these liquids to add to the *Yes* list on the board:

ranch dressing

water

motor oil

gasoline

pancake batter

ink

maple syrup

Mrs. Cook points out that the class has listed liquids that feel very different from one another.

Next, she asks them again about their ideas and how they thought about them during the categories lesson today, a skill that is still new to these students.

Mrs. Cook: Shari thought at first that items in the *Yes* column all came from fruit of some kind. Many of you agreed with her. Kass?

Kass: Well, one was from oranges and one was from apples.

Todd: My mom says that soda pops like orange and cherry don't have real fruit in them. They only taste like they do.

Mrs. Cook: When did we know that our first category idea was wrong? Dea?

Dea: When you wrote iced tea.

Jeremy: Well, it would fit if she wrote raspberry iced tea.

Marcy: But she didn't. We can only go by what was on the board. We can't add anything to what it says.

Mrs. Cook: What was our next guess for the category? Jon?

Jon: Eric and Ronnie thought the category was things we can drink. We thought it might be that until you wrote corn oil in the *Yes* column. Then we changed it to things we can eat.

Richard: Yes, but we could eat everything on both lists then.

Miriam: Not pennies!

Richard: We could eat them if they were cinnamon jelly pennies.

Miriam: But they aren't. Mrs. Cook wrote Elmer's glue next, and nobody eats glue.

Even though this is a fairly new skill for these students, they manage to weave through each hypothesis as it was offered in the course of the lesson. They could remember why some ideas seemed to work and why others did not. Mrs. Cook brings this lesson to a close by quickly reviewing the critical attributes of solids and liquids. As their "ticket out the door," she asks each child to whisper a solid and a liquid in her ear as they line up to go to art class.

For tonight's homework assignment, Mrs. Cook asks her students to make a list of all the liquids their family members use after school today until they go to bed tonight. Tomorrow, the class will look at the different kinds of liquids the students recorded and find ways to categorize items on the complete class list.

Case Study 5.1: Post-Lesson Reflection

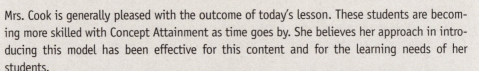

Mrs. Cook is generally pleased with the outcome of today's lesson. These students are becoming more skilled with Concept Attainment as time goes by. She believes her approach in introducing this model has been effective for this content and for the learning needs of her students.

She first introduced Concept Attainment using exemplars of everyday items in the *Yes* columns—breakfast cereals, sports shoes, and so on. Once the basic format of Concept Attainment was familiar to her students, Mrs. Cook began using the model with academic content. She started with material already learned by her students, such as even and odd numbers in math and nouns and verbs in language arts. When she felt they were ready, Mrs. Cook used Concept Attainment as the vehicle for new learning. In their last Concept Attainment lesson, the students discovered the category of dairy foods—one of the basic food groups they had been learning about in their nutrition unit. Mrs. Cook didn't want her students to become bored by the model, but she did use sponge activities that involved categories to keep the basic skill alive in between formal Concept Attainment lessons.

The students' ability to discriminate between items in the *Yes* and *No* columns has become increasingly more sophisticated. She remembers that at first the "guesses," as the hypotheses were then called, were seldom backed up by reasons. By working initially with simple categories and by asking the right questions, she was able to elicit students' reasons for their guesses. Public think alouds let the students hear how their friends were thinking about the items in each column. The final group think aloud reviewed the process one more time. This step of the model provides the practice some students may need to attain the concept firmly.

Mrs. Cook has seen these students become more analytical thinkers as a result of having to think out loud for everyone. Students' critical thinking has become sharper as they have had to describe their thinking, and students have also become more articulate in their descriptions of their thinking, or their **metacognition**. She notices now that this is a kind of chicken-and-egg benefit of using Concept Attainment. Speaking about their thinking process actually assists their thinking. Thinking out loud assists students in giving more-precise explanations, or what they "really mean." Although she was prepared for it, Mrs. Cook is relieved that in today's lesson, no one confused "solids that are wet" with liquids. Tomorrow she may clarify the difference between the two concepts. She had already prepared an example in case this question was asked in class. Solids that are wet are still solids, not liquids. Water on a washcloth makes the washcloth wet, but the washcloth is still a solid. The water is a liquid. After considering this, Mrs. Cook decides to leave well enough alone. She will deal with this question only if it comes from one of her students. One child whispered "Jell-O" as a liquid as he lined up for art class. Mrs. Cook whispered back that Jell-O was something special, and they might be talking about it later in the unit. Could he think of another example of liquid? The student did so easily. Again, Mrs. Cook was satisfied. She may choose to address the concept of colloids in a lesson later in the unit; however, colloids are a difficult concept, and she will have to think carefully about how they might be taught to young children.

Tomorrow, Mrs. Cook plans to extend this morning's science lesson to the current math unit on graphing. She thinks she can further students' understanding of bar graphs using the data from tonight's homework. She will wait and see the data her students collect. Mrs. Cook does have one major concern about today's lesson. She worries that she is inconsistent in expecting students to always raise their hands to speak during a full-group lesson. This was less of an issue when Mrs. Cook ran a resource room. In this class of 22 students, she wants to maintain order, but she also wants to promote quick-paced discussions as much as possible. She plans to think about this expectation and to speak with one of the more experienced general education teachers on the staff. Several teachers at Mrs. Cook's school are experimenting with the Concept Attainment model, and she thinks they will help her think about this issue further.

The Stages of the Concept Attainment Model

Concept Attainment requires preparation prior to the lesson to ensure student success and to maintain smooth momentum during the lesson. This preparation supports teachers' flexibility when they use any model of teaching, but it is particularly important for Concept Attainment lessons. While the stages of Concept Attainment first appear easy to follow, the sequence is not rigid and requires the teacher to make some quick and important decisions as the lesson progresses.

Preparation for Using Concept Attainment

While most veteran teachers have learned to "think on their feet" and find appropriate, spontaneous exemplars when faced with students' questions, they still plan ahead carefully and choose the clearest exemplars to use. Thorough preparation is crucial to the success of beginning teachers.

Earlier this week, as she was planning for today's lesson, Mrs. Cook developed two lists of items. The first list contained exemplars of liquids. She tried to brainstorm liquids with different individual attributes—thin, thick, edible, nonedible, variously colored, and used for a variety of purposes. The second list contained **nonexemplars** of items of varying shapes, textures, edibility, and usefulness. Mrs. Cook next began to consider how best to sequence the first list so that the order of the items prompted students' initial hypotheses. The exemplars list was finally organized in this way:

Exemplars	salad dressing
orange soda pop	rain
apple juice	vinegar
iced tea	milk shake
milk	sports drink
corn oil	fingernail polish
Elmer's glue	floor cleaner
lemon juice	smoothie

Next, she developed a list of nonexemplars. Again, Mrs. Cook used variety in her selection. She decided to include two gases in this second list, ones that she thought her students would understand. Once she completed her second list, she tried to sequence each item in relation to the exemplars list. The nonexemplars list looked like this:

Nonexemplars	soccer ball
penny	helium
cookie	picture frame
loaf of bread	chair
scrambled egg	hook
clouds	scooter
computer	washcloth
plastic pitcher	glass
brick	cup

The first four items in each list were chosen to begin her lesson, and they were chosen with care. These first pairs were intended to jump-start students' thinking. She took a look at the first four items from each list and wrote them as pairs.

Exemplars	*Nonexemplars*
orange soda pop	penny
apple juice	cookie
corn oil	loaf of bread
milk	scrambled egg

Mrs. Cook generated several more exemplars in sequence than she believed she would actually need in this lesson because she has misjudged the necessary number before and had to think of more exemplars on the spot. On one memorable occasion, Mrs. Cook's spontaneous exemplars missed the mark and confused a number of students in her class. She promised herself to be more thorough in her lesson planning after that experience.

A lengthier list of both exemplars and nonexemplars is always helpful in case students' hypotheses require the teacher to shift gears. It also might have been necessary for Mrs. Cook to move through the sequence of exemplars and nonexemplars in a different order than she anticipated depending on her students' responses. Either way, she felt prepared with strong exemplars to present in this Concept Attainment lesson.

Several times before today's lesson, Mrs. Cook reviewed each list in sequence carefully. Once she had reviewed the lesson again the night before she taught it, she created a lesson prompt by writing the lists side by side on a 3 × 5 inch index card. She kept this card in her hands as the children worked through this Concept Attainment lesson.

Introduction of Exemplars and Nonexemplars

Once preparations are complete, the stages of Concept Attainment are not difficult to understand. The teacher's sequential actions are clear. The timing for using each stage of the model and the specific use of exemplars and nonexemplars during the lesson will require flexibility. As with every other model of teaching, facility and ease come only with time and experience.

To initiate a Concept Attainment lesson, teachers must begin by presenting exemplars and nonexemplars to their students—many teachers identify these as "Yes" and "No" exemplars of the concept. Two or three sets of exemplars are adequate to begin a lesson, although some teachers choose to provide a greater number of exemplars for students right away. Once you have taught a number of Concept Attainment lessons, you may find that you prefer one way or the other. You may also find that your students respond better to one than to the other.

Once the first data set of exemplars and nonexemplars is given to the students, ask them to identify specific attributes of the concepts in the exemplar list. If your students have never worked with Concept Attainment before, it is probably best to limit the number of attributes the positive exemplars have in common. For example, in the case study, Mrs. Cook limited the critical attributes of liquids to *take the shape of their container* and *take up space*. She could have narrowed the concept to differentiate between liquids with different viscosities, but that would not have been appropriate given the day's objective. The complexity of thick liquids might have confused second graders at their stage of understanding the states of matter.

Generating Hypotheses

When the attributes of the positive exemplars have been analyzed, students might have an initial hypothesis. You can choose to elicit this right away, or you can choose to give another pair of exemplars against which they can check their hypothesis. The age of your students, as well as their facility in Concept Attainment, may help you decide this move. Younger students might need to state their hypotheses before you add another pair of exemplars. Older students may be able to handle another pair or multiple pairs of exemplars against which to test their hypotheses privately. A full-group discussion of initial hypotheses is in order, whenever you elicit them.

As students begin to state their hypotheses, your job is to listen and facilitate their rationale for their first efforts. The thinking strategies of each student who explains a hypothesis must be made explicit for the rest of the class. The class, in turn, has the job of pointing out how a hypothesis may be correct, or in what ways it is off the mark. This occurred in our case study when Karyl noticed that Rebecca's hypothesis, things to eat, could not be the category because the *No* list contained cookies, bread, and eggs. Collectively, the group can work its way through each initial hypothesis until it can be restated in a revised version that satisfies everyone.

Testing and Affirming Hypotheses

A formal test of any hypothesis consists of reviewing it against a new set of exemplars. Does the hypothesis still hold true for the entire exemplar set? If so, students should be asked to generate new ideas given the criteria for exemplars. Again, each proposed exemplar is examined against the criteria. If the new exemplars do not match the criteria for the first hypothesis, a new hypothesis must be considered. You may choose to add a new exemplar pair or two to the lists. The cycle of generating hypotheses and then testing them against new exemplar pairs continues until the concept has been identified correctly.

Once you affirm the correct hypothesis, your job is to name the concept and review the critical attributes of exemplars. Mrs. Cook did this when she wrote the attributes of solids on the board and compared them with the attributes of liquids, the new category. Students may continue to offer additional exemplars that can be evaluated against the attributes of the concept. Students have attained the new concept when each additional exemplar fits the criteria accurately.

Teachers must be prepared to move in the direction of their students' thinking during a Concept Attainment lesson.

Analyzing the Cognitive Road Map

When Mrs. Cook first began using Concept Attainment with this class, the students resisted the final step of the model, which is to analyze the path of their thinking throughout the lesson. Since they had already "thought those thoughts," as one student put it, why did they need to think about them again? To get around this resistance, she decided to approach the task in another way. Mrs. Cook knew that her students enjoyed puzzles of any kind and mysteries, a new literary genre for them. She asked them what another teacher might be able to figure out about their lesson if the three lists remained on the board but no one was in the classroom to answer questions about what happened. How might this teacher figure out the way they discovered today's category? This tactic was successful, and since then, this class has enjoyed reviewing how a "detective teacher" would unravel the way they had figured out their category puzzle.

Mrs. Cook has developed an increased appreciation for the benefits of this final collective memory stage of Concept Attainment. Students with fewer cognitive strategies have multiple opportunities to learn from other students as the class reviews the road map of their thinking processes out loud. The class's pool of strategies also increases as a result of participating in these discussions. She has noticed

| Table 5.1 | The Stages of Concept Attainment |

Stage	Teacher Action	Students' Response	Notes
Preparation	Creates lists of positive and negative exemplars		Make sure you have prepared enough exemplars
Introduction of the first exemplar pairs	Asks students to consider the unique attributes of exemplars and nonexemplars	Discuss exemplar attributes	
Hypothesis 1	Calls for first hypothesis	Generate first hypothesis and define concept	Write down hypothesis
Testing hypothesis 1	Provides another pair to challenge initial hypothesis or support it	Respond to new exemplars with either Hypothesis 2 or other possibilities for exemplar list	Write down new hypotheses
Additional hypothesis-testing cycles	Same	Same	Same
Affirmation of hypothesis	Affirms correct hypothesis, names concept, reviews critical attributes of concept	Offer additional exemplars	Write down additional exemplars
Analysis of student thinking	Requests a road map of students' hypothesis building, initiates discussion of effectiveness of strategies	Recount how they "got there" individually and as a group	Write down the road map if helpful; record multiple strategies

that some students create new strategies as they describe ones they have already used successfully.

A friend of Mrs. Cook's, a fifth-grade faculty member who is also experimenting with Concept Attainment this semester, has commented that her students have even more sophisticated reasoning behind their hypotheses. Given their maturity, this is to be expected. These fifth graders are beginning to recognize patterns in their successive hypotheses, and they are becoming quite adept, even enthusiastic, about sharing their thinking with the rest of the class.

Case Study 5.2: Fifth Grade, Math

Ms. Fernandes teaches fifth-grade math in a team of teachers who have chosen to share their teaching responsibilities by subject. Her teammates teach language arts, social studies, and science. She teaches four fifth-grade classes each day and has a math lab for high-achieving math students the last period of her day. The students in each fifth-grade class were heterogeneously grouped at the beginning of the school year, so there is a range of skill levels in each of these classes.

Last year as fourth graders, Ms. Fernandes's students were introduced to prime numbers. Rather than beginning her fifth-grade series of lessons on prime numbers with a traditional review followed by Direct Instruction, she has decided to use the Concept Attainment model of teaching to assess her students' understanding. She knows that each group of fifth graders will come in knowing the model because their social studies teacher uses it from time to time. One thing she appreciates about Concept Attainment is that the model's structure supports students' interactive critical thinking. How her students formulate and explain their hypotheses and challenge one another's ideas will give her an informal assessment of their thinking about prime numbers. She will be modifying the model in two ways today. One modification is to ask her students to name the critical attributes from both the *Yes* and *No* lists, and the second is to allow them to work in pairs and table groups.

This is her first math class of the day. She will have the opportunity to change this lesson based on what she learns this period. Ms. Fernandes has chosen to show the numbers in the *Yes* and *No* columns in their numerical order. She thinks this will be the most effective procedure, but she may decide to mix up the order of the numbers in later lessons. She has written "Please take your seats" on the front board. Once she counts backward from 10, the students know that she will begin the class with a mental math problem. These problems have gotten longer recently, and her students prepare for the countdown with enthusiasm.

Ms. Fernandes: Ten, nine, eight, seven, six, five, four, three, two, one. Are you ready? 6 times 4, divided by 2, times 3, plus 4, times ½, times 8, divided by 4, minus 4, minus 24, divided by 4. The correct answer is 3. If one of you is ready to give the mental math problem at the beginning of class, prepare one, and we'll schedule a day for you.

Today we are going to work with yes and no exemplars of numbers to see if you can figure out the differences between the two sets. You will be looking for the critical attributes of each set. You have done this type of lesson with Mrs. Gallagher in social studies class. Remember, you need to be forming a hypothesis as the exemplars are revealed. There is scratch paper in the middle of your tables and pencils in case you want to use them as you think. I'll ask for your ideas after we have a few of each set. Two is a *Yes*. Three is a *Yes*. Five is a *Yes*. Four is a *No*. Take a good look at the list so far. If you and a partner want to talk quietly, that's fine.

Yes	No
2	4
3	
5	

Let's not share hypotheses just yet. Let me give you one more example. Six is a *No*. (*She provides wait time.*) Any ideas? Thomas?

Yes	No
2	4
3	6
5	

Thomas:	My hypothesis depends on the next *No* number. I am thinking that the numbers in the *Yes* column are doubled on the right.
Ms. Fernandes:	Who would like to comment on Thomas's idea? Meyly?
Meyly:	I understand why he thinks that, but if every number on the *Yes* column is doubled on the *No* column, you can't give the name of either set. You are only using an operation to get the second number.
Ms. Fernandes:	What is that?
Meyly:	You are multiplying by 2.
Ms. Fernandes:	So, this hypothesis does not provide a critical attribute?
Meyly:	No.
Ms. Fernandes:	Any other thoughts on this idea? Joel?
Joel:	Go back to what Thomas first said. If his idea is true, then every number on the *No* list would end up on the *Yes* list, also.
Ms. Fernandes:	How can you be sure?
Joel:	We need more *Yes* and *No* numbers to see.
Ms. Fernandes:	Beatrice?
Beatrice:	I don't think Joel's idea is true because number four isn't in the *Yes* list and five is already past four.
Ms. Fernandes:	Comments? Sarah, your hand shot up quickly. Did you want to say something about Beatrice's comment?
Sarah:	Well, no. I had another idea. Are they lists of odd and even numbers? Wait, wait, it can't be that because when we count even numbers, we begin with two, and two is on the *Yes* list.

| | | | Ms. Fernandes: | Let's look at a few more exemplars. Seven is a *Yes*. Eight is a *No*. Nine is a *No*. Ten is a *No*. Eleven is a *Yes*. What can we say about Thomas's hypothesis now? Was his hypothesis correct or incorrect and why? Olivia? |

Yes	No
2	4
3	6
5	8
7	9
11	10

Olivia: No. Five times 2 is not 8, and 7 times 2 is not 9.

Ms. Fernandes: Do you see anything new in the exemplars? Douglas?

Douglas: Well, 9 is an odd number, so that is another reason that Thomas's hypothesis isn't correct, and also a reason that Sarah's isn't either. The other thing is that so far, the numbers in the *Yes* list have been smaller than the number across from them. But 11 is larger than 10.

Ms. Fernandes: Meyly, you are looking so agitated. What is on your mind?

Meyly: We still aren't looking for something that unites the numbers in the *Yes* column. And, anyway, Ms. Fernandes, I think I already know the answer.

Ms. Fernandes: Meyly, keep it to yourself. You can write it on a small piece of paper, and I'll check it in just a moment, but please keep it to yourself. I am going to put several more exemplars in each list. Listen, look, and think; 13, 17, and 19 are all *Yes* numbers, and 12, 14, and 15 are all *No*s. At your table groups, talk about what you see in common in each set of numbers. Meyly, you may show me what you have written down.

Yes	No
2	4
3	6
5	8
7	9
11	10
13	12
17	14
19	15

Ms. Fernandes: (*Several minutes have passed.*) Let's hear your ideas. Lillian's table.

Lillian: We think Meyly was right about the operation business, but we did find things in the lists that we think mean something. Two times 2 is 4. Two times 3 is 6. Two times 5 is 10. Two times 7 is 14. That is as far as we can go with 2, but we can start at the top of the lists again with 3. Three times 4 is 12. Three times 6 is 18, so it might be a *No* number, but we can't say for sure until you put that number somewhere.

Ms. Fernandes: We'll see in a moment. A new idea about the critical attributes of these numbers?

Lillian: We didn't get any further than that. We needed more exemplars to see if our pattern fits.

Ms. Fernandes: A few more exemplars, then. Twenty-three is a *Yes*. Twenty-nine is a *Yes*. At your tables, think about what number should come next in the *No* column. Dina, you're waving your hand.

Yes	No
2	4
3	6
5	8
7	9
11	10
13	12
17	14
19	15
23	
29	

Dina: Yes, I think I know the name of the *Yes* numbers.

Ms. Fernandes: OK, Dina. Have Meyly check your answer. She was correct. But both of you should stay with your table groups. (*A few minutes pass.*) Let's see where you are. Angela?

Angela: We decided to count from 2 and see where we thought the next number would go based on that. It wouldn't matter which direction we bounced around, we just needed to count in order. So, we began with 2. Then we counted from 3 to 15, the last number on the *No* list. We have to put 16 somewhere, right? Because you gave us numbers up to 29? After 15, if the next number to be placed is 16, it has to go in the *No* list because the next *Yes* numbers is already 17. We think 16 and 18 both go in the *No* column.

Ms. Fernandes: Angela, would you please draw the path of numbers the way you just talked it out? We need to make sure that everyone understands what you are saying because you are making an important point. (*Angela does so.*) Did you come up with a name for either the *No* or *Yes* columns?

Angela: No. But we still think we are right.

Ms. Fernandes: Did any other tables come up with 16 as the next *No* number? Every table? Can you tell us why? Mary?

Mary:	There are no other even numbers on the *Yes* side, so we think it goes in the *No* side.
Ms. Fernandes:	Did any tables come up with the next *Yes* number or numbers?
Gabriel:	Well, my table was talking about something else, but if we keep doing what Angela's table did with the counting, if 16 is a *No*, and 17 is a *Yes*, and 19 is a *Yes*, then 18 has to be a *No*.
Ms. Fernandes:	Did other tables consider this? (*Two other tables respond.*) Here are a few more exemplars. Tell me where you think these should go—one finger for *Yes*, two for *No*. (*She calls out 20, 21, 22, 24. The students respond correctly.*) You nailed every one. Gabriel, what other idea was your table talking about?
Gabriel:	Simon came up with the idea of number families. He noticed that all the *No* numbers had number families.
Ms. Fernandes:	Interesting observation, Simon. (*To the entire class:*) What is a term we could use instead of *number families*? Joanie?
Joanie:	OK. Factors. We have been talking about factors. I remember something about this but not enough to explain it.
Ms. Fernandes:	Meyly and Dina, don't jump ahead to giving us the term for these *Yes* numbers; please think about where we left off in our thinking together. Take us from number families. (*Dina nods to Meyly.*)
Meyly:	OK, we can say number families because we can make different equations using the same numbers for any of the numbers in the *No* column. You can't do that with the *Yes* numbers.
Ms. Fernandes:	Can you give us an example, Dina?
Dina:	Sure. I'll use 12 because it is a really good example. Two, 3, 4, and 6 are factors of 12. We can make lots of equations with combinations of those numbers using all four operations, like 3 times 4 is 12 or 12 divided by 2 is 6. You can't do that with any *Yes* numbers. Their only factors are themselves and 1.
Meyly:	Like 5. Five has only two factors, 1 and itself. Five cannot be divided by any other number.
Ms. Fernandes:	So, if they are correct, what might we call the *No* numbers? Aaron?
Aaron:	Dividable numbers?
Ms. Fernandes:	Does anyone know what we call the *Yes* numbers? Sergio?
Sergio:	When Meyly was explaining, I remembered. We call them prime numbers. They are kind of like the cheese. They stand alone.
Ms. Fernandes:	Does anyone remember what we call the *No* numbers?

Meyly:	No, I don't.
Ms. Fernandes:	We call them *composite numbers* because they can be "composed" by factors, sometimes several, like Dina's example of the factors of 12. Can anyone provide an example of a *Yes* or *No* number—prime or composite—that is out of numerical order? (*Students offer a few correct exemplars.*) Tomorrow we will review prime and composite numbers and learn how to use the Sieve of Eratosthenes to find all the prime numbers up to 100. Tonight at home, make a list of the prime numbers we worked with today, and see if you can add five or six more to each list. For the rest of our time together today, I would like you and a partner to write down what you remember about today's lesson as it unfolded. What hypotheses were offered? What critical attributes were suggested?

Case Study 5.2: Post-Lesson Reflection ◆

Ms. Fernandes knew that the fifth-grade social studies teacher has been using Concept Attainment in her classes. These students had recently been working with factors, and last year they were introduced to prime and composite numbers. She thought that using familiar content in today's Concept Attainment lesson was appropriate. In the past, she would have informally assessed her students' knowledge of primes and composites through full-group discussions. Because of the intention of this model, Ms. Fernandes did not want to ask them about those concepts directly. Her hope was that they would rediscover these familiar concepts without too much difficulty.

As it turned out, the Concept Attainment experience today provided Ms. Fernandes with a more accurate assessment of her students' understanding. They were unable to transfer their knowledge of factors to this lesson right away. After the lesson, she could see that a traditional review of prime and composite numbers would not have been the best beginning for these students. If she began a direct instruction lesson on the Sieve of Eratosthenes using a focus activity with prime numbers, she would find out right away that she needed to start from scratch with those concepts. Today's Concept Attainment lesson also helped prepare her students for tomorrow; they have had a conceptual experience with prime and composite numbers.

At first, Ms. Fernandes's students struggled with the task itself. Initially, one student wanted to use basic operations to find relationships between numbers, and that was understandable given the subject. However, in a Concept Attainment lesson, the items in the *Yes* and *No* columns should have no cause or effect relationships with one another. The critical attributes have to be illustrated clearly by the items in the *Yes* and *No* columns. The student who distinguished the concepts of odd and even numbers was on target in terms of the task (odd and even are concepts), but his hypothesis was incorrect. He named a critical attribute of each list, just the wrong one.

Ms. Fernandes saw that in formulating hypotheses, her students had to travel through those initial, familiar ways of thinking about numbers before they could develop the concept of primes. In fact, they had to rediscover the concept of composites before they could see how the primes were different. Eventually, their hypotheses about operations and the even and odd status of numbers did help the class to piece together the concept of primes and composites. Beatrice's comment about 5 being past 4 was important. Ms. Fernandes wonders if she should have waited longer for comments or asked a follow-up question about this idea before opening the discussion again. While she thought Beatrice's idea would have helped develop the group's thinking earlier, she did not want to engineer the lesson. She also wonders if she should have worked more with Simon and Joanie's contribution before moving on to Meyly's and Dina's ideas. She had discovered what she needed to know for tomorrow's lesson. However, she thinks she could have done a better job for her students had she continued to question their thinking processes.

Ms. Fernandes decides that she will teach her next class of fifth graders using the *Yes* and *No* exemplars in numerical order, as well. She could see that her first class needed the numbers in that order to begin hypothesizing. Their ideas were all based on the assumption that the exemplars in each column would remain in numerical order. While she doesn't expect the second lesson to play out exactly like the first, she believes that this organization is still the best way to begin. She might decide to give some *Yes* and *No* numbers out of numerical order later in the next lesson, once the students have started hypothesizing. For this first class, she waited until later in the lesson and then asked them to provide those exemplars. While she is curious to know whether any of her fifth-grade classes could begin with *Yes* and *No* numbers out of numerical order, she realizes that approach would probably be too much for them today.

Brief Background of Concept Attainment

Concept Attainment was developed by Jerome Bruner (1961; Bruner et al., 1959) with the intention of introducing, teaching, and nurturing students' critical thinking skills. Bruner wanted these skills to become an integral part of students' cognitive repertoire over time and to transfer from subject to subject. In Bruner's initial investigations with Concept Attainment, he focused on students' attaining familiar concepts. Once the process of Concept Attainment itself was in place, students would be ready to discover new concepts. This progression from familiar to unfamiliar is still the most appropriate way to introduce students to Concept Attainment.

Concept Attainment and Research on Teaching

The effectiveness of the Concept Attainment model has received little formal study. Studies in the 1980s indicated that teachers required much practice to work with the model but that the model's benefits for students were many (Tennyson &

Cocchiarella, 1986). Tennyson and Cocchiarella's research (1986) also stresses that teachers should begin each Concept Attainment lesson with very clear exemplars. Less apparent exemplars are best left to the later stages of the lesson, when students have developed ideas and are testing exemplars against their various hypotheses.

The final stage of Concept Attainment, which asks students to analyze how they arrived at each concept, improves their understanding of that concept and also provides the opportunity to review the metacognitive skills they used to attain the concept. This analysis of metacognitive strategies has a collective benefit as well as an individual one. Joyce and Calhoun (1996) describe uses of Concept Attainment that provided indisputable benefits to classmates as they shared and discussed their diverse thinking strategies with one another. In one study (Baveja, 1988), pairs of students began their hypothesizing about multiple attribute concepts in a variety of ways. The pairs were each asked to record their thinking processes as they were discerning appropriate concepts. Later, the pairs were asked to share their road maps to each concept. As a direct result of these exchanges, students gained others' perspectives and intellectual tools as problem solvers.

Since the 1960s, Concept Attainment has been used with students at every grade level, including higher education. The structure of Concept Attainment has not been revised since it was developed in the 1960s. However, it is typical for individual teachers to modify the model. Modifications may occur prior to the lesson as the teacher plans for instruction, but it may also occur during the lesson itself as teachers respond to students' contributions.

Concept Attainment and Constructivism

In the constructivist view of learning, students construct meaning and make sense of information individually. Students' minds interpret the world through their personal lenses of prior knowledge and experience. Teachers must acknowledge that students will learn different things from the same lesson (Nuthall & Alton-Lee, 1990). A constructivist might say that teachers are teaching as many lessons as there are students in the classroom.

Rather than present information directly, teachers who use a constructivist approach provide students with meaningful tasks that require them to engage with rich ideas. We know that learning is related to the amount of time students spend on lesson content (Nuthall & Alton-Lee, 1990). Unlike direct instruction lessons, which are fast paced and have predetermined end points, constructivist lessons often lead to further, student-driven investigations over extended periods.

The Concept Attainment model is one example of constructivist lesson design. With one concept in mind, teachers sequence exemplars and nonexemplars to begin each lesson. The juxtaposition of specific exemplars with nonexemplars will affect students' thinking in various, sometimes circuitous, ways depending on their prior experience with items on either list. Students will offer hypotheses or suggest exemplars depending on how they are constructing meaning from the list items as they emerge. Constructivist teachers help students explain their cognitive processes as they develop hypotheses by asking strategic questions (Confrey, 1990).

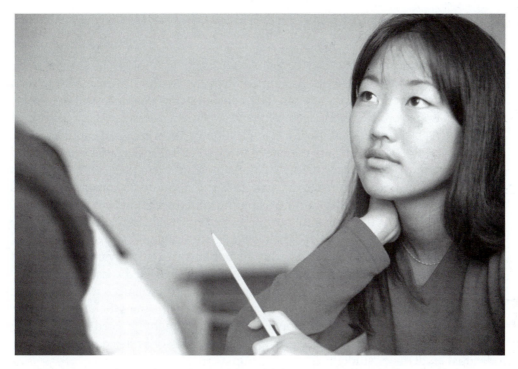

Concept Attainment provides students with multiple opportunities to reflect on their cognitive processes.

In Ms. Fernandes's lesson on prime numbers, some students moved immediately to hypothesizing cause and effect relationships between numbers while others rejected that idea and first hypothesized categories. Neither idea was correct, but moving through these hypotheses supported students' individual construction of meaning. Working with each hypothesis also supported the class as it collectively worked to discover the concept. Ms. Fernandes's job was to keep students focused on the lists by continuing to question their ideas rather than by providing positive reinforcement for a correct answer early in the lesson. This practice is a hallmark of constructivism.

Concept Attainment and the Cognitive Processing Philosophy of Curriculum and Instruction

The cognitive processing philosophy of curriculum and instruction advocates learning experiences that help students discover content as they develop critical thinking skills (Eisner & Vallance, 1974). Furthermore, students should be encouraged to think about how and why their discovery moments occurred. The structure of the Concept Attainment model provides students with sequenced opportunities to see relationships among ideas, hypothesize, analyze, categorize, verbalize their cognitive strategies, critique the strategies of others, and observe how their own cognitive skills have progressed over time.

Concept Attainment and Technology

Concept Attainment lessons can be enhanced using technology in several ways. Technology can move Concept Attainment from a reading-focused lesson to a creative visual experience for students. The concept being examined will determine whether it is appropriate to use technology in a particular lesson. Many lessons in science and social studies that involve classification of items are good candidates.

Many models of teaching are enhanced through online tasks or CD-ROMs, and Concept Attainment is no exception. Additional positive exemplars can be found on Web sites and in reference materials such as Encarta. Students can print pictures they have found or access them online using the computer and projector at school. You can use these pictures directly during a Concept Attainment lesson when the time comes for students to provide their own exemplars and test their hypotheses. Pictures will help the class decide whether or not a new exemplar fits the criteria of the hypothesis being tested. This approach would have provided a visual experience for students in Case Study 5.1. If you choose to do this, you will need to provide time for students to locate pictures. If you are working on strengthening students' research experiences, then the additional time required might be worthwhile. Online and CD-ROM experiences can also provide follow-up lessons related to concepts for individual students or students in small groups.

Along the same lines, a digital camera can be effective in developing students' conceptual understanding in a follow-up lesson after their first Concept Attainment experience. Students can capture photographs of exemplars in nature, at home, or in other environments, and their classmates can classify the pictures as either exemplars or nonexemplars. These images can be loaded easily on the computer and projected for full-class viewing. They could also be printed in conventional form and serve as material for a center activity that reinforces the new material. Again, the digital camera could be used as a meaningful tool in the first Concept Attainment case study lesson itself and in follow-up lessons.

The Smart Board is a recently developed technological tool that has many uses in the classroom. The **Smart Board** can best be described as a large electronic whiteboard connected to a computer that has a projector. The large screen can be portable or mounted on the wall so that an entire class can view sites on the Internet, word processing documents, CD-ROMs, DVDs, and videos directly on the board. Electronic markers allow the user to work in many different fonts and colors. Teachers and students can save and print original text written directly on the screen, Web sites or materials found online, and original or imported graphics. It has touch-screen capability so that the user can manipulate all figures or text written on the board and move back and forth between screens that have been saved. The Smart Board can be used during Concept Attainment lessons or for follow-up activities. Children can draw additional exemplars and nonexemplars electronically on the board and manipulate the images. Exemplars can also be found online and manipulated on the screen. Pictures of exemplars from traditional and online sources can be imported for use. Since it is capable of saving many screens in order, student hypotheses and their intellectual tracks can be recorded and kept to review and print if desired.

Some Concept Attainment lessons lend themselves to being organized around visual images. The teacher can introduce both exemplars and nonexemplars at the beginning of the lesson using pictures imported from a digital camera or videotape. Images can be located using Internet resources. Students can also use these resources to locate additional exemplars. Technology should always be used in the service of learning and not used for its own sake. Once you feel you have become conversant with the Concept Attainment model of teaching, you may decide to explore some of these ideas for incorporating technology and discover your own.

The National Educational Technology (NET) Standards for Students given below are paired with specific performance indicators for those standards.* Following the indicators are brief descriptions of class activities involving technology that can be used with the Concept Attainment model to support student learning.

GRADES K–2

NET Standard 1: Basic Operations and Concepts

NET Standard 2: Social and Ethical Human Issues

NET Standard 5: Technology Research Tools

Performance Indicator 5: Work cooperatively and collaboratively with peers, family members, and others when using technology in the classroom.

Concept Attainment Extension

Have the students find additional positive exemplars using digital camera, CD-ROM, or other software, or through online research. They can do this as a teacher-directed activity individually or in small groups.

GRADES 3–5

NET Standard 2: Social, Ethical, and Human Issues

NET Standard 3: Technology Productivity Tools

NET Standard 4: Technology Communication Tools

NET Standard 5: Technology Research Tools

NET Standard 6: Technology Problem-Solving and Decision-Making Tools

Performance Indicator 5: Use technology tools (e.g., multimedia authoring, presentation, Web tools, digital cameras, scanners) for individual and collaborative writing, communication, and publishing activities to create knowledge products for audiences inside and outside the classroom.

Performance Indicator 9: Determine when technology is useful and select the appropriate tool(s) and technology resource to address a variety of tasks and problems.

---

*National Educational Technology Standards for Students: Connecting Curriculum and Technology by ISTE. Copyright © 2000 by International Society for Technology in Education (ISTE), 800–336–5191 (US & Canada) or 541–302–3777 (Int'l), iste@iste.org, www.iste.org. All rights reserved. Reproduced with permission of ISTE via Copyright Clearance Center. Reprint permission does not constitute endorsement by ISTE.

Concept Attainment Extension

Have students write brief descriptions of the attributes of concepts explored through lessons, provide additional visual exemplars using technology resources—individually or in small groups—and create handouts or brochures for the class and other classes.

GRADES 6–8

NET Standard 4: Technology Communication Tools

NET Standard 5: Technology Research Tools

NET Standard 6: Technology Problem-Solving and Decision-Making Tools

Performance Indicator 6: Design, develop, publish, and present products (e.g., Web pages, videotapes) using technology resources that demonstrate and communicate curriculum concepts to audiences inside and outside the classroom.

NET Standard 5: Technology Research Tools

NET Standard 6: Technology Problem-Solving and Decision-Making Tools

Performance Indicator 8: Select and use appropriate tools and technology resources to accomplish a variety of tasks and solve problems.

Concept Attainment Extension

Have students use digital camera or desktop publishing to create a booklet that describes and illustrates concepts embedded in the generalizations being explored in a current unit. The text and visuals can provide the critical attributes of each concept and present them in various settings.

GRADES 9–12

NET Standard 2: Social, Ethical, and Human Issues

NET Standard 4: Technology Communication Tools

NET Standard 5: Technology Research Tools

NET Standard 6: Technology Problem-Solving and Decision-Making Tools

Performance Indicator 3: Analyze advantages and disadvantages of widespread use and reliance on technology in the workplace and in society as a whole.

Performance Indicator 8: Select and apply technology tools for research, information analysis, problem solving, and decision making in content learning.

Performance Indicator 10: Collaborate with peers, experts, and others to contribute to a content-related base by using technology to compile, synthesize, produce, and disseminate information, models, and other creative works.

Concept Attainment Extension

Concept Attainment can be used to structure a lesson on advantages and disadvantages of technology. That lesson can be the basis for research, writing, and visual products that illustrate the critical attributes that distinguish advantages and disadvantages of technology.

Concept Attainment, Content Standards, and Benchmarks

As you review the content standards and benchmarks given below, consider which concepts can be explored using exemplars and nonexemplars to illustrate them. These examples, from the *Michigan Curriculum Framework* (1996), illustrate standards and benchmarks for which Concept Attainment may be appropriate.*

English Language Arts

CONTENT STANDARD 2: All students will demonstrate the ability to write clear and grammatically correct sentences, paragraphs, and compositions.

Early Elementary Benchmark 4: Begin to edit text and discuss language conventions using appropriate terms. Examples include action words, naming words, capital letters, and periods.

Action words can be taught using exemplars and nonexemplars.

Social Studies (Economics)

CONTENT STANDARD 1: All students will describe and demonstrate how the economic forces of scarcity and choice affect the management of personal financial resources, shape consumer decisions regarding the purchase, use, and disposal of goods and services, and affect the economic well-being of individuals and society.

Early Elementary Benchmark 1: Identify ways families produce and consume goods and services.

Goods and services can be contrasted using a modified version of Concept Attainment in which goods are taught through exemplars and services through the nonexemplars.

---

*Excerpts from the *Michigan Curriculum Framework* are reprinted with permission of the Michigan Department of Education.

> ### Math (Patterns, Relationships, and Functions)
>
> **CONTENT STANDARD 1:** Students recognize similarities and generalize patterns, use patterns to create models and make predictions, describe the nature of patterns and relationships, and construct representations of mathematical relationships.
>
> **Elementary Benchmark 1:** Recognize, describe, and extend numerical and geometrical patterns.
>
> **Middle School Benchmark 1:** Describe, analyze, and generalize patterns arising in a variety of contexts and express them in general terms.
>
> **High School Benchmark 1:** Analyze and generalize mathematical patterns, including sequences, series, and recursive patterns.

Patterns appear in the mathematics curriculum across the grade levels. In early childhood classrooms, Concept Attainment can be used visually to compare and contrast simple geometric or color patterns. In middle and high school, Concept Attainment can provide a change of pace from direct instruction in this strand of the math curriculum. Secondary students bring a lot of prior knowledge to their work with patterns, and Concept Attainment can build on this knowledge in creative ways.

Benchmarks across the curriculum employ *classify* or *categorize* as behavioral terms or ask students to describe attributes or characteristics. The following benchmarks from the science curriculum provide examples.

> ### Science: (Using Scientific Knowledge From the Life Sciences in Real-World Contexts)
>
> **CONTENT STANDARD 1:** All students will apply an understanding of cells to the functioning of multicellular organisms and explain how cells grow, develop, and reproduce.
>
> **High School Benchmark 1:** Classify cells/organisms on the basis of organelle and/or cell types. (Key concepts: Cell parts used for classification—organelle, nucleus, cell wall, cell membrane)
>
> **CONTENT STANDARD 2:** All students will use classification systems to describe groups of living things, compare and contrast differences in the life cycles of living things, investigate and explain how living things obtain and use energy, and analyze how parts of living things are adapted to carry out specific functions.
>
> **Middle School Benchmark 1:** Compare and classify organisms into major groups on the basis of their structure.

Clearly, it would be inappropriate to use Concept Attainment in every instance in which it might be used. Of course, that is true of every model of teaching. Instructional variety promotes student interest, and it also provides students with daily opportunities to think in a variety of ways.

Why Choose Concept Attainment?

These questions will help you to decide whether Concept Attainment is an appropriate model for teaching specific material or for developing students' reasoning skills:

1. Do your students have difficulty seeing relationships among items or ideas?

2. Is categorization of items an important component of an instructional unit?

3. Do you notice that students are having difficulty "thinking out loud" as they solve problems, sequence past events, or explain their reasons for making decisions?

4. Do your students need support in learning how to "shift gears" when the need arises?

5. Do your students need greater opportunity to work with others but require monitoring as they do so?

6. Do your students need practice and flexibility in using familiar concepts?

Summary

Concept Attainment was developed by Jerome Bruner more than 40 years ago with the express purpose of strengthening students' critical thinking skills. Concept Attainment requires students to compare and contrast exemplars and nonexemplars to determine the critical attributes of new concepts. Students also learn to formulate and test hypotheses by suggesting additional exemplars of concepts. Opportunities for students to describe their metacognition as they develop and revise their hypotheses occur throughout lessons following the Concept Attainment model.

This model provides an alternative to direct instruction for teaching concepts. It is particularly valuable to teachers because it can be used successfully in most grade levels and can be tailored to address specific developmental needs. When teachers prepare for these lessons with carefully chosen exemplars and nonexemplars, the model is flexible and effective.

Putting It Together

1. In your state curriculum guide, find suitable content for two Concept Attainment lessons for any grade level or subject. Create an initial list of exemplars for each lesson.

2. Prepare one Concept Attainment lesson and teach it to a field placement class or even to friends. Record what you notice about your students' problem-solving strategies during this lesson.

3. Develop a second Concept Attainment lesson and teach it to a field placement class or to friends. After this lesson, recall points at which you were aware you needed to modify your instruction "on your feet." Also record any changes since your earlier lesson in your students' facility in describing how they developed their hypotheses.

Student Study Site

The Companion Web site for *Models of Teaching: Connecting Student Learning With Standards*
www.sagepub.com/delloliostudy
Visit the Web-based student study site to enhance your understanding of the book content and discover additional resources that will take your learning one step further. You can enhance your understanding by using the comprehensive Study Guide, which includes chapter learning objectives, flash cards, practice tests, and more. You'll find special features, such as the links to standards from U.S. States and associated activities, Learning from

Journal Articles, Field Experience worksheets, Learning from Case Studies, and PRAXIS resources.

References

Baveja, B. (1988). An exploratory study of the use of information-processing models of teaching in secondary school biology science classes. Doctoral dissertation, Delhi University. Delhi, India.

Bruner, J. (1961). *The process of education*. Cambridge, MA: Harvard University Press.

Bruner, J., Goodnow, J., & Austin, G. A. (1959). *A study of thinking*. New York: Wiley.

Confrey, J. (1990). What constructivism implies for teaching. In R. Davis, C. Maher, & N. Noddings (Eds.), *Constructivist views on the teaching and learning of mathematics* (Monograph 4). Reston, VA: National Council of Teachers of Mathematics.

Eisner, E., & Vallance, E. (1974). *Conflicting conceptions of the curriculum*. Berkeley, CA: McCutchan.

International Society for Technology in Education. (2000). *National educational technology standards for students: Connecting curriculum and technology*. Washington, DC: Author in collaboration with the U.S. Department of Education.

Joyce, B., & Calhoun, E. (1996). *Creating learning experiences: The role of instructional theory and research*. Alexandria, VA: Association for Supervision and Curriculum Development.

Michigan Department of Education. (1996). *Michigan curriculum framework*. Lansing: Author.

Nuthall, G., & Alton-Lee, A. (1990). Research on teaching and learning: Thirty years of change. *Elementary School Journal, 90*, 546–570.

Tennyson, R. D., & Cocchiarella. M. (1986). An empirically based instructional design theory for teaching concepts. *Review of Educational Research, 56*, 40–71.

chapter

The Inductive Model

Attached to the refrigerator at home, we (J. M. D. and family) have a small white wipe-off board where we keep a running list of things we need from the store over the course of a few days. This list is never organized; we just write items down as they occur to us. When it is time to go to the store, we need to make sense of the contents on the board. I have my own system. First, I mark each item to be purchased at the grocery store. Those items usually make up the bulk of our list at home. Two large grocery stores are near our house, and we have found that each has consistently better prices than the other on certain items. Since neither store has the better price for all items on our list and since the stores are fairly close to one another, I visit both of them.

The next thing I do is separate the grocery items by type of food—meats, cereals, vegetables, and so forth, until all my food items are categorized. If this is a two-grocery-store day, I mark which items we purchase at grocery store A and which at grocery store B. Now I move on to a new type of item on our list. Since I have found that cleaning supplies and paper goods are priced advantageously at the superstores, I mark those differently. If there are items to buy at the bookstore or home improvement store, I mark them, too.

Since I know the layout of each grocery store, I can take a mental walk through the aisles and make a master shopping list based on how things will appear in each store from left to right. This always saves me time, and I hope it keeps me away from things I do not need to purchase. When I am in stores I know less well, like the home improvement store, I need to read the aisle signs, walk up and down looking for what I want, or, on a good day, locate someone to help me. Obviously this takes more time, even if I need just one item. If I have difficulty locating items at the bookstore, it is usually because I have gotten sidetracked by the discount tables or the most recent arrivals. Finally, I plan my itinerary: which store to visit first, which second, and so on.

Planning my shopping requires me to think about a number of things: the nature of the shopping task, relationships among items on the shopping list, the best way to group items, and how to organize the trip to make efficient use of my time. These are skills that do not come naturally to most people but have to be learned and practiced. Preparing my shopping certainly isn't the most important organizing task I do, but the skills required are essential in many endeavors at school, at work, in my family life, and in how I interact with the world.

The next model of teaching we will present is the Inductive Model of teaching. **Inductive thinking** requires students to observe data carefully, see patterns in data, describe those relationships, and then come to some conclusions. The Inductive Model of teaching provides students with opportunities to generate their own information, organize that information, make sense of what they have collected, and communicate their understanding to others.

The Inductive Model of teaching was developed by Hilda Taba, an influential curriculum developer in the 1960s who advocated many changes in the way we teach the social studies. Like Concept Attainment, presented in Chapter 4, the Inductive Model uses carefully crafted questions to structure each lesson. This model helps students develop concepts as they generate and examine information, explore connections, make comparisons, and write summary statements.

Unlike Direct Instruction, once an Inductive Model lesson begins, the direction of the lesson will be determined by the way students respond to their teacher's series of questions. Which philosophy of curriculum and instruction do you think an Inductive Model lesson exemplifies? As you review the first case study, consider how the organization of the lesson differs from Direct Instruction and Concept Attainment.

Case Study 6.1: First and Second Grade Multiage, Social Studies

Using the Inductive Model to Assess Prior Knowledge

Ms. Herchold and Ms. Quesnel team teach first and second grade multiage homeroom classes at a small suburban school. They use flexible grouping throughout the school week to meet the diverse needs of their combined students. Today they are using the Inductive Model to assess their students' prior knowledge of holidays. The study of holidays is one component of the early childhood curriculum. This lesson will be the initiating experience that begins the holiday unit. Here is the long-term objective for their unit:

The learner will define, illustrate, and write two sentences about activities his or her family does on each national holiday.

Here is the objective for today's lesson:

The learner will list, categorize, and label group-generated terms associated with the word *holidays*.

The information these teachers acquire about their students' understanding during this lesson will help the teachers plan for lessons to come. Today they have decided to work with their combined group of children. Both classes assemble in one classroom on the large rug area in front of the chalkboard. The children have been instructed to sit comfortably on the rug. Ms. Quesnel is just learning the Inductive Model, and today Ms. Herchold is modeling the first day of this lesson for her. Ms. Herchold will facilitate the brainstorming stage of this lesson. Ms. Quesnel will list on the board the items the children brainstorm.

Ms. Herchold: Most of you have found a quiet seat on the rug. Great! You remembered the directions I gave while we were in line outside! We are still waiting for a few of you to find a quiet seat. Brian has just found a place. So has Annie. I can tell that you are all ready for today's lesson.

I am going to show you some pictures that give you an idea about what we will be studying next in social studies. Our very first lesson will be today. Please don't call out names or information about any picture. Just take a good look at each one. Ready? (*She shows each picture for a few seconds before moving on to the next: firecracker, turkey, hearts, parades, shamrock, community workers, U.S. flags, and three ships.*) Wave to me if you think you know what we will be studying for the next few weeks. Josie, what do you think?

Josie: Holidays, Ms. Herchold.

Ms. Herchold: You bet! We will be spending several days in class talking and learning together about holidays in the United States. I know that we are always excited at school when a holiday is coming up. Raise your hand if you can tell us what a holiday is. (*She pauses*.) Many hands are up! Quickly whisper what a holiday is to your neighbor. Raise your hand to tell us what your partner told you about holidays. Sam, how did your partner describe a holiday?

Sam: She said it was a special day when fun things happen.

Ms. Herchold asks for other responses. She limits these to five. Following these exchanges, she asks why some days might be special and a reason to celebrate with fun activities. Several children reply that holidays help us remember important events, like Thanksgiving or a person's birthday. Other holidays are days when we show special people we love them, like Mother's Day or Father's Day.

Ms. Herchold: Absolutely right! We are going to list on the chalkboard everything we know about holidays. I will call on each of you when you raise your hands. Ms. Quesnel will write down what she hears you say. We want to hear from everyone on the rug today. It is important that you remember the brainstorming rules. What is the first thing we should remember about brainstorming? Emma?

Emma: You can say whatever you know about what we are talking about.

Ms. Herchold: Right. What else? Jon?

Jon: No one can tease you about anything you say?

Ms. Herchold: Right! Why is that important? Charlie?

Charlie: We want to hear everybody's ideas and not hurt anybody's feelings.

Ms. Herchold: Looks like we are ready to begin. What do you think about when you hear the word *holiday*?

As the children call these items out, Ms. Quesnel writes each one on the board. The class comes up with this list:

Christmas	Thanksgiving	turkeys
presents	birthdays	trees
Valentine's Day	oranges	Easter
candles	Easter Bunny	Santa Claus
pumpkin pies	candy	eggs
Halloween	witches	costumes
church	piñata	New Year's
St. Patrick's	Mother's Day	Father's Day

July 4th	Hanukkah	no work
lots of food	traveling	driving a long way
sleeping	football	parades
family	no school	snow
projects	making cards	cookies
shopping	in school	Ramadan
parties	picnics	decorations
decorating	house	Passover
Kwanzaa	bunnies	reindeer
chicks	shamrocks	egg hunts
Santa suits	elves	pictures at the mall
stickers	dragons	Cinco de Mayo
Chinese New Year	Dewali	New Year
dreidel	latkes	

Ms. Herchold: You came up with a terrific list! So many different ideas that have to do with holidays! Tomorrow we will be looking at this list again and working with it some more. Be ready to think about how we might categorize the items we listed on the board.

Ms. Herchold and Ms. Quesnel have ended the social studies lesson for this day because these children are young and their attention span is relatively short.

The next day, the second stage of the lesson gets under way. The teachers kept the students' brainstorming list on the chalkboard. Ms. Herchold helps the students summarize what was accomplished yesterday.

Ms. Herchold: Yesterday you did a terrific job brainstorming what you remember about holidays. We came up with a long list of words that tell us something about holidays. We are ready to do some important work with this list today. I am going to ask a few of you to read columns of this list aloud for everyone to hear again. Ms. Quesnel will point to each word as it is read. Who would like to volunteer? (*Several children read a portion of the holiday list aloud for everyone to review.*)

Good job, readers! Everyone! Think carefully now. Do any of these items seem to belong together? Do any two seem like partners? When you can think of two things that might go together, put your hand on your head. (*She pauses.*)

I am going to trade places with Ms. Quesnel, and I will mark with a check which things from our holiday list you think go together. She will make lists for us on this chart paper. Who can tell us two things that belong together from the board? Georgia?

Georgia: Christmas and Thanksgiving.

Ms. Herchold:	Why do they belong together, Georgia?
Georgia:	Because they are both names of big holidays.
Ms. Herchold:	What do you mean by a "big holiday," Georgia?
Georgia:	One where my whole family gets together. We do special things at home.
Ms. Herchold:	Right. What other holidays might go with Thanksgiving and Christmas? Can you name just one?

Ms. Herchold asks additional questions about the nature and reason for each holiday as the students mention it. From their brainstorming, the children listed the names of these holidays as belonging together, which became List A:

Christmas	Thanksgiving	Valentine's Day
Easter	Halloween	New Year's Day
St. Patrick's Day	Mother's Day	Father's Day
July 4th	Hanukkah	Cinco de Mayo
Chinese New Year	birthdays	Kwanzaa
Ramadan	Dewali	

Ms. Herchold:	What name might we give this list? What name describes each item on the list? Joanna?
Joanna:	Like Georgia said, these are all names of big holidays that we celebrate.
Ms. Herchold:	Ms. Quesnel will label our first list by writing "Names of Big Holidays" at the top of the paper. Besides the names of holidays, what other items from our first list also seem to belong together? Can we make a new category? Can any other items go together?

Ms. Herchold marks each new group with a new symbol so that all the children can see. Ms. Quesnel makes a separate list on chart paper. As they continue to group items together, the children come up with these lists:

B	C	D
traveling	pumpkin pies	chicks
parades	candy	elves
make projects in school	turkeys	menorah
shopping	eggs	Easter Bunny
decorating the house	oranges	shamrocks
put on costumes	eat cookies	Santa Claus
drive a long way		bunnies
go to parties		candles
have our pictures taken at the mall		reindeer
go to church		Santa suit

B	C	D
no work		make cookies
sleeping		dreidel
make cards		dragons
go to picnics		trees
have egg hunts		
buy presents		
get presents		
break a piñata		
eat lots of food		
play football		
watch football		
red envelopes		
put stickers on presents and pictures		
light the menorah		

They named these lists as follows:

List B: Things we do on holidays

List C: Things we eat on holidays

List D: Things we see on holidays

Ms. Quesnel asks Amy to explain why *red envelopes* belong on List D. Amy tells the class that on Chinese New Year, her relatives give her red envelopes with money inside them. Ms. Quesnel says she will ask Amy to tell the class more about Chinese New Year later in this unit. Ms. Herchold then asks about the items on the big brainstorming list that haven't been placed in a group:

Ms. Herchold: Think carefully, now. Where do these things belong: *family* and *snow*? Sally?

Sally: I think that snow should go under "Things we do on holidays." I play in the snow on Christmas and sometimes on Thanksgiving.

Ms. Herchold: Do we all agree? Andy?

Andy: We don't play in the snow on every holiday. We don't have snow on Easter.

Ms. Herchold: That's true. Do we need another category for things that belong on another list? Turn to your neighbor and see if you can come up with another way to place items in our "Things we do on holidays" list. (*She pauses for a few moments.*) Carrie?

Carrie: Paul and I said that we might put things we do on summer holidays and things we do on winter holidays on different charts.

Ms. Herchold: Did anyone else come up with that idea?

Several hands go up. One pair of students says that Easter is neither a summer nor a winter holiday. Maybe a better idea is to separate into warm weather holidays and cold weather holidays. The class agrees. Together they separate activities on this list into two new lists. Two children tell the group that some things on the list really belong on both activities lists. Ms. Quesnel puts these two children in charge of making up three new lists for holiday activities: warm weather holiday activities, cold weather holiday activities, and holiday activities for all seasons.

Ms. Herchold: So, it looks like you found out that some items on our first big list might go in more than one category. Did any partners come up with different ideas for new categories? Barbara?

Barbara: Brenda and I said that we go to church on some holidays, but on others we don't.

Several children agree, but one child mentions that his family goes to synagogue, not church, on Jewish holidays. Ms. Quesnel asks how the class can name new lists to include both these things. Two second graders suggest that they call this list "Different Religious Holidays."

Ms. Herchold asks the class on which list *family* belongs? Ben thinks a new list should be made that includes people we do things with on the holidays. Ms. Herchold answers that right now we have only *family* to put on this list. What else might belong there? Several children suggest that *friends*, *relatives*, and *neighbors* be added to this list. The class agrees.

Ms. Quesnel asks if anyone sees any other items on the first list that belong in a separate group. Sarah says that her family celebrates Cinco De Mayo because they are Mexican American, but she knows that not all families do. The class decides that some of the holidays on the first list are not traditional U.S. holidays but holidays from other countries. Some families still celebrate these holidays even though they now live in the United States. The students end up with these separate lists made from their original brainstorming list:

List A: Holiday brainstorm

>   Sublist 1: Holidays in our country

>   Sublist 2: Different religious holidays

>   Sublist 3: Holidays from other countries

List B: Things we do on holidays

>   Sublist 4: Things we do on warm weather holidays

>   Sublist 5: Things we do on cold weather holidays

>   Sublist 6: Things we can do on every holiday

List C: Things we eat on holidays

List D: Things we see on holidays

List E: People we do things with on holidays

Ms. Herchold asks the class to think in pairs about what they might say about the lists they made today and what they know about holidays. How can they say in just one sentence, one big idea, something about all these groups they talked about today? She stresses that there is no one right answer to this question, and she gives them some quiet time to think it over. These are the groups' responses:

Families do special things on important days called holidays.

When we want to remember something important that happened, we choose a day to celebrate it every year.

Holidays are important days when people do fun things together.

We have holidays during each year.

Families eat some foods only on holidays.

Case Study 6.1: Post-Lesson Reflection ◆

As a result of this Inductive Model lesson, these two teachers have learned a lot about what their students know about holidays. After the entire lesson was completed, they discussed what occurred over the two days and shared what insights they have about designing and beginning the holiday unit.

Ms. Quesnel notes that most of the major national holidays were mentioned during the first brainstorm, but not all U.S. holidays made that list. Memorial Day did not show up on the list the children made, nor did Labor Day. Even though children often make craft projects for Columbus Day, it was not mentioned either. Ms. Herchold reminds Ms. Quesnel that they could have made the choice during this lesson to prompt the children and possibly elicit those holidays, but she did not want to interfere with student thinking.

Since several were mentioned, and to be inclusive in this lesson, the teachers chose to make a separate category for "religious holidays." Here they followed the lead of the two second graders who explained what *religious* meant. Ms. Herchold found that the majority of the students understood the differences between religious and secular holidays but did not have *religious* in their vocabulary. She didn't expect them to use the terms "national" or "secular" with regard to holidays. There will be times during the unit to extend students' concepts about these holidays if they decide it is appropriate. Both teachers were pleased that the brainstorming list reflected the diversity of their class.

During this two-part Inductive Model experience, the teachers assessed the depth of their students' understanding with as little prompting as possible. This was unfamiliar territory for Ms. Quesnel, who is more conversant with teacher-directed lessons. As a first experience for her, Ms. Herchold thought it best not to ask the children to group items on the first day. She wanted Ms. Quesnel to experience the uninterrupted brainstorming of the lesson. She believed this choice would help Ms. Quesnel begin to understand the process of the model better. Ms. Herchold decided to forgo grouping and explanations of groupings until the second day.

The Inductive Model is one way to assess students' prior knowledge at the beginning of an instructional unit—to find out what your students know, or think they know, about a topic. The information these two teachers learned about their students' knowledge will help them decide what concepts need to be reviewed, what new concepts need to be introduced, and how they can best develop this unit.

The Stages of the Inductive Model

Hilda Taba created the Inductive Model of teaching to provide students with opportunities to develop concepts, to increase their depth of understanding of those concepts, and to begin building bigger ideas as they see relationships among concepts. While the stages of the model are described in a sequential way, there is flexibility in how you orchestrate them in your lessons. As you read through the stages of the model, notice the questioning stance of the teacher and the ways students' critical thinking is promoted throughout the lesson.

Preparation for the Inductive Model

Many Inductive Model lessons begin by providing students time to examine a **study print**. A study print is a poster-size photograph that serves as a visual catalyst for a lesson. Study prints can depict any combination of people in settings or situations, eras in history, activities, emotions, weather, and so forth. Study prints provide true inductive learning experiences because all the ideas that come into play during the lesson will be supplied directly by students. Whatever students see happening or displayed in the study print is what they will list, group, and label in response to the teacher's questions. Two separate groups of students may list items from the same study print with different emphasis. For example, a detailed study print representing an urban setting during the Great Depression can provide a multilayered, conceptually rich inductive experience for students. One group of students may focus initially on the activities of people in the study print, such as individuals standing in bread lines. However, students in another class may begin by making observations related to the tattered apparel of people in the print or other examples of poverty during that era, such as Hoovervilles. Every new idea generated by students' observations of the study print will serve as a catalyst for the next idea. As students move through the brainstorming stage of the Inductive Model, their unique juxtaposition of ideas will provide scaffolding for their concept development. Teachers hope that concepts they have targeted for these study print lessons will emerge during the course of the inductive experiences provided by the model. If they use the model as designed, teachers will not influence students' study print observations by teaching any concepts directly during the lesson. They will instead facilitate students' concept development by asking the specific questions that form the structure of the Inductive Model. Follow-up lessons may be more teacher directed.

Textbook series often include a set of study prints for each grade level that teachers can use in a number of ways. Public libraries and curriculum libraries in colleges and universities may also have collections of study prints. If you find appropriate photographs in magazines or books, color copiers can now reproduce those photographs and enlarge them in several poster sizes. Commercial teacher stores have posters that may be appropriate for you to use. Your opening question might be as simple as, What do you see in this picture? Examine the picture closely yourself so that you are aware of everything your students might notice. Some teachers prepare by brainstorming their own list and deciding how the items might be categorized, but be prepared for your students to categorize differently.

If your Inductive Model lesson is for the purpose of pre-unit assessment, as in the case of Case Study 6.1, or formative assessment during a unit, you need to consider a question to begin the lesson. Make sure you have phrased it well and have used developmentally appropriate vocabulary. If you are unsure, ask a mentor teacher. State the content of the lesson, briefly explain why you have chosen the Inductive Model, and ask about the validity of your opening question. Ms. Herchold used a short series of pictures to motivate her students, but her Inductive Model lesson actually began when she asked a straightforward question about holidays.

The next thing you need to consider as you prepare is how you will record the data that you collect during the brainstorming part of the lesson. Because you will be categorizing many items, you will need an expanse of space. Chalkboards or whiteboards immediately come to mind, but these can record data only temporarily unless you transfer the students' ideas to paper later in the day. If you have access to one in your building, a Smart Board is ideal for brainstorming because you can work with various colors, save each screen electronically, and print the screens if you choose to do so. Many teachers use a series of chart paper sheets taped across the board. Chart paper also allows you to use color as your students begin categorizing, and it can easily be kept for reference during another lesson.

If you begin your lesson with a question, you need to consider whether you want your students to briefly explain why they respond as they do immediately or whether all brainstormed responses will be recorded without comment. Your decision here rests on the students' needs, the nature of the content, your intentions, and possibly your students' facility with the Inductive Model. In this case study, the teachers chose to have the children group items and explain their groups in the second lesson.

Time is always a resource in the classroom. You may find that completing all stages of this model during one class session is not possible or necessary, given your objective. Ms. Herchold and Ms. Quesnel chose to split the experience into two lessons because of the age of their students. Waiting a day also provides time for reflection or consultation and time to revise the lesson if necessary. On the other hand, you may want to move to later stages in one day. This decision can also be an on-the-spot one that you make as you observe your students' progress during the lesson. Some teachers wait on Stages 6 and 7 (explained below) until the students are very conversant with the model.

Each stage of the model is explained below in the order devised by Taba originally and summarized in Table 6.1, but you may decide to skip some stages or vary their order from lesson to lesson.

Stage 1: Brainstorming Responses

In the initial stage of the Inductive Model, students brainstorm their responses to the teacher's first question. This first question frames the inquiry of the lesson and requires thoughtful consideration by the students. Whether the model is used to assess prior knowledge, develop new concepts, or assess student learning, the beginning question must be open ended and impossible to answer with any one response. The purpose is to provide students with an opportunity to enumerate many and varied responses to the question. For Inductive Model lessons to work effectively, student responses should number at least 25. These responses will be used as data to analyze throughout each stage of the lesson.

Stage 2: Grouping Items

In Stage 2, students are asked to find pairs of items on the initial list that they think go together in some way. Items that students pair first will tell you something right away about the students who contribute and the nature of the connections they are making. You will see whether other students follow their line of thinking, as you perceive it, or whether they want to move on. You may want to let students know that items may be used more than once.

You will want to spend some time on the first group of similar items and not move on to another pair too quickly. As items are linked, you must use symbols to indicate which ones are being grouped together. Teachers often use geometric shapes because it is easy to change colors and use those shapes several times as the entire list of items is grouped. It is wise to leave ample space in between items as they are being recorded. You may need room for more than one symbol if an item is cross-categorized.

Stage 3: Providing Rationales

Stage 3 provides an opportunity for students to develop their metacognitive abilities as they explain the rationale behind their pairings. You might choose to have students describe their reasoning at this point in the lesson. Teachers also have the option of waiting until all the lists are formed before asking students for their rationales. This choice will depend on your intentions and objectives. If you ask for rationales earlier in the lesson, you may break the students' momentum. In Case Study 6.1, the teachers reviewed the rules for brainstorming to prevent this digression at the beginning of their lesson. However, if students are experiencing the Inductive

Model for the first time, it may be a wise choice to have them explain their thinking during Stage 3.

Stage 4: Naming Lists

In Stage 4, students are asked to name the lists they have developed, and a full discussion of students' reasoning will come into play. If students are familiar with the Concept Attainment model, you might describe Stage 4 as determining the critical attribute for the items on each list. Students must reach a consensus on the name of each list. You might also have students add items to individual lists once they have been named. It is often effective to end the first day of a two-day lesson once the names of the groups are agreed on by consensus and recorded.

Stage 5: Cross-Categorizing

In Stage 5, students move into higher levels of analytical thinking. They will consider multiple attributes of items so that they can be cross-categorized (placed on more than one list). Even young children can **cross-categorize**. For example, attribute blocks, a common early childhood math manipulative, ask young children to categorize flat geometric shapes by size (small, medium, or large), by color (red, yellow, or blue), by shape (circle, square, or triangle), and by multiple attributes (small shapes that have sides, large shapes that are round). In Stage 5, it is important for the development of students' metacognitive abilities to have them explain in detail why they think items can belong in two or more groups.

Had their objective been different, Ms. Quesnel and Ms. Herchold might have moved into Stage 5 of the model. In the data generated by their students, some cross-categorizing was certainly possible. For example, *menorah* could be categorized as belonging to both the B group, things we do on holidays (lighting the menorah), and the D group, things we see on holidays (menorahs as a holiday symbol).

Stage 6: Grouping Differently

Stage 6 of the Inductive Model takes the students into the synthesis level of Bloom's taxonomy. Using the same initial brainstorming list, students are asked to develop groups totally different from the ones they have already used to categorize their items. Teachers ask that students provide the rationale for their new groupings and give each new group a name. Given the nature of this task, it is possible that items in these new groups can also be cross-categorized in different ways. Again, the use of symbols and color will organize the new groupings visually, and they should be recorded separately from the original set.

Stage 6 can also be a follow-up lesson. In fact, students' preparation for this follow-up lesson may be assigned as homework the night before to give them time to consider possibilities for new groups. Some teachers provide time for small groups to work together before the full group assembles for a Stage 6 follow-up lesson. Some teachers choose to forgo Stage 6 or move it to a different place in the sequence.

In an Inductive Model lesson, categorizing and cross-categorizing items on the initial brainstorm list provide opportunities for students to develop their metacognitive skills.

Others use Stage 6 as an individual or small-group enrichment activity for students who need a greater challenge.

Stage 7: Identifying Subgroups

In Stage 7, teachers ask students whether there are subgroups in any existing groups that have already been identified and named. If students have ideas for subgroups, teachers ask them to explain their rationale for these hierarchies, and typically a discussion will ensue.

In Case Study 6.1, for example, six subgroups were identified early in the lesson, three in List A and three in List B. The teachers could have chosen to forgo this Stage 7 activity until later in the lesson. Following the students' lead, they created the subgroups. More subgroups could have been established if an objective of the lesson was to reinforce conceptual hierarchies. For example, List A consisted of holidays;

Table 6.1   The Inductive Model

Stage and Question	Teacher Action	Students' Response	Notes
Stage 1 What do you notice about this picture? What comes to mind when I say the word _____?	Records responses on the board, chart paper, etc.	Call out items individually	Make sure students can all see the display; allow students to brainstorm freely
Stage 2 What two items on this list might belong together?	Identifies students' groupings visually on the display (symbols, color, etc.)	Identify items that can be grouped together	Option: Indicate that these items might also belong to other groups
Stage 3 Why do you think these items belong together?	Asks clarifying questions to ensure the understanding of the class	Explain why these items belong together	Ask why the items belong together, either as each new group is identified or after all groups have been formed
Stage 4 What might we call this group?	Records labels	Give a label to each group that summarizes its items' characteristics	Facilitate the discussion without influencing the direction or substance
Stage 5 Could some of these items belong in more than one group?	Asks for rationale for new cross-categorizing and marks additional groups visually	Identify alternative groupings	Find clear way to reorganize data visually on the display (new color, unique symbols, etc.)
Stage 6 Could we begin this exercise again and come up with groups that are totally different from the ones we have used already?	Asks rationale for new groupings and records new groups on a different visual space	Identify alternative groupings	May be appropriate in some instances, but not all; may be done during a follow-up lesson
Stage 7 Are any of these groups subgroups of larger groups?	Asks rationales for hierarchies and records them on a different visual space	Identify subgroups	Facilitate student thinking without overt direction
Stage 8 Can we find one sentence that summarizes an important idea about all these groups?	Records all summary statements	Develop a summary sentence individually, in pairs, or in small groups	Facilitate student thinking to ensure that all groups have been included in the summaries

SOURCE: From *A Teacher's Handbook to Elementary Social Studies* by H. Taba, M.C. Durkin, J.R. Fraenkel, and A.H. McNaughton. Copyright © 1971 by Addison Wesley Publishing. Reprinted by permission of Pearson Education, Upper Saddle River, NJ.

however, both *Hanukkah* and *dreidel* could have been given their own group, items associated with Jewish holidays. *Eight days of celebration, candles, menorah,* and *gelt* could have been added to that list. Ms. Herchold and Ms. Quesnel could have chosen to continue working with conceptual hierarchies, but that activity would need to take place on another day. It would not be germane to their current purpose, which was to assess their students' prior knowledge about holidays.

Stage 8: Summarizing Concepts

In Stage 8 of the Inductive Model, students synthesize the major points of all their lists into a single sentence. In addition to the content they include, this stage provides teachers with a quick assessment of students' facility in developing summary statements. Younger children who have not had much experience with this model often write statements that focus on individual groups rather than developing a summary of the entire set. This happened in Case Study 6.1. With greater exposure to the model and continued experience developing summaries, students can make statements that are more conceptually complex. Sometimes teachers are tempted to halt the inductive experience at this moment and provide instruction in writing a superior summary statement, but they should continue working inductively with students instead. Although there is some flexibility regarding some of the other stages of the Inductive Model, all Inductive Model lessons should end in this Stage 8 activity. The summary statements provided in Stage 8 serve as an assessment of students' conceptual understanding that will help their teachers make informed decisions about subsequent lessons.

In all stages of this model, an additional challenge for the teacher is to continue asking students questions to facilitate their thinking, as opposed to providing praise for "right" answers. There are no right answers in an Inductive Model lesson; there are only answers that students generate though their interactions. Holding back immediate positive reinforcement is not easy for teachers new to the Inductive Model.

Case Study 6.2: Fifth Grade, Social Studies

Using the Inductive Model as Formative Assessment

The Inductive Model can also be used to assess collective student knowledge at any point in a unit. Used in this manner, the model can be an effective way to help students review unit content. As you read this last case study, consider how the sequenced questions of the model give the teacher a formative assessment.

Mrs. Pacheco teaches fifth grade in a large urban school. Her class has just finished studying the native populations in North, Central, and South America prior to European exploration and colonization. The current unit focuses on Europe in the 15th century during the Age of Exploration. When possible, Mrs. Pacheco has chosen to use reprints of primary source documents, stories and novels, movies, documentaries, and Internet research in this unit, as well as the textbook.

The following benchmarks for upper elementary students helped inform Mrs. Pacheco's development of this unit:

Measure chronological time by decades and centuries.

Recount the lives of a variety of individuals who impacted the exploration, settlement, and colonization of the early Americas.

Trace the national origins of items and agricultural products and the trade flows that brought them to the United States. (Michigan Department of Education, 1996)

Mrs. Pacheco has found ways for her students to work with these benchmarks throughout the course of this unit, and the benchmarks will be strengthened in subsequent units as well.

In concert with those benchmarks, Mrs. Pacheco is using a **generalization** as a unifying theme for her students' yearlong examination of this period in history. A generalization is a statement that relates two or more concepts and provides a broad perspective. We call these statements generalizations rather than facts because they are generally true. The following generalization will be one focus of social studies this year:

All people, cultures, and religions have contributed to our cultural heritage—there has been much borrowing, trading, and diffusion of ideas, goods, and practices.

A number of concepts from the social studies make up this generalization: people; cultures; religions; cultural heritage; and borrowing, trading, and diffusion of ideas, goods, and practices.

In today's lesson, Mrs. Pacheco wants to assess her students' understanding of these objectives:

The learner will describe Europe in the 1400s and identify major reasons for exploration.

The learner will describe technological developments in the 1400s that supported global exploration.

The learner will summarize Spain's and Portugal's search for Asia and their subsequent settlements in North, Central, and South America.

Summarize the events and consequences of the French, English, and Dutch explorations.

Describe and evaluate the impact of European settlement on the native populations in the Americas.

Just as important, she wants to know how her students are thinking about what they have learned. This information will help her decide whether any material needs to be reviewed, what ideas most engaged the students' minds and hearts, and how she might proceed with the next lessons.

Mrs. Pacheco: We have been studying Europe in the 15th century during the Age of Exploration, a very exciting time and one not unlike our own time, with the advances in technology and space exploration. I want to get an idea of what has struck you as being important in our unit so far. This will help me plan for our next lessons. Let's spend a few minutes brainstorming what you have learned. I need two volunteers to write our list on the board. Brad and Jill? Please take turns writing down what you hear.

What comes to mind when you think of the Age of European Exploration? (*Over the next several minutes, the students participate enthusiastically, and they generate their list.*)

Columbus	Ferdinand	Isabella	trade
Spain	Portugal	Marco Polo	Italy
cross-staff	rudder	lateen sails	astrolabe
Christianity	Muslim maps	Indians	John Cabot
French	English	rats	3 voyages
shipbuilding	caravels	carrack	Portugal colony
Prince Henry	da Gama	Dias	Vespucci
Cape of Good Hope	Nina	Pinta	scurvy gold
Northwest Passage	spices	salted foods	silk
Asia	Australia	bananas	pineapple
Coronado	Cortes	Balboa	De Soto
Magellan	Aztec	Inca Moctezuma	Mexico
Dutch	Sir Francis Drake	Henry Hudson	smallpox
Verrazano	Cartier	South Pacific	North America
Canada	South America	Central America	chocolate
houses	pumpkins	sugar cane	

As a vehicle for content review, the brainstorming step of the Inductive Model reveals to Mrs. Pacheco once again the strength of collaborative learning. Individual students are provided with an additional opportunity to review the unit material and make associations after hearing entries called out by their peers. She is not surprised that the students have listed so many items during the brainstorming, and she hopes the activity that comes next will reveal a complex understanding of how these items relate to one another.

Mrs. Pacheco followed the Inductive Model through Stage 4. The students placed the items in their list into these categories:

List A	List B	List C
Columbus	expedition	England
Magellan	colony	France

da Gama
Dias
Polo
Balboa
Coronado
Cortes
Vespucci
Verrazano
Cartier
Hudson
Cabot
Drake

expansion
Mexico
Peru
West Indies
Colombia
Canada
South America
Central America
North America
Australia
South Pacific

Italy
Spain
Portugal
Netherlands

List D

Indians
Aztec
Incas
Moctezuma

List E

3 voyages of Columbus
caravels
carracks
rudder
lateen sails
shipbuilding
Niña
Pinta
Santa Maria

List F

diseases
smallpox
scurvy
food
water
rats

List G

gold
trade
Asia
spices
silk
territory
spread of Christianity

List H

chocolate
bananas
pumpkins
smallpox
horses
chickens
sugar cane

List I

cross-staff
lateen sails
caravel
shipbuilding
astrolabe
rudder
maps

As a result of grouping their entries, the class has a spirited discussion of 15th-century technology. They agree that lists E and I are very similar, as the sciences of astronomy and navigation and the craft of shipbuilding constituted much of the technological advancement of the 15th century. Mrs. Pacheco reminds the class that it is getting ahead of itself because the students have not yet found labels for each of the categories. As she moves into Stage 4, she divides the lists among small groups of students and asks them to come up with names that describe each list, to be reviewed by the full group. Her students come up with these labels:

List A—Explorers

List B—Places explored

List C—Countries financing expeditions

List D—Native American populations

List E—Ships and voyages

List F—Problems on the voyages

List G—Reasons for exploring the New World

List H—Items traded between Europe and the New World

List I—15th-century technology

One student reminds the group that Italy did not actually finance voyages of its own. Italian sailors who wanted to explore often sailed for countries other than Italy, like Christopher Columbus and John Cabot. List C needs to be changed somehow. The teacher directs this problem to the class. Another student suggests that Italy be taken off the list. Perhaps a new list can be made for countries that provided sailors for expeditions.

Once this is addressed, Mrs. Pacheco asks whether the lists are now complete, whether any material should be added, or whether the lists should be changed in any other way. Various students make these observations:

List A could be subdivided by nationality of the explorer or by the country for which each explorer sailed.

List B also has subcategories that reflect more precise relationships, such as Canada's being part of North America.

List F contains "smallpox" as an entry, although smallpox was a problem for the native populations as a result of European exploration, not a problem on the expeditions for the explorers.

List H can also be divided between items brought to the New World from Europe (horses, chickens, etc.) and those coming from the New World to Europe (chocolate, bananas, etc.).

Mrs. Pacheco asks that List H be divided accordingly because this observation relates directly to one generalization she wants to reinforce through this unit of study: how borrowing, trading, and diffusion of ideas, goods, and practices have enriched our culture. She directs two students to take charge of separating the items on List H, and she asks the class to brainstorm additional things that belong on these two new lists. The group recalls these items:

cattle	pigs	corn
sheep	potatoes	squash
sugar cane	sweet potatoes	wheat
tobacco	tomatoes	

A brief discussion helps students remember which items traveled in which direction across the Atlantic Ocean.

To bring closure to the lesson, Mrs. Pacheco asks small groups to come up with summary statements they might make about the Age of Exploration based on the material they have reviewed today. The groups record these statements to share with the class:

1. Many European countries sent sailors to explore and settle in the New World.

2. European explorers found native people already living in the new land.

3. Because they were not immune, the native people sometimes suffered from diseases that came from the European settlers.

4. Ships in the 15th century used state-of-the-art technology to promote the success of the voyages.

5. Countries and sailors had many reasons for wanting to explore new lands. The main reason was to find gold and bring back fancy goods.

6. In our lives, we use goods that the explorers took back to Europe and things that native people in the Americas learned about from the explorers.

7. Europe and the New World exchanged many goods and foods because of the explorations.

The nature of these statements, their amount of detail, and the level of their conceptual and factual accuracy provide Mrs. Pacheco with information that will help direct the next social studies lessons she teaches in this unit.

Case Study 6.2: Post-Lesson Reflection

Mrs. Pacheco has mixed feelings about today's lesson. As in the first case study, using the Inductive Model as an assessment activity has provided her with a view of her students' understanding of the content of this unit. The stages of the model have allowed her to see not only what facts the students remember but also whether they have grasped the concepts so far.

When Mrs. Pacheco uses the Inductive Model at the beginning of a unit, students' responses are idiosyncratic; they rarely follow patterns. She has attributed this to her belief that as she assesses students' prior knowledge, the students are contributing directly from their individual experiences rather than from experiences mediated through shared instruction. Because she used the Inductive Model as a formative assessment today, she expected that her students' responses would follow a pattern during the brainstorming, for example the explorers, then countries, and so on. However, Mrs. Pacheco noticed at the beginning of this lesson that her students' responses did not fall into patterns. She will continue to think about this because she has no ready explanation.

As she reviewed the charts at the end of the lesson, she could see which of her unit objectives were reflected in the students' data. The brainstorming, categorizing, and naming included references to the reasons for explorations and technological developments in the 15th century. One aspect of the unit that did not surface today was the differences among the Spanish, Portuguese, French, Dutch, and English explorations. Because her students' grasp of this aspect is a foundation for the next part of the unit, the colonization of the New World, Mrs. Pacheco will consider how to revisit this material in a creative way as the class moves on to study European settlements in North America.

At one point in today's lesson, Mrs. Pacheco decided to intervene as her students were grouping their data. Because she wanted to prompt their thinking about the economic aspects of European exploration, she asked that List H be divided. She rarely steps into the action in Inductive Model lessons, but she chose to today to help herself plan for the next component of the unit. She wanted to see how her students were internalizing key ideas in economics. She was relieved to see that her actions did not stop the momentum of the lesson.

However, she believes it is important that they be able to differentiate among goods that were exchanged between the old and new worlds. Furthermore, it isn't enough for them to know in which direction the goods traveled; they also need to know why. She had hoped her students would provide more information or context for the items in List H, for example that chocolate and potatoes traveled east because they were not plants native to Europe.

Mrs. Pacheco was also disappointed in the summary statements written by the groups. With one exception, she does not think they were inclusive of the material her students have studied so far. Each one was an individual statement that could be sequenced to tell the story of the unit, as opposed to a summary statement that encompassed the major ideas in the whole unit so far. Summary statement number six came closest to the mark. In language arts, Mrs. Pacheco will spend time with her students reviewing how to write summary statements of longer text selections. She hopes that these improved skills will transfer to her students' work in social studies.

A quick glance at her benchmarks and objectives shows Mrs. Pacheco that her students are moving toward a solid, but still incomplete, grasp of the concepts and generalization in this unit to date. While their brainstorming list revealed recall of facts, her students' summary statements did not reflect the concepts she thinks are important. She knows that she needs to address these ideas again before moving to the next component of the unit.

Brief Background of the Inductive Model

For the past several decades, most discussions of curriculum development acknowledge the contribution of Hilda Taba (1962; Taba, Durkin, Fraenkel, & McNaughton, 1971) and her associates in the United States and around the world (Costa & Loveall, 2002; Fraenkel, 1988, 1992, 1994; Fraenkel, McNaughton, Wallen & Durkin, 1969; Hertzberg, 1971, 1981, 1989; Isham, 1982; Bernard-Powers, 1999; Parry, 2000). Although her work focused on the social studies, Taba made a lasting impact on K–12 curriculum development across the disciplines.

As in a Concept Attainment lesson, all students benefit from contributing their ideas and hearing and critiquing their classmates' ideas during an Inductive Model lesson.

Beginning in the mid-1960s, Taba's ideas revolutionized both instructional methodology and the organization of social studies content. Typically, students had experienced social studies instruction in elementary and middle school as little more than reading from a textbook and answering questions at the end of the chapter. Rather than following this traditional approach, Taba's work centered on students' cognitive development as they produced, organized, and analyzed information. Traditional social studies content consisting of facts—names, dates, places—would always be significant, but the more substantial ideas that encompassed those facts would serve students' understanding better over time. Taba believed students would gain long-lasting and flexible knowledge in key concepts and generalizations across the social studies if they interacted directly with intellectually rigorous ideas. In the second case study, Mrs. Pacheco used concepts and generalizations embedded in her state standards and benchmarks as building blocks for her unit. This practice, introduced by Taba, provides the social studies curriculum with texture often absent in traditional social studies materials.

The Inductive Model and Research on Teaching

Unlike the Direct Instruction or Jigsaw models, the Inductive Model's effects on student achievement have received little study. The literature does contain articles that document how curriculum developers and teachers began to understand and implement Taba's ideas about the reorganization of the social studies curriculum and her model of inductive teaching (Banks, 1985; Graham, 1993; Hertzberg, 1987; Parry, 2000).

Along with Jerome Bruner, Taba suggested that the integration of K–12 social studies include sociology, anthropology, economics, and political science, as well as history and geography, even for the early childhood grades. Not everyone agreed that these ideas would move social studies curriculum and instruction in a positive direction. For example, while curriculum developers in Australia were genuinely enthusiastic about Taba's reorganization of social studies content, many classroom teachers were not impressed. Opponents of Taba's work were skeptical about integrating the social studies and preferred the clarity of teaching history and geography as separate disciplines. They also believed that the organization of the content into concepts and generalizations would confuse students. Many teachers found these additional content requirements unfamiliar and unwieldy, and they resented the need for extensive retraining in subjects they had taught for years (Parry, 2000). Like Concept Attainment, the Inductive Model requires that teachers become comfortable with unexpected directions that these lessons might take. Also like Concept Attainment, the Inductive Model is very complex and requires significant practice (Banks, 1985; Fraenkel, 1992; Isham, 1982). However, Taba's social studies student books and teacher guides published in the late 1960s were "one of the most respected and influential curriculum projects that emerged during the new social studies reform movement" (Banks, 1985). Very few of her books are currently in print.

The Inductive Model and Learning Theory

As mentioned in Chapter 5, constructivist learning theory states that students construct meaning from hands-on experiences. They should be provided with opportunities to work directly with information in a variety of ways. The Inductive Model illustrates one way that students can construct knowledge though collaborative interaction. Rather than being given new information from the teacher or another source, such as a textbook or computer software, students work directly with data they have been actively engaged in generating.

In the course of addressing each question in the successive stages of the Inductive Model, students are asked to enumerate, categorize, label, and generalize, thinking skills that move them up the levels of Bloom's taxonomy. When students create

Table 6.2	Constructivist Principles and Taba's Inductive Model

Constructivist Principles	Taba's Inductive Model
Teachers must assess students' prior knowledge.	The brainstorming activity that begins the lesson provides information about students' prior knowledge.
Prior knowledge should be taken into consideration in a teacher's plan for instruction.	The outcome of an Inductive Model lesson provides information about students' skills in observation, categorization, analysis, and evaluation of data and their fluency in using concepts and generalizations. This information provides formative assessment.
Students should discover knowledge collaboratively.	The Inductive Model is a full-group experience.
Teachers need to facilitate this discovery directly rather than through immediate Direct Instruction.	The teacher's role in Inductive Model lessons is to ask a series of questions and facilitate student thinking.
A variety of critical thinking skills should be employed in the service of learning new content.	Each level of Bloom's taxonomy is addressed in Inductive Model lessons: • Knowledge and comprehension (brainstorming) • Application (categorizing) • Analysis (categorizing—naming subgroups) • Synthesis (creating new categories) • Evaluation (justifying and challenging connections or analyses of the data and the ideas of others)
Students must have opportunities to learn about and reflect on their own learning processes.	Students have multiple opportunities to provide rationales for their contributions.

SOURCE: Constructivist principles adapted from Brooks & Brooks, 1999.

subgroups or write summary statements in inductive lessons, the processes of the model also provide opportunities for ideas to be revised and refined. Brooks and Brooks (1999) stress several principles of constructivist learning theory that can be applied to classroom practice. The structure and intellectual tasks provided by the Inductive Model are aligned with each of these constructivist principles, as shown in Table 6.2.

The Inductive Model and the Cognitive Processing Philosophy of Curriculum and Instruction

The Inductive Model relates to the cognitive processing philosophy of curriculum and instruction. You will remember from Chapter 2 that the cognitive processing philosophy considers the development of students' intellectual skills to be the primary goal of schooling. This is not to say that academic content is seen as unimportant for students. The cognitive tasks exercised in Inductive Model lessons, such as collecting, organizing, and interpreting data and forming generalizations, will provide the context for students to remember factual content in an organic and meaningful way.

During Inductive Model lessons, teachers can assess the quality of students' critical thinking and then use this information to design additional lessons to further develop specific skills. Like Concept Attainment, the Inductive Model provides students with opportunities to reflect on their own and others' thinking. In follow-up lessons to both case studies presented, the teachers can return to the lists, classifications, labels, and interpretations made by the students with an eye to helping them understand the increased sophistication of their thinking about those concepts over time.

Technology and the Inductive Model

Technology can be incorporated into Inductive Model lessons during the lessons or after the full-group lesson as extension activities. Using a computer with a projector, additional items for the initial list or specific categories can be located on a CD-ROM, educational software such as the Encarta encyclopedia, or online.

Digital cameras can be used in follow-up activities for students to record images that reflect the list titles and summary statements developed by the class. Videotape clips can be located and placed into PowerPoint presentations to further illustrate concepts developed during these lessons. These ideas can all be applied to the content of the two Inductive Model case studies, holidays and the Age of Exploration.

When Smart Boards are available, teachers have the advantage of being able to record the brainstorm list and save it to recall during the lesson, print it, and copy it for everyone in the class. Having their own copy of the initial list may be helpful to students for follow-up lessons in the unit. Since the board works with a computer, teachers can also go online during full-group lessons.

The Smart Board has other features that make it especially creative with these lessons. Electronic markers can change colors to assist in visual clarity as the brainstorm items are categorized. To create and name categories, items on the list can be manipulated to a new position directly on the board and easily moved again.

Collections of Smart Board lesson materials can also be accessed once they are downloaded from the Smart Technology Web site. For example, one resource in this collection is a comprehensive set of maps that can be used in many ways. In some Inductive Model lessons, the maps can provide a visual dimension to the concept being developed. A world map could be used in both of this chapter's case study lessons: to locate holidays' countries of origin and to chart the origins and destinations of the goods imported and exported between the Old and the New Worlds. One feature of the many Smart Board maps is that they can be divided, then reassembled like puzzle pieces. Adapting this feature could structure follow-up lessons for both case studies.

In the language arts curriculum, students working individually or in pairs can expand summary statements into short compositions using word processing programs. Desktop publishing software can be used to create "newsletters" about the concepts under examination. In the case studies, that could mean feature articles about holidays or the "recent voyages" of the Italian explorers who sailed for countries other than their own. Online or software resources can be used to illustrate these newsletters for classroom publication.

The National Educational Technology (NET) Standards for Students (International Society for Technology in Education, 2000) are given below and paired with specific performance indicators developed for those standards.* Following the indicators are brief descriptions of class activities that can be used as extensions of Inductive Model lessons.

GRADES K–2

NET Standard 2: Social, Ethical, and Human Issues

NET Standard 5: Technology Research Tools

Performance Indicator 4: Use developmentally appropriate multimedia resources (e.g., interactive books, educational software, elementary multimedia encyclopedias) to support learning.

Performance Indicator 5: Work cooperatively and collaboratively with peers, family members, and others when using technology in the classroom.

Inductive Model Extensions

Have students use technology resources to locate additional items for the initial list.

In pairs, have students locate illustrations that describe or illustrate summary statements.

GRADES 3–5

NET Standard 2: Social, Ethical, and Human Issues

NET Standard 3: Technology and Productivity Tools

NET Standard 4: Technology Communication Tools

Performance Indicator 5: Use technology tools (e.g., multimedia authoring, presentation tools, Web tools, digital cameras, scanners) for individual and collaborative writing.

Inductive Model Extension

Have students extend the initial list or categories or write about and illustrate summary statements—individually or collaboratively—as an independent activity.

---

*National Educational Technology Standards for Students: Connecting Curriculum and Technology by ISTE. Copyright © 2000 by International Society for Technology in Education (ISTE), 800–336–5191 (US &Canada) or 541–302–3777 (Int'l), iste@iste.org, www.iste.org. All rights reserved. Reproduced with permission of ISTE via Copyright Clearance Center. Reprint permission does not constitute endorsement by ISTE.

GRADES 6–8

NET Standard 2: Social, Ethical, and Human Issues

NET Standard 4: Technology Communication Tools

NET Standard 5: Technology Research Tools

NET Standard 6: Technology Problem-Solving and Decision-Making Tools

Performance Indicator 6: Design, develop, publish, and present products (e.g., Web pages, videotapes) using technology resources that demonstrate and communicate curriculum concepts to audiences inside and outside the classroom.

Inductive Model Extension

Have students, individually or in pairs, produce written and illustrated handouts that further develop concepts explored through the model or contribute to a class Web page that discusses the summary statement.

GRADES 9–12

NET Standard 2: Social, Ethical, and Human Issues

Performance Indicator 1: Identify capabilities and limitations of contemporary and emerging technology resources and assess the potential of these systems and services to address personal, lifelong-learning and workplace needs.

Performance Indicator 4: Demonstrate and advocate legal and ethical behaviors among peers, family, and community regarding the use of technology and information.

Inductive Model Extension

In both performance indicators above, students can brainstorm the advantages and disadvantages of technology, as well as examples of legal and ethical behaviors that can be categorized into groups for further analysis. This content would be an excellent writing assignment as a follow-up to the full class discussions of these topics.

The Inductive Model, Content Standards, and Benchmarks

State standards and benchmarks are sometimes written as behavioral objectives by which the specific actions of the student can be assessed easily. This format is of great help to teachers who are beginning to use the Inductive Model. In Michigan, for example, the first content standard in geography is stated in a measurable way:

> ### Geography
>
> **CONTENT STANDARD 1:** All students will describe, compare, and explain the locations and characteristics of places, cultures, and settlements.

The following generalizations relate to this standard:

The mosaic of people, places, and cultures expresses the rich variety of the earth. Natural and human characteristics meld to form expressions of cultural uniqueness, as well as similarities among peoples.

Culture is a group of people's way of life, including language, religion, traditions, family structure, institutions, and economic activities.

The generalizations above relate to all people and places that students will encounter in PK–12 social studies. For example, the first generalization can relate to the Roman Empire or to the contemporary United States. The second generalization can relate to the Inuit living in the Arctic coasts or the Aborigines living in Australia. Regardless of the particular unit, teachers need to find a variety of ways to provide learning experiences and assess students' abilities to describe, compare, and explain locations and characteristics of the many peoples and settings that they will study in school.

The Inductive Model is particularly useful when the content to be learned requires that students notice detail, see relationships, and compare and contrast. Review the following benchmarks from the Michigan curriculum framework as they relate to the two generalizations above. Taba advocated that the social studies curriculum be organized in this conceptually progressive manner.

> **Early Elementary Benchmark:** Describe the human characteristics of places and explain some basic causes for those characteristics. (Content focuses on family and community)
>
> **Later Elementary Benchmark:** Locate and describe the major places, cultures, and communities of the United States and compare their characteristics. (Content focuses on Native American populations, Northern, Middle, and Southern states in colonial America, ancient world cultures)
>
> **Middle School Benchmark:** Describe and compare characteristics of major world cultures, including language, religion, belief systems, and gender roles and traditions. (Content focuses on Canada and Mexico, Central and South American countries)

High School Benchmark: Describe how major world issues and events affect various people, societies, places, and cultures in different ways.

In each grade level, students will develop the concepts embedded in these benchmarks—human and geographical characteristics, places, and cultures—with significantly greater complexity, level of detail, and level of abstraction.

Teachers can use the Inductive Model when their students are learning about historical eras, the roles of family members in societies past and present, cultural artifacts, or works of art. Many of these topics will be enhanced through the use of study prints to begin each lesson. Listed below are additional examples of content standards and benchmarks that can be explored using the Inductive Model.

Geography

CONTENT STANDARD 2: All students will describe, compare, and explain the locations and characteristics of ecosystems, resources, human adaptation, environmental impact, and the interrelationships among them.

Early Elementary Benchmark 1: Describe how people use the environment to meet human needs and wants.

Elementary students living in rural areas can study the variety of local agricultural and dairy industries. The use of study prints can be an effective way to begin an Inductive Model lesson.

High School Benchmark 1: Describe the environmental consequences of major world processes and events.

Secondary students can examine the worldwide effects of global warming in an Inductive Model lesson using a world map in lieu of a study print. Or such a lesson could begin with the simple question, What do you know about the effects of global warming?

History

CONTENT STANDARD 3: All students will reconstruct the past by comparing interpretations written by others from a variety of perspectives and creating narratives from evidence.

Later Elementary Benchmark 1: Use primary sources to reconstruct past events in the local community.

An Inductive Model lesson could begin with the question, What was it like living in colonial America?

Small groups examining facsimiles of various colonial-era newspapers could answer the same question to begin an Inductive Model lesson. Each small group would have unique information to contribute to the brainstorm.

Using the Life Sciences in Real-World Contexts

CONTENT STANDARD 1: All students will use classification systems to describe groups of living things; compare and contrast differences in the life cycles of living things; investigate and explain how living things obtain and use energy; and analyze how parts of living things are adapted to carry out specific functions.

Early Elementary Benchmark 1: Compare and classify familiar organisms on the basis of observable physical characteristics. (Key concepts: Plant and animal parts—backbone, skin, shell, limbs, roots, leaves, stems, flowers. Real-world contexts: Animals that look similar—snakes, worms, millipedes; flowering and nonflowering plants—pine tree, oak tree, rose, algae.)

This benchmark can be explored with the question, Can you give examples of all living things we will find in the ocean? as the starting point.

This is also excellent content for an Inductive Model lesson using one or more study prints.

The Inductive Model is an easy fit with the social studies and science curriculums, and the flexibility of the model makes it applicable for every grade level. The products of the different stages of this model—lists, group names, reorganization of data, and summary statements—can be used as catalysts for additional lessons, in-class work, or homework assignments.

Why Choose the Inductive Model?

The following questions can help you determine whether the Inductive Model can provide an appropriate learning experience for your students:

1. If students were to discover the lesson content on their own in a group context, what thinking skills would be required? Are these skills exercised during the stages of the Inductive Model?

2. Are the classification of items and the labeling of groups an integral component of the content to be studied?

3. What opening question might elicit at least 25 student responses?

4. How might you classify and label responses to your opening question?

5. Can students collect or provide data, independently or with support by the teacher, to examine the content to be studied? How might you structure this task?

6. Can the data be retrieved and displayed for the entire class to examine collectively? How might you best display the data in your classroom?

Summary

The Inductive Model developed by Hilda Taba provides full-group interactive learning experiences in the social studies. In this model of teaching, students brainstorm many items in response to the teacher's initial question, find relationships among items in the data they have generated, organize and reorganize their data, name their groups, and write summary statements that communicate their interpretations. The successive stages of this model can be used in one extended lesson or divided into several lessons, depending on the developmental level of the students, the daily instructional objective of the teacher, and time considerations.

The Inductive Model illustrates students' construction of knowledge as described by constructivist learning theory. Rather than being teacher directed, these lessons are driven by the actions and reactions of the students as they respond to teachers' questions and work with data they have generated. The focus of the Inductive Model is on critical thinking skills orchestrated by the teacher in flexible stages: observation, categorization, analysis, synthesis, and evaluation.

Putting It Together

1. Review your state or district curriculum guide for one grade level. Choose topics in social studies or science that might lend themselves to the Inductive Model. Write an appropriate lesson objective for an Inductive Model lesson addressing the content you have chosen.

2. Write opening questions for your lessons or locate study prints that would be appropriate to use.

3. Develop a list of possible brainstorming items, and categorize and name your lists.

4. Consider a social studies lesson or science lesson that you have observed in the field. How might you teach this lesson using the Inductive Model? Explain why you believe that this model might have been a good choice.

Student Study Site

The Companion Web site for *Models of Teaching: Connecting Student Learning With Standards*
www.sagepub.com/delloliostudy

Visit the Web-based student study site to enhance your understanding of the book content and discover additional resources that will take your learning one step further. You can enhance your understanding by using the comprehensive Study Guide, which includes chapter learning objectives, flash cards, practice tests, and more. You'll find special features, such as the links to standards from U.S. States and associated activities, Learning from Journal Articles, Field Experience worksheets, Learning from Case Studies, and PRAXIS resources.

References

Banks, J. A. (1985). *Teaching strategies for the social studies: Inquiry, valuing, and decision-making* (3rd ed.). Reading, MA: Addison-Wesley.

Bernard-Powers, J. (1999). Composing her life: Hilda Taba and social studies history. In M. S. Crocco & O. L. Davis, Jr. (Eds.), *Bending the future to their will: Civic women, social education, and democracy,* (pp. 185–206). Lanham, MD: Rowman & Littlefield.

Brooks, J. G., & Brooks, M. G. (1999). *In search of understanding: The case for constructivism.* Alexandria, VA: Association for Supervision and Curriculum Development.

Costa, A. L. & Loveall, R. A. (2002). The legacy of Hilda Taba. *Journal of Curriculum and Supervision, 18*(1), 56–62.

Fraenkel, J. R. (1988). Remembering Hilda Taba. *Teaching Education, 2*(1), 82–85.

Fraenkel, J. R. (1992). Hilda Taba's contribution to social studies education. *Social Education, 56*(3), 172–178.

Fraenkel, J. R. (1994). The evolution of the Taba curriculum development project. *Social Studies, 85*(4), 149–158.

Fraenkel, J. R., McNaughton, A. H., Wallen, N. E., & Durkin, M. C. (1969). Improving elementary-school social studies. *Elementary School Journal, 70*(3), 154–163.

Hertzberg, H. W. (1971). *Historical parallels for the sixties and seventies: Primary sources and core curriculum revisited.* Boulder, CO: Social Studies Education Consortium.

Hertzberg, H. W. (1981). *Social studies reform 1980–1980.* Boulder, CO: Social Studies Education Consortium.

Hertzberg, H. W. (1989). History and progressivism: A century of reform proposals. In P. Gagnon & the Bradley Commission on History in Schools (Eds.), *Historical literacy: The case for history in American education,* (p. 73). Boston: Houghton-Mifflin.

International Society for Technology in Education. (2000). *National educational technology standards for students: Connecting curriculum and technology.* Washington, DC: Author in collaboration with the U.S. Department of Education.

Isham, M. M. (1982). Hilda Taba, 1904–1967: Pioneer in social studies curriculum and teaching. *Journal of Thought, 17*(3), 108–124.

Parry, L. (2000). Transcending national boundaries: Hilda Taba and the "new" social studies in Australia, 1969 to 1981. *Social Studies, 91*(2), 69–78.

Taba, H. (1962). *Curriculum development: Theory and practice.* New York: Harcourt Brace & World.

Taba, H., Durkin, M. C., Fraenkel, J. R., & McNaughton, A. H. (1971). *A teacher's handbook to elementary social studies.* Reading, MA: Addison-Wesley.

chapter 7

Reciprocal Teaching

On a recent trip, I (T. D.) was relaxing with a good book, a novel set in New England. Most of the time, I was reading at a very relaxed pace, fully enjoying and understanding the twisting plot of the story. This reading was purely for pleasure and required very little concentrated effort on my part. Even more recently,

I was reading a technical research report. This experience was quite different. The content and vocabulary were unfamiliar. I had to concentrate on what I was reading and whether it was making sense to me. This meant slowing down my reading pace, rereading passages, and even talking to myself to make sure I understood what I was reading. You have probably had similar kinds of experiences. Some readings are smooth and easy, and others require you to monitor your comprehension of the text carefully. For the latter, we often use a variety of processes or strategies, such as making predictions about what will come next or seeking clarification of unknown words or a poorly written paragraph. These are strategies that many of us have learned to use over time and in the course of many experiences with reading, including those that occurred in school.

For most teachers, helping students increase comprehension and retain information they are reading is a primary task—one that takes many forms. When I was a young student, I sometimes just skipped over the parts of stories or other text that I found difficult. I remember that my teachers would ask me questions or give me tasks to help me. Sometimes I was asked to summarize a passage or predict what would happen next. Other times, we talked about unfamiliar vocabulary or phrases. I doubt that I understood at the time what my teachers were trying to do, but as a teacher, and now as a teacher educator, I understand that these questions and tasks had two objectives: to increase my reading comprehension and to help me regulate my understanding of text.

Reciprocal Teaching is a model for improving reading comprehension and helping learners develop comprehension-monitoring skills. It was developed by Annemarie Palincsar and Ann Brown (1983, 1984, 1986), teacher educators and researchers. In Reciprocal Teaching, students and teachers ultimately exchange roles as they work with text to generate questions, clarify information, make predictions, and summarize.

As you read the next case study, think about how the students begin to assume the teacher role as they discuss the text they are reading. Notice how students are assisted in monitoring their own understanding of the text and how this fosters their reading comprehension. Finally, it may also be helpful to consider how the cognitive processing perspective provides a helpful way of understanding this model.

Case Study 7.1: Fifth Grade, Reading

Ms. Darcy is a fifth-grade teacher in a large urban school district. She is a relatively new teacher and has given considerable amounts of time, energy, and focus to helping her students increase their reading comprehension. Many of her students can decode words well, but her own observations and standardized test scores reveal that a significant number of students in her classroom have limited comprehension of the texts they are engaged with. She has noticed that many read the words with little assistance, but they struggle with creating meaning and retaining the information they have read. Consequently, she has decided to assist her students with both enhancing and monitoring their comprehension using the Reciprocal Teaching model.

As Ms. Darcy considered ways to support her students, she was mindful of the content standards, benchmarks, and grade-level content expectations produced by the state board of education. One of these guided her choice: Students will "use a combination of strategies when encountering unfamiliar texts while constructing meaning. Examples include retelling, predicting, generating questions, mapping, examining picture cues, analyzing word structure, discussing with peers, analyzing phonetically, and using context and text structure" (Michigan Department of Education, 1996, p. 15). She considers the Reciprocal Teaching model to be an excellent fit with her own concerns and the goals of the standards, benchmarks, and grade-level content expectations.

Ms. Darcy also wants the use of Reciprocal Teaching to be a genuine part of her curriculum. She wants students to learn the model but to learn it in the process of learning content that is part of the normal fifth-grade curriculum in her district. Consequently, she has decided to use the Reciprocal Teaching model with small reading groups as they study the systems of the human body—a component of her district's science curriculum for fifth graders. She sees this as a valuable opportunity to use expository text during her reading group time and as a way to integrate the science and language arts components of her curriculum.

In four earlier lessons, Ms. Darcy introduced students to the Reciprocal Teaching model. She has told them why they are using Reciprocal Teaching and what her intentions are: improved comprehension and comprehension monitoring. She also introduced, explained, and provided examples of the terms *generating questions*, *clarifying*, *summarizing*, and *predicting*. In addition, she modeled her own use of these processes by reading sections of the text and then doing a think aloud—telling students what she was thinking as she was involved in a process of making meaning from the text. Finally, she began to encourage active participation in the process by inviting students to assume the teacher role by asking questions and directing the discussion of the text.

In this lesson, Ms. Darcy will continue to orient the students to the use of Reciprocal Teaching. She knows that this process will take several weeks to complete. The students will also be focused on the nervous system, using a section of their science text, part of a series adopted by their district and shown in Figure 7.1. She has the following objective for today's lesson:

The learner will use Reciprocal Teaching terminology and strategies (question generating, clarifying, summarizing, and predicting) to discuss text about the human nervous system.

At the beginning of the lesson, Ms. Darcy calls a group of five students to the round table she uses for reading groups. She passes out a copy of the science book to each group member.

Ms. Darcy: Today we are going to continue our readings about how the systems of the human body work. As we read and discuss today, we are also going to keep

Figure 7.1 **Student Text for This Lesson**

Our Nervous System: Automatic Protection

Have you ever touched something really hot and practically without thinking about it pulled your hand away from the object? Or maybe you have poured a glass of milk and just as you were about to take a drink of it, you realized that the milk had gone sour and you stopped just in the nick of time. Perhaps you have experienced a ball being thrown at you in gym class and just before it hit you in the eye, your eyelid closed and your hands moved up to protect your face. We have all had similar experiences. In fact we have these split-second reactions many times on any day when our bodies seem to react almost automatically. How is it that our bodies can react so quickly and without much thinking on our part? The answer can be found by looking at one of the systems of our body known as the nervous system.

What Is the Nervous System?

The nervous system is made up of two major parts—the brain and the spinal cord. Sometimes it is easiest to think of these as being like a very complex computer system. The brain would be the hard drive, and the spinal cord would be the wires that travel to the computer monitor, the printer, and the keyboard. Like the computer hard drive, the brain controls all the functions of our bodies. Messages are sent from your brain to all the other parts of your body and then sent back again to the brain. The spinal cord is like the wires attached to your computer hard drive. It is filled with nerves that are encased in the spinal column. These nerves then branch out and spread throughout your body. This network of nerve cells is responsible for carrying the messages back and forth to your brain. Look at the picture on the next page to see how these parts of the nervous system are connected.

How Do Messages Travel to and From the Brain?

Messages to and from the brain are constantly moving at very high speeds, as your brain monitors all the functions of your body. Thinking of this as an expressway during rush hour may be helpful. Like the cars traveling at high speeds in many directions, nerve signals travel from every part of the body to and from the brain. The nerve signals travel along axons. To get from one axon to another, these signals jump across synapses—like crossing a highway bridge.

The speed with which these messages travel helps to explain how our bodies can react to things without stopping to think about them. As your finger touches a hot pan, messages are sent back and forth along the nerve cells in a split second, and your body reacts to protect itself. It's a good thing too! You wouldn't want to have to think too long before you moved your hand off a hot plate! In a similar way, very quickly traveling messages between your brain and your nerve endings cause you to stop before drinking a glass of spoiled milk and protect your face from a fast approaching ball.

working on asking questions, clarifying, summarizing, and predicting. Some of you will also get the chance to be the leader. I'd like you to open your book to page 92. (*She pauses and looks around to make sure that everyone has found the correct page*.) Look at the first heading and read it to yourself. (*The title reads: "Our Nervous System: Automatic Protection."*) What do you think we will be reading about today?

Dalton: I think that this part will be about nerves. I think those are the things in our body that help us know when we hurt.

Ms. Darcy: That's a good prediction, Dalton. Let's all see if that's what this section is about. Read the first paragraph silently, and then we'll all talk about it together. I'll be the leader for this first paragraph.

Everyone begins reading the first paragraph silently. It reads as follows:

Have you ever touched something really hot and practically without thinking about it pulled your hand away from the object? Or maybe you have poured a glass of milk and just as you were about to take a drink of it, you realized that the milk had gone sour and you stopped just in the nick of time. Perhaps you have experienced a ball being thrown at you in gym class, and, just before it hit you in the eye, your eyelid closed and your hands moved up to protect your face. We have all had similar experiences. In fact, we have these split-second reactions many times on any day when our bodies seem to react almost automatically. How is it that our bodies can react so quickly and without much thinking on our part? The answer can be found by looking at one of the systems of our body known as the nervous system.

Ms. Darcy: When you are finished reading, please look up at me so that I'll know when everyone is ready to discuss this paragraph. (*After a few moments, everyone is looking at Ms. Darcy*.) I have some questions. What do all these things like removing your hand from a hot object and protecting your face from a ball have in common? How are they alike?

Mackenzie: Well, they are the things we do when something is hurting us or when something is going to hurt us.

Mike: Yeah. In the title it says that our nervous system protects us automatically, and all those things are automatic. You don't really think about them. You just do them.

Ms. Darcy: Those are good answers. Does it tell us how our nervous system protects us automatically?

Jillian: Well, not really. The last sentences just say that you can find out by learning about the nervous system.

Ms. Darcy: I see. I wonder if the rest of this section might tell us that part. Are there any things you'd like to clarify? Words or things you're not sure about?

Maura: Well, I'm not sure why they call it a system. I mean, I'm not sure what a system is exactly.

Ms. Darcy: Perhaps I can clarify that one. You can think of a system as a group of things that work together. So, our nervous system has different parts in our body, and they work together. Does that help, Maura? (*Maura nods to indicate that she understands*.) Is there anything else that needs to be clarified? (*There are no responses*.) Okay, then let me give a summary. This paragraph is about finding out how we react to things, like protecting our face when a ball is coming toward it, by learning about our nervous system. Does anyone have anything to add to that? (*Several students shake their heads to indicate* no.) I also want to make a prediction about the next paragraph. I like what Jillian said about the last sentences and how they tell us that we can learn about why our bodies are able to react quickly and protect us by learning about the nervous system. My prediction is that the next paragraph will tell us about the parts of the nervous system and how they work. Who would like to be the leader for the next paragraph? (*Dalton tentatively raises his hand*.) Great! Dalton will be our teacher for the next paragraph. Let's all read it silently and then look at Dalton when we are finished.

Everyone begins reading the next paragraph silently. It reads as follows:

What Is the Nervous System?

The nervous system is made up of two major parts—the brain and the spinal cord. Sometimes it is easiest to think of these as being like a very complex computer system. The brain would be the hard drive, and the spinal cord would be the wires that travel to the computer monitor, the printer, and the keyboard. Like the computer hard drive, the brain controls all the functions of our bodies. Messages are sent from your brain to all the other parts of your body and then sent back again to the brain. The spinal cord is like the wires attached to your computer hard drive. It is filled with nerves that are encased in the spinal column. These nerves then branch out and spread throughout your body. This network of nerve cells is responsible for carrying the messages back and forth to your brain. Look at the picture on the next page to see how these parts of the nervous system are connected.

As they finish, group members look at Dalton to indicate that they are ready to discuss this paragraph.

Dalton: Okay. I'm not sure what to ask.

Ms. Darcy: Maybe it would help to begin your question with *why* or *how*.

Dalton: Oh, okay. My question is, How is the nervous system like a computer? (*He sees Mike raise his hand.*) Mike?

Mike: It has parts like a computer. The brain is like the hard drive, kind of the main part of the computer. The spinal cord is like the wires on a computer, except the spinal cord has nerves that carry messages instead of electricity.

Dalton: Good. I think that's right. Does anyone else have a question? Mackenzie?

Mackenzie: Yes. What do they mean when they say that the nerves are encased in the spinal column? I guess I don't really understand exactly what *encased* means.

Dalton: I'm not really sure either. Can anyone else clarify this? (*No one responds.*)

Ms. Darcy: What could we use to find out what *encased* means? Maura?

Maura: We could use a dictionary or that thing in the back of the book that tells you what words mean.

Ms. Darcy: Yes, we could use a dictionary or the glossary. But to help us save time and stay focused on this paragraph, let me try to clarify. *Encased* means covered. So they mean that the nerves are covered by the spinal column.

Maura: So you mean that nerves are in the middle of the spinal column? And the bone goes all around it?

Ms. Darcy: Right. Does that help? (*Maura nods to indicate that it does.*) Okay, Dalton. Can you summarize this paragraph by telling us the main idea?

Dalton: I'll try. My summary is that this paragraph is about how the brain and spinal cord are the important parts of the nervous system.

Ms. Darcy: Are there any other important ideas in this paragraph?

Dalton: Oh, it does tell us about nerves in the spinal column. I guess that's important too.

Ms. Darcy: Yes, good point. Do you think that the point the author is trying to help you understand is how the brain, spinal cord, and nerves work together as part of the nervous system?

Dalton: Oh, maybe I didn't include enough. Can I try again? My summary is that this paragraph tells us that the brain, spinal cord, and nerves make up the nervous system and send messages to other parts of our bodies. I have a prediction too. My prediction is that the next paragraph will tell us more about the messages.

Ms. Darcy: Good work, Dalton. Let's see if his prediction is right. Who would like to be our leader for the next paragraph? (*Jillian raises her hand.*) Okay, let's all read the next paragraph to ourselves, and Jillian will be our leader for this section. Look up at Jillian when you are finished so that she will know you are ready.

All group members begin reading the paragraph, titled "How Do Messages Travel to and From the Brain?" It reads as follows:

Messages to and from the brain are constantly moving at very high speeds, as your brain monitors all the functions of your body. Thinking of this as an expressway during rush hour may be helpful. Like the cars traveling at high speeds in many directions, nerve signals travel from every part of the body to and from the brain. The nerve signals travel along axons. To get from one axon to another, these signals jump across synapses—like crossing a highway bridge.

As Jillian finishes, she looks up to see that all group members have finished and are now looking at her.

Jillian: My question is, Where do the nerve signals go?

Mackenzie: It says that they go from the brain to every part of our bodies.

Ms. Darcy: Good. I would like to ask a question too. Why are axons important?

Maura: Well, they are kind of like the roads that the messages travel on. If you didn't have them, the messages wouldn't be able to move from one place to another even if the brain wanted to send them. It wouldn't have a way to get them anywhere. Oh, and the synapses are important too, or the message couldn't get from one axon to another.

Ms. Darcy: Yes, that would make them very important. I like the idea of thinking about them as highways with cars that are traveling very fast. Jillian, do you have any other questions you'd like to ask us?

Jillian: No. Does anyone want us to clarify something?

Mackenzie: Well, I'm a little bit confused about one thing. It said that the messages go from one axon to another and that they have bridges. I think they called those *synapses*. But I don't really get how they move. Is it like electricity or something?

Maura: It doesn't really say, but maybe it's like water or something that goes from axon to axon.

Jillian: I'm not really sure.

Ms. Darcy: That's a really good question. It is a little bit confusing because the paragraphs don't really seem to say how that works. Perhaps this time we could write down that question and see if the rest of the chapter will help us understand that better. (*She writes this on a piece of paper on the flip chart next to her.*)

Jillian: Is there anything else we need to clarify? (*No one responds with a question.*) Okay, then I will try to give a summary. My summary is that the messages from our brain to our body move through axons and synapses very quickly.

My prediction is that the next part will tell us how our body reacts to those messages. But I have to tell you that I cheated a little bit and read the first sentence in the next paragraph. (*Everyone laughs.*)

Ms. Darcy: That's a good prediction, and it reminds me of how the first sentence in a paragraph can often tell you what the rest of the paragraph is about! Besides, your prediction fits well with the information we have already read. Nice work.

The class continues to read the next several sections, alternating leaders and continuing the process of generating questions, clarifying, summarizing, and making predictions. Ms. Darcy continues to coach the students throughout this process.

Case Study 7.1: Post-Lesson Reflection ◆

Ms. Darcy was very happy with the way today's lesson went, both because it showed the progress her students were making in using the Reciprocal Teaching model and because it provided her with a window into the way her students explore expository text. She could see that after only four lessons using this model, her students were beginning to use the terminology and related processes. They used these to frame the way they talked about the text—a kind of outline for their explorations of the information. More important, they were using the model to actively increase and monitor their understanding. The lesson also provided Ms. Darcy with valuable insights into how to enhance their comprehension of text in the future.

Ms. Darcy's objective for this lesson was met. As the students talked about each section of the text, they consistently used the terminology she had explained and modeled in earlier lessons. She knows that students benefit from this model best when they employ its terms (King & Johnson, 1999). It provides them with a way to explore, think, and talk about the text in a very specific and helpful way. For example, without the use of the terminology and embedded processes, student conversation may drift into unimportant details versus a summary statement that demonstrates that they do indeed comprehend the text. She wants to utilize these terms for future discussions about text and knows that students will need to use them to guide their talk. Ultimately, she wants students to be able to internalize these processes, something that good readers frequently demonstrate. Having her students use the terms may help them to do so.

Ms. Darcy was also happy to see the active engagement with the text by all group members. In the past, she has observed that her students did not demonstrate comprehension-monitoring behaviors when reading expository text. They appeared to read the words but often seemed to be skimming over sections or words they did not understand. In this lesson, students asked questions about the meaning of vocabulary words or a section of the text that was unclear to them. These attempts to clarify what they did not know or understand showed earnest efforts to make meaning from what they were reading.

In this lesson, students also showed their active engagement with the group discussion process. In the past, some students showed only minimal participation, allowing other group members to respond to questions or other tasks related to understanding the text. During today's lesson, group members took a lively role by asking and responding to questions, seeking and providing clarification, and leading the group. Ms. Darcy attributes this participation to an essential component of Reciprocal Teaching: having students assume the teacher role. Because responsibility for assuming leadership is shared, students can become more involved in the process. She believes that this kind of participation is critical to comprehension of the text.

Ms. Darcy was also able to use this lesson to guide her in what to do next. She knows that she will have to continue to model Reciprocal Teaching processes for her students. She also sees a need to continue coaching students on such things as how to ask an important question about the text or how to summarize. Although her students showed an increasing ability to demonstrate the processes of Reciprocal Teaching and were able to begin assuming leadership, they will need many opportunities to see it being done and to have assistance as they try to do it themselves. She knows they will require additional lessons using the Reciprocal Teaching model, and she looks forward to their progress.

As children learn to use the Reciprocal Teaching model, they begin to actively assume the roles that have been modeled for them by their teachers.

Figure 7.2   Essential Components for Introducing Students to Reciprocal Teaching

Explanation: Define terms (*Reciprocal Teaching, generating questions, clarifying, summarizing,* and *predicting*) and help students gain an explicit understanding of the reasons they are using Reciprocal Teaching.

Instructions: Provide students with sample opportunities to practice each strategy: summarize a paragraph together, make lists of helpful questions, and the rest.

Modeling: As the teacher and as a reader, show students your own use of the Reciprocal Teaching strategies by demonstrating or using a think aloud procedure.

Guided practice: As students begin to take an active role, alternate leadership with them and serve as a coach for their efforts (ask questions, rephrase their attempts, etc.).

Praise: Provide praise as needed and appropriate to guide students toward an accurate demonstration of behaviors and use of the Reciprocal Teaching processes.

Teacher judgment: Use your own perceptions and observations to decide when students need more modeling or instruction.

SOURCE: Adapted from Palincsar & Brown, 1986, p. 773.

The Components of Introducing Reciprocal Teaching

In Case Study 7.1, Ms. Darcy selected Reciprocal Teaching to help her students increase both their comprehension of text and their comprehension-monitoring behaviors. She also wanted to see her students take a more active role in group discussions of text. She knew that this process would take time and several opportunities for her to model the strategies of Reciprocal Teaching. Prior to the lesson described here, she began introducing her students to the model using several components described by Palincsar and Brown (1986): explanation, instructions, modeling, guided practice, praise, and teacher judgment (see Figure 7.2).

Explanation

Palincsar and Brown (1986) suggest that you begin using the Reciprocal Teaching model by explaining to students the strategies of generating questions, clarifying, and so on. They also note that students should understand explicitly why they are using these strategies, as well as how to use them. During earlier lessons, Ms. Darcy explained each of the terms and defined them for students. She also talked about how she wants them to improve their comprehension and comprehension-monitoring skills, as well as her belief that the Reciprocal Teaching model will help them accomplish this. She discussed the procedures they will use for assuming leadership and the importance of using the terminology in their discussions.

Instructions

Along with her explanations, Ms. Darcy also provided her students with brief instructions for each of the strategies. For example, she selected and gave them a sample paragraph and helped them summarize it, avoiding a focus on the details (something they tended to do) and instead capturing the essence of the paragraph. She wanted to make sure that her students understood each of the processes and what they would be expected to do in the group discussions of text.

Modeling

After the brief explanation and instructions, begin modeling, showing students what the processes look and sound like. As Ms. Darcy and the students began using text, she modeled her own use of the Reciprocal Teaching processes. She would often employ a think aloud as she modeled. For the students, she would literally say out loud what she was thinking as she was involved in the processes. This allowed them to see how she was generating questions, seeking clarification, summarizing, and predicting when reading. Often she would invite students to add their own questions, clarifications, or attempts at summarizing and predicting. It is important that students become active participants in the process as soon as possible.

Guided Practice

As students begin to take a more active role, encourage them to take increasing responsibility for the discussions by assuming the teacher's role and leading the discussion. Dalton and Jillian each volunteered to provide leadership for a segment of the content and direction of the discussions. Ms. Darcy provided guided practice by alternating with students and acting as a coach. She asked questions to help students expand their responses ("Are there any other important ideas in the paragraph?"). She assisted them by providing advice ("Maybe it would help to begin your question with *why* or *how*"). Perhaps most important, she modeled the process while students were involved with trying to learn and demonstrate it.

Praise

Providing appropriate praise will encourage student attempts and help them determine when they were using a strategy accurately. Throughout this introductory process, Ms. Darcy provided praise for students when and where appropriate. She knew that the processes in the Reciprocal Teaching model would be unfamiliar terrain for her students and that they would need this reinforcement as they practiced.

Teacher Judgment

The final component recommended by Palincsar and Brown (1986) is teacher judgment. Here, the teacher must determine when modeling or more instruction is needed (p. 773). In Ms. Darcy's case, this was a critical element of preparation for the students. She does not want them to see the process as rigid or teacher dominated.

| Figure 7.3 | Reciprocal Teaching Strategies and Processes |

Generating Questions: *What do all these things like removing your hand from a hot object and protecting your face from a ball have in common?*

Predicting: *My prediction is that the next paragraph will tell us more about the messages.*

Clarifying: *What do they mean when they say that the nerves are encased in the spinal column?*

Summarizing: *My summary is that this paragraph tells us that the brain, spinal cord, and nerves make up the nervous system and send messages to other parts of our body.*

She also wants them to consider her a helpful participant, not the final authority on issues of clarification or question generating. To accomplish this, and to provide knowledgeable guidance, she will have to carefully consider when further modeling and instruction would be advisable.

It should be noted here that the components described above are not restricted to introducing students to Reciprocal Teaching, although some may more consistently serve that purpose than others. Rather, you will interweave these components in your use of this model on an ongoing basis. From time to time, students will need to be reminded why they are using this model and how they can participate in the discussion.

The Strategies and Processes of Reciprocal Teaching

After using the components described above to introduce your students to the Reciprocal Teaching model, shift attention to the use of the four processes or strategies at the heart of this model: generating questions, clarifying, summarizing, and predicting (see Figure 7.3). We have chosen to present them in the order we would most typically use them in a class discussion, but their order can vary. In fact, in the natural course of a discussion, students will often alternate between questions and points for clarification, for example. Initially, though, students may develop more confidence if you guide them to use the strategies in the order given.

Generating Questions

After students read a small section of text (initially a paragraph or two), they form questions to be answered by group members. In forming the questions, the learners must rely on the information provided by the author or on their own background information (Ruddell, 1999).

Creating good questions can often be difficult for students and may require you to provide a good deal of modeling and coaching. One reason for students' difficulty may be that they simply are unaccustomed to being in the role of questioner in school settings, where teachers more traditionally assume this role. Practice and continued praise for attempts may be the prescription here. However, sometimes the tentativeness demonstrated by students may be a sign of uncertainty about how to form a good discussion question. In these cases, modeling or coaching will be most helpful. For example, in the case study, Dalton simply said, "I'm not sure what to ask." Ms. Darcy responded with a prompt to consider beginning the question with *why* or *how*. In this case, the coaching she provided was enough to help him formulate an initial question.

As students begin generating questions, it is important to help them move beyond the literal to the interpretive. Often students ask questions that can be answered easily by providing a detail listed in the text. For example, Jillian asked, "Where do the nerve signals go?" Students could easily locate the answer in the explicit details provided by the author: "It says that they go from the brain to every part of our bodies." Ms. Darcy followed up this question by simply modeling one that required more interpretation by the learner: "Why are axons important?" Literal questions and answers certainly have a useful purpose. However, a steady dose of them, to the exclusion of more interpretive ones, should be avoided. As with all the processes of Reciprocal Teaching, **generating questions** will take practice, encouragement, modeling, and coaching.

After the leader and group members have completed their questions and answers, typically the leader asks for any points that require clarification—confusing words or content that might limit comprehension.

Clarifying

As skilled readers move through text, they engage in a constant process of **clarifying**. Sometimes this involves checking a word or phrase for understanding, perhaps because it doesn't seem to fit with what they've already read. Other times it might require the reader to reread a passage that was unclear or clarify who is being referred to by the author's use of a personal pronoun. Less-skilled readers may not engage in this process of clarification, choosing instead to skip over parts or simply believing that an ability to decode and say the words is all that is essential for reading. In the Reciprocal Teaching model, learners are provided with an opportunity to stop and clarify anything they may not fully understand. The model assumes this practice will ultimately become an internalized process for all readers.

In Case Study 7.1, a number of examples of the process of clarifying can be observed. Maura said she did not completely understand the meaning of the term *system*. Ms. Darcy provided clarification by telling her, "You can think of a system as a group of things that work together." On another occasion, it was information that was missing from the paragraph that created confusion and needed to be clarified. Mackenzie was confused about how the messages actually move along axons to synapses, wondering whether it was similar to how electricity moves in an electrical cord. Because that information was not included in the paragraph, Ms. Darcy wrote the question down on a chart pad for future clarification. Regardless of the cause, it is important to provide students with regular opportunities to consider things that are unclear, as well as strategies for dealing with them.

Another issue you may want to consider when clarifying is the potential use of this time to introduce students to resources that may be helpful, such as dictionaries, glossaries, and other reference tools. In our example, Ms. Darcy considered this when Mackenzie asked what was meant when the authors said that "nerves are encased in the spinal column." Ms. Darcy posed the following question to the group to consider: "What could we use to find out what encased means?" They then briefly talked about the use of dictionaries and glossaries, but she elected not to use them at that time. In some cases, it may be worthwhile to stop briefly and demonstrate the use of an appropriate resource. Students could benefit from seeing how these tools are helpful at the point when they are needed, rather than performing an isolated exercise in their use. At other times, you may wish to follow Ms. Darcy's example and stay focused on the passage itself, avoiding interruptions in the flow of the reading experience.

Another issue to consider is the importance of making Reciprocal Teaching an exercise in using cooperative learning principles. As the teacher, you may find it tempting and more efficient to simply do all the clarifying for students. Indeed, modeling how to clarify is important. However, Reciprocal Teaching is best done when students assume the responsibility for clarifying information for each other through an active exchange of ideas. These discussions help students share and test ideas. They can take charge of finding information and become less reliant on the teacher.

Summarizing

After all clarifications have been made, the group leader summarizes the major points in the paragraph or text that has just been read. **Summarizing** text demonstrates both an accurate reading of the text and the use of higher-order thinking skills in processing the information. Skilled readers summarize the text as they read, sequencing ideas, making inferences, synthesizing information, and so on. In the Reciprocal Teaching model, readers have the opportunity to practice this process out loud and to hear the attempts and contributions of other group members.

Young readers and less-sophisticated readers tend to summarize by simply restating the details found in the text. For example, in the case study, Dalton attempted to summarize a paragraph on the components of the nervous system and their relationship to each other in sending messages throughout the body. Rather than stating a summary, he used a detail: the brain and spinal column as important parts of the nervous system. Ms. Darcy then asked him questions to help broaden his summary. This kind of coaching may be necessary for an extended period of time for many readers as they attempt to sort out details from main ideas in text.

Predicting

Teachers have long valued the task of engaging students in **predicting** upcoming text as a means of increasing their reading comprehension. Skilled readers make internal predictions using a variety of text resources (headings, relevant background information, etc.) and continually test each hypothesis as they read (Gunning, 1992). A large inconsistency may cause them to stop and recheck what they have read. For example, reading a long passage about the desert and then starting to read a sentence about a large lake might cause readers to stop to make certain they have read the information correctly. On the other hand, congruent predictions and text will add to the flow of the reading and increase comprehension. Therefore, the Reciprocal Teaching model provides students with opportunities to practice making and testing their predictions, more skills that will ultimately be internalized.

One important issue worth noting is the need to keep students focused on the passage and relevant background when making predictions. Students sometimes tend to make predictions based on information that is not relevant to the text. For example, one of Ms. Darcy's students might have begun talking about a neighbor's ulcer surgery, a topic with no relevance to the text about the human nervous system except that both involve the body. This kind of conversation may be helpful for other purposes but contributes little to students' abilities to make predictions based on the reading.

In a high school setting, Reciprocal Teaching helps students monitor and increase their reading comprehension of content area texts.

The Reciprocal Teaching model provides an opportunity to model use of the text, headings, illustrations, and relevant background information to make predictions, just as skilled readers do. For example, although she humorously referred to it as "cheating," Jillian used the topic sentence of the upcoming paragraph as she predicted what would come next in the reading. The strong discussion component of the Reciprocal Teaching model allows readers to hear what others are using as they internally structure their predictions.

Although we have listed predicting as the final phase of each Reciprocal Teaching discussion, it can also be an important feature of the beginning of a lesson, before any reading has occurred. You can ask your students to use chapter headings, subheadings, illustrations, and other text features to predict what a reading will be about. Such a prediction sets a purpose for reading, namely, to see if the prediction is accurate. It can also activate the learners' prior knowledge (Palincsar & Brown, 1986). Both reading purposefully and activating prior knowledge are very important in fostering reading comprehension.

As you read the next case study, consider how each of the processes of the Reciprocal Teaching model is configured as we observe its use in a high school setting.

Case Study 7.2: High School, Content Area Reading

Mr. Keur is a high school resource room teacher in a small rural school district. Most of his students are categorized as learning disabled, and many have significant problems reading the high school texts used in most of their courses. They come to Mr. Keur for assistance throughout the day, primarily with the content and assignments related to their mainstreamed classes. In addition to working directly with the students, Mr. Keur often meets formally and informally with their teachers to monitor student progress and coordinate coverage of assignments and content. He then develops plans for students that support what is being covered in their classes and provides more-specific learning strategies.

In considering ways to both support his students in their mainstreamed course work and provide additional assistance with their reading concerns, Mr. Keur has elected to use the Reciprocal Teaching model with small groups of his students. His overarching goal is to help his students develop **metacognitive skills**: to think about their own thinking as they read and process information. He also wants them to have a common language for talking about their thinking, especially as it relates to reading. He believes that by making this process transparent, the concept of "thinking about your thinking" will transfer to other tasks that students face, from content area courses to vocational training.

Another reason Mr. Keur has selected the Reciprocal Teaching model is his concern that many of his students have struggled with reading in general, and much of their emphasis has consequently been centered on decoding skills. Few of his students seem to have the reading comprehension skills he believes Reciprocal Teaching will provide. In addition, Mr. Keur is well aware that the content standards and benchmarks provided by his state emphasize reading comprehension skills in content areas. Indeed, his students will all participate in the annual state assessment process that reflects these standards and benchmarks.

Two of the students in Mr. Keur's resource room are tenth graders taking a course in U.S. government. In consulting with the instructor for this course, Mr. Keur has determined that the students have little difficulty understanding course concepts that are discussed orally. However, they struggle with content and concepts that must be gleaned from their reading of texts. Mr. Keur has introduced them to the Reciprocal Teaching model and has spent a number of weeks helping them understand how to generate questions, clarify misunderstandings, summarize text, and make predictions. In this lesson, he wants to work with the content that is being emphasized in their government class and help them use the Reciprocal Teaching model as they read a short newspaper article related to this content. Consequently, he has multiple objectives for today's lesson, but we will list only the objective related to his use of Reciprocal Teaching:

> The learner will use Reciprocal Teaching to demonstrate metacognitive strategies for reading and discussing text about the U.S. government.

Figure 7.4 | **Student Text for This Lesson**

Politics and the Supreme Court

Most Americans recognize and appreciate the balance of power in the U.S. form of government. The executive, judicial, and legislative branches of government envisioned by the founders were intended to insure that no one segment of the government would dominate and that politics in general would not completely dictate the laws of the land, nor their interpretation. While politicians take center stage in the executive and legislative branches, most Americans have assumed that the judicial branch was free from the influence of politics. Recent decisions handed down by the United States Supreme Court, the highest level of the judicial branch, have many people reevaluating those assumptions.

Over the years the Supreme Court has heard cases on a number of issues that are hotly debated in political circles. Decisions on abortion, racial quotas, and the role of religion in governmental conduct are just a few of these issues. While elected officials in the executive and legislative branches openly bring their political perspectives to these discussions, as they represent the constituents who brought them to office, many Americans assume that the justices on the U.S. Supreme Court maintain an objective stance as they consider issues and interpret the U.S. Constitution. However, several of the written decisions issued by the courts show a clear division among justices taking conservative and liberal positions on the law. The recent 4 to 5 ruling on the display of the Ten Commandments in government buildings illustrates this division.

Perhaps nothing better illustrates the influence of politics on the U.S. Supreme Court than the debates and proceedings surrounding the appointment of a new justice. When Justice Sandra Day O'Connor announced her decision to resign from the court, some observers began to refer to the process to find her replacement as "the presidential election of 2005." Replacing O'Connor, who was often the swing vote in 5 to 4 decisions, became one of the most talked and written about topics in the media and political circles—with many political groups attempting to influence the selection and decision-making process. With so much talk about the political and ideological leanings of Supreme Court nominees, many Americans are left wondering just how separate the judicial branch is from the influence of politics.

At the beginning of the lesson, Mr. Keur sits down at a small table with Nathan and Allison, the two students who are in his classroom for a portion of the day to receive additional help with their government class assignments, especially those that deal with reading content text. He passes out copies of the newspaper article that they were assigned to read for class the next day.

Mr. Keur: Today I want to spend some time with you reading over the newspaper article Mr. Toppen assigned to you. I really have two goals in mind, though. I want to make sure that you have done a careful reading of this article, but I also want to use it to continue practicing the Reciprocal Teaching model that we have been working on. I just want to remind you that one of the reasons we are using it, besides helping you understand this article better, is to help you use the strategies of clarifying misunderstandings, summarizing information, making predictions, and asking good questions in other situations. For example, if you know how to summarize this article, you can summarize other readings too. So let's go ahead and get started. I'd like you to begin by reading over the first paragraph of the article on your own.

Both the students begin reading the first paragraph silently. It reads as follows:

Politics and the Supreme Court

Most Americans recognize and appreciate the balance of power in the U.S. form of government. The executive, judicial, legislative branches of government envisioned by the founders were intended to insure that no one segment of the government would dominate and that politics in general would not completely dictate the laws of the land, nor their interpretation. While politicians take center stage in the executive and legislative branches, most Americans have assumed that the judicial branch was free from the influence of politics. Recent decisions handed down by the United States Supreme Court, the highest level of the judicial branch, have many people reevaluating those assumptions.

When they finish reading, the students look at Mr. Keur.

Mr. Keur: As you remember, what we want to do with this paragraph is come up with some questions, clarify anything we don't understand, summarize what we've read, and then predict what will be in the next paragraph. You know that this is something that good readers do when they are reading this kind of informational text. Of course, those are also things we do when we are trying to understand lots of things—even things like math problems. Let's start with some questions. My question is, Why are some people reevaluating their assumptions about the influence of politics on the Supreme Court?

Nathan: Well, the article says that the court has made a lot of decisions lately that are making people wonder. Maybe they mean things like their decisions about the 2000 presidential election. That's something we talked about in class yesterday. Maybe that's my prediction about what will come up later in this article.

Allison:　Yeah, it doesn't really give much information about why people are wondering. It just says that they've made recent decisions that are making people wonder.

Mr. Keur:　I agree. There's not much here yet that tells us the why part of my question. But I think that how my question led you to make a prediction, Nathan, is really helpful. Are there any other questions? (*Both shake their heads to indicate that they do not have any other questions*.) Okay, are there any things you need to clarify so that you'll feel like you really understood this paragraph?

Allison:　Yes. I know that I should know this, but I always get confused about it. Who are the people in the legislative and executive branches again?

Mr. Keur:　Well, before we answer that, maybe we should talk for a minute about places where we could locate that information—just for future reference. Any ideas?

Allison:　Well, I know it's in my government book and I know I could find it on the computer pretty easily.

Mr. Keur:　Yes, I think both of those would be good sources. For right now, though, let me just remind you that the executive branch has the president, vice president, and cabinet members. The legislative branch is the one with senators and representatives. How could we summarize this paragraph?

Nathan:　Well the writer seems to think that even though we all know that the executive and legislative branches are political, many people are now starting to see how politics influences the judges too.

Mr. Keur:　That's a good summary, I think. Now, we already have the prediction you made earlier, Nathan, so how about if we use that as we read the next paragraph? Before we do that, though, I just want to remind you both that one of the reasons we make these predictions is to help you be better readers of this kind of informational text. You know how sometimes you can be reading the word on the page but you are really thinking about something else the whole time—like what you might have for lunch? And then you get to the end of the reading and have no idea what you just read? (*Both students nod their heads and laugh*.) Well, if you are looking for something in the paragraph, it's more likely you'll read it more closely. So, if you are trying to see if your prediction is right, you'll be more focused on what you are reading. So let's see if the next paragraph talks about the decisions that have been made that have people wondering if the Supreme Court is influenced by politics.

Mr. Keur and the students read the next paragraph silently. It reads as follows:

Over the years the Supreme Court has heard cases on a number of issues that are hotly debated in political circles. Decisions on abortion, racial quotas, and the role of religion in governmental conduct are just a few of these issues. While elected officials in the executive and legislative branches openly bring their political perspectives to these discussions, as they represent the constituents who brought them to office, many Americans assume that the justices on the U.S. Supreme Court maintain an objective stance as they consider issues and interpret the U.S. Constitution. However, several of the written decisions issued by the courts show a clear division among justices taking conservative and liberal positions on the law. The recent 4 to 5 ruling on the display of the Ten Commandments in government buildings illustrates this division.

As the students finish reading, Mr. Keur resumes the discussion.

Mr. Keur: Okay, which of you would like to walk us through this part of the article?

Allison: I'll try this time. So, let's start with a question. Maybe we should start with a question about Nathan's prediction. So, my question is, does the paragraph tell us what the decisions were that the Supreme Court has made that make some people wonder if politics is influencing them?

Nathan: Yeah, they do mention a few things. At the end it talks about the decision they made on whether or not you can display the Ten Commandments in a government office building. They also mention things like the decisions they have made about abortion and having quotas based on race.

Allison: Well then, I have another question. They have to make decisions, right? So why do some people think that it's politics that is pushing them to make them?

Nathan: I'm not really sure about that.

Mr. Keur: I think that when this writer here talks about politics, he means that the justices interpret the law and the Constitution from different viewpoints. Some of those reflect a more conservative political perspective on the issue and some a more liberal. I don't think he means that they are directly influenced in any way by politicians themselves or the way politicians are influenced because of what their constituents want.

Nathan: That makes some sense. Hey, thanks for the clarification. (*They all laugh.*)

Allison: Speaking of that, is there anything we need to clarify?

Nathan: No, I think I get the rest of it pretty well.

Allison: Okay. Let me try a summary. I say that this paragraph is about how Supreme Court Justices can be either liberals or conservatives when they make decisions and interpret laws and the Constitution. I'll make a prediction too. I think that the next paragraph will talk about the decision they made about the Ten Commandments, since that is what this one ended with.

Mr. Keur: Nice job of summarizing, Allison. I think your prediction could be helpful, too, since authors often use the last point they made in one paragraph to start the next paragraph. Let's go ahead and read this last paragraph silently, and then maybe Nathan can lead us.

The students read the last paragraph to themselves.

Perhaps nothing better illustrates the influence of politics on the U.S. Supreme Court than the debates and proceedings surrounding the appointment of a new justice. When Justice Sandra Day O'Connor announced her decision to resign from the court, some observers began to refer to the process to find her replacement as "the presidential election of 2005." Replacing O'Connor, who was often the swing vote in 5 to 4 decisions, became one of the most talked and written about topics in the media and political circles. With so much talk about the political and ideological leanings of Supreme Court nominees, many Americans are left wondering just how separate the judicial branch is from the influence of politics.

As they all finish reading, Mr. Keur and Allison look to Nathan to start the discussion.

Nathan: I'd like to start with a clarification. I'm a little confused by what it means when it says that finding the replacement for that justice was like the presidential election of 2005. What's it talking about?

Allison: I'm not positive, but I think he meant that lots of people would want a justice with the same opinions as theirs. You know, like when you vote for a president, you're trying to elect someone who has the same opinions that you do. So maybe people who are conservative would want a conservative person to be the new justice.

Nathan: That helps, but I'm still a little bit confused. I mean, we don't vote for people to be on the Supreme Court, right?

Mr. Keur: I'm curious, Nathan. What makes you wonder about that?

Nathan: Well, it says it was like a presidential election.

Mr. Keur: Now I think I see what you are thinking. Let me clarify. People in this country don't vote for Supreme Court justices. But there is a selection process. The president nominates someone, and of course he gets lots of advice from other folks. The nominee then has to go before the members of the Senate Judiciary Committee, who ask about the nominee's views on a variety of topics. After that, the nominee still has to be confirmed by the Senate. And on top of that, there are all sorts of groups with particular views trying to influence the senators to pick someone with views they like. Of course, this gets lots of media attention too. So in a way, the justice is elected and the whole process is similar to a presidential election. I like the way you're thinking that through, Nathan. It would be easy to just ignore it instead of trying to figure it out.

Nathan: Thanks. I don't really have any questions. Do you, Allison?

Allison: Not really.

Nathan: Okay, so I'll try to make a summary of this paragraph. This paragraph says that the biggest political influence on the Supreme Court comes from how they are selected.

The students and Mr. Keur read the rest of the article, Nathan and Allison alternating roles and focusing on both the content of the article and their thinking processes.

Case Study 7.2: Post-Lesson Reflection ◆

Mr. Keur was very pleased with how this lesson transpired and felt that it met his objective well. Allison and Nathan understood the information in the assigned article, and they focused on their thinking process in important ways. Both students were able to use the Reciprocal Teaching terminology to label what they were doing as they read and also when they were preparing to read a new section of the text. They freely discussed things that confused them, tried to clarify misunderstood terms and passages, made predictions based on what they had read, and were able to use what they learned to summarize the text they had read. Mr. Keur was especially pleased about this because Allison and Nathan had previously spent little time processing texts they were reading but rather focused on just reading the words—a legacy of the heavy emphasis on decoding skills in their earlier reading experiences. In this reading, they focused on both the meaning of the text and the way they were understanding it.

Mr. Keur also appreciated the way the discussion had progressed. He remained able and willing to model or clarify as needed, but he was encouraged because both Allison and Nathan participated actively and were able to carry on the conversation on their own. As high school students who have struggled with reading, both Allison and Nathan have sometimes been reticent to participate in discussions about text. However, as both students gained confidence in their abilities, through the processes involved in Reciprocal Teaching, they have become active participants who are even willing to direct their own learning. Perhaps they have achieved this milestone because asking questions and seeking clarification are explicitly valued in this model.

It is also interesting to note that the discussion in this case study was more fluid than it might be with younger students. As high school students, Allison and Nathan might feel too restricted by a process that required rigid adherence to steps. Consequently, Mr. Keur encouraged a more natural conversation by allowing the students to use the strategies of questioning, clarifying, summarizing, and predicting when and if needed—avoiding a lockstep approach. This approach allowed the students to have a discussion of the content and how they were thinking about it rather than completing an exercise in using the Reciprocal Teaching model.

Mr. Keur has also developed an appreciation for how Reciprocal Teaching can serve as an assessment tool for him. As the students asked questions and sought clarification, he was able to hear their thinking about the specific content as well as see how they were reading and comprehending the text. For example, when Nathan was confused about how the selection of a Supreme Court justice might be comparable to a presidential election, Mr. Keur was able to probe his thinking with a question, note his train of thought, and provide clarification. This insight into how Nathan sometimes processes such metaphorical language will help Mr. Keur plan for working with him in the future, which is the goal of formative assessment.

Finally, Mr. Keur is convinced that Allison and Nathan's reading comprehension skills are improving as a result of their use of the Reciprocal Teaching model and that he is able to help them understand how the strategies are helpful in an explicit way. For example, when he talked to them about making predictions, he was able to demonstrate how predicting increases comprehension by keeping readers focused on the text as they look for specific information—as opposed to thinking about lunch menu choices! The Reciprocal Teaching model provided the language and process for focusing on this important comprehension strategy. We believe that such conversations in the context of reading have much greater potential than an isolated skills lesson on making predictions.

Brief Background of Reciprocal Teaching

Reciprocal Teaching was developed by Annemarie Palincsar and Ann Brown (1983, 1984, 1986) as a model for increasing both students' comprehension of text and their comprehension-monitoring processes. Begun with a pilot study in 1982, Reciprocal Teaching extended work done by Manzo (1968, cited in Palincsar & Brown, 1983) on a reciprocal-questioning intervention known as ReQuest, as well as work done by Frase and Schwartz (1975, cited in Palincsar & Brown, 1983) on a system in which students took turns developing and responding to questions.

The Reciprocal Teaching model is more elaborate than the Manzo or Frase and Schwartz models, which focused primarily on the role of questions and answers and the student's part in generating them. Also, unlike its predecessors, Reciprocal Teaching has teachers and students alternating roles to create summaries of text read, make predictions about upcoming passages, and seek clarification of confusing text or vocabulary.

Reciprocal Teaching has been used with a variety of grouping patterns and age groups. In the original studies (Brown & Palincsar, 1985), the teacher was a researcher, and she met with students either individually or in pairs. As the results of this early work proved successful, efforts were made to make the work with students more reflective of real classrooms. Since then, many classroom teachers have successfully used Reciprocal Teaching with small groups, in peer-tutoring situations, and in large-group settings. Reciprocal Teaching is also used with a variety of age groups, including elementary, middle, and high school students. Even nonreaders can use a modified version of Reciprocal Teaching if the text is read to them.

Finally, the original work with Reciprocal Teaching focused primarily on content area reading. This is a sensible use of the model since in many ways it provides students with a means for studying the content of a reading selection. However, Reciprocal Teaching can also be modified rather easily to fit narrative text selections and to focus on the main elements of a story (Reutzel & Cooter, 1992).

Reciprocal Teaching and Research on Teaching

The original studies conducted by Palincsar and Brown (1983, 1984, 1986) demonstrated significant benefit for students judged to have adequate decoding skills but low comprehension of text. Subsequent research supports their conclusions. Reciprocal Teaching has been shown to be effective with a variety of grouping patterns and levels of support in both special populations of learners and general classroom situations.

Evidence also indicates that students who have been taught to use Reciprocal Teaching and who have been given adequate scaffolding can use it effectively with a minimal level of monitoring by the teacher (Klinger & Vaughn, 1996). This suggests that Reciprocal Teaching holds much promise for meeting the demands of teachers and school settings that require flexibility and emphasize collaborative work among students.

Many of the earlier efforts to implement Reciprocal Teaching used experts in the model (researchers and doctoral candidates) working with students (Rosenshine & Meister, 1994). More recent efforts have explored the success of implementation by classroom teachers (Kelly, Moore, & Tuck, 1994; King & Johnson, 1999). One report on Reciprocal Teaching suggested that parents might be trained to use the model with their children (Carter, 1997). Thus, with appropriate training and background, many members of the school community could employ Reciprocal Teaching with positive results. In other words, it appears to be a simple and effective model for improving reading comprehension.

Reciprocal Teaching has also been shown to be effective with special populations of learners. Klinger and Vaughn (1996) used this model with English as a Second Language students who were also categorized as learning disabled. They reported overall improvement in reading comprehension and have suggested that the model may be appropriate and effective in general education classrooms that include special education or English as a Second Language students as well as in classes structured specifically to meet the needs of these populations.

Recent research has explored the use of Reciprocal Teaching in general education classrooms, places characterized by multiple demands and tasks for teachers and large groups of students. These studies (Kelly et al., 1994; King & Johnson, 1999) showed positive results for students in these regular classroom settings. They further suggest that Reciprocal Teaching is an appropriate and manageable model for the repertoire of classroom teachers.

In their review of the research on Reciprocal Teaching, Rosenshine and Meister (1994) noted an important issue: scores on researcher-created measures of reading comprehension showed significant gains after exposure to Reciprocal Teaching in controlled studies. However, improvements on standardized tests of reading comprehension were less significant. This difference may be explained by differences in the tests themselves. For example, the tests created by the researchers often used reading passages that were longer than the passages on standardized tests, and the longer passages allowed the students to benefit from more context clues. Other reports (Lysynchuk, Pressley, & Vye, 1990; Carter, 1997), however, show significant gains on standardized tests by students who have used Reciprocal Teaching, and more study may be warranted to resolve this inconsistency.

Reciprocal Teaching and Learning Theory

Reciprocal Teaching reflects a constructivist view of learning, which holds that individuals construct unique understandings of the world around them through mediated interactions with other people and the environment. An important way in which we build these understandings is through the use of scaffolding, which is emphasized in the Reciprocal Teaching model.

Scaffolding is a useful way of considering how learning occurs in general, as well as with Reciprocal Teaching. In a construction project (such as creating a new building), a scaffold is placed around the beginning stages of the structure to provide support. As the structure becomes capable of supporting itself, the scaffolding is carefully and increasingly removed. In Reciprocal Teaching (and other models of teaching as well), students are provided with considerable teacher support in the early stages of using the model. The teacher models and then gradually allows students to assume more and more responsibility. As students become more confident and capable, the teacher continues to withdraw, providing support only when needed.

Also important to the constructivist view of learning is the importance of interaction with others. As discussed by Vygotsky (1978), most learning occurs as individuals scaffold for each other rather than in isolation. In students' early experiences with Reciprocal Teaching, the teacher is often a critical partner in learning, encouraging, providing corrective feedback, and guiding the students. Ultimately, group members become "experts," sharing their understanding of the text with each other. In this way, students construct their understanding of the text with each other.

Reciprocal Teaching also reflects some elements of information processing theories of learning, specifically the development of metacognition. Metacognition refers to the intentional use of cognitive processes. Reciprocal Teaching was designed specifically to highlight and develop such processes. In addition, metacognition involves an awareness of one's own thinking (as illustrated especially in Case Study 7.2). In Reciprocal Teaching, the deliberate use of language that reflects the mental processes students are using (summarizing, clarifying, predicting, and questioning) provides a mechanism for increasing students' own awareness of these processes. Such awareness may also increase the potential for internalizing the processes, which is the ultimate goal of Reciprocal Teaching.

Reciprocal Teaching and the Cognitive Processing Philosophy of Curriculum

Reciprocal Teaching easily fits the cognitive processing philosophy of curriculum, as described by Eisner and Vallance (1974). This orientation emphasizes the development of intellectual processes (p. 6), something Brown and Palincsar (1985) considered fundamental to the Reciprocal Teaching model. Indeed, in describing Reciprocal Teaching, they have said, "We have always regarded the procedure as a form of general education in thinking critically rather than a specific form of reading instruction" (p. 50). As students learn and gain confidence in the use of the Reciprocal Teaching model, they develop specific cognitive processes related to critical thinking.

When teachers model and coach students in the use of Reciprocal Teaching, they use it to further students' understanding of the curriculum and to assist students in internalizing the intellectual processes embedded in the model. In Case Study 7.1, Ms. Darcy uses Reciprocal Teaching to focus on the required curriculum, namely, a study of the systems of the human body. She is also meeting a criterion encouraged by her state standards: providing students with a strategy to use when encountering unfamiliar texts. However, underlying all this is her concern for modeling intellectual processes (generating questions, clarifying, summarizing, and predicting) that she hopes her students will eventually internalize. Modeling and even naming the processes you as a teacher use to comprehend text provides your students with a schema and language for their own use.

The cognitive processing philosophy also suggests that these internalized cognitive processes should be transferable to other situations, something that has been demonstrated by the work of Palincsar and Brown (1986). For example, they documented a significant jump in percentile ratings in science and social studies classes for students who were trained using the Reciprocal Teaching model. Students who began at the 20th percentile or lower dramatically improved their performance, moving up to the 50th percentile and even higher in some cases (p. 775).

Technology and Reciprocal Teaching

Technology can be used in at least two significant ways with the Reciprocal Teaching model. First, it can be used to facilitate the actual teaching process. Second, technology can be used as a resource tool when preparing to use the model or during the process itself.

A Smart Board would work well with the text being read. The teacher can project the text for all to see in a shared reading experience, providing many explicit opportunities for modeling how to use the text to ask questions, clarify, predict, and summarize. For example, as students summarize a text, they need to learn to consider the major concept in the passage rather than isolated details. Using the Smart Board, the teacher would be able to highlight various details in different colors and then show how they contribute to a summary statement. Similar kinds of visual opportunities would be possible while modeling how to make predictions, generate questions, and use the text itself to clarify confusion.

Computers can be used as a resource tool in Reciprocal Teaching in at least two ways. First, multiple databases can be used to find texts for which Reciprocal Teaching strategies are well suited. Second, students can use various databases and computer programs to locate information that relates to an issue or term raised for clarification. For example, in the second case study, Allison suggested that information helpful to understanding the three branches of government could be found easily by searching on a computer.

A sampling of National Educational Technology (NET) Standards for Students and performance indicators (International Society for Technology in Education, 2000), along with some suggested classroom applications of the Reciprocal Teaching model, is provided below.* Because the model focuses primarily on reading comprehension and comprehension-monitoring strategies, the listing below includes only standards and indicators related to the English language arts.

GRADES PK–2

NET Standard 3: Technology Productivity Tools

NET Standard 4: Technology Communications Tools

NET Standard 5: Technology Research Tools

NET Standard 6: Technology Problem-Solving and Decision-Making Tools

Performance Indicator 9: Use technology resources for problem solving, communication, and illustration of thoughts, ideas, and stories.

Reciprocal Teaching Extensions

Use the Smart Board or individual PCs to (a) highlight details in passages to show how they contribute to a summary, (b) indicate details in the passage that lend support for making a prediction, and (c) highlight terms that need clarification and then demonstrate how various computer programs or databases can be used to find the needed information.

GRADES 3–5

NET Standard 5: Technology Research Tools

NET Standard 6: Technology Problem-Solving and Decision-Making Tools

Performance Indicator 9: Determine when technology is useful and select the appropriate tool(s) and technology resources to address a variety of tasks and problems.

Reciprocal Teaching Extension

Make a list of terms and items that require clarification in a passage being read by the students. Discuss which tools will be most efficient and productive in finding the needed information. For example, when looking up a term, discuss which tool is most helpful, a printed dictionary or a computer program.

GRADES 6–8

NET Standard 5: Technology Research Tools

NET Standard 6: Technology Problem-Solving and Decision-Making Tools

Performance Indicator 8: Select and use appropriate tools and technology resources to accomplish a variety of tasks and solve problems.

Reciprocal Teaching Extension

For a particular subtopic within a content area, have students use personal computers to locate a variety of text sources, including primary sources, that can be used for practice with the strategies involved in the Reciprocal Teaching model.

GRADES 9–12

NET Standard 4: Technology Communication Tools

NET Standard 5: Technology Research Tools

NET Standard 6: Technology Problem-Solving and Decision-Making Tools

Performance Indicator 7: Routinely and efficiently use online information resources to meet needs for collaboration, research, publications, communications, and productivity.

Reciprocal Teaching Extension

When students need to clarify their understanding, have them use computer databases and programs to find helpful information.

Reciprocal Teaching, Content Standards, and Benchmarks

The Reciprocal Teaching model is designed to promote reading comprehension and comprehension monitoring skills. As a result, you will easily be able to connect the use of this model with your state's content standards and benchmarks that relate to English language arts. It will also be possible to connect your use of this model with standards and benchmarks that are specific to the subject of the text you are reading. However, for the sake of providing clear and direct examples, we have limited the standards and benchmarks listed below to English language arts. All standards and benchmarks listed below are taken from the *Michigan Curriculum Framework* (Michigan Department of Education, 1996).*

---

*Excerpts from the *Michigan Curriculum Framework* are reprinted with permission of the Michigan Department of Education.

English Language Arts

CONTENT STANDARD 1: All students will read and comprehend general and technical material.

Early Elementary Benchmark: Employ multiple strategies to construct meaning, including word recognition, skills, context clues, retelling, predicting, and generating questions.

Later Elementary Benchmark: Employ multiple strategies to construct meaning, including the use of sentence structure, vocabulary skills, context clues, text structure, mapping, predicting, retelling and generating questions.

Middle School Benchmark: Employ multiple strategies to construct meaning, such as generating questions, studying vocabulary, analyzing mood and tone, recognizing how authors use information, generalizing ideas, matching form to content, and developing reference skills.

High School Benchmark: Selectively employ the most effective strategies to construct meaning, such as generating questions, scanning, analyzing, and evaluating for specific information related to a research question and deciding how to represent content through summarizing, clustering, and mapping.

CONTENT STANDARD 3: All students will focus on meaning and communication as they listen, speak, read, and write in personal, social, occupational, and civic contexts.

Early Elementary Benchmark: Employ strategies to construct meaning while reading, listening to, viewing, or creating texts. Examples include retelling, predicting, generating questions, examining picture cues, discussing with peers, using context clues, and creating mental pictures.

Upper Elementary Benchmark: Employ multiple strategies to construct meaning while reading, listening to, viewing, or creating texts. Examples include summarizing, predicting, generating questions, mapping, examining picture cues, analyzing word structure and sentence structure, discussing with peers, and using context and text structure.

Middle School Benchmark: Select appropriate strategies to construct meaning while reading, listening to, viewing, or creating texts. Examples include generating relevant questions, studying vocabulary, analyzing mood and tone, recognizing how authors and speakers use information, and matching form to content.

High School Benchmark: Employ the most effective strategies to construct meaning while reading, listening to, viewing, or creating texts. Examples include generating focus questions; deciding how to represent content through analyzing, clustering, and mapping; and withholding personal bias.

Why Choose Reciprocal Teaching?

1. As you observe students reading, do you notice them skipping over sections that pose difficulties for them, especially with expository text? Could

Reciprocal Teaching provide them with strategies and processes that would be helpful in monitoring and enhancing their reading comprehension?

2. Do all students take an active role in group readings and discussions of text? If not, could Reciprocal Teaching provide a framework for improved participation?

3. Do you have students who seem to read (decode) words but have low comprehension of text? Could the Reciprocal Teaching model provide them with strategies and processes for monitoring their own comprehension of text?

4. Do students view the teacher as the authority on issues related to questions and answers, clarification of words, and unclear passages? Would the Reciprocal Teaching model help them broaden their base of resources to include one another, as well as such appropriate resource tools as dictionaries and thesauruses?

5. Do students demonstrate the use of appropriate strategies to read text for meaning?

Summary

Reciprocal Teaching has been shown to be an effective model for improving both reading comprehension and comprehension-monitoring skills. Teachers and learners are encouraged to exchange roles as students practice and then internalize the cognitive strategies of generating questions, clarifying information, summarizing, and making predictions about the text they are reading. As readers incorporate these strategies, they begin to process text in ways that have been identified in readers with strong comprehension skills.

The Reciprocal Teaching model helps teachers scaffold learning for students until the learners can use the model independently. It ensures active participation and engagement with the text itself as the learner assumes more and more of the teacher's role. This quality also makes Reciprocal Teaching an effective model for students working in various groupings, including collaborative groups that work with little teacher support.

The Reciprocal Teaching model offers many advantages to teachers and learners. It can be used in a variety of settings and with support from numerous trained members of the school community. Perhaps most important, it has a demonstrated success rate for improving reading comprehension.

Putting It Together

1. Consider your own reading of text when comprehension and retention are important. What strategies do you use to monitor your own reading? Try to identify those that are consistent with the Reciprocal Teaching model.

2. Select a reading that will require your attention for comprehension, perhaps a textbook that you are currently using for a course or for independent study. Divide it into small sections. At the end of each section, generate questions, determine issues that need clarification, summarize it, and write down your predictions for the next section.

3. Select a textbook or other reading text that students will be using. Take one section and divide it into smaller sections. To prepare for modeling Reciprocal Teaching, at the end of each section, write down appropriate questions (perhaps using the QAR model discussed in Chapter 8), potential words or passages for clarification, a one-sentence summary, and your predictions for the upcoming section.

4. Survey your state or local curriculum documents. Locate strategies that are recommended for monitoring and improving reading comprehension. Consider their fit with the Reciprocal Teaching model.

Student Study Site

The Companion Web site for *Models of Teaching: Connecting Student Learning With Standards*

www.sagepub.com/delloliostudy

Visit the Web-based student study site to enhance your understanding of the book content and discover additional resources that will take your learning one step further. You can enhance your understanding by using the comprehensive Study Guide, which includes chapter learning objectives, flash cards, practice tests, and more. You'll find special features, such as the links to standards from U.S. States and associated activities, Learning from Journal Articles, Field Experience worksheets, Learning from Case Studies, and PRAXIS resources.

References

Brown, A. L., & Palincsar, A. S. (1985). *Reciprocal teaching of comprehension strategies: A natural history of one program for enhancing learning* (Report No. CS-008–029). Washington DC: Office of Educational Research and Improvement. (ERIC Document Reproduction Service No. ED257046)

Carter, C. (1997, March). Why reciprocal teaching? *Educational Leadership, 64–68.*

Eisner, E., & Vallance, E. (1974). *Conflicting conceptions of the curriculum.* Berkeley, CA: McCutchan.

Gunning, T. G. (1992). *Creating reading instruction for all children.* Boston: Allyn & Bacon.

International Society for Technology in Education. (2000). *National educational technology standards for students: Connecting curriculum and technology.* Washington, DC: Author in collaboration with the U.S. Department of Education.

Kelly, M., Moore, D. W., & Tuck, B. F. (1994). Reciprocal teaching in a regular primary school classroom. *Journal of Educational Research, 88*(1), 53–61.

King, C. M., & Johnson, L. M. (1999). Constructing meaning via reciprocal teaching. *Reading Research and Instruction, 38*(3), 169–186.

Klinger, J. K., & Vaughn, S. (1996). Reciprocal teaching of reading comprehension strategies for students with learning disabilities who use English as a second language. *Elementary School Journal, 96*(3) 275–293.

Lysynchuk, L. M., Pressley, M., & Vye, N. J. (1990). Reciprocal teaching improves standardized reading comprehension performance in poor comprehenders. *Elementary School Journal, 90*, 471–484.

Michigan Department of Education. (1996). *Michigan curriculum framework.* Lansing: Author.

Palincsar, A. S., & Brown, A. L. (1983). *Reciprocal teaching of comprehension-monitoring activities* (Report No. CS-006–981). Washington DC: Office of Educational Research and Improvement. (ERIC Document Reproduction Service No. 225135)

Palincsar, A. S., & Brown, A. L. (1984). Reciprocal teaching of comprehension-fostering and comprehension-monitoring activities. *Cognition and Instruction*, *1*(2), 117–175.

Palincsar, A. S., & Brown, A. L. (1986). Interactive teaching to promote independent learning from text. *Reading Teacher*, *39*(8), 771–777.

Reutzel, R. D., & Cooter, R. B. (1992). *Teaching children to read: From basals to books.* New York: Macmillan.

Rosenshine, B., & Meister, C. (1994). Reciprocal teaching: A review of the research. *Review of Educational Research*, *64*(4), 479–530.

Ruddell, R. B. (1999). *Teaching children to read and write: Becoming an influential teacher.* Boston: Allyn & Bacon.

Vygotsky, L. S. (1978). *Mind in society: The development of higher psychological processes.* Cambridge, MA: Harvard University Press.

chapter

Question-Answer Relationship

You can probably recall many of the features of literacy learning from your own experiences as a young student. Often the teacher would assign a reading, or you might read together as a group. During and afterwards, there was a discussion time with questions about the text. Who is the story about? What did they do? What happened at the end? Perhaps you were asked to fill out a worksheet with similar kinds of questions. Your response may have been to page back through the text and search for the answer or simply to rely on your memory of the reading. I (T. D.) still have memories of these searches for *the* answer. In many instances, I was looking for things at the most literal or explicit level—a name, a color, and like answers. However, in recent years, reading has often been redefined with a focus on the reader's ability to create meaning from text. Consequently, it is clear that students must go beyond an emphasis on the literal.

What may not have occurred to many of us as young readers is that there are relationships between the questions and answers in text we read and write. Explicitly knowing this relationship may help a student comprehend text at a level that includes, but also extends beyond, the literal level (what the author tells you). Students may also begin to understand where to find sources for the answers they are looking for.

Question-Answer Relationship (QAR) was developed by Taffy Raphael (1982, 1986; Raphael & Pearson, 1985). This model can be used for content area reading or narrative types of text. It is useful for helping students find the relationships between questions and their answers and for providing language to describe those relationships. This model is also a potential vehicle for teachers as they examine their own question-asking behaviors, something that will be discussed later in this chapter. As you read Case Study 8.1, think carefully about how the teacher helps students understand the process of connecting questions with answers and finding the sources for answers, as well as how he provides them with the language of QAR for future use. It may also be helpful to think about how the cognitive processing philosophy is useful for understanding the QAR model.

Case Study 8.1: Third Grade, Language Arts

Mr. Zucco teaches third grade in a self-contained classroom in Laketown, a small community bordering one of the Great Lakes. His language arts curriculum is based on the use of whole texts and the integration of content area readings that focus on themes. Recently he has been reflecting on his students' answers to questions he has posed about their readings and to questions included in the texts. The students often seem to respond with a simple yes or no or with a brief detail. Mr. Zucco sees a need to move the students toward a deeper level of thinking and responding. He has selected the QAR model to assist them.

For the past several months, the students have focused on the theme of communities, a topic frequently discussed in the content standards and benchmarks produced by their state board of education. The class is currently learning about the way homes are designed, given the topography, climate, and other factors affecting a community.

In an earlier lesson, Mr. Zucco had the students read a short story about the town's early settlers and how they used the natural resources and terrain to plan and build the town. Before, during, and after this reading, he asked the students questions. As they responded, he asked them to put each answer into one of two broad categories of question-and-answer relationships: In the Book answers, which could be found in the text itself, and In My Head answers, which use the reader's background knowledge. The students practiced this way of categorizing until he felt they were comfortable with it.

In this lesson, Mr. Zucco will introduce four subcategories of question-and-answer relationships. He plans to make them an integral part of the class language and procedures for dealing with text in the future.

Mr. Zucco has selected a pamphlet developed by the local chamber of commerce as the reading (see Figure 8.1).

Figure 8.1 **Chamber of Commerce Brochure Excerpt**

Housing

Much of the housing in Laketown reflects the Victorian style that was so popular among the lumber barons who established the town in the 1900s. Tall peaked roofs tower over the large porches that are so perfect for hot summer evenings spent watching the neighborhood children play on the front lawn.

Many of these homes are located in the center of town on Elm Boulevard and Oak Street. Most have recently been restored to their original designs and colors and have such modern necessities as gas heat and air-conditioning. Tours of these homes are held every spring during the local garden club's annual garden festival.

In a newer development in Laketown, homes have also been built using the Victorian style that was so popular when the town was founded. These homes can be found in the marina section of town, mostly along Little Station Street and Harbor Lights Avenue. Walking through this area on a warm summer night is a must for all visitors. This area is also usually included in local tours of the marina district.

The founders of Laketown built their homes for beauty and also to fit with the changing climate of this lakeshore community. The more recent additions of modern heating units, air-conditioning, and other innovations have only made them more livable for current residents.

Mr. Zucco has also prepared a chart that illustrates QAR (see Figure 8.2): the two categories from the earlier lesson and the subcategories for today's lesson. He has the following objective for today's lesson:

> The learner will use QAR terminology to categorize responses to questions about written text and will show the sources used for responses.

For this lesson, Mr. Zucco has chosen to work with students in small reading groups. He calls the first group to the rectangular table he uses for such work. On the wall, he has placed the QAR chart he prepared in advance. Next to it on an easel is a flip chart to record student responses. He passes out a copy of the brochure for each student.

Figure 8.2   Mr. Zucco's Wall Chart

In the Book

Right There

The answer is in one place in the text. Words from the question and words that answer the question are often "right there" in the same sentence.

Think & Search

The answer is in the text. Readers need to "think and search," or put together different parts of the text, to find the answer. The answer can be within a paragraph, across paragraphs, or even across chapters and books.

In My Head

On My Own

The answer is not in the text. Readers need to use their own ideas and experiences to answer the question.

Author & Me

The answer is not in the text. To answer the question, readers need to think about how the text and what they already know fit together.

SOURCE: From *Super QAR for Testwise Students: Grade 8 Teacher Guide* by Kathy Au and Taffy Raphael. Used by permission of The McGraw-Hill Companies, Inc.

Mr. Zucco: Today we are going to continue reading about our community here in Laketown. Some of you have seen this brochure before. It was made by the Chamber of Commerce to help people learn about our town. I'd like you to take a few minutes to look it over. Be sure to pay attention to the illustrations and captions too.

The students spend the next few minutes looking over the brochure and quietly pointing out the things they notice to each other.

Mr. Zucco: Let's turn to the section that is titled "Housing." Raise your hand if you would like to volunteer to begin reading the first paragraph of this section while the rest of us follow along. (*Keenan raises his hand to volunteer.*) Thank you, Keenan.

Keenan: Housing. Much of the housing in Laketown reflects the Victorian style that was popular among the lumber barons who established the town in the 1900s. Tall peaked roofs tower over the large porches that are so perfect for hot summer evenings spent watching the neighborhood children play on the front lawn.

Mr. Zucco:	Let's stop there for a moment and talk about what we have learned so far about how houses were built here in Laketown. Are the roofs on the houses flat? (*Several children raise their hands.*) Crystal, what do you think?
Crystal:	No.
Mr. Zucco:	That's right, Crystal. Tell us how you knew that was the answer.
Crystal:	It says the houses have peaked roofs, so they can't be flat. That means that the roof has a point like this. (*She demonstrates with her hands.*)
Mr. Zucco:	How did Crystal know that the roofs weren't flat? Brian?
Brian:	It says it right on the page.
Mr. Zucco:	Did we have to look anywhere else? (*Several students shake their head to indicate no.*) The authors tell us the answer right there in that sentence. Now let's look at the chart I've placed here on the wall. Remember how we talked about how answers can be in the book or in our head? Which type is this? Amy?
Amy:	In the Book because it says it right on the page.
Mr. Zucco:	I'm glad that you remembered that, Amy. Now today I want to show you how there are two kinds of answers that can be found in the book. When the author tells us the answer in one sentence, we can call that a Right There answer. (*He points to the box labeled Right There on the wall chart.*) Here I've written a reminder to us that answers to questions that we can find in one sentence are Right There. Let's take that sentence that Crystal found in the brochure and write it under the Right There title I have written on this page on the easel. (*He writes, "Tall peaked roofs tower over the large porches."*) Raise your hand if you'd like to read the next paragraph in the brochure. Josh?
Josh:	Many of these homes are located in the center of town on Elm Boulevard and Oak Street. Most have recently been restored to their original designs and colors and have such modern necessities as gas heat and air-conditioning. Tours of these homes are held every spring during the local garden club's annual garden festival.
Mr. Zucco:	Thanks, Josh. Who would like to continue? Kelsey?
Kelsey:	In a newer development in Laketown, homes have also been built using the Victorian style that was so popular when the town was founded. These homes can be found in the marina section of town, mostly along Little Station Street and Harbor Lights Avenue. Walking through this area on a warm summer night is a must for all visitors. This area is also usually included in local tours of the marina district.
Mr. Zucco:	Let's stop here for a moment. We know that Laketown has two areas with Victorian houses. Can visitors to our town ever get to see them? (*Several hands go up.*) Alex?

Alex: Sure. It says that there are tours during the garden festival and that you can go to the other one if you go on a tour of the marina district.

Mr. Zucco: I see. Were those answers found in the book or in your head, Alex?

Alex: They are right in the book. (*He points to the passages.*)

Mr. Zucco: Okay. Are they right there in one sentence, like the last one we looked at?

Alex: No, you have to look in these two different places.

Mr. Zucco: Let's look at this chart I've made again. We know that the answer to this question is in the book. We also know that you have to put information together to find the whole answer. These kinds of answers are called Think and Search. (*He shows this category on the chart.*) I've also written a reminder here that these kinds of answers are in the story but that you have to put different parts of the writing together to find the answer. Let's write the two sentences with the answer on the easel here. (*He writes, "Tours of these homes are held every spring during the local garden club's annual garden festival" and "This area is also usually included in local tours of the marina district."*)

We are learning a lot about the houses in our town. Let's read this last paragraph together. Would someone like to read? Crystal?

Crystal: The founders of Laketown built their homes for beauty and also to fit with the changing climate of this lakeshore community. The more recent additions of modern heating units, air-conditioning, and other innovations have only made them more livable for current residents.

Mr. Zucco: Thank you, Crystal. Let's all think for a minute about what we now know about houses in Laketown. What makes these Victorian homes such a good match for the climate we live in?

Keenan: Well, it says that they have big porches for watching kids play on warm nights in the summer, and that would be a good way to stay cool in the summer. It gets really hot sometimes in the summer.

Alex: Yes, and the air-conditioning would really help in the summer too. It gets so hot sometimes that I can't even sleep unless we turn on the air-conditioning.

Kelsey: But it gets really cold here in the winter, too, so having new heaters is really important.

Josh: Yes, plus my mom told me that having peaked roofs, like this brochure says, is really important. Then the snow will slide off your roof. Otherwise it will get really heavy and your roof will cave in.

Mr. Zucco: Good thinking! Did the authors use sentences that tell you how the climate fits with the houses in Laketown? Amy?

Amy: Not really, but they did give us clues, like saying you need heaters and air-conditioners. Plus, I live here, too, so I know that we get lots of snow and it gets hot in the summer.

Mr. Zucco: So, for this question, did you find the answer in the book or in your head?

Amy: In my head.

Mr. Zucco: Yes. Let's look at our chart again. These kinds of answers are called Author and Me. The answer isn't right in the text. You have to put together what you know and what the author tells you. Let's write this answer on our flip chart. (*Paraphrasing, he writes, "We know there is lots of snow in Laketown, and it can get very cold and hot here. The author tells us there are big porches for hot summer nights, air-conditioning, and heaters in the homes, and the roofs are peaked. We know peaked roofs allow snow to slide off."*)

Mr. Zucco asks a few more questions that he has constructed in advance to give students practice with this category of relationships. As the lesson ends, he helps students begin to understand the final category of relationships.

Mr. Zucco: Before we end for today, let's just talk about a few more things. When I walk by the Victorian homes in the center of town, I always wonder what it might have been like to live there nearly a hundred years ago. What do you think it might have been like?

Alex: I think it would have been fun because they played really fun games in the yard that my grandpa told me about when we went to the museum.

Kelsey: I think it would be hard. They didn't even have dishwashers, so you'd have to do all the dishes in a sink or tub. My brother and I have to do the dishes after dinner, and we'd hate that!

Mr. Zucco: Let's take one last look at this chart on the wall. To answer my last question about living in those homes a hundred years ago, where did you get your answer? Was it in the book or in your head?

Josh: It was in my head because there aren't any sentences that talk about that.

Mr. Zucco: Good point. Does the author tell you anything about what it was like living in these houses a hundred years ago?

Alex: No, not really. I knew that stuff because my grandpa and I saw some toys in the museum and he told me about it.

Mr. Zucco: Okay. So you could really answer that question even without reading this brochure, couldn't you? These kinds of answers are called On My Own.

(*He points to the appropriate box on the chart.*) These answers come from what you already know, not what the author tells you. Let's write Alex's and Kelsey's answers on the chart paper on the easel. (*He writes, "At the museum, Alex's grandpa told him about fun games that were played a hundred years ago. Kelsey knew that dishes had to be washed in a sink or tub."*) Now here is a list of questions that I've made up about our reading today. This time I've written the answers too! I'd like you to go back to your group tables and work together. Next to each answer, I'd like you to write which type it is. Let me know if you need any help. Nice work today.

Case Study 8.1: Post-Lesson Reflection ◆

Mr. Zucco was very pleased with this lesson. His reason for selecting QAR had been, in part, to begin moving students beyond answering just yes or no to questions. Although this was a beginning exercise, he was encouraged to hear the students mixing their own experiences and background knowledge with what the authors told them explicitly in the text. This was particularly true in their brief discussion about the match between the climate and home design in Laketown. He is now even more convinced that the QAR model will prove to be a useful tool for helping his students "dig deeper" as they think about and respond to text.

Mr. Zucco also found this lesson helpful to his own development as a teacher. He had suspected that one reason his students responded at such a literal level to questions about text related to his own question-asking skills. As he reflected on his own teaching, he began to see that the questions he posed to students, as well as those often included in the teacher guides, did not always provide students with opportunities to analyze, synthesize, or use other forms of higher-order thinking. Explicitly using QAR was helping him explore the relationship of questions and answers for himself and then transfer this understanding into more helpful experiences for his students (Reutzel & Cooter, 1992).

The objective Mr. Zucco designed for this lesson involved helping his students understand the language of QAR, categorize their responses to questions, and show their sources. Given that this was only their second lesson, he was happy with the results. He knows that the students will need many more experiences with this model before it will be incorporated fully into their vocabulary, routines, and schema.

As he looks ahead, Mr. Zucco plans to provide more teacher-directed experiences using QAR. He will also arrange for more independent practice so that he can see how students understand the use of this model (Ruddell, 1999). He will deliberately use both narrative and expository texts. He wants students to recognize and explore the relationships of questions and answers in all types of text.

Finally, Mr. Zucco hopes to move beyond teacher-centered instruction in QAR and toward integration of this model and language into daily discussions of text. Whenever they are working on text comprehension, in science or geography or with a novel, he would like his students to see the question-answer relationships inherent in text, as well as the sources for answers, and to use the QAR language to describe them, even when question-answer relationships are not the focus of a lesson or discussion.

The Stages of QAR

Mr. Zucco began by teaching the relationships between questions and answers quite explicitly. As his students begin to understand this process and use the language to describe their thinking, Mr. Zucco will spend less time teaching it and more time using it for class discussion and their written responses to text. Thus, the ultimate purpose of QAR is to use it to think and talk about text. Consequently, we will describe how QAR is introduced to students, assuming that once taught, it will be used for multiple purposes.

Use of the QAR model will assist you in posing better questions to your students. Your own understanding of question-answer relationships will help you develop questions that promote higher-order thinking skills.

Often when working with models, we have a tendency to see them as a step-by-step process. We do step A first, followed in tight sequence by step B. In some cases this may in fact be quite helpful. This discussion will describe a common sequence for introducing QAR (Raphael, 1986; Reutzel & Cooter, 1992). However, once students have fully understood the process, it can be used very flexibly to frame the relationship between questions and answers rather than as steps to be followed in a specific sequence. In fact, later you may even design lessons that emphasize only one or two categories or that use QAR only incidentally as part of a text discussion or written response.

The QAR model consists of two broad categories and four subcategories. To teach the process itself, Raphael (1986) recommends starting with the broad categories, In the Book and In My Head. Once students have gained an understanding of them, you can introduce the four subcategories: Right There, Think and Search, Author and Me, and On My Own, shown in Figure 8.3.

Figure 8.3 QAR

A Sequence for Initial Instruction

Step 1: Introduction of broad categories

Using a preselected text or one prepared in advance for this lesson, introduce students to In the Book and In My Head.

In the Book: Readers are asked to locate or recall information using what the author tells them.

In My Head: Readers answer using their own background knowledge and understanding as well as what is suggested by the text. Sometimes the answer is independent of the text.

Step 2: Introduction of the In the Book subcategories

When asking students about the text, distinguish between the two text-dependent types of question-answer relationships:

Right There: Readers can locate the answer in one line of the text.

Think and Search: Readers can locate parts of the answer in different places within the text.

Step 3: Introduction of the In My Head subcategories

When asking students about answers that require the use of their own background knowledge and understanding, distinguish between those that are somewhat text dependent and those that are completely independent of the text.

Author and Me: Readers use information found in the text as well as in their background to make interpretations or applications.

On My Own: Readers rely solely on their own background knowledge, independent of the text.

SOURCE: Adapted from Reutzel & Cooter, 1992; Raphael, 1986.

In the Book

In the Book relationships are just what the name implies. The reader is asked to locate information that the author explicitly tells the reader (Raphael, 1986). The questions asked can be answered by surveying the information provided by the author. In the case of Mr. Zucco, questions about how the author describes the homes and the streets they are located on all fit in this category.

Teaching this category first has the advantage of familiarity. From their earliest experiences with text, learners are asked questions at this level. You may recall these experiences with books yourself when a parent asked you to look at the illustrations and name the objects there or to read a brief description and tell what the character did. The source for your answers was on the page itself, and you were able to locate it there.

As a teacher, you may want to prepare some passages for your students to read in advance or select a passage from a text that is part of your curriculum. This text should supply students with answers to your questions that can be found in either one sentence or in multiple sentences in the text. The key here is that the relationship between the questions and the answers should be explicit. Students should not have to interpret what the author is saying. Questions such as, When can people tour these homes? would work here because the answer can be found right in the text. A question such as, Why would people want to tour these Victorian homes? would require too much interpretation to fit under this category even if a part of the answer could be found in the text Mr. Zucco provided.

Once the text has been selected, it may be helpful to put it on an overhead, Smart Board screen, or piece of chart paper for everyone to see at the same time. After you and the students have read the text, begin asking the questions you have prepared in advance to fit this category. Following each answer, ask the students to tell you the source of their answer. When a student says, "It's right on the page" or gives some similar response, introduce the language of QAR by reframing the statement into one like, "Oh, so you found that answer in the book," which provides you with an opportunity to talk about the text itself—what the author explicitly tells the reader— as one source for answers.

Of course, many answers to questions we ask about readings are not found explicitly in the text itself but require readers to combine what they already know with what the author tells them. In some cases, the answers do not even require the learner to read the text. In these instances, the relationship falls into the next broad category: In My Head. Early in the teaching of QAR, it is important to help students to distinguish these relationships from the In the Book types. In fact, you may want to intersperse these types of questions and answers in the initial exercises, asking students questions from both categories until you have evidence of their understanding and their ability to distinguish between them.

In My Head

Oftentimes as we are reading and trying to locate information, we are called on to make interpretations using our own background knowledge and understanding.

In some instances, the author may provide some information to use in finding an answer, but in others the author simply does not make the answer explicit, or the question itself is only loosely connected to the text. For example, when Mr. Zucco asked students about the relationship between the design of Victorian homes and their suitability to the climate of Laketown, students were able to combine information given to them by the author (peaked roofs) with their prior understanding (the snow we get in Laketown could collapse a home with flat roofs). However, Mr. Zucco's final question about what it might have been like to live in a Victorian home required the students to rely primarily on their own background knowledge to formulate an answer. In fact, he could have asked this final question before the students had even read the text.

Students will also have some level of familiarity with this category of relationships. You may recall early reading experiences such as looking at an illustration of someone walking into a barn with a pail and being asked what the person will do in the barn. However, unlike In the Book relationships, these require more application and analysis. As a consequence, they frequently seem to be more difficult for students, especially if their reading experiences have generally required literal responses to text. It may be helpful to provide many examples of In My Head questions to give students a thorough understanding of these types of relationships and the sources of the answers.

As a teacher, you will want to select or prepare in advance many questions that can be classified as In My Head. Again, in the initial sessions these should be interspersed with In the Book questions. One useful way to begin is to ask questions related to the text before the students actually look at or read it. A question like Why do you think the older homes in Laketown were built as they were? would work well. As students begin to answer, you can assist them in understanding rather easily that their responses are independent of the text itself and dependent on their own prior understanding. Such questions also have the potential advantage of setting a purpose for their reading, namely, seeing what the text may add to their understanding.

It may prove helpful to list the questions and student responses on an overhead, Smart Board screen, or chart paper. As responses are recorded, you can begin to label them using the QAR language, further helping your students distinguish between categories of questions and answers and the location of the answers. If they can also see a chart that provides a key to the various categories, students can easily sort out the various types of questions and answers.

After you are comfortable with your students' understanding of In the Book and In My Head categories, you will want to move on to the subcategories, beginning with Right There and Think and Search.

Right There

Question-and-answer relationships fitting into the Right There category are the most literal types. Answers to questions can be found "right there" in one sentence of the text (Raphael, 1986). Thus the source for these answers is what the author tells the reader, and typically, the reader is required only to locate or recall the information (Ruddell, 1999). For example, Mr. Zucco asked the class whether the roofs on the homes in Laketown were flat. Crystal and Brian explained that they were not. As he asked them for their source or proof, they explained by pointing out the sentence in the brochure that said roofs on these homes were in fact peaked, and therefore they could not be flat.

It should be noted here that the literal nature of Right There questions and answers should not diminish their value. Locating and recalling information that is explicitly stated in text is a valuable skill, both for reading and for using text to learn about content. For example, being able to locate or recall an author's description of the physical characteristics of a story character will contribute a great deal to an appreciation of the role of that character in a story. Likewise, it would be important to be able to locate and recall the parts of an amoeba described in a science text. It may be most helpful here to remember that Right There questions and answers represent one type of relationship and that equal time needs to be given to the others if we want our students to gain facility with all of them. To monitor your own use of QAR, it may be helpful to keep an informal tally of the types of questions you ask, with an eye to achieving balance.

Sometimes Right There questions are used to do instant checks of student comprehension. Often in group reading situations, the teacher will stop periodically and ask students a question that relies on the location or recall of information just provided in the text. This can provide the teacher with useful information when done as a review or as a way of clarifying understanding. In fact, you have probably been encouraged to do this very thing in coursework and textbooks on classroom management procedures. However, a practice we would discourage is the frequent and abrupt use of Right There questions for drilling students or checking for attentiveness. Reading should not feel like a testing situation. In fact, such an atmosphere might work to weaken comprehension of text and should be avoided. However, when used for important purposes and when done in moderation, Right There questions and answers can be helpful for students and teachers alike.

Think and Search

Question-and-answer relationships fitting into the Think and Search category require the reader to look for parts of the answer in more than one place in the text. The source for the answers is again what the author tells the reader. However, readers will find parts of the answer in more than one sentence and then will typically have to make some inferences or draw a conclusion to put together an answer (Ruddell, 1999). In Case Study 8.1, Mr. Zucco asked his students when visitors might be able to visit the two sections of town built in the Victorian style. Alex said that they could visit during the garden tour and when they were taking a tour of the marina district. His conclusion was based on the information presented by the author in two different sections of the text.

Understanding that text is constructed in this way, seeing connections between isolated facts in text, and understanding the need to actively look for information in a text are important skills for readers. For example, you might assign your students a geography study of a particular state. While reading a Web site that provides information on the topography of the state of California, it would be important for your students to continue looking for information beyond a description of the beach areas. To be accurate in describing the state, they would need to put information together from parts of the text that describe the mountainous areas, the desert areas, and other features. Likewise, when students are reading a novel and are asked to describe the setting, they might well have to look in several parts of the story to describe its multiple components: a house, a yard, a city park, and so forth.

As you introduce your students to QAR, you will want to demonstrate in a physical way the need to put information together. One way is to put the text on an overhead or Smart Board screen and simply underline the different parts of the answer with a marker. Another way would be to give students a photocopy of the text. As they are reading and locating parts of an answer, instruct them to underline the parts lightly with pencil. As you talk about the sources for the answer together, they can check their own underlining, adding or deleting as necessary.

Perhaps the biggest difference between this category of questions and answers and the Right There type is the readers' need to draw conclusions or make inferences about gathered pieces of information as they construct a response. In the example about California, students might be asked to describe the topography of the state. A student who responds, "California has it all!" has drawn a conclusion by putting together specific and explicit information provided throughout the text by the author of the Web site.

After students have demonstrated that they understand the subcategories of In the Text questions, you can introduce them to the two subcategories of In My Head.

Author and Me

In My Head question-and-answer relationships that fit into the Author and Me subcategory use information found in the text plus information in the reader's own background and understanding. Consequently, these types of relationships may require learners to interpret or apply what they learn from the text (Jacobson, 1998).

Mr. Zucco asked the students why the housing described in the brochure would be a good match for the climate of Laketown. The author said this is the case but did not give a detailed explanation. In responding, the students applied their own experience with the snowfall in Laketown to what the author told them. For example, Josh said that Laketown has lots of snow and that it can get very heavy on rooftops. He also recalled his mother's telling him that heavy snow would make a flat roof collapse. In responding, he applies this background information to the detail in the brochure: the roofs in Laketown are peaked, not flat. Using his background information and the information from the text, Josh has concluded that the peaked roofs on the homes in Laketown make them a good match for the climate because the snow will roll off the roofs.

As you help your students understand and use Author and Me questions and answers, it will be necessary to keep them focused on using the information provided by the author. Our own classroom experiences are filled with discussion moments only marginally related to the text itself. Although such diversions have some value in and of themselves, they may not increase students' understanding or use of QAR. Asking students to "prove" they got part of the answer from the text by, for example, physically pointing to it will help them stay focused on the text and ultimately on the relationships.

On My Own

As teachers, we often want to help our students think about the content of a text we are using by asking questions that rely solely on their own background knowledge or understanding (Gunning, 1992; Ruddell, 1999). Frequently these are the kinds of questions we ask before reading a text or as we talk about it afterwards. After they had read the brochure, Mr. Zucco asked his students what it might have been like to live in a Victorian home. He might just as easily have asked this question before the students read the text, given that their responses would be based on their own experiences rather than on what the author told them.

As with all the categories of QAR, as you introduce students to the On My Own subcategory, you will want to ask them for the source for each of their responses. It will also be advisable to write each question and response and then label them on your chart or overhead to further cement the idea that an important source for answering some questions is the reader, not the author.

The On My Own category of relationships can be beneficial as a gauge of what students know and understand before reading the text: their prior knowledge. In many cases, we cannot fully comprehend a text without some level of prior knowledge. For example, students reading a book such as *Number the Stars,* by Lois Lowry, would need to have some understanding of the context for this story: the persecution of Jewish people during World War II. Asking On My Own questions before the reading would allow you to evaluate your students' background knowledge and then make adjustments before or during the reading of the book to increase their potential for comprehension. You might discover that students' prior knowledge in this area is so weak that you want to supplement it before you begin reading the text.

Yet another way to use On My Own is to ask questions that use students' prior knowledge to set the stage or purpose for reading. Asking at the beginning of the daily lesson what students know about the holocaust would provide them with a mental framework for the reading. As they read, they would be prepared to look for information that expands their current understanding.

The most important thing to emphasize with your students is that the relationship between some questions and answers is dependent on one specific source—themselves.

Two Additional Thoughts

Although QAR implies that the teacher ask a question, we would urge you to consider framing some of your "questions" to students differently. Oftentimes, a question, such as Do you like Victorian homes? can be answered simply with a yes or a no. Rephrasing it as a request, such as "Tell me what you like about Victorian homes," is more expansive. It allows students to respond in multiple ways, including specific information: "My favorite part is the big porches. They would be fun to play games on, and you could have a porch swing." As you construct potential questions in advance of a reading, try framing them in this manner. (Case Study 8.2 provides more examples.)

One other aspect of question and answer behaviors that is worth mentioning here is the importance of "wait time." This involves asking a question and then giving your students time to think before responding. We teachers often call on the first student who raises a hand, which results in a kind of rapid-fire discussion. Providing students with time to think before you call on anyone will increase their participation. It may also let students know that we appreciate thoughtful and reflective responses.

Case Study 8.2: Middle School, Science

Ms. Huizenga teaches a seventh-grade general science course at a small private school located in a large metropolitan area. She has developed a unit on the body systems with a particular focus on how these systems can be affected by environmental conditions. Her primary goal is to have students understand each system. In addition, she wants them to see how these systems can be influenced by diverse factors, such as access to recreational opportunities for exercise or diseases induced by air pollution. In part, her aim is to help students develop healtful practices that will protect and strengthen the body systems they are learning about. This unit has allowed her to address several science content standards and benchmarks, as well as those that focus on improving content area reading—a particular goal in her school.

Ms. Huizenga's students are studying the segment of her unit dealing with the respiratory system. A small group is considering how asthma, a disease impacting children in disproportionate numbers in their city, might be influenced by environmental conditions. These students are also interested in learning how this disease can be managed. For today's small-group lesson, Ms. Huizenga has used a variety of sources to construct an information sheet on asthma, its impact on individuals, and its management (see Figure 8.4).

Earlier in the year, Ms. Huizenga noted that a number of her students were struggling with the structure of the informational text that dominates her content area readings. She believed that student reading levels were adequate and that they could understand science concepts that were presented orally. However, she suspected that her students had not had adequate work with informational text in the past. In particular, they seemed to have difficulty responding to questions beyond the Right There level. Therefore, Ms. Huizenga has worked with her students using the QAR model with their textbook and primary source readings. As a result, her students have become far better consumers of informational text. Specifically, they are able to use the QAR model and related terminology to find information in a passage and connect it with other parts of a reading. In addition, they are better

---

Figure 8.4 | **Ms. Huizenga's Asthma Information Sheet**

What is asthma?

According to the American Lung Association, "Asthma is a chronic inflammation of the airways with reversible episodes of obstruction, caused by an increased reaction of the airways to various stimuli. Asthma breathing problems usually happen in 'episodes' but the inflammation underlying asthma is continuous" (American Lung Association, 2005).

What is an asthma episode?

"An asthma episode is a series of events that result in narrowed airways. These include: swelling of the lining, tightening of the muscle, and increased secretion of mucus in the airway. The narrowed airway is responsible for the difficulty in breathing with the familiar 'wheeze'" (American Lung Association, 2005).

What can cause an asthma episode?

Many things can initiate an asthma episode. Some people have episodes that are induced by exertion—such as exercise or participating in a sport. For others, episodes can be triggered by a virus. Environmental conditions can also promote asthma reactions. These conditions can range from pollens released into the air to pollution from automobiles or smoke.

What are the treatments for asthma?

Currently there is no cure for asthma. Individuals who live with asthma need to learn to manage this disease—both long term and during episodes.

A variety of options exist.

Doctors: It is important for individuals with asthma to see their doctors regularly. At these meetings, doctors can monitor asthma symptoms, medications, and treatment options.

Medications: Many individuals with asthma manage the disorder with medications. These can range from daily pills and inhalers (medication delivered in vaporized form and inhaled directly into the lungs) to injections of steroids.

Asthma equipment:

Peak flow meter—a tool that measures the lung capacity of asthmatics. These meters vary in size and shape. In all types, the individual blows into one end of the instrument. The air flow is then measured by the meter. A doctor helps the individual interpret the results. Typically, scores fall within three color-coded ranges: green (healthy), yellow (caution), and red (danger). Depending on the results, individuals follow the plan developed by their doctor.

Nebulizer—a machine that delivers vaporized medication into the lungs of asthmatics as they inhale through a mouthpiece.

Rescue inhaler—a small instrument used to introduce medication into the lungs of an asthmatic either during an asthma episode or prior to its onset, as directed by the individual's physician.

Environmental issues affect asthma.

Since many asthma episodes are triggered by environmental conditions, individuals are urged to avoid or minimize certain types of exposure. In particular, exposure to smoke, pollen, dust, mold, and animal dander can be problematic and should be avoided by those who live with asthma.

---

at connecting information between texts and using their prior knowledge of a topic. Pleased with these results, Ms. Huizenga has continued to emphasize QAR whenever reading is done in her class.

In this Case Study, Ms. Huizenga is working with students who have decided to use the relationship between asthma and the environment as the focus of a project on the respiratory system. Although she has many content-related learning objectives for this unit, we will list only the objective related to her use of the QAR model:

The learner will use QAR to demonstrate comprehension while reading and discussing text about asthma.

Ms. Huizenga and the five students meet at a small table in the back of the room. Behind them is a chart (similar to Figure 8.2) they developed when learning about QAR earlier in the year. It shows each of the relationships and continues to be used as a reference tool for students as they read and discuss text.

Ms. Huizenga: Today we are going to spend a little bit of time reading about asthma to help you get started on your project. I have an information sheet we are going to read today, but before we do that, I thought it would be helpful to explore what you already know about this disease.

Drew: Well, part of the reason that I wanted to do this project on asthma is because my sister has asthma and I already know some things about it, but I also thought it might be good to learn more about it too.

Betsy: I know a lot of kids at this school who have asthma. One of the girls on my softball team had an asthma episode during one of our games, and I thought it would be good to know how to help her if it ever happened again.

Michael: I read once in the newspaper that kids in this city have a lot more problems with asthma than kids in other places, and they said it had a lot to do with the air pollution from all the cars and buses. I want to know if that's true, and if it is, we should do something to change that.

Ms. Huizenga: So we know that asthma affects a lot of people, and according to what Michael is telling us, that may be because we have more air pollution in this city than in other places. If that is true, how do you see this as related to the respiratory system?

Nicky: Well, air pollution is obviously not good for our lungs, which are important parts of the respiratory system. I don't know for sure, but maybe it's the dirty air that causes asthma, or it could just make it worse. I know my friend Meg can't be around people who are smoking or even around campfires because they cause her to have asthma problems.

Ms. Huizenga: That seems to be a good connection between what we are learning about the respiratory system and asthma. I just want to point out here too that it is clear that you already know a lot about asthma. Using our QAR language for this, we could say that your answers to my questions were developed on your own, right? As we read this information sheet, I just want to remind you to use the question-answer relationships we have explored to help you understand this sheet and increase your understanding of asthma. Let's go ahead and start reading. (*She distributes the information sheet to the students.*) I think it might be useful if we start by reading parts of it together out loud. Any volunteers?

Ian: Sure. I'll start. (*He reads.*) What is asthma? According to the American Lung Association, "Asthma is a chronic inflammation of the airways with reversible episodes of obstruction, caused by an increased reaction of the airways to various stimuli. Asthma breathing problems usually happen in 'episodes' but the inflammation underlying asthma is continuous."

Ms. Huizenga: Okay, let's stop there for a minute. That definition is quite a mouthful. Let's see if we all understand it before we go on. Tell me what you think this definition of asthma is saying.

Drew: One thing it says right there in the first sentence is that it is an inflammation of the airways. I know that sometimes when things get inflamed, they swell up, because that happened to my toe one time when I had an infection.

Betsy: It also says that it is chronic. I have chronic bronchitis, which means that I keep getting it. So that must mean that the inflammation keeps happening—which seems to make sense.

Ms. Huizenga: Nice work there. You've said that the author told you that it is a chronic inflammation. And then you used your own experiences with a toe and repeated bronchitis to figure out what that phrase means.

Ian: It also says that there are reversible episodes of obstruction. I was watching this show on television last night, and this lady was choking. The doctor said that she had an obstruction in her throat, instead of just saying that she was choking. So, an obstruction must mean that there is something in the way so that the air can't get through, and with asthma it can be reversed so that you can breathe again.

Nicky: It also says that inflammation is caused by a reaction to various stimuli. We learned about stimuli last month when we where talking about things like food and salivation. That makes me think that things in the environment could be the stimuli; things like smoke or other pollution.

Ms. Huizenga: Makes sense to me. You've done a nice job again of using the words on the sheet and also using your own experiences to figure this one out. Let's try reading the next two sections silently, and then we can talk about them. (*The students read the sections entitled "What is an asthma episode?" and "What can cause an asthma episode?"*)

Drew: Well one thing I noticed is that the author says here that an asthma episode is a series of events that result in narrowed airways. So, if you put that together with what they said before about the inflammation, it would mean that the airways swell up and that's what makes it hard to breathe during an asthma episode.

Michael: Yes, and it also says here that one thing that can trigger an asthma episode is air pollution. That fits with what Nicky was saying earlier about how smoke and other kinds of pollution can be the stimuli for an asthma episode.

Betsy: Right. Of course it also mentions that other things that aren't part of the environment can cause asthma episodes too, but now we know that air pollution is one of the things that cause people to have an asthma episode.

Ms. Huizenga: Again, you are doing a really fine job of reading carefully and putting information from different sections together to find what you are looking for. Now I'm curious. Does what you have read so far tell you what causes asthma or how to cure it?

Ian: Well, it doesn't really say that. So far, this sheet just says what causes someone to have an asthma episode, but it doesn't really say what causes the disease itself or how you would cure it.

Ms. Huizenga: Try reading this next section with those questions in mind. Again, let's just each read silently. (*They all read the section entitled "What are the treatments for asthma?" on their own.*)

Nicky: Well, in the first line of this section it answers part of that question you asked us to think about. The author tells you that there is no cure for asthma. It doesn't really say what causes someone to have it, though, and I am guessing that they probably don't know, and that is why they don't have a cure for it.

Michael: Yeah, the rest of it talks about how to manage asthma, not how to cure it. And when you manage something, you are controlling it. Like my dad is the manager of his department at work, and he just tries to keep things moving along and avoid problems. So, the author gives ways to prevent problems with asthma and what to do if you have an episode.

Betsy: Right, and the author does say that avoiding certain things in the environment that can trigger an asthma episode is one way to manage asthma. That could be the focus of our project. We could talk about how air pollution causes asthma episodes and what people could do to help eliminate some of those things in our environment.

Ian: We could talk about how air pollution impacts the lungs and other parts of the respiratory system for all of us but especially how and why it can be a problem for someone with asthma. Then we could talk about what we can do about it.

Ms. Huizenga: Sounds to me like your reading of this information sheet has given you some good links between our study of the respiratory system and your project on asthma. I think you are ready to continue. One last thing I'd urge you to do is to go to the Web site for the American Lung Association that is listed on the information sheet to get even more information on asthma and its impact on the respiratory system.

Case Study 8.2: Post-Lesson Reflection

In this lesson, Ms. Huizenga demonstrated her beliefs that students need to master seventh-grade science content and that she has a responsibility to teach reading in her content area. Her use of the QAR model was designed to do both. Although Ms. Huizenga had often heard the saying that students learn to read in the first few grades of school and then read to learn in middle and high school, she did not embrace this way of thinking, nor did her school district. Students at all levels need opportunities to enhance their reading skills. While many students are excellent consumers of narrative stories (a particular focus in many elementary classrooms), they struggle with informational text. Narrative and informational texts do not have the same structure, and each needs to be learned for competent reading fluency and comprehension. Given that many content areas at the secondary level rely heavily on such informational texts, it is imperative that secondary teachers use various reading models and strategies to ensure their students' comprehension of these texts.

Ms. Huizenga's use of this model sounded quite different from the use of QAR in Case Study 8.1. In her classroom, students talked about question-answer relationships with some references to the terminology used in the QAR model she was employing, but they did so very informally. The students in Case Study 8.1 were learning to use the model. To ensure clarity and accurate use of the model, repeated use of the terminology of QAR was important. Ms. Huizenga's students had been using the model for quite some time and had integrated it into the way they read and discussed text. As a result, they were able to talk casually about question-answer relationships. Second, secondary students can sometimes respond to repeated uses of terminology, such as On My Own and In My Head, with something less than enthusiasm. Developmentally, they can benefit from an initial use of such terms and phrases, but once they have integrated the underlying concepts, they may prefer to express them in words they find more appropriate.

This case study also demonstrated clearly the use of On My Own questions and answers to set the stage for reading the text (Raphael, 1986). At the beginning of the lesson, Ms. Huizenga told the students to explore with each other what they already knew about asthma from their own experiences before they read the information sheet. This allowed the ensuing discussion to both frame the reading and activate students' prior knowledge of the topic. Both are important ways to strengthen comprehension of text to be read. We encourage the use of On My Own questions and answers in this way when appropriate.

Finally, Ms. Huizenga encouraged students' responses by avoiding yes-no questions. For example, after the students had read the first section of the information sheet,

Ms. Huizenga said, "Tell me what you think this definition of asthma is saying." This prompted the students to actively explore what the author said and to use their own experiences to enrich the text. In contrast, a question such as "Does the author provide a definition for asthma?" could result in a simple yes response that functions at the lowest level of most taxonomies of thinking about and responding to text. If you want your students to respond at higher levels, practice reframing your questions.

Brief Background of QAR

In response to what was considered a lack of research on children's question-related behaviors, Taffy Raphael (1982, 1986) developed QAR to improve students' abilities in answering comprehension questions. QAR was based largely on the work of Pearson and Johnson (1978), who had developed a question taxonomy that suggested that questions and answers should be related "to both the text and the reader's background knowledge" (Raphael, 1986, p. 516). Pearson and Johnson grouped questions and answers into three categories: Text Explicit, Text Implicit, and

Secondary students are often expected to read informational text in both primary source readings and textbooks. QAR can provide secondary teachers with an important model for helping their students to be better consumers of this type of text.

Script Implicit. Raphael altered these terms to make them more user friendly for children. She called them Right There, Think and Search, and On My Own. The purpose of QAR was to teach the relationships between questions and answers, as well as where to locate appropriate responses to questions. In exploring these relationships, students could also develop strategies for finding answers (Raphael, 1982; Reutzel & Cooter, 1992).

After her introduction of QAR, Raphael (1986) modified the terms and the process, in large part on the basis of input of teachers who had used QAR with their own students. In the revised version, she expanded the subcategories of question-and-answer relationships in the model from three to four, adding Author and You, now called Author and Me. In addition, she changed Think and Search to Putting It Together. This label was thought to avoid the confusion some children experienced when they found answers without having to search extensively. However, in recent publications, she has returned to Think and Search for this subcategory (Raphael & Au, 2005). In the revised version of QAR, Raphael also discussed how the model would work differently for students of various ages and how the use of QAR helps students gain a better understanding of text structures, such as cause and effect (Raphael, 1986; Raphael & Au, 2005).

QAR and Research on Teaching

The early research on the effectiveness of QAR was conducted in the 1980s, when the model was developed. This research showed that students using QAR outperformed others in answering reading comprehension questions based on text (Ezell, Hunsicker, & Quinque, 1996). In addition, students using QAR tended to be more strategic readers when reading and answering questions. They demonstrated behaviors that showed an ability to consider various sources of information—the text and their own background knowledge (Raphael, 1986).

The early research also indicated that the amount and type of instruction using QAR varied on the basis of students' age. For example, a first-grade class might benefit most from concentration on two categories (In the Book and In My Head) for an extended period. However, an eighth-grade class might learn the categories in one or two sessions and then focus on exploring text structures using QAR (Raphael, 1986).

More recent research has focused on maintenance (whether or not students continue to use QAR over time) and on whether teacher or peer assisted instruction is more effective. In a study conducted by Ezell et al. (1996), two groups of students were observed during fourth and fifth grades. These researchers found that the students were indeed able to maintain the use of QAR over time. In another study (Ezell, Hunsicker, & Quinque, 1997), the same researchers determined that QAR instruction could be effective in increasing reading comprehension regardless of whether the instruction was delivered through peer- or teacher-assisted procedures. However, the authors of this study indicated that the teacher-assisted procedure involved students more actively, by having them come up with and discuss questions about text, than did a more traditional approach, in which the teacher asks the questions and students answer them.

Some recent research has shifted to the application of QAR to content area reading and the use of expository texts. McIntosh and Draper (1996) have described their successful efforts using QAR to help students read math text and applying QAR to logic problems and general problem solving in mathematics. Similarly, Ouzts (1998) has reported positively on QAR as applied to social studies. Furthermore, Ezell et al. (1996) found that students using QAR were able to answer questions about "fact-focused" and "character-focused" text equally well (p. 66). These reports demonstrate the versatility of QAR: It is effective in various content areas and with both expository and narrative text.

On the other hand, Ezell et al. (1996) have suggested that student effectiveness in answering On My Own questions based on their background knowledge is not as well demonstrated or successful. Even after instruction in QAR, many students continue to have difficulty answering questions that rely on their own prior understanding and experiences. This may indicate the need to consider the unevenness of students' prior knowledge and experiences in any given topic and the importance of providing students with background information or experience before they read a text.

QAR and Learning Theory

QAR can be connected to information processing theory. Information processing theorists suggest that learning and memory can be facilitated in a variety of ways, such as by organizing a group of random items into a list by specific characteristics. (All the red things go into one group, all the blue things into another, and so on.) They also suggest that developing an awareness of your own thinking and your "intentional use" of cognitive processes will enhance learning (Ormrod, 1998). This awareness is referred to as metacognition.

In QAR, students are specifically directed toward increasing metacognition. They are asked to discuss their own thinking by providing rationales and sources for their answers to questions. The language of QAR provides them with a mechanism for this discussion. It also allows them to be consciously aware of their thinking processes and ultimately, those of others.

As teachers give repeated instruction in the use of QAR, they are providing students with opportunities to be intentional about the processes they use, and, according to information processing theory, such opportunities increase their potential for learning. Repeated exposure to and practice with this language and the QAR model will ultimately allow students to use these processes independently.

QAR and the Cognitive Processing Perspective on Curriculum

It is most useful to think of QAR as reflecting the cognitive processing perspective on curriculum. As discussed earlier in this text, Eisner and Vallance (1974) suggest that this orientation to curriculum focuses on "sharpening intellectual processes and developing a set of cognitive skills that can be applied to virtually anything" (p. 6). This perspective helps us view QAR as a way of orienting students to multiple ways of thinking about question-and-answer relationships that can be applied to nearly all their encounters with text—and perhaps to experience in general. Eisner and Vallance refer to this orientation as providing students with a kind of "intellectual autonomy" (p. 6).

In Case Study 8.1, Mr. Zucco showed students that questions and answers about text can be categorized by the sources they use. Although he used a content area (homes and community) to demonstrate this, his objective was to help his students understand a way of thinking—a set of cognitive processes. Specifically, students are asked to develop and use such mental skills or processes as classifying, inferring, and synthesizing (Burns & Brooks, 1974). For example, students must classify question-answer relationships based on the source of the answers. As students consider what the text says, they are asked to infer what might be meant. They are required to synthesize their own experiences with what they discover in the text. All are mental processes involved in problem solving that can be attached to their future interactions with text or transferred to other efforts.

As teachers, we can certainly appreciate how QAR can promote mental skills or processes that can be applied to other learning situations and content areas. QAR and the processes it fosters can be applied to students' own writing efforts, using original documents like the Declaration of Independence in social studies or a story problem in mathematics.

Technology and QAR

Technology can be used in two primary ways with QAR. First, certain applications can be helpful in teaching the model itself. For example, in a classroom equipped with a Smart Board, the teacher can display the text being read. As each of the question-answer relationships is determined, the appropriate sections of the passage can be highlighted and labeled, providing a graphic demonstration for students. For example, in Case Study 8.1, Mr. Zucco asked the students when visitors could see the Victorian-style sections of the town. They pulled their responses from two sections of the passage, and Mr. Zucco could have used the Smart Board to highlight these sentences. He could also draw a line from one sentence to the other or literally put them together by using a cutting and pasting feature of the technology.

A second application could involve students' or teachers' finding text via a Web search. This would allow students to apply QAR to "real-world" print sources, including primary sources and a wider variety of texts than can often be provided in a classroom. Students could use these sources to demonstrate their understanding of QAR by making charts or other graphic organizers with the various relationships as titles and "cut and pasted" sentences or paragraphs from the passages listed with the relevant title.

A sampling of National Educational Technology (NET) Standards for Students (International Society for Technology in Education, 2000) that can be reinforced with QAR is listed below, along with specific performance indicators for those standards and a brief description of possible classroom applications.[*]

GRADES PK–2

NET Standard 3: Technology Productivity Tools

Performance Indicator 2: Use a variety of media technology resources for directed and independent learning activities.

QAR Extension

Use the Smart Board (teacher) or individual personal computers (students) to highlight or electronically cut and paste passages of text to graphically demonstrate question-answer relationships.

GRADES 3–5

NET Standard 3: Technology Productivity Tools

NET Standard 4: Technology Communication Tools

Performance Indicator 4: Use general purpose productivity tools and peripherals to support personal productivity, remediate skill deficits, and facilitate learning throughout the curriculum.

Performance Indicator 5: Use technology tools (e.g., multimedia authoring, presentation, Web tools, digital cameras, scanners) for individual and collaborative writing, communication, and publishing activities to create knowledge products for audiences inside and outside the classroom.

QAR Extension

Have students locate primary source texts related to a content area using a classroom computer. Have pairs of students take one section of a text and develop questions and answers that demonstrate their understanding of each subcategory of QAR.

GRADES 6–8

NET Standard 5: Technology Research Tools

Performance Indicator 5: Apply productivity/multimedia tools and peripherals to support personal productivity, group collaboration, and learning throughout the curriculum.

QAR Extension

Have students conduct standardized test preparation in reading comprehension by developing test questions about a passage. Then students can develop a PowerPoint presentation for their peers that demonstrates the question-answer relationship required by items from the test.

QAR, Content Standards, and Benchmarks

The QAR model is designed to promote reading comprehension of text, both narrative and expository. Consequently, as you examine your state curriculum framework, it is likely that you will connect this model most easily with content standards and benchmarks related to the English language arts. In particular, look for standards and benchmarks that relate to question development or question-answer relationships. Below are a few examples of this type of connection. All standards and benchmarks listed are from the *Michigan Curriculum Framework* (Michigan Department of Education, 1996).[*]

English Language Arts

CONTENT STANDARD 1: All students will read and comprehend general and technical materials.

Early Elementary Benchmark: Employ multiple strategies to construct meaning, including word recognition skills, context clues, retelling, predicting, and generating questions.

Later Elementary Benchmark: Employ multiple strategies to construct meaning, including the use of sentence structure, vocabulary skills, context clues, text structure, mapping, predicting, retelling, and generating questions.

CONTENT STANDARD 3: All students will focus on meaning and communication as they listen, speak, view, read, and write in personal, social, occupational, and civic contexts.

Later Elementary Benchmark: Employ multiple strategies to construct meaning while reading, listening to, viewing, or creating texts. Examples include summarizing, predicting, generating questions, mapping, examining picture cues, and analyzing word and sentence structure.

---

*Excerpts from the *Michigan Curriculum Framework* are reprinted with permission of the Michigan Department of Education.

> **Middle School Benchmark:** Select appropriate strategies to construct meaning while reading, listening to, viewing, or creating texts. Examples include generating relevant questions, studying vocabulary, analyzing mood and tone, recognizing how authors and speakers use information, and matching form to content.

Recall also that QAR can be used across the curriculum to help students understand text. For example, if students are reading primary sources or a textbook in science, you will want to examine your state's content standards and benchmarks in science. Explore the match between the topic you are studying and QAR strategies suggested in the benchmarks. It is likely that you will be able to see a connection with the QAR model there too.

Why Choose QAR?

1. Do your students often answer questions with one- or two-word answers? Do their answers often seem unconnected to the text?

2. Can your students benefit from an explicit understanding of question-answer relationships? Would knowing the specific sources for answers help them to comprehend text better?

3. Will QAR help you ask better questions? Will it give you a better understanding of how to ask questions that rely on multiple and varied sources for answers?

4. Do you have ways to explore students' prior understanding and experiences related to comprehension of the texts you are or will be using? Could QAR help you do this?

5. Do you and your students have a common language for talking about question-answer relationships? If not, could QAR work?

6. Do you (or does your district) measure student comprehension of text by asking questions, either orally or with testing (placement, state assessments, etc.)? Could students demonstrate their understanding better if they understood question-answer relationships and sources for answers?

Summary

Using QAR has many benefits for students and teachers. This model helps students explicitly understand the relationship between questions and answers, as well as the sources that can be used to answer questions. Armed with this knowledge, students can more strategically read text for meaning and ultimately increase their reading comprehension. QAR also provides students and teachers with a common and understandable language for exploring and talking about a text and what they are learning from the experience of reading it.

For teachers, QAR provides a framework for constructing questions and monitoring their question-asking behaviors. Questions can be prepared that ask students to use a variety of sources for their answers and avoid an overreliance on explicitly stated information provided by the author or on single-word responses. This variety can enliven discussions of texts and help students become more engaged in the proceedings.

QAR also provides students opportunities to improve or develop higher-level thinking processes. As students use various sources for exploring question-answer relationships, they begin to infer, synthesize, make applications, and cultivate sophisticated ways of thinking.

Much of how we judge learner comprehension is based on responses to questions. Therefore, taking the "mystery" out of question-answer relationships by helping students understand them is a worthy enterprise. QAR provides a useful and attainable means of doing so while ultimately improving reading comprehension.

Putting It Together

1. Raphael (1986) has suggested that students can learn about formal text structures using QAR subcategories. For example, as students work with the Think and Search subcategory, further group their answers into examples of cause and effect, compare and contrast, list and example, or explanation.

2. Select a textbook and a novel. Using a small section of each text, develop questions and answers that reflect each of the subcategories of QAR and label them. Continue to practice this until you are comfortable with your understanding of each category and how to develop each kind of question.

3. Locate an assessment test that measures reading comprehension. Look at each question, its answer, and the source of the answer. Label each with the appropriate QAR subcategory.

4. Review your state or district documents. Highlight each benchmark that would either require an understanding of question-answer relationships and sources or be assisted by this knowledge.

Student Study Site

The Companion Web site for *Models of Teaching: Connecting Student Learning With Standards*

www.sagepub.com/delloliostudy

Visit the Web-based student study site to enhance your understanding of the book content and discover additional resources that will take your learning one step further. You can enhance your understanding by using the comprehensive Study Guide, which includes chapter learning objectives, flash cards, practice tests, and more. You'll find special features, such as the links to standards from U.S. States and associated activities, Learning from Journal Articles, Field Experience worksheets, Learning from Case Studies, and PRAXIS resources.

References

American Lung Association. (2005). *Asthma & children fact sheet.* Retrieved May 23, 2006, from www.lungusa.org/site/pp.asp?c=dvLUK900E&b=44352

Au, K. & Raphael, T. *Super QAR for Testwise Students: Grade 8 Teacher Guide.* New York: McGraw-Hill.

Burns, R.W. & Brooks, G.D. (1974). Processes, problem solving, and curriculum reform. In E. Eisner & E. Vallance (Eds.), *Conflicting conceptions of the curriculum* (pp. 37–47). Berkeley, CA: McCutchan.

Eisner, E., & Vallance, E. (1974). *Conflicting conceptions of the curriculum.* Berkeley, CA: McCutchan.

Ezell, H. K., Hunsicker, S. A., & Quinque, M. M. (1996). Maintenance and generalization of QAR reading comprehension strategies. *Reading Research and Instruction, 36,* 64–81.

Ezell, H. K., Hunsicker, S. A., & Quinque, M. M. (1997). Comparison of two strategies for teaching reading comprehension skills. *Education and Treatment of Children, 20*(4), 365–382.

Gunning, T. G. (1992). *Creating reading instruction for all children.* Boston: Allyn & Bacon.

International Society for Technology in Education. (2000). *National educational technology standards for students: Connecting curriculum and technology.* Washington, DC: Author in collaboration with the U.S. Department of Education.

Jacobson, J. M. (1998). *Content area reading: Integration with the language arts.* New York: Delmar.

Lowry, L. (1989). *Number the stars.* Boston: Houghton Mifflin.

McIntosh, M. E., & Draper, R. J. (1996, Jan.-Feb.). Using the question-answer relationship strategy to improve students' reading of mathematics texts. (National Standards: Pro and Con). *Clearing House, 69,* 154.

Michigan Department of Education. (1996). *Michigan curriculum framework.* Lansing: Author.

O'Donnell, M. P., & Wood, M. (1999). *Becoming a reader: A developmental approach to reading instruction.* Boston: Allyn & Bacon.

Ormrod, J. E. (1998). *Educational psychology: Developing learners* (2nd ed.). Upper Saddle River, NJ: Merrill.

Ouzts, D. T. (1998, March-April). Curriculum concerns: Enhancing the connection between literature and the social studies using the question-answer relationship QAR. *Social Studies and the Young Learner, 10*(4), 26–28. (ERIC Document Reproduction Service No. EJ596087)

Pearson, P., & Johnson, D. D. (1978). *Teaching reading comprehension.* New York: Holt, Rinehart and Winston.

Raphael, T. E. (1982). Question-answering strategies for children. *Reading Teacher, 36,* 186–190.

Raphael, T. E. (1986). Teaching question answer relationships, revisited. *Reading Teacher, 39,* 516–520.

Raphael, T. E., & Au, K. H. (2005). QAR: Enhancing comprehension and test-taking across grades and content areas. *Reading Teacher, 59*(3), 206–221.

Raphael, T. E., & Pearson, P. D. (1985). Increasing students' awareness of sources of information for answering questions. *American Educational Research Journal, 22*(2), 217–235.

Reutzel, R. D., & Cooter, R. B. (1992). *Teaching children to read: From basals to books.* New York: Macmillan.

Ruddell, R. B. (1999). *Teaching children to read and write: Becoming an influential teacher.* Boston: Allyn & Bacon.

chapter

Jigsaw

Most of us have participated in a group, in school or at work, when an important assignment is to be accomplished by everyone working together. Too often, a single member of the group ends up doing the lion's share of the work, and that member is often responsible for the grade given the assignment or the evaluation of the task. Sometimes that single member is the dominant personality in the group and tends to take over every time the group members meet. Other times, that member is the person who cares most about the assignment and is willing to do the lion's share to make sure the job is accomplished well. Beginning teachers often say

Table 9.1	Johnson and Johnson's Five Essential Components of Cooperative Learning
Positive interdependence	Cooperative tasks are designed so that each student's contribution is required for the group's success.
Face-to-face interaction	Students relate directly to one another as they work together to solve problems and complete assignments.
Individual accountability	Groups may be evaluated on the quality of their work; however, individual students will always be held responsible for mastery of the content.
Social skills development	Students must be taught a range of social skills that will help them be productive and appreciated group members.
Group processing opportunities	Group members must be given time after cooperative learning experiences to reflect on how well they worked with one another. Areas of strength and social skills that require improvement need to be identified and addressed.

SOURCE: Chart adapted with permission from *The New Circles of Learning: Cooperation in the Classroom and School* by Johnson, D. et al. The Association for Supervision and Curriculum Development is a worldwide community of educators advocating sound policies and sharing best practices to achieve the success of each learner. To learn more, visit ASCD at www.ascd.org.

that they were the students who shouldered more than their share of responsibility when they worked on group projects in school. Am I describing you? Your experience was bound to be frustrating and unfulfilling. It is very unlikely that you learned positive group work skills and the true value of collaboration.

Cooperative learning is an approach to instruction that provides both the opportunity and the organization for balanced, successful, and satisfying group learning experiences. Not all small-group work in classrooms can be considered true cooperative learning. In *Circles of Learning*, David and Roger Johnson (1997), describe five essential components for cooperative learning experiences, shown in Table 9.1.

There are many ways of organizing cooperative learning, which Spencer Kagan (1990, 1997) calls **cooperative learning structures**. This chapter will introduce one of the most widely used and most sophisticated cooperative learning structures, Jigsaw. When teachers use Jigsaw to its fullest potential, each of the five essential components of cooperative learning is met.

Jigsaw is a type of cooperative learning experience that promotes both academic and social goals for students. When you put a jigsaw puzzle together, each interlocking piece is an integral part. Without every piece of the jigsaw puzzle, you cannot complete the entire picture. Jigsaw learning works on the same principle. The model requires students to work collaboratively on an academic task. Each member of a Jigsaw group has one portion of the total content to be learned, and the members will each teach their portion to all the other group members. Without everyone's contribution to the Jigsaw, the group will be missing information it needs. Because of the way the Jigsaw lesson operates, no one student can dominate the group.

Jigsaw is a popular and effective instructional choice that can be used with many grade levels. In most cases, Jigsaw learning can be introduced as early as third grade, depending on the particular makeup, maturity, and **social skills** of the class. The structure of the model promotes interdependence among students. Jigsaw also provides a sense of autonomy and responsibility in students, and with careful preparation on your part, they rise to these occasions. Students generally respond well to Jigsaw learning because it provides opportunities for discussion, decision making, variety, and movement in the classroom.

Jigsaw is also very flexible. Like all effective models of teaching, it can be modified in a number of ways to meet the specific needs of students, and it can be used to address many content areas. Once students have learned the model, they can use it to learn many concepts in the core academic curriculum. Social studies is a natural fit for Jigsaw learning, but teachers have found creative ways to use Jigsaw to address other subjects as well.

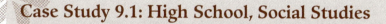

Case Study 9.1: High School, Social Studies

Mrs. Litera teaches social studies in a large urban high school. She has lived in this neighborhood with her family for more than 20 years, and she has been teaching in this school since she was a student teacher 25 years ago. In the past 10 years, the student population at her high school has become increasingly diverse.

Mrs. Litera's Global Studies class has been examining some of the historical developments that have contributed to or impeded human rights across the centuries. This unit has been of particular interest to the class because many of these students' families immigrated to the United States from countries where human rights violations were not uncommon—Cambodia, Bosnia, Guatemala, Laos, China, El Salvador, Iran, Sri Lanka, and Chile. The content of her unit addresses one of the state benchmark objectives in history for high school students and also serves as her long-term objective:

The learner will evaluate the responses of individuals to historic violations of human dignity involving discrimination, persecution, and crimes against humanity.

Here is Mrs. Litera's objective for today's lesson:

The learner will describe, compare, and contrast human rights violations in three specific settings: The West Indies c. 1530, a slave market in 1846, and the Maidenak concentration camp in 1944.

Earlier this week, Mrs. Litera's class reviewed both the Universal Declaration of Human Rights (1948) and passages from the Helsinki Accord (1975). Today her class will be reading eyewitness accounts of human rights violations in various eras. Because of the sensitive nature of the material, as well as the challenging reading levels, Mrs. Litera has chosen the

Jigsaw model to use in today's class. Block scheduling at her high school allows for the class time needed to accomplish her activity in one session today with a follow-up session later this week. None of Mrs. Litera's students have participated in Jigsaw learning before, so they are unfamiliar with the procedure.

Prior to yesterday's class, Mrs. Litera divided her 26 students into **expert groups** of 4 or 5 students for each historical period. To form the groups, she used **heterogeneous grouping** with regard to gender, ethnicity, leadership ability, and facility with written texts. Homework was assigned to prepare for today's class. Each group was responsible for reading one eyewitness account of a historical event: Spanish atrocities against native peoples in the West Indies, c. 1530; a slave market sale in 1846 South Carolina; or deaths that occurred in Maidanek, a Nazi extermination camp, in 1944 (Carey, 1997). Students were required to read their account carefully, summarize the events recorded, then interpret and describe the attitude of the writer toward the incidents witnessed. The students were also asked to highlight difficult words or phrases from their readings.

As students assemble today in class, it is clear from their comments that last night's readings affected them greatly. On the chalkboard, Mrs. Litera has written a brief direction for students to sit at the table cluster labeled by the date of their event. Before class, she placed the tables in these configurations, shown in Figure 9.1.

After a quick look around the classroom, most students located their group. To begin class, Mrs. Litera asks the students to write three questions they would ask if their eyewitness appeared in class later that week. She addresses their puzzled looks by stating that her students will need to use their imaginations. She asks them not to share their questions with their group members yet. These questions will play an important role later in today's lesson. Mrs. Litera allows five minutes for students to develop their questions. She gives them a one-minute warning before she calls time.

Mrs. Litera directs students' attention to the handouts on each desk. They will notice that at the top of the handout, a column along the left side of the matrix indicates their first grouping for today (Table 9.2). Students are already placed in these groups, which Mrs. Litera calls the expert groups. She now explains the expert groups' first task.

Each student will need to take notes throughout the various discussions today. To begin, members of each expert group will work together to clarify any difficult passages or vocabulary in their reading. Next, the expert groups will collaborate on a **document analysis** of their reading. These students have done document analyses individually and in groups in several of their social studies classes. Mrs. Litera adapted a Document Analysis Worksheet from the Web site of the National Archives and Records Administration (1998). Her students will record their document analysis on the worksheet shown in Table 9.3.

The document analysis prepared by each group will help the students share some of the most important facts from their readings with the rest of the class later on.

Once their document analysis is accomplished, group members will discuss how the subjects of their reading were deprived of basic political, economic, and social rights. Next, they will share their interpretation of the eyewitness's thoughts and feelings about the event described as it took place and afterward. Finally, from among their individual

(Case study text continues on page 251)

Figure 9.1 **Table Organization for Six Expert Groups**

Table 9.2 **Expert and Home Groups**

	1530		1846		1944	
	Student	**Home Groups**	**Student**	**Home Groups**	**Student**	**Home Groups**
Expert Group 1	Mel	A	Leah	A	Joseph	A
	Christina	B	Andrew	B	Jay	B
	Jack	C	Kallie	C	Anna	C
	Olivia	D	Philip	D	Randy	D
Expert Group 2	Andrea	E	Susan	E	Camille	E
	Anthony	F	Danny	F	Frankie	F
	Bennette	G	Laurie	G	Rosa	G
	Avi	H	Mary	H	Adrienne	H
	Stuart		Tanya			

Table 9.3   **Written Document Analysis Worksheet**

<table>
<tr>
<td>1.</td>
<td colspan="3">TYPE OF DOCUMENT (Check one):</td>
</tr>
<tr>
<td></td>
<td>○ Newspaper
○ Letter
○ Patent
○ Memorandum</td>
<td>○ Map
○ Telegram
○ Press Release
○ Report</td>
<td>○ Advertisement
○ Congressional Record
○ Census Report
○ Other</td>
</tr>
<tr>
<td>2.</td>
<td colspan="3">UNIQUE PHYSICAL CHARACTERISTICS OF THE DOCUMENT (Check one or more):</td>
</tr>
<tr>
<td></td>
<td colspan="2">☐ Interesting Letterhead
☐ Handwritten
☐ Typed
☐ Seals</td>
<td>☐ Notations
☐ "RECEIVED" stamp
☐ Other</td>
</tr>
<tr>
<td>3.</td>
<td colspan="3">DATE(S) OF DOCUMENT:</td>
</tr>
<tr>
<td>4.</td>
<td colspan="3">AUTHOR (OR CREATOR) OF THE DOCUMENT:

POSITION (TITLE):</td>
</tr>
<tr>
<td>5.</td>
<td colspan="3">FOR WHAT AUDIENCE WAS THE DOCUMENT WRITTEN?</td>
</tr>
<tr>
<td>6.</td>
<td colspan="3">DOCUMENT INFORMATION (There are many possible ways to answer A-E.)

A. List three things the author said that you think are important:

B. Why do you think this document was written?

C. What evidence in the document helps you know why it was written? Quote from the document.

D. List two things the document tells you about life in the United States at the time it was written.

E. Write a question to the author that is left unanswered by the document:</td>
</tr>
</table>

SOURCE: Designed and developed by the Education Staff, National Archives and Records Administration, Washington, DC 20408.

(Continued from page 248)

questions, they will choose from three to five relevant questions for their group to ask the author if he or she were to visit their class today. These questions should relate to the Universal Declaration of Human Rights adopted by the United Nations General Assembly in 1948. They can also address other aspects of the eyewitness's experiences.

Mrs. Litera points out that each of these task components is written on the second worksheet students found on their desks at the beginning of class (see Table 9.4). She tells her students that they have 25 minutes to complete these tasks. Since the expert groups are large today, she asks that each group appoint a Leader to make sure the group progresses through the task, a Scout to keep track of the time, and an Encourager to make sure that everyone in the group participates. She reminds her students that they need to practice active listening today and pay special attention to how they critique one another's ideas.

Table 9.4 Human Rights Jigsaw: Experts' Task

Title of your document _____

1. How were the subjects of your reading deprived of their basic human rights?

   Political rights

   Economic rights

   Social rights

2. What is your interpretation of your eyewitness's thoughts and feelings about the event described?

3. In your group, choose three to five questions for your eyewitness from among the ones you each developed.

While these students have not worked in Jigsaw groups before, they have worked collaboratively in the past. At the beginning of the term, Mrs. Litera spent ample time in team building and communication building exercises. These exercises not only helped create a strong class spirit but also provided opportunities for her students to review facts and concepts in social studies. Over the course of the term, she has also used a number of other cooperative learning strategies with her students in pairs, trios, or groups of four (Kagan, 1997).

The classroom is alive with discussion. Mrs. Litera notices that one element of the expert task that particularly engages each group is deciding to whom the writers addressed their eyewitness accounts. As she moves from group to group, she suggests that this question be raised during the next phase of the Jigsaw. She serves as a resource when issues arise in each discussion. Her main role during the expert-group period is to listen to her students, note common themes or points made in each expert group, and generally absorb a bird's-eye view of these conversations so that she can facilitate the full-class discussion later. She also provides assistance when groups experience difficulties working together by asking questions about their process to help them find their own solutions.

A two-minute warning serves as a signal to wrap up the expert phase of the Jigsaw. As directed, the groups check to make sure each component of the task has been completed. Every group completes the expert tasks by the allotted time, and each feels confident about its document analysis.

Mrs. Litera gives the final signal for the expert discussions to come to a close. She directs students' attention back to the matrix in their handouts. Expert groups have been recorded in three horizontal rows on the chart. Since the expert phase of the Jigsaw is completed, she asks them to find their individual names in the vertical columns of the matrix. Each vertical column organizes the class into eight groups of three (and one of five, to accommodate everyone), called **home groups**. Every home group has a representative from each expert group. She asks the students to form these new groups by changing seats and pulling the desks into circles.

Home-group tasks are listed on a third worksheet (Table 9.5). In turn, experts will provide the name of their readings, and then they will briefly explain their analyses of the documents and the nature of the eyewitness accounts. Experts will close their presentations by listing the questions their groups would ask the writer of each document if he or she were to visit the class. Home groups have also been asked to include any additional questions they may have in response to the readings. Mrs. Litera has requested that the documents be discussed in chronological order. Home groups are given 25 minutes to share their information and analyses.

As she did before, Mrs. Litera visits each group silently and notices the substance and tenor of the discussions. She especially notices how themes or ideas that surfaced in the expert groups reappear as the home groups share.

Rather than give a two-minute warning this time, Mrs. Litera moves silently from circle to circle to assess how much each group has accomplished. It appears as though all the home groups but one will be finished on time. In a subdued voice, she announces that the groups have three additional minutes to work. When these three minutes are up, Mrs. Litera requests that each group open up its circle so that everyone in class is visible in a larger circle.

It is time now for the full class to compare and contrast the similarities of events in the three readings and the eyewitnesses' responses to those events. Mrs. Litera mentions that as they were working, each home group drew parallels between the three narratives and the news reports about events in Kosovo in 1998–1999, from Iraq prior to 2003, and more recently since the fall of Saddam Hussein. Several students had also chosen to share the incidents that prompted their families' immigration to the United States. Mrs. Litera had hoped this would occur. She asks the class about the impact of the events in the Balkans and the Middle East in light of the eyewitness accounts examined today. How are they similar, and how do they differ?

| Table 9.5 | **Human Rights Jigsaw: Home-Group Tasks** |

First eyewitness account:

_____

Document analysis information:

Nature of eyewitness account:

Three to five expert group questions:

Additional questions?

Second eyewitness account:

_____

Document analysis information:

Nature of eyewitness account:

Three to five expert group questions:

Additional questions?

Third eyewitness account:

_____

Document analysis information:

Nature of eyewitness account:

Three to five expert group questions:

Additional questions?

Before she dismisses the class, Mrs. Litera asks each of the home groups to report the questions they would want to ask the writers of each narrative. She lists these questions on the whiteboard, comparing and contrasting questions across the centuries. Later this week, she tells the class, they will watch a videotape of a network correspondent's report from Kosovo in June 1999. The class will examine whether the correspondent could answer similar questions about the events she reported. Mrs. Litera's students will also review the efforts of global organizations such as Amnesty International in addressing human rights violations in the late 20th and early 21st centuries.

Case Study 9.1: Post-Lesson Reflection ──────────────◆

Mrs. Litera is pleased with the outcome of today's class. The time she spent at the beginning of the semester with team-building activities has paid off for her students. Jigsaw is one of the most sophisticated models of cooperative learning, and success in using it requires that students be comfortable with less-directive styles of teaching and prepared to take on different roles. Mrs. Litera eased her students into Jigsaw by pairing them first in twos for class exercises and outside projects. Over the course of the term, she expanded the size of the groups, depending on the learning goals she set for her students. They have worked in groups of four or five, but never in a Jigsaw lesson before.

In order to emphasize the "social" in social studies, her students also examined what makes a group effective and productive. During the semester, Mrs. Litera gave them plenty of opportunities to practice complex social skills, such as active listening and critiquing ideas without criticizing individuals. Regarding their success using the Jigsaw model today, she is confident that her students will leave her classes possessing much more than just social studies facts.

Because the material today was sensitive, and also personal for some of the students, Mrs. Litera believes the small, intimate expert and home groups were effective. She was surprised and pleased that all students fully participated today in both groups, and she credits this to the atmosphere of trust developed in class.

The eyewitness accounts used in the Jigsaw today seemed to be on target. Mrs. Litera decides to continue searching for eyewitness accounts from other historical periods. She particularly likes to use eyewitness accounts for document analysis in class because they may generate multiple interpretations. Mrs. Litera hopes that as a result of the Jigsaw, her students are gaining a greater appreciation for the work historians do, as well as a genuine excitement about history.

Mrs. Litera believes that by relating the readings to the experiences of students' families, her students will better understand and value the Universal Declaration of Human Rights. She also believes that the task of developing questions in response to the readings will promote students' analytical thinking about current news reports. She is planning further class activities and homework assignments along these lines.

Today's full-class discussion after the home groups met was full of energy and insight. When she first began using Jigsaw in the 1980s, Mrs. Litera split the Jigsaw into a two-day lesson because she was limited to 50-minute class periods. She remembers that she used the final discussion as time for a traditional lecture presentation. Over the years, Mrs. Litera has steadily improved her questioning skills, and she has found that the final wrap-up of her lessons can be less formal. By trusting the intelligence of her students and by designing engaging learning experiences for them, she has found less need to lecture in class. Her students' experience with Jigsaw today reinforces this belief.

Since she began using this model of teaching, Mrs. Litera has experimented with the structure of Jigsaw and adapted it for several purposes in class. In the past, she used it as a way for students to help one another master social studies facts and concepts. However, in the past few years, she has adapted Jigsaw for open-ended, interpretive tasks such as the one today. She prizes the flexibility of the Jigsaw model to support student learning in a variety of ways.

After class, several students asked additional questions about Amnesty International and wanted to know whether this organization and others like it might be the subjects of their upcoming research projects. She thinks that the level of participation and responsibility required by Jigsaw promotes students' authentic interest and investment in the content of the lesson.

Mrs. Litera decides that from now on when she uses cooperative learning of any kind, she will stress all five essential components in a more focused way than she has so far this year (Johnson & Johnson, 1987; Johnson, Johnson, & Holubec, 1994). So far she has discussed the importance of students' **face-to-face interaction** with one another, their need for **positive interdependence** as they work together on their tasks, their **individual accountability** for the unit material when they are evaluated, and time spent developing the many social skills required for them to function successfully with one another. What she plans to do next is focus their attention on **group processing** skills: how they perceive their work together in groups. She will work with them to find the right vocabulary and manner for discussing how well their group functioned and how they might improve the next time they meet. Whether she uses Jigsaw or another strategy, more time spent on group processing will be important for her students' success in all cooperative learning lessons.

The Stages of the Jigsaw Model

While Jigsaw has distinct stages, these stages can be adapted to address specific student needs or demands of the curriculum. As with all models of teaching, the preparation time prior to the actual lesson is of paramount importance for the lesson to be successful. Jigsaw preparation is more involved than preparation for other models of teaching. However, once it is accomplished the first time, it is less time consuming for the teacher the next time the lesson is taught.

Preparation for Jigsaw

Consider the involved preparation you do for a Jigsaw lesson as an investment because it will greatly affect the success of the experience for the students and for you. To begin, you must consider your lesson content and determine whether Jigsaw learning fits your instructional objectives. Consider whether the lesson content can be examined, learned, and then taught by expert groups independently (with your support, of course), without Direct Instruction. Differentiating the three branches of the United States government is one example of content that students might work with in a Jigsaw lesson; explaining the functions of various parts of a plant cell may be another. Appropriate content for a Jigsaw lesson can be divided into component parts; two, three, or four separate Jigsaw pieces work best. Too many expert categories may lead to a prohibitively long home-group period as each piece of the Jigsaw is shared.

Having your students work informally in pairs or trios helps prepare them for working in structured Jigsaw groups.

Time is another important factor to consider. As you are planning a Jigsaw experience, it is always wise to forecast how much time you think students will need to work through their expert-group tasks, change groups, and then work through their home-group tasks. The time needed for a full-class debriefing after the Jigsaw must also be estimated.

Once you have fully prepared for the Jigsaw lesson, it is always wise to consider your time forecasting once again. As with most classroom activities, each stage of the Jigsaw will probably take more time than originally planned. If the lesson seems to take more time on paper than you have available in a typical class period, it may be that the text selections are too lengthy or too numerous. You may need to reconsider the scope of the lesson, possibly reconfiguring the material or spreading the content over two days.

Teachers at the elementary level generally have more flexibility in their schedules and can add more time if students need it to complete a Jigsaw activity. Secondary teachers, unless they have the luxury of block scheduling, may need to schedule the Jigsaw for two regular class periods. Once their students are comfortable with the Jigsaw format, upper elementary, middle school, and high school teachers may assign the expert material to be read or reviewed as homework so that the in-class expert stage will take less time.

Another factor to consider when planning a Jigsaw lesson is group size. Eliot Aronson, creator of the Jigsaw model, suggested that teachers use home groups of six for Jigsaw lessons (Aronson et al., 1978). Over time and with experience with cooperative learning, students may work effectively in groups of six. However, many teachers choose smaller groups as they introduce Jigsaw to their classes, sometimes beginning with foursomes for the expert groups and pairs for the home groups.

Group size may also be determined by the length and nature of the material to be learned during the Jigsaw. There may be some natural divisions in the complete text to be used, such as subheading sections or short chapters. Teachers must consider student readiness, type of material, and the number and length of the selections as they determine the sizes of both the expert and the home groups. If expert groups appear to be too large, they can be split into more than one group, as Mrs. Litera did in the first case study.

When a class is working through its first Jigsaw lesson, less is more. It is a better choice to focus on less material and provide enough time for each stage of the lesson than to risk an unsuccessful Jigsaw experience because students have to rush through the group tasks. The final discussion also deserves adequate time for summarizing what students have learned, as well as for processing the class experience of the Jigsaw model.

Once decisions have been made as to how the content will be divided, the actual Jigsaw materials must be prepared. Some teachers make cards or duplicate handouts of the separate expert-group selections. Selections from textbooks can also be identified as expert-group material as long as each selection is clearly assigned. Teacher decisions and preparations of the Jigsaw materials are crucial for the success of any Jigsaw lesson. Time spent carefully considering the best format is a wise investment.

The next step in preparation is forming the Jigsaw groups. It is always best for teachers to compose the Jigsaw groups because students do not always make the best choices if they are allowed to form their own groups. (In most cases, students of all ages understand that they may not do their very best work if they are grouped with friends. Teacher control of Jigsaw group formation will not become an issue if students are given regular opportunities to make choices about other groups and activities in class.)

The original intent of Jigsaw learning was to provide children from diverse backgrounds the opportunity to work effectively and interdependently with one another. Even if students are racially or culturally homogeneous, diversity, which is manifested in many different ways in U.S. classrooms, should always be a goal. Teachers should consider gender, age, ethnicity, culture, language factors, academic ability, exceptionalities, social and emotional maturity, learning styles, and leadership qualities as they compose groups.

Decisions about group composition will also be affected by the content of the lesson. Students' prior knowledge or experiences may be a relevant consideration. For example, if the class is studying the national parks, students who have visited them should be seen as class resources and distributed throughout the groups.

The final step in preparation for the Jigsaw lesson is to decide how to tell students which expert and home groups they are assigned to. Some teachers post Jigsaw groups on the board or a chart visible to everyone. Because they often move from room to room, many secondary teachers prepare a handout listing expert and home groups. If tables can be arranged prior to class, the teacher can fold large index cards into signs that list who should be seated where for each group. This approach requires the teacher to consider student movement from expert to home group.

Thorough preparation of the Jigsaw material and the formation of the groups is key to a rewarding and profitable learning experience for students. Remember, the groundwork is accomplished the first time a Jigsaw lesson is used in a course, and much less time is required to prepare for the same lesson the following year. The entire process of Jigsaw preparation gets easier over time, and it is well worth the effort.

Working Through the Jigsaw

Steps in the Jigsaw model, listed in Table 9.6, are few and very straightforward. Students first work in expert groups to learn material they will be responsible for sharing with their home groups later in the lesson. The expert-group task has time segments: time to learn, time to check for understanding, and time to prepare for teaching.

Adequate time must be allotted for expert groups to learn what they will be sharing. Students need to review their material thoroughly, grapple with the complexity of their Jigsaw contribution, and seek counsel from the teacher when either academic or group process questions arise. Time for this task will vary depending on the nature of the material to be learned. Expert groups learning about new land formations—isthmus, archipelago, and so on, for example—may need considerably less time than groups reviewing written text, as in Case Study 9.1.

Each member of the home group is responsible for teaching expert material to the rest of the group and then checking for understanding of the material. You can determine the order of sharing ahead of time or leave it to the discretion of the group. Sometimes the content of the lesson determines how the material will be shared—chronological material would best be shared in chronological order, for example. Alphabetical or numerical order may be important in home-group sharing. In addition, you may suggest or require that home groups, to help fuel the full-class discussion, compile a list of their questions or concerns about what they learned.

You will be moving from group to group during this time to serve as a resource for students. You may hear comments during both the expert- and home-group periods that you want to bring to the full-group discussion. You will also be on the lookout for improvements in the group process to share with the class as you bring closure to the Jigsaw. Your role in both the expert-group and the home-group stages will vary from lesson to lesson.

A final full-class meeting will bring closure to the Jigsaw experience. You will highlight the academic content of the Jigsaw lesson in some way. This may be accomplished through discussion, question and answer, or even a quiz, in which each student is held individually accountable for the material. The teacher may also provide time for the full class to comment on the experience of working in expert and home groups, the way they worked together, and whether they believe Jigsaw was an effective choice for the lesson. This stage is called debriefing.

In addition to a full-class discussion, teachers should allow time for members of each home group or expert group to discuss their experience working with one

Table 9.6 Jigsaw: Stages and Tasks

Stage	Teacher's Tasks	Students' Tasks

Preparation	Forecast time requirements
	Prepare materials:
	    Expert readings
	    Task sheets
	Compose groups; consider
	    gender
	    age
	    culture
	    exceptionality
	    language skills
	    ESL concerns
	    prior knowledge	

Expert group	Move among groups to facilitate process Address content questions Assess readiness for home-group stage	Review or learn material Accomplish any specific expert tasks Check expert-group members' understanding of the material Decide how to teach expert content

Home group	Move among groups to facilitate the process
	
	Address content questions as groups assemble the Jigsaw material
	
	Assess readiness for full-class debriefing
		Share or teach material
		    round robin
		    chronologically
		    numerically
		    student-chosen order

Debriefing	Conduct full-class discussion Highlight specific content Ensure that concerns of the home groups are addressed Assign homework or other follow-up tasks to groups or individuals	Participate fully in the discussion Raise questions arising from the full-class discussion
Group processing	Provide time for small-group (expert or home group) or full-class discussion of the Jigsaw process Structure group processing with specific questions Help students set goals to improve group work and social skills	Focus on the improvement of ongoing home-group collaboration Brainstorm improvements for the expert-group process Brainstorm improvements for the full-class discussion Set goals for improving group work and individual contributions

Individual accountability	Design assessment to hold students accountable for what they learned
	    quiz or test
	    journal entry
	    project
	    homework
		Prepare for individual assessment

SOURCE: Adapted from Aronson & Goode, 1980.

Full-class discussions provide time for students to reflect openly on their Jigsaw experience.

another. Opportunities for small-group processing can be especially important for home groups that have worked together several times. Home groups may be working on specific improvements in their collaboration that they or you have identified. You may even choose to make group processing an individual journal assignment. Journals can provide an opportunity for you and each student to have a private discussion of the group experience.

Adaptations of the Original Jigsaw Structure

Jigsaw's original format can be modified to suit particular needs or constraints in your classroom. Assigning the expert reading for homework has already been mentioned. Expert review of materials at home is best suited for middle school or high school students, but upper elementary students may be able to accomplish it as well, depending on the nature of the material and the academic skills of the group members. However, if you are introducing Jigsaw for the first time or if you and your students are not yet comfortable with the model, it is best for students to experience each step of Jigsaw during class time.

You may also consider having the expert groups share their material with the full class. One reporter from each group can make the presentation. Modifying Jigsaw in this way may be effective if you have planned something extra for the class as each expert group presents, such as a set of specific questions or a short video selection. The expert-group task might also include the creation of a poster or other kind of visual aid for presenting the material or the production of a role play or skit to highlight what the group learned.

You may feel that eliminating home-group sharing in favor of full-group sharing weakens the social component of Jigsaw as envisioned by its creators. You can preserve the valuable social aspects of Jigsaw, however, through your skill in developing expert-group tasks, composing solidly diverse groups, and providing other opportunities for home groups to function well together.

Aronson and his colleagues (1978) recommended that home groups work together repeatedly. Having multiple opportunities to work together provides time for groups to work out their differences, see their progress in becoming an effective team, and learn to appreciate one another's individual strengths and talents. If you choose to follow this recommendation, you will need to assess carefully the rhythm of the group process over time and make wise decisions about when to reconfigure your home groups. A natural opportunity for change occurs when major units of study have been completed. Some teachers decide to create new home and expert groups each time students engage in a Jigsaw lesson. This modification of the original Jigsaw format allows students to work with many of their classmates over time. You may choose this approach for introductory Jigsaw learning experiences when your primary objective is for students to participate effectively in both expert and home groups rather than focus on specific content. You will observe and learn what is best for your students during the school year and use this insight as you adapt Jigsaw to meet their needs.

Robert Slavin and Spencer Kagan, who have both developed materials and written extensively about cooperative learning, have developed additional versions of the Jigsaw model. Jigsaw II, developed by Slavin (Knight & Bohlmeyer, 1990), has a competitive component. In Jigsaw II, heterogeneous teams are awarded points for individual members who improve their quiz performances over time. In Jigsaw II, all students read the same selections, and each one is also given a topic on which to become an expert. Jigsaw III was developed by Spencer Kagan (Knight & Bohlmeyer, 1990) for bilingual classrooms. Jigsaw III groups consist of one English speaker, one non-English speaker, and one person who speaks both languages. Materials used in each Jigsaw III group are bilingual.

Using Jigsaw as an Assessment Tool

An authentic assessment of social skills and group-process skills can be accomplished by observing students in a Jigsaw lesson. In fact, Jigsaw may be one of the most effective ways to observe, record, and assess student improvement in these skills over time. Many state K–12 curriculums include social skills and collaborative work skills as a component of the social studies curriculum. Some school districts have composed their own list of abilities that will be stressed in all K–12 classrooms, such as effective communication and decision making. Individual districts may be working with commercially designed programs such as Megaskills (Rich, 1998) and Lifelong Guidelines (Kovalik & Olsen, 2002). These programs stress students' abilities in working effectively with one another and participating fully in the community. Students' individual and group behavior related to the elements of these programs can be examined during Jigsaw experiences. If teachers choose to use Jigsaw in these ways, each student in the class must understand the Jigsaw process clearly.

Case Study 9.2: Sixth Grade, Online Research: A Jigsaw Modification

Mrs. Concannon teaches sixth grade in a rural part of her state. Most of the people in the community know one another. There is only one section of each grade in her K–12 building. Mrs. Concannon's school district recently purchased enough computers to create a computer lab adjacent to the library. Until this time, each classroom had only two computers, one for the teachers to use and one for the students. Very few of Mrs. Concannon's students have computers at home.

While Mrs. Concannon's students have done Jigsaw work before, she wants to add a new dimension to it. In small groups, her students will research one of the six simple machines, create a poster and matching trifold brochure that illustrates their machine, and then teach the second-grade class about the machine. Her students' research must be done online in the computer lab with a second-grade audience in mind.

Mrs. Concannon used the NETS Performance Indicators for Grades 6–8 directly as her long-term objective for this unit:

> The learner will design, develop, publish, and present products (e.g. Web pages, videotapes) using technology resources that demonstrate and communicate curriculum concepts to audiences inside and outside the classroom.

So far, her students have used word processing and desktop publishing programs to create newsletters and curriculum-based documents. They have also become adept at creating and editing videotapes as a result of working with the high school media teacher. He will be teaching her class how to create Web sites later in the year.

Here is Mrs. Concannon's objective for this project:

> In small groups, the learners will use online resources to research one of the simple machines, create a poster and make a trifold brochure that describes and illustrates how it is used in everyday life.

Besides having her students work as reading buddies with children in the kindergarten class, Mrs. Concannon has never tried this kind of cross-age project before. She has been working with the second-grade teacher, Mr. Lyon, to organize and schedule what their students will be doing. Three of her students have siblings in the second-grade class, and she thinks they will be especially pleased to take part in this project.

After lunch, Mrs. Concannon's students find their tables, take out the library books in their desks, and read silently. She joins them for 20 minutes, and then she quietly gives the class signal, "Sixth graders, give me five!" Once she has everyone's attention, she begins.

Mrs. Concannon:	At the beginning of the year, when I was getting to know you better, I asked everyone what projects your class had done in other grade levels that you remember as being the most interesting. Lenora?
Lenora:	You also said "fun." My favorite things were the school trips we made each year to the state park, where we had team sports all afternoon.
Mrs. Concannon:	You are right, I did say fun. But field trips that are fun aren't necessarily for material you are learning in class. Many of you talked about projects you remember that were connected to what you were learning in class. There was a project you had completed one winter that many of you agreed was a favorite. Everyone thought the project, and the teacher, were pretty neat. Elizabeth?
Elizabeth:	Everyone liked making the toys from the simple machines we had been learning about . . . and we all liked Mr. Lyon a lot. But we didn't say "neat," Mrs. Concannon. We said "cool." The project was "cool."
Mrs. Concannon:	OK . . . since so many of you enjoyed that project, and so many of you liked being in Mr. Lyon's class, I talked to Mr. Lyon at the beginning of the school year and asked him if you could be part of that project again. He was very enthusiastic about that, and today we will begin. Billy?
Billy:	Do we get to make those toys again, Mrs. C?
Mrs. Concannon:	No, you are sixth graders now, and the toys are a special school project for the second-grade students. What you will do is help Mr. Lyon teach his class about simple machines. We will be doing Jigsaw learning with his class. In Jigsaw learning, what word do we use to name the people who first become knowledgeable about a subject? Everyone?
Class:	Experts!
Mrs. Concannon:	Yes. And what word do we use to name the groups who will be learning that new information?
Class:	Home groups.
Mrs. Concannon:	Right. You will be in expert groups, and the second graders will be in home groups.
	Who remembers how many simple machines there are? Show me with your fingers. Great! Everyone remembers six simple machines. Turn to your neighbor and see if you can quickly name each one. (*They do so.*)
	Last night I assigned each of you to a small group. Each group will be in charge of one simple machine. You will be researching your

machine online, creating a display poster and a trifold brochure, and teaching your simple machine to groups of second graders. Mr. Lyon will be placing your posters on the walls of his classroom. Each second grader will get a set of brochures to keep. In the middle of your tables, printed side down, you will see a green sheet of paper. There should be enough for each of you at your table. Let's read through these directions one at a time. Whomever I call on also has to tell us why they think that step is important. Josh?

Josh: "Find three sites online about simple machines that you think most second graders can read." That is important because the posters will stay in Mr. Lyon's class, and his students might need to look at them again and again. Any writing we use from a site has to be what second graders can read for themselves.

Mrs. Concannon: And if you use a quote from a site? Jeff?

Jeff: We write the site information out at the bottom of our chart.

Mrs. Concannon: So far, so good. Amy? The next direction?

Amy: "Find pictures on your sites or other sites that might be good ones to use on your posters." The second graders have to be able to see what we are describing. Just our definition of the simple machine won't be enough. Mrs. C, what if those pictures are small?

Mrs. Concannon: What do you think? Dale?

Dale: We can enlarge the size of many pictures on the Internet or on a copy machine. Then we can use them on our posters.

Mrs. Concannon: You probably won't have time to do much more than that today, and we have only 30 minutes in the computer lab this afternoon. Who will read the last steps in your project so that you all have an idea of the entire project? Susan?

Susan: OK.

"Find pictures online and in magazines that show your simple machine in everyday life.

"Create a poster for the second graders. You will need to include the name of your machine on poster board, a definition of your machine that second graders can read, and the pictures you have located that illustrate your simple machine.

"Create a trifold brochure to accompany your poster so that each second grader will have a personal set that describes each of the simple machines."

Mrs. Concannon: Thanks, Susan. Once you have completed your posters and brochures, you will be spending two afternoons with Mr. Lyon's second graders. The first afternoon, three groups will be teaching their machines. Mr. Lyon's class will be spending a few days learning more about those machines, doing experiments, and drawing pictures on their own. Once his class is ready to learn about the next three, the groups that have not presented will go to his room. On both presentation days, Mr. Lyon will have your groups set up at three different tables in his room. The second graders will rotate through each of your centers. Michael?

Michael: So, we will be teaching our center three different times?

Mrs. Concannon: Yes, there will be four or five of you in your groups, and you can split up the presentations any way you like. It will be interesting to hear from you what your different experiences are as you teach each group of second graders.

I also want everyone to consider what roles might be needed in each expert group to make sure the assignment gets done well and on time. In the past, we have used leaders, readers, scouts, encouragers, and recorders. You may or may not think that those roles will be helpful in your groups. You might want to create new roles. I am going to let you decide. Each day you work together, different roles may be needed. That will be up to you.

Mrs. Concannon checks her students' understanding of what they will be doing in their groups once they get to the computer lab today. She asks them to bring paper, pencil, and their green sheets with them. Next, she calls out the names in each group and asks that each group line up at the door.

The sixth-grade expert groups work through each step of the assignment and do an excellent job on their posters and brochures. After a few days of working together, they are ready to teach Mr. Lyon's second graders about the six simple machines.

Case Study 9.2: Post-Lesson Reflection ◆

Mrs. Concannon thought that her students would be excited about helping Mr. Lyon teach his second graders material they had enjoyed learning as second graders themselves, and she was right. This project was highly motivating for her students, and Mr. Lyon's class felt that they must be very special for sixth graders to prepare the posters and brochures just for them.

She also believes that modifying the original Jigsaw model was effective for this project for two reasons. First, her students will be doing an individual research project soon, and she wants to give them practice using Internet resources. She thinks that having them work in groups will provide a shared experience that they can refer to as they work on their own projects. Second, when she and Mr. Lyon were discussing how to organize and run the home-group instruction, they knew that it would be foolish to have each group of sixth graders present their simple machines on the same day. To have everyone engaged at once, the sixth graders would have to teach their machine six times, and the second graders would be overwhelmed with too much information. Mr. Lyon thought that three groups on each of two days, spread about a week apart, would work best. The sixth graders' presentations would serve as overviews. He would be teaching a number of follow-up lessons and doing activities focused on each of the simple machines over the next few days. After the first presentation day, Mrs. Concannon could see that their plan worked out well for everyone.

Mrs. Concannon's first expert groups taught their simple machines to seven or eight children at a time, which turned out to be a good home-group size. These experts had a lot to tell the rest of the class about their Jigsaw experience overall, and every expert group had its own humorous stories about the differences among the second-grade groups. The first set of experts advised the others to practice their presentations carefully before they spoke to the second graders. The first experts wished they had spent more time preparing to teach. Even though they had found Internet resources at an early-childhood level to help them create their posters and brochures, the change in vocabulary and pacing as they taught second graders took them by surprise. They had not encountered communication challenges when they served as experts in their sixth-grade class.

They also recommended that each group have a simple machine worksheet or coloring page for their second graders in case they finished their presentations before the other groups were finished. One group of second graders became antsy, and it was difficult to keep them occupied as they waited. Mrs. Concannon closed the discussion by saying that anyone who became a teacher would experience these challenges every day in the classroom.

Mrs. Concannon provided the first three simple machine groups with private time to discuss how they worked together as a team and what they would change the next time they worked on a Jigsaw assignment in class. They were also asked to summarize their group discussion in their journals and write any personal observations they had not felt like sharing with their group members. Mrs. Concannon will review these journals with an eye to spending more class time on group processing skills prior to the next Jigsaw activity. She thinks she will place her students in these same groups so that they can work directly on the items they identified today.

Mrs. Concannon is looking forward to speaking with Mr. Lyon today after school about his experience with her students. She is also looking forward to hearing the experiences of the other three expert groups next week. Mr. Lyon's simple machine unit will end when his second graders invite the sixth graders to their classroom to view the toys they have made from simple machines.

Additional Cooperative Learning Structures

Spencer Kagan (1997) has described a number of cooperative learning structures that fulfill various purposes in the classroom. He has categorized these as team - building, class-building, and communication-building structures; and mastery, concept-development, and multifunctional structures. Jigsaw is one of the multi-functional structures. Teachers often use these additional cooperative learning structures not only because they are inherently valuable but also because they want to prepare their students for Jigsaw learning. Table 9.7 provides an example of cooperative learning structures in each of these categories.

Brief Background of Jigsaw

Eliot Aronson developed the Jigsaw model in response to students' socialization problems in desegregated schools in the 1970s (Aronson, Blaney, Stephan, Sikes, & Snapp, 1978; Aronson & Goode, 1980). Aronson, a psychologist from the University of Texas at Austin, was asked to examine why the district's efforts at school integration were unsuccessful. Technically, the schools were now integrated by law, but the true goals of integration—students' deeper understanding, acceptance, and celebration of one another's differences—were not evident. This was the first time most of the students had shared schools and the new social circumstances, and Aronson called the situation "highly explosive" (2000, p. 1). How could this state of affairs be explained, and how could it be remedied?

Several difficulties in the Austin schools needed to be addressed. Aronson and his associates found that traditional instruction and an overemphasis on competition had resulted in students' having few opportunities to get to know one another in the classroom and to establish trusting relationships. There was an "atmosphere of suspicion, fear, distrust, and physical violence" (Aronson, 2000, p. 1). In addition, many students of color experienced a drop in self-esteem after the integration of the schools. These were not the desired effects of integration in Austin (Aronson, 1978), and Aronson was asked to institute changes to alleviate them.

One of Aronson's objectives when he developed Jigsaw was to provide opportunities for students from different races and cultures to work together to understand and master their school studies. A second, and equally important, objective was to engender students' appreciation for the unique gifts and talents of the diverse individuals in their classrooms. Jigsaw proved to be effective in achieving both these objectives (Aronson et al., 1978). Since its inception, Jigsaw has become one of the most widely used models of teaching in the United States. It has also been the subject of hundreds of studies that indicate its effectiveness in the classroom.

Table 9.7 Cooperative Learning Structures

Structure	Brief Description	Functions, Academic and *Social*
Team Building		
Round robin	Each student in turn shares something with his or her teammates.	Expressing ideas and opinions, creating stories *Equal participation, getting acquainted with teammates*
Class Building		
Corners	Each student moves to a corner of the room representing a teacher-determined alternative. Students discuss within corners, then listen to and paraphrase ideas from other corners.	Seeing alternative hypotheses, values, and problem-solving approaches *Knowing and respecting different points of view, meeting different classmates*
Communication Building		
Match mine	Students attempt to match the arrangement of objects on a grid of another student, using oral communication	Vocabulary development *Communication skills, role-taking ability*
Mastery		
Numbered heads together	The teacher asks a question, students consult in their groups to make sure everyone knows the answer, then one student is called on to answer.	Review, checking for understanding, comprehension *Tutoring*
Concept Development		
Think-pair-share	Students think to themselves about a topic provided by the teacher; they pair with another student to discuss it; then they share their thoughts with the class.	Sharing personal information such as hypotheses, reactions to a poem, conclusions from a unit *Participation, listening*
Multifunctional		
Inside-outside circle	Students stand in pairs in two concentric circles. The inside circle faces out; the outside circle faces in. Students use flashcards or respond to teacher questions as they rotate to each new partner.	Checking for understanding, review, processing, helping *Tutoring, sharing, meeting classmates*

SOURCE: Adapted with permission from "The Structural Approach to Cooperative Learning," Spencer Kagan, *Educational Leadership*, vol. 47, no. 4, December 1989/January 1990. Used with permission. The Association for Supervision and Curriculum Development is a worldwide community of educators advocating sound policies and sharing best practices to achieve the success of each learner. To learn more, visit ASCD at www.ascd.org.

Jigsaw and Research on Teaching

The research on Jigsaw needs to be placed within the broader context of research on cooperative learning. Cooperative learning models of teaching have a strong research base (Johnson & Johnson, 1987; Slavin, 1991, 1995). Positive effects are seen in academic achievement of students of all ability levels in Grades 2–12; in students' attitudes toward themselves, others, and schooling (Brandt, 1987; Ellis & Fouts, 1993; Slavin, 1986, 1987); and in urban, suburban, and rural schools (Slavin, 1991). Cooperative learning has also been shown to be more effective than competitive work in the classroom (Johnson, Johnson, & Holubec, 1994). It is important to note that Slavin (1991) found cooperative learning to be effective only when both group goals and individual accountability are present.

Jigsaw has been used for more than 30 years in U.S. classrooms at all levels of schooling, including colleges and universities. In elementary schools, Jigsaw has become a familiar pattern in the fabric of everyday classroom life. It is less prevalent in secondary schools. One reservation about the use of Jigsaw in secondary classrooms was suggested by Newmann and Thompson (1987). They agreed with Slavin that secondary teachers were less likely to provide group rewards and individual accountability when they used Jigsaw. However, teachers well versed in these essential components of cooperative learning as defined by David and Roger Johnson (1994) will incorporate them.

Initial research on Jigsaw took place when the model was developed and implemented in the 1970s (Aronson et al., 1978). Several studies examined the effect of the model on White and minority students' attitudes toward school, attitudes toward their group members, and academic achievement. These initial studies demonstrated that Jigsaw is beneficial to students in a variety of ways. Jigsaw teaching lessened the emphasis on competition in classrooms. As a result of their Jigsaw experiences, both White and minority students held a more favorable view of school. Students not only liked the members of their Jigsaw groups more; they also demonstrated genuine appreciation for the strengths of others and empathy in difficult situations (Aronson, 2000). These improved attitudes about others were joined by enhanced self-esteem and feeling of self-efficacy. Academically, students of color in Jigsaw classrooms did as well or better than students of color in conventional classrooms. White students were found to do equally well in either Jigsaw or traditional classrooms (Aronson et al., 1978). Aronson's latest discussion of the positive social effects of Jigsaw can be found in "Nobody Left to Hate: Teaching Compassion After Columbine" (2000).

The most recent writings about Jigsaw have focused on its efficacy in instruction in specific curriculum areas. Educators have found Jigsaw to be effective in teaching secondary-level biology (Colosi & Zales, 1998), math (Draper, 1997), and geology (Fenster, 2000).

The use of technology in U.S. classrooms increases exponentially each academic year. We should not be surprised to see future research document the positive effects of the Jigsaw model when used to organize classroom assignments and projects using the Internet and other technology.

Jigsaw and Learning Theory

The Jigsaw experience relates to either behaviorist or constructivist views of learning, depending on how the teacher uses it. As mentioned earlier, Spencer Kagan has classified cooperative learning structures according to purpose: class building, team building, communication building, concept development, concept mastery, and multiple purposes (Kagan, 1997). Kagan considers Jigsaw to be a multiple-function cooperative learning structure serving both social and academic purposes. However, the way a teacher chooses to use Jigsaw determines the model's relationship to learning theory in a particular lesson. Jigsaw moves in either a behaviorist or constructivist direction, depending on the teacher's intention, what she wants the students to learn, and how she wants the students to learn.

In Case Study 9.1, Mrs. Litera is using Jigsaw as a constructivist. Students in both expert and home groups in her lesson are constructing meaning from their readings by working collaboratively. Because of the discovery emphasis in this lesson, there is room for student analysis and multiple interpretations of text. Rather than focusing on rote memorization of facts, her students are working as historians to construct the meaning of their documents contextually. Both expert- and home-group discussions in this Jigsaw are active and exploratory. These are features that make constructivist experiences so powerful for students.

In Case Study 9.2, Mrs. Concannon and Mr. Lyon modified the Jigsaw model and used it in different ways. Mrs. Concannon's sixth-grade students already knew about simple machines. In this Jigsaw experience, they were learning how to work interdependently on their group projects. Since she provided them with opportunities to make many of their own decisions, she used Jigsaw in a constructivist manner. Mr. Lyon wanted his second-grade students to learn the names and examples of the six simple machines. His students experienced Jigsaw for the purpose of content mastery in a behaviorist manner.

Jigsaw and the Social Reconstructionism and Cognitive Processing Philosophies of Curriculum and Instruction

Given the origin of Jigsaw, its relationship to the goals of the social reconstructionist perspective on curriculum can easily be seen. Initially, it was hoped that the Jigsaw experience would help relieve racial tensions in the schools. Early research indicated that students involved in Jigsaw classrooms did learn to value the contributions of each member of their groups regardless of race or culture. In doing so, students and teachers helped to "reconstruct" society.

Social concerns that prompted the development of Jigsaw are still present in U.S. society and in our schools. The current social climate in the United States demands that teachers continue to address students' acceptance and appreciation of their classmates' diversity. While all structures of cooperative learning address these issues, Jigsaw learning is especially designed to promote these goals effectively and responsibly in the classroom.

Jigsaw also relates to the cognitive processing perspective on curriculum. When Jigsaw is used to facilitate content discovery, teachers can design tasks for expert and home groups that focus on specific critical thinking skills. Mrs. Litera designed expert-group tasks in this way in her lesson. The first component of the expert groups' responsibilities was to analyze their document. The document analysis in turn fueled the expert groups' discussion and helped structure the way the document would be shared with the home groups. The questions Mrs. Litera included in the document analysis moved her students from the analysis level of critical thinking to evaluation. This essential feature of her lesson connects the Jigsaw experience directly to the cognitive processors' philosophy of the purposes of schooling.

Technology and Jigsaw

The National Educational Technology (NET) Standards for Students (International Society for Technology in Education, 2000) provide a structure for teachers to integrate technology opportunities for students into the classroom. Technology can work in tandem with different models of teaching, and the Jigsaw experience connects with technology in several dimensions. Technology can support Jigsaw learning experiences of both content mastery and collaboration among students.

Students in most grade levels can locate a teacher-assigned Web site or Encarta entry to find Jigsaw material. Many can also locate additional material on the Web. These experiences can include lessons in skills such as downloading and documenting to enhance students' technical abilities.

The National Archives Digital Classroom (1998) Web site provides templates for analyses of several kinds of primary-source documents (artifact, cartoon, written document, map, photograph, poster, sound). Mrs. Litera used the written Document Analysis Worksheet in her Jigsaw lesson on human rights. Oral history data can be audio or video recorded in live interviews with family or community members to share with expert Jigsaw groups. Jigsaw material can also be collected via telecommunications projects directed by the school or classroom teacher.

The following NET indicators can be reinforced during Jigsaw lessons.[*] Following the indicators are brief descriptions of class activities that can be used to support Jigsaw learning.

GRADES PK–2

NET Standard 1: Basic Operations and Concepts

NET Standard 2: Social, Ethical, and Human Issues

Performance Indicator 1: Use input devices (e.g., mouse, keyboard, remote control) and output devices (e.g., monitor, printer) to successfully operate computers, VCRs, audiotapes, and other technologies.

Performance Indicator 2: Use a variety of media and technology resources for directed and independent learning activities.

Performance Indicator 5: Work cooperatively and collaboratively with peers, family members, and others when using technology in the classroom.

Performance Indicator 6: Demonstrate positive social and ethical behaviors when using technology.

Jigsaw Extension

In small groups, have the students learn specific word processing skills (cut-and-paste, changing the font, etc.) and then teach these skills to their home groups.

NET Standard 1: Basic Operations and Concepts

NET Standard 2: Social, Ethical, and Human Issues

Performance Indicator 1: Use input devices (e.g., mouse, keyboard, remote control) and output devices (e.g., monitor, printer) to successfully operate computers, VCRs, audiotapes, and other technologies.

Performance Indicator 4: Use developmentally appropriate multimedia resources (e.g., interactive books, educational software, elementary multimedia encyclopedias) to support learning.

Performance Indicator 5: Work cooperatively and collaboratively with peers, family members, and others when using technology in the classroom.

Performance Indicator 6: Demonstrate positive social and ethical behaviors when using technology.

Jigsaw Extension

Have expert groups research and prepare handouts or worksheets reflecting content they will be teaching to their home-group members.

GRADES 3–5

NET Standard 1: Basic Operations and Concepts

NET Standard 5: Technology Research Tools

NET Standard 6: Technology Problem-Solving and Decision-Making Tools

Performance Indicator 1: Use keyboards and other common input and output devices (including adaptive devices when necessary) efficiently and effectively.

Performance Indicator 8: Use technology resources (e.g., calculators, data collection probes, videos, educational software) for problem solving, self-directed learning, and extended learning activities.

Performance Indicator 10: Evaluate the accuracy, relevance, appropriateness, comprehensiveness, and bias of electronic information sources.

Jigsaw Extension

In expert groups, have students evaluate the bias and author's voice in a primary-source document. This task could include, but not be limited to, finding appropriate documents from the Digital Classroom Web site (National Archives). The experts can present their findings to their home groups.

GRADES 6–8

NET Standard 2: Social, Ethical, and Human Issues

NET Standard 3: Technology Productivity Tools

NET Standard 4: Technology Communication Tools

NET Standard 5: Technology Research Tools

NET Standard 6: Technology Problem-Solving and Decision-Making Tools

Performance Indicator 5: Apply productivity/multimedia tools and peripherals to support productivity, group collaboration, and learning throughout the curriculum.

Performance Indicator 6: Design, develop, publish, and present products (e.g., Web pages, videotapes) using technology resources than demonstrate and communicate curriculum concepts to audiences inside and outside the classroom.

Performance Indicator 7: Collaborate with peers, experts, and others using telecommunication and collaborative tools to investigate curriculum-related problems, issues, information, and to develop solutions or products for audiences inside and outside the classroom.

Performance Indicator 8: Select and use appropriate tools and technology resources to accomplish a variety of tasks and solve problems.

Jigsaw Extension

Have each home group create a desktop-published brochure, digital story, or PowerPoint presentation from the information given by each of its experts.

GRADES 9–12

NET Standard 4: Technology Communication Tools

NET Standard 5: Technology Research Tools

NET Standard 6: Technology Problem-Solving and Decision-Making Tools

Performance Indicator 6: Evaluate technology-based options, including distance and distributed education, for lifelong learning.

Performance Indicator 10: Collaborate with peers, experts, and others to contribute to a content-related base by using technology to compile, synthesize, produce, and disseminate information, models, and other creative works.

Jigsaw Extension

Representing home groups that are researching different topics, , students can work in expert groups to share strategies for compiling, synthesizing, producing, or disseminating information. When home groups reassemble, they will have a leader in each of those facets of production.

Jigsaw, Content Standards, and Benchmarks

Creative teachers can find additional ways to use the Jigsaw model, or an adaptation of the model, across the curriculum. Jigsaw is effective when the content to be learned can be broken into equal components. When the assignment is divided among small groups, each expert group can be responsible for learning the material, then deciding how it can best be taught to the home groups. You may choose to provide teacher-prepared materials for students to use, or you may decide that the first part of the expert-group task will be to research information electronically or with traditional research resources. Some teachers prefer to use Jigsaw only when the sequence of the material is not necessarily important. Other teachers like to use Jigsaw in social studies expressly for the home groups to create a time line of the information each expert group has gathered.

Here are a few examples of ways Jigsaw might be used to teach material in typical social studies, science, and math content standards and benchmarks from the *Michigan Curriculum Framework* (Michigan Department of Education, 1996):[*]

History

CONTENT STANDARD 2: All students will understand narratives about major eras of American and world history by identifying the people involved, describing the setting, and sequencing the events.

Later Elementary Benchmark: Identify and explain how individuals in history demonstrated good character and personal virtue.

In expert groups, students can choose one important figure from the pre-Revolutionary era to research, collaboratively write a two-page essay, and create a graphic organizer for their home groups to record information about that person.

Geography

CONTENT STANDARD 2: All students will describe, compare, and explain the locations and characteristics of ecosystems, resources, human adaptation, environmental impact, and the interrelationships among them.

Middle School Benchmark: Describe the consequences of human/environment interactions in several types of environments.

---

*Excerpts from the *Michigan Curriculum Framework* are reprinted with permission of the Michigan Department of Education.

In expert groups, students can create tables that record information about the way people living in these settings modified their environment and how their environment has affected the development of their cultures over time: India, Tibet, Kenya, Greece, the Falkland Islands, and Hawaii. This information will be shared with their home groups.

Science

CONTENT STANDARD 2: All students will use classification systems to describe groups of living things; compare and contrast differences in the life cycles of living things; investigate and explain how living things obtain and use energy; and analyze how parts of living things are adapted to carry out specific functions.

High School Benchmark: Explain how living things maintain a stable internal environment. (Key concepts: Related systems/cells/chemicals—excretory system, endocrine system, circulatory system, hormones, immune response, white blood cell, bacteria, virus. Factors/mechanisms under control—temperature disease/infection. Real-world contexts: mechanisms for maintaining internal stability, such as body temperature and disease control.)

Depending on the progress of the unit, expert groups can research one of the concepts, and each student will create a three-dimensional model to demonstrate that concept to their home groups.

Math: Probability and Discrete Mathematics

CONTENT STANDARD 2: Students investigate practical situations such as scheduling, routing, sequencing, networking, organizing, classifying, and analyzing ideas like recurrence relations, induction iteration, and algorithm design.

Elementary Benchmark: Explore, develop, and invent their own algorithms to accomplish a task or to solve numerical problems.

Using a handout in expert groups, students can organize multiple algorithms they have learned (e.g., traditional, partial products, and lattice method multiplication) for an operation and develop an original algorithm to add to the handout. They then teach these new algorithms in their home groups.

As you review your state's standards and benchmarks and the grade-level expectations in your district, you will find many more instances in which Jigsaw teaching will be effective and will provide variety of instruction in your classroom.

Why Choose Jigsaw?

1. Is the lesson content "Jigsaw friendly"? Can it be easily divided into separate expert sections of equal length and level of difficulty?

2. Do your students have enough experience working in cooperative learning groups? Are they ready to move from working in pairs or trios to working in groups of four or five?

3. Can the lesson content be learned independently without direct teacher intervention?

4. Do students need any specific social skills that can be emphasized by participation in Jigsaw lessons?

5. Are you ready to give up total control of the classroom so that your Jigsaw groups can function as they were designed to function?

Summary

Jigsaw has widespread appeal among educators, and it is easy to see why. Jigsaw learning addresses in full measure several components of what we know to be effective learning environments for students: clearly stated learning goals combined with lesson flexibility, high levels of student engagement, opportunities for focused social interaction and student interdependence, and opportunities for mastery learning. Jigsaw is also developmentally appropriate for students of many ages because the structure of any Jigsaw lesson can be modified to fit the needs of different ages, grade levels, or content areas.

Many areas of the curriculum are well served by Jigsaw. However, the social studies are consistently a solid match for Jigsaw learning across most grade levels. Content in each strand of the social studies—geography, history, civics, and political science, as well as inquiry processes—can be organized into Jigsaw lessons. The format of Jigsaw and the high level of student involvement also provide an authentic experience of responsibility in a democratic society. Working as members of two separate groups during a complete Jigsaw, students have multiple opportunities to think, speak, and listen to one another. These opportunities allow students to appreciate the important contributions of their classmates.

Teachers benefit from using the Jigsaw model because it provides the opportunity to observe their students in joint academic and social situations. By facilitating rather than specifically directing student learning, teachers have the time to document and then assess individual and group behavior. Teachers are also provided the opportunity to observe students' critical thinking skills in action during Jigsaw lessons.

Putting It Together

1. Consider any Jigsaw experiences you have had in the classroom, either K–12 or college. What was appealing about these experiences? Do you perceive any disadvantages in Jigsaw learning?

2. Review your state or district documents and find appropriate content for Jigsaw lessons in two or three grade levels of the social studies curriculum. Describe how you might organize these lessons.

3. Review your state or district documents and find appropriate content for Jigsaw lessons in two or three grade levels of the curriculum in another academic subject. Describe how you might organize these lessons.

4. Choose a document analysis template from the Digital Classroom Web site. Find four or five examples of documents that can be analyzed using that template. Do not limit yourself to historical documents.

Student Study Site

The Companion Web site for *Models of Teaching: Connecting Student Learning With Standards*
www.sagepub.com/delloliostudy

Visit the Web-based student study site to enhance your understanding of the book content and discover additional resources that will take your learning one step further. You can enhance your understanding by using the comprehensive Study Guide, which includes chapter learning objectives, flash cards, practice tests, and more. You'll find special features, such as the links to standards from U.S. States and associated activities, Learning from Journal Articles, Field Experience worksheets, Learning from Case Studies, and PRAXIS resources.

References

Aronson, E. (2000). Nobody left to hate. *Humanist, 60*(3), 17–21.

Aronson, E., Blaney, B., Stephan, C., Sikes, J., & Snapp, M. (1978). *The jigsaw classroom.* Beverly Hills, CA: Sage.

Aronson, E., & Goode, E. (1980). Training teachers to implement jigsaw learning: A manual for teachers. In S. Sharan, P. Hare, & C. D. Webb (Eds.), *Cooperation in education* (pp. 44–65). Provo, UT: Brigham University Press.

Brandt, R. (1987). On cooperation in schools: A conversation with David and Roger Johnson. *Educational Leadership, 45*(3), 14–19.

Carey, J. (Ed.). (1997). *Eyewitness to history.* New York: Avon.

Colosi, J. C., & Zales, C. R. (1998). Jigsaw cooperative learning improves biology lab courses. *BioScience, 4,* 118–124.

Digital Classroom. (1998). Lesson plans, NARA educators and students, information for educators: Teaching with documents. Retrieved May 22, 2006, from www.archives.gov/education/

Draper, R. J. (1997). Jigsaw: Because reading your math book shouldn't be a puzzle. *Clearing House, 71,* 33–36.

Ellis, A., & Fouts, J. (1993). *Research on educational innovations.* Princeton Junction, NJ: Eye on Education.

Fenster, M. S. (2000). A jigsaw exercise in classification of coasts. *Journal of Geoscience Education, 48*(5), 579.

Helsinki Accord. (1975). Woodrow Wilson International Center for Scholars. Retrieved May 22, 2006, from www.wilsoncenter.org/subsites/ccpdc/pubs/addm/osce.htm

International Society for Technology in Education. (2000). *National educational technology standards for students: Connecting curriculum and technology.* Washington, DC: Author in collaboration with the U.S. Department of Education.

Johnson, D., & Johnson, R. (1987). *Learning together and alone: Cooperative, competitive, and individualistic learning*. Englewood Cliffs, NJ: Prentice Hall.

Johnson, D., Johnson, R., & Holubec, E. J. (1994). *The new circles of learning*. Alexandria, VA: Association for Supervision and Curriculum Development.

Kagan. S. (1990). The structural approach to cooperative learning. *Educational Leadership, 47*(4).

Kagan, S. (1997). *Cooperative learning in the classroom* (2nd ed.). San Juan Capistrano, CA: Resources for Teachers.

Kovalik, S. J., & Olsen, K. D. (2002). *Exceeding expectations: A user's guide to implementing brain research in the classroom* (2nd ed.). Covington, WA: Books for Educators.

Knight, G. P., & Bohlmeyer, E. M. (1990). Cooperative learning and achievement: Methods for assessing causal mechanisms. In S. Sharan (Ed.), *Cooperative learning: Theory and research* (pp. 1–22). New York: Praeger.

Michigan Department of Education. (1996). *Michigan curriculum framework*. Lansing: Author.

Newmann, F. M., & Thompson, J. A. (1987). *Effects of cooperative learning on achievement in secondary schools: A summary of research*. Madison: National Center on Effective Secondary Schools: Wisconsin Center for Education Research, University of Wisconsin.

Rich, D. (1998). *Megaskills*. Boston: Houghton Mifflin.

Slavin, R. E. (1986). *Education psychology: Theory into practice*. Englewood Cliffs, NJ: Prentice Hall.

Slavin, R. E. (1987). *Student teams* (2nd ed.). Washington, DC: National Education Association.

Slavin, R. E. (1991). Synthesis of research on cooperative learning. *Educational Leadership, 48*(5), 71–82.

Slavin, R. E. (1995). *Cooperative learning: Theory, research, and practice* (2nd ed.). Boston: Allyn & Bacon.

Universal Declaration of Human Rights. (1948). Retrieved May 22, 2006, from en.wikisource.org/wiki/Universal_Declaration_of_Human_Rights

chapter 10

Role Playing

There are times when most of us wish we could "replay" a difficult moment when we believe we acted inappropriately in a social or work situation. Sometimes our problem lies in not knowing what to do, and under stress we do the wrong thing. If we had one more chance to "get it right," we would be sure to know what to do, know what to say, know what to ask, or perhaps know not to say anything at all. Even the most poised of teachers may say something hurtful to a student in moments of anger or frustration. As professionals, we must learn to handle stress involving students, parents, or colleagues without erupting and to disagree without offending. Our livelihood depends on it.

Students of all ages come to school with varying degrees of behavioral self-control. Many students come from homes where they have seen adults handle disagreements in healthy ways. They have had strong, positive models of the normal give-and-take of family life, and that experience transfers to their social interactions with friends and with teachers. However, too often students come to school with inappropriate ideas about dealing with conflict and getting along with others. These students may be exposed to unsuitable ways of handling stress at home, or their role models may be violent television or movie characters. As professional educators, we have the job of helping students be caring, open minded, fair, and flexible in their relationships, especially in times of disagreement. As you can imagine, this is not an easy task if students have few positive role models at home.

Role Playing is a model of teaching that facilitates social problem solving. Role Playing has been shown to be effective in, among other things, helping students learn positive ways of handling interpersonal conflict wherever it occurs (Chesler & Fox, 1966; Shaftel & Shaftel, 1982). Role Playing allows students to clarify an interpersonal problem and then experiment with a variety of ways to address that problem when it occurs again. As originally conceived, Role Playing focused on social values and relationship issues; however, Shaftel and Shaftel (1967b) also experimented with using Role Playing to enrich the academic curriculum. We will focus first on the use of Role Playing to address interpersonal problems; later, we will briefly discuss creative applications of the model in designing learning experiences.

Case Study 10.1: Middle School, Anger on the Playing Fields

Mr. Liben is certified to teach English and social studies at the secondary level. He teaches these subjects to seventh-grade students at an alternative middle school in a large Midwestern city. Mr. Liben teams with Ms. Meredith, who teaches math and science to the same groups of students. In addition to their teaching responsibilities, all faculty members at this alternative school teach an elective and coach coed intramural sports teams. Because their elective classes and sports teams are made up of seventh, eighth, and ninth graders, teachers at this school get to know the entire student body very well, not just their subject area students. Several of the teachers have remarked that their most difficult moments during the school week occur when students argue over the rules, official calls, or suspected cheating by their opponents on the playing field.

As part of his masters degree work in social studies education, Mr. Liben has become adept at leading Role Playing exercises with his students. He has also instructed his fellow teachers at the middle school in how to use the model in their classrooms. Today these skills are needed because several fights broke out during the softball games yesterday afternoon. Contentious disagreements, just short of fisticuffs, included runners knocking down fielders, pitchers hitting the batters, thrown bats hurting catchers, and several instances of teacher umpires being accused of missing illegal maneuvers on the field. Today the teachers have decided to run a Role Playing session for pairs of teams before the sports period. They intend to focus on the kinds of difficulties the players experienced yesterday. While school counselors are on site two days a week, they are never on the playing fields with the sports teams, so the teachers are taking the sports situation into their own hands. Mr. Liben and Ms. Meredith's teams will be working together today. They have arrived at the following objective for today's lesson:

The learner will participate in role plays that illustrate effective ways of handling conflict during a softball game.

This lesson supports the following long-term objective:

The learner will participate in collaborative problem solving using discussion, compromise, and consensus rather than resorting to verbal or physical confrontation.

Early in the fall, Mr. Liben and Ms. Meredith recognized the need to provide social problem-solving tools for a significant number of their students. Many students at their middle school need support as they learn to make positive choices when they find themselves in increasingly difficult social situations at home and in their neighborhoods. Although these difficulties may not seem related to academic content at first, they are directly related to these middle school benchmarks:

Social Studies: Use laws and other ethical rules to evaluate their own conduct and the conduct of others.

Language Arts: Speak confidently, listen, and interact appropriately. Demonstrate how communication is affected by connotation and denotation, and why one particular word is more effective than others in a given context.

Mr. Liben and Ms. Meredith begin this class session by reviewing yesterday's sports period before moving into the first role play. Their challenge this afternoon is to promote authentic responses to the problems at hand yet keep the students detached enough to focus on role play cycles without getting carried away by yesterday's emotions.

Mr. Liben: All right, yesterday was not our finest hour as a school community. You may remember during the games that you had a lot of trouble getting along with one another. Many of you thought that your opponents were cheating on the field and generally not playing fairly. I'm sure you've heard that there were similar problems during most of the games yesterday and that the teachers were not happy about things that were said and done.

We expect more from you all because you are middle school students. We're going to spend some time today looking at what happened on the field and trying to address some of those problems. You've all worked with Role Playing before. Cynthia, you've just transferred here, so sit tight and watch the procedure. Now, what specific things do you remember that happened yesterday that you argued about? Clinton, just tell us one, and I'll write it down on the board. Don't mention any names now.

Clinton: Pitchers were hitting the batters on purpose. That happened on my sister's team, too.

Trina: (*calls out*) Clinton, you don't know that for sure. You got so mad over nothing. And besides, you weren't the only one that happened to yesterday.

Clinton: Well then, that makes it even worse if I wasn't the only one. And it wasn't nothing. I saw that ball coming right at me.

Mr. Liben: Hey, that's enough. Let's just list the things you were upset about, and we'll work them out later. What else do you remember? Malik?

Malik: I was playing shortstop, and runners kept knocking me down so I couldn't catch the balls that were thrown to me. That happened three whole times!

Mr. Liben: OK, I got that. Who else? Alejandro?

Alejandro: Mr. Liben, you didn't see it when runners missed the bases. They would cut corners, and you missed it a lot.

Mr. Liben: I'll put that down, Alejandro. This happens in at least one game every afternoon. Trina?

Trina: I didn't like the calls you made either, Mr. Liben. You were way off a lot yesterday.

Mr. Liben: Well, we can't always help that, but I've got it down. Alma?

Alma: People kept throwing their bats around. Everyone knows that can really hurt someone, and some people did it on purpose.

Susan: (*calls out*) You don't know that, Alma. You can't be sure of that.

Alma: Yeah, well, that's what it looked like to me.

Mr. Liben: Now this is just the way the trouble started yesterday afternoon. Let's look at the problems you've mentioned today. This is a good start. The other teachers mentioned similar problems during their games. While it is OK to ask whether rules are being followed as well as they might be, it's definitely not OK to curse one another, push someone around, or threaten to beat someone up after school. Our role playing today should help us figure out what to do and say the next time we have difficulty getting along on the field.

Let's start with the first one you mentioned: pitchers' being accused of throwing balls to hit batters deliberately. That is a dangerous situation. We need two of you to act out the first role play. Let's take two people from the same team this first time. Perhaps that will keep our tempers in check. Who'd like to volunteer to get us going? Jeff, I know you were very upset yesterday, come on up. Jeff and . . . Noemi, great. Good to see you volunteer. Come up to the front of the room. (*They do.*)

Ms. Meredith: Jeff and Noemi are going to set up the scene for us during the first role play. Remember, right now our jobs as observers are to watch how accurately they set up the problem and then be ready to analyze their motives and reactions to one another. Don't respond to them during the role play. We'll all get a chance to discuss what we saw after Mr. Liben calls "Cut!" like the directors do in the movies. A lot of you started yelling yesterday afternoon in support of your team members when they were having problems. Even though that sometimes happens during professional games, it's definitely not all right, and it can't happen here. Just keep cool today, and let the players work their scenes.

Mr. Liben: Noemi, I am going to ask you to be the pitcher during this role play. Jeff, you'll be the batter. We'll begin the action right after you have been struck by the ball that Noemi pitched. Noemi, Jeff thinks you threw that last ball to hit him on purpose. Set up the problem for us. Let's see what happens. Now, both of you, it's fine to show that you are angry, but please watch your language. And don't think you need to be funny. We need to take this seriously.

Jeff: (*Yelling in pain, he throws down a bat in pantomime and advances toward Noemi.*) Noemi, you threw that ball right at me. You could have broken my arm.

Noemi: Yeah, well, I didn't hit you on purpose.

Jeff: Yes, you did!

Noemi: What do you think I am, crazy? Liben is here, and he'd throw me out of the game if he saw that. Besides, if I wanted to hit you on purpose, I'd have done a real good job.

Jeff: Yeah, well, your team is behind three runs, and one of those runs was mine. You just wanted to hurt me so that I'd be out for the rest of the game. Chicken.

Noemi:	That's not true. You stepped into that pitch to get me thrown out of the game. This is your fault, not mine. And that makes you the chicken.
Jeff:	(*rubbing his arm*) You shouldn't be pitching if you have so little control of your pitches.
Noemi:	I can control my pitches. This has never happened to me before. You know that. You're just trying to make me look bad. You're still mad that we have some female pitchers on our teams.
Jeff:	What do I care about that? You're just trying to change the subject now. You know that you hit me on purpose, Nomi.
Noemi:	It's No-emi, and I did not!
Jeff:	(*stops the action*) Mr. Liben, after talking like this for a while yesterday, people started pushing one another around on my team, and then Ms. Meredith had to break it up. You don't want us to do that now, do you?
Mr. Liben:	No! You set the stage for us well and reacted the way some people did yesterday. So, how was this problem resolved yesterday? Ernest?
Ernest:	Well, they resolved it by getting benched for the rest of that game. Is that what you mean?
Ms. Meredith:	Yes, but how else might they have handled the problem before getting benched? What else could have happened? Owen?
Owen:	Well, I would have just walked off the field. I would have been that mad.
Ms. Meredith:	What do you think about that? Leslie?
Leslie:	You sure could have done that, Owen, but it would have hurt your team if you were out of the lineup for the rest of the game.
Owen:	You bet.
Ms. Meredith:	Any other ideas? Lee?
Lee:	Waiting for a teacher to listen to both sides of the story might help. It would at least keep them out of trouble. If my sister gets into another fight, Mr. Elwell said she's out of here.
Ms. Meredith:	Would it be easy for any of you to sit on your anger long enough to call over a teacher? Catalina?
Catalina:	It would be easier for some of us than for others. That's a good one to role play.
Ms. Meredith:	Let Jeff and Noemi act it out. Jeff and Noemi, please try the scene again from the beginning, but this time, try out Lee's idea to deal with one

another. Watch to see whether or not you think the second solution would have worked better yesterday. (*Jeff and Noemi begin again.*)

Jeff: Noemi! You threw that ball right at me! You could have broken my arm!

Noemi: No, I didn't mean to throw the ball at you. And don't get so mad. Just ask Ms. Chillemi. She was watching. Calm down and call her over. She'll tell you that I didn't do that on purpose.

Jeff: OK, let's call her over. She'll say that you threw that ball to hurt me on purpose.

Noemi: Look, at least this will give us both a chance to explain. I really didn't mean to hurt you. Seriously. Ms. Chillemi! Chillemi!

Mr. Liben: Great! What was different about the way Jeff and Noemi handled it this time? Elna?

Elna: Well, they didn't yell at each other, but being that calm and polite would never happen here, and don't you know it. Someone would get in your face.

Vanessa: No, I think that Noemi trying to prove that she didn't hit Jeff on purpose was good. If Ms. Chillemi was looking where she was supposed to, then she'd say so to Jeff. Chillemi sees Noemi during her practices and her games, and she sees her in homeroom, so she would know if it had been on purpose.

Mr. Liben: So by her asking for help, you think that everyone would have settled down?

Elna: Right. Well, maybe not. How is Ms. Chillemi really going to know? She can't just jump inside Noemi and feel whether or not she is telling the truth. This isn't the Psychic Hotline.

Jack: Elna's right. Things could still get worse if Ms. Chillemi agrees with one over the other. Then everyone would just get angry all over again, just like the first time.

Mr. Liben: So perhaps asking for help may work sometimes, but not always. If we can give Noemi the benefit of the doubt, what might we say about the kind of person she is? What is important to her, based on her willingness to talk things out with a teacher?

Tyra: Do you mean is she a good person?

Ms. Meredith: Let's try to go beyond "good" or "bad." Can we say something specific to describe her offer, Tyra?

Tyra: Well, if I get what you mean, I think we can say that she wants people to know that she is honest. Not the kind of person to hurt someone intentionally.

Alex: Yeah. She's not trying to get away with something.

Mr. Liben: It sounds like you're saying that our actions on the outside always say something about who we are inside. Let's look at this problem differently. Is there another way we could react in this situation? A new idea? Vanessa, what do you think?

Vanessa: Well, whether or not Noemi meant to hurt Jeff, she didn't apologize. When there is an apology, then usually people can still keep talking about whatever happened.

Mara: Only if the apology is for real, and if it sounds phony, then people will just get mad all over again, and it'll be even worse.

Mr. Liben: Well, you have a point there. Let's try that for the second role play. A real apology. Jeff and Noemi, you did a great job getting us started. We need two new players. Vanessa, do you want to try out your idea? And . . . Danny, why don't you be the batter who is hurt. (*The players exchange positions.*) The rest of you need to decide whether the apology given is real, works, and might lead to a better resolution.

Danny: Vanessa! I can't believe you hit me on purpose with that pitch! What do you think you are doing? You should be thrown out of the game.

Vanessa: Look, I didn't mean to hurt you. I'm sorry if you think I did. I guess that pitch just got away from me. I really am sorry.

Danny: I probably won't be up to bat again in this game. This really hurts! You ruined my chance for a double or triple. I can't even try to advance the runner at second base.

Vanessa: So look. I'll try the pitch again, and we'll see how you do.

Mr. Liben: Let's stop it right there. So what about this solution? Tyler?

Tyler: Sounds shady to me. First of all, everybody knows that if a batter is hit by a pitch, the batter gets to walk to first base. (*general agreement*) Danny can't bat again this inning. Maybe Vanessa just made that offer to look like the good guy when maybe she did mean to hit Danny on purpose.

Victor: Tyler, you must not think much of a person to think she'd try to get away with all that.

Mr. Liben: So, Tyler, what if Vanessa had just apologized and left it at that?

Tyler: Well . . .

Deb: Look, if someone apologizes, then that's it. That's good enough. It's not like Vanessa does this all the time, with Danny or anybody else. Apologies just have to be accepted, otherwise we'd always be angry with one another all the time.

Mr. Liben: So, let's try this again. How about playing the scene when an apology is really meant, and it is accepted graciously. Do any of you here think you can be gracious?

The class experimented with three different solutions in several role play cycles. Each time, the students found another way to deal with the hurt and angry feelings experienced by the players in these scenes. The class made the most of the role play cycles that focused on the first problem they listed today.

Ms. Meredith asked the entire group what could be said about what they learned today. If they could sum it up in one sentence, what would the "headline" be for today's role plays? The group agreed that one of the things they liked most about their school was the organized sports emphasis. It gave them a sense of belonging at the school, and no one wanted to jeopardize their opportunities to play. If they could not learn to get along better when things got rough, they all might lose that. Ms. Meredith asked whether people should control their tempers only out of their self-interest. The class began a lively discussion about self-interest, working for the common good, and our motivations for acting as we do. The period ended after 50 minutes, and overall the teachers were hopeful that players would get along well on the field today. In the hallways on the way to the playing fields, other teachers remarked that the role play sessions in every class seemed to be successful.

Case Study 10.1: Post-Lesson Reflection

These teachers are pleased that a family feeling exists at their school. Mr. Liben knew that working through the volatile emotions expressed yesterday during the games period would have been much more difficult if the students had not felt genuinely positive about their teachers and about one another. This fact made his job that much easier today. However, Mr. Liben also knew that he took a risk by conducting this particular role play session as he did. Shaftel and Shaftel (1967a) originally suggested that role play sessions should center on composed problem situations, stories that described a social predicate familiar to students. (Table 10.1, "Money for Marty," later in the chapter, is an example.) Mr. Liben's students first learned how to role play using these situations. He was familiar with some shorter scenarios written by Shaftel and Shaftel that focus on situations similar to the ones the class worked on today. However, Mr. Liben felt it was necessary to deal head-on with inappropriate student behaviors as experienced by the students yesterday. He felt that addressing this problem directly would serve to reinforce the severity of the problem school-wide. The rhythm of today's session and the level of engagement and care exhibited by the observers and the participants led him to believe that he had made the right choice.

Once again, Mr. Liben appreciated how the Role Playing model supported the diverse personalities and learning styles of his students. The structure of Role Playing provided time and opportunity for individual voices to be heard. Quick and facile solutions seldom lead to quality role plays. Taking time to think through ideas and their consequences was highly valued by the students today, and Ms. Meredith helped facilitate that approach. Mr. Liben noticed that several of his soft-spoken students who are often shy during regular class periods contributed to the role play discussions today. The multiple rounds of today's role play provided several opportunities for these students to contribute. Obviously, Mr. Liben counted on the more talkative students to propel the session, and he usually relies on more-verbal students to get role plays off to a good start. However, he was pleased to see that Jeff wanted to begin today's session. Jeff is generally one of the quieter students in class. Because he is a team cocaptain for the softball games, he was particularly distressed by the outbreaks of temperament yesterday.

When this class first began learning Role Playing, several students used the opportunity to clown around and move the role plays in the direction of unacceptable humor. While Mr. Liben expected this to a degree, he was concerned that some key students in this class would never make the transition to appropriate role playing behavior. It has been a while since this class worked with Role Playing, so he was pleased that Vanessa rose to the occasion today. In the past, she tended to sabotage some of the role plays by making jokes or unsuitable remarks. Yesterday on the softball diamond, Vanessa was accused of cheating by not touching one of the bases on a triple play. She was furious that her integrity was challenged during the game. Mr. Liben noticed that Vanessa took the role playing seriously today, and she contributed to the discussion in a meaningful way: as a team player.

Another small victory occurred today when Alejandro spoke for the first time on his own. The most recent immigrant student at this school, Alejandro spoke no English when he arrived. He has been reticent to speak up in any class unless he received much encouragement. Role Playing, Reader's Theater, and Reciprocal Teaching have provided engaging and supportive opportunities for Alejandro to communicate in class using English. Mr. Liben has also had the pleasure of watching other ESL students' English proficiency strengthen in class, and he credits Role Playing, as well as other active learning experiences, for this increased fluency.

Mr. Liben felt that the entire class was thoroughly engaged during the role plays. Of course, the relative success or failure of these role plays cannot be evaluated until after the next softball games. What happens during today's games will shed light on the students' progress in dealing with conflict on the field. Tomorrow during lunch, the teacher coaches and team captains will have a joint meeting. Mr. Liben hopes that behavior problems will not dominate the discussion.

The Stages of Role Playing

If your students have never participated in Role Playing before, then you need to prepare them for what is expected during a Role Playing session. Like many models of teaching, especially cooperative learning models that require social skills, it is best to ease into Role Playing gradually. Some teachers begin with short, commercially written materials. Working with situations that are not very complex helps prepare students for Role Playing that explores detailed or nuanced situations. Gregory

> ### Table 10.1   Money for Marty
>
> **The problem:** The issue is honesty. If someone has cheated you, is it fair to cheat him in return? Bryan owes Marty for money he has borrowed but not paid back in spite of Marty's repeated requests. Marty has a chance to get his money back; he can steal it in a way that will cause Bryan much trouble.
>
> **Introducing the problem:** Say to the group, "Have you ever lent something to a friend who just never gets around to giving it back? If you have, you can remember how provoked you felt. This story is about such a happening. The story stops but is not finished. As I read it, think of ways in which you might end it."
>
> Marty had put his foot on a shiny dollar. Nearby, on hands and knees, Bryan was searching in the grass carefully parting the blades to peer between them for a silvery telltale glint.
>
> "Marty, help me," he pleaded. "I've lost my dollar!"
>
> "Too bad," Marty said. "Too bad you didn't pay me what you owe me before you lost that money."
>
> "Oh, I couldn't pay you out of *that* dollar!"
>
> "Oh, no? Well, you are, chum, you are," Marty said to himself. He was really disgusted with Bryan. He had lent Bryan money for a movie just the week before, when Bryan already owed him for a hot dog and a Coke. But Bryan, who was good at mooching, always managed to forget any debts he owed.
>
> "I couldn't pay you from *that* half dollar," Bryan explained, "because it isn't mine. Besides, it's special. It's a coin from my Dad's collection. I brought it to school to show Mr. Dolan. He collects coins. I didn't tell my Dad I was taking it. He doesn't like me to mess with his collection. Besides, this coin isn't worth just a dollar. It's scarce, so it's worth a lot more. Dad'll really be sore!"
>
> "So you're in trouble," Marty thought. "Well, go ahead and squirm. You got it coming to you." Then Marty thought of Bryan's father. He'd be really rough on Bryan. Marty almost lifted his foot, almost said, "Hey, look . . ." but checked the impulse. Bryan needed a lesson.
>
> But this would be so tough a lesson.

SOURCE: From *Role-Playing for Social Values: Decision-making in the Social Studies* by Fannie R. Shaftel and George Shaftel. Published by Allyn & Bacon, Boston, MA. Copyright © 1967 by Pearson Education. Reprinted by permission of the publisher.

Stock's *Kids' Book of Questions Revised for the 21st Century* (2004) is an excellent source of brief prepared situations that can be adapted for Role Playing. Lawrence Kohlberg used complex situations, **moral dilemmas,** to evaluate boys' stages of moral development (1963), and these might be appropriate for use in your classroom. In their excellent books about Role Playing, Shaftel and Shaftel (1967a, 1967b) have provided many classroom-ready problem situations of varying lengths and complexities that you may use directly or adapt. An example is reproduced in Table 10.1. You may also find that you have a flair for developing these materials on your own based on the typical problems your students encounter.

Role Playing requires students to think on their feet and be vulnerable in ways that are usually uncommon in classrooms. Students will feel comfortable Role Playing only in a learning environment that supports and values sensitivity and

Many typical school situations, such as gossiping or socially excluding students, are appropriate material for Role Playing sessions.

honesty along with risk taking and creativity. To ensure that kind of environment, certain ground rules must be established: no put-downs or sarcastic humor at another's expense, and no interrupting one another at any time during the role play or discussion. Any student should have the right to pass at being a player, although everyone should be encouraged to join in group discussions.

Students experience authentic conflicts in everyday social situations. Some of these conflicts, such as stealing, gossiping, cheating, and friendship concerns, may be common to most groups of students. Others, such as bullying, tattling, and sharing, are more age specific. While it is not the teacher's job to manipulate student responses or solutions toward particular ends, it is wise to review the specifics of a given conflict and imagine possible directions a role play may lead. This preparation will help you defuse any tense situations should they arise and will inform the way you begin each role play session. The stages of Role Playing are discussed below and then summarized in Table 10.2.

Warming Up the Class

Shaftel and Shaftel suggest that you begin each session by warming up the students (1967a). Time will always be a limiting factor, especially for secondary school teachers who are not on block scheduling. However, every Role Playing session requires a brief warm-up period. Students need a moment to shift gears from their last class or activity to a proper mind-set for Role Playing. Warming up may be as simple as reviewing what the group understands about a previous problem or briefly presenting a new situation in an engaging way. In Case Study 10.1, Mr. Liben set the stage by opening a brief discussion of the difficulties experienced yesterday on the softball fields. He elicited the students' input in this discussion by asking them to recall the disturbances during their games and the feelings that were engendered.

Choosing the First Set of Participants

It is always best to begin role plays with volunteers, students who are willing to take a risk. When you introduce Role Playing for the first time, it helps to stress that the collective intention for the class is to explore interpersonal problems and characters' actions and reactions, not to win an Academy Award. Role plays are not expected to be funny. Student volunteers or teacher-selected players are usually the best choices. Nominations from the other students can conceal ulterior motives or some form of peer retribution (Shaftel & Shaftel, 1982). Mr. Liben felt that his first two players had a vested interest in the positive outcome of these role plays, especially Jeff, who is a team captain. Since the content of these role plays is a pressing issue and highly charged emotionally, Mr. Liben was wise to go with volunteers who would help set a positive and serious tone for today's session.

Establishing the Problem, Characters, and Setting

Whether you are working with prepared materials or with problems that are close to home, the specifics of the first role play need to be established. As Johnson, Johnson, and Holubec remind us, when we teach social skills, students need to understand a problem exists and agree to work together toward a remedy (1994). This public consensus on the situation of each role play alleviates performance anxiety for some students because it reminds them that they are not creating a scene from scratch.

Once the problem is clarified, the characters must be described, and the scene must be set for place and time. You can help the students by asking these kinds of questions:

Who are our characters?

Why have we chosen these characters?

Where is this scene taking place, and why?

What time of day does our scene occur?

What are the characters doing as the scene begins?

In our case study, Mr. Liben and Ms. Meredith were working from a real-life problem that had occurred the day before. As he assessed students' comments during the warm-up, Mr. Liben suggested that the first role play focus on the batters' being hurt by wild pitches. Everyone in the room knew exactly which characters and what time and place were involved.

Preparing the Observers

To fuel the group discussion to come, you may want to direct the observers' attention to particular behaviors or reactions by the players. You may want the group to watch and evaluate the plausibility of each character's emotional response to a situation. Another possibility is to have students focus on the choice of vocabulary or vocal expression used during the role play. You will want to prompt the observers before each new setup if the focus or intention of the role play has changed. Ms. Meredith gave two separate instructions to the group. She advised the observers to notice the players' motivations and reactions, and she also reminded them that during the role play itself, they should not call out to any character in response to what they see and hear. That kind of behavior contributed to the problems on the field the day before.

Role Playing the First Scene

The first set of participants chosen will role-play the situation with improvised character actions and reactions to the problem and to one another. The players must establish the situation, characters, and setting. If the situation comes from real life, the beginning of the scene must reflect what actually happened. How long the role play continues may vary in several ways. In some cases, the players can continue the role play through the first solution. Once the first solution has been illustrated, the teacher stops the action. The content and nature of the first solution will prompt questions relating to the problem situation. These questions will fuel your students' first full-group discussion. In other cases, you may want to stop the action for discussion prior to the first solution.

In the case of Mr. Liben's class, Jeff, the team captain, stopped the action of the first role play himself by asking Mr. Liben how to proceed. He and Noemi had been asked to set up the scene, and it was clear that they were moving toward the emotions and responses generated during the games the day before. Since Jeff had stopped the action, Mr. Liben turned the discussion over to the group. This is an example of the fluidity of the Role Playing model in practice. Like Mr. Liben, you will need to make swift decisions about how to use your time and which direction to proceed during every role play. These moments provide an immediacy and energy to this model of teaching.

Stopping Action for Discussion and Evaluation

Each discussion interval will play out in a unique way. Most of these discussions will begin with students' reactions to what they saw and heard in the role play. This may happen with little intervention by the teacher, or skilled questioning might be required, depending on the makeup of the class and the students' sophistication with the Role Playing process. The questions below might be useful in the first discussion:

Have you seen this situation in your experiences?

Talk about how the scene was or wasn't played on target as we described the situation.

Did the solution look and sound and feel on target? Why? Why not?

Did you think these characters would react to one another in these ways?

Why or why not?

What would have happened if . . . ?

What is (name) feeling now? Why do you think so?

What does (name) character's response tell you about what he or she thinks is important?

Your manner in engaging the group through questioning is central to the overall success of a role play session and the degree of student learning. One measure of teachers' skills in leading role plays is whether they can keep a nonevaluative stance during the discussion periods (Shaftel & Shaftel, 1967a). Emphasizing follow-up questions that ask why will help keep you less judgmental yet still keep you honest in your reactions to the group's response to each role play. It is wise to steer clear of questions that can be answered with a simple yes or no because they may cut off further analytical or critical thinking. Shaftel and Shaftel (1967a) also suggest that teachers structure questions to inquire, What might happen next? or What will happen next? rather than, What should happen next? *Should* questions can shut down honest dialogue because they seem to prescribe the direction any further thinking must take.

However, Role Playing cannot be described as a value-free model of teaching. The model was conceived to serve as a powerful interactive learning experience whose ultimate goals were decidedly moral. Given the social turbulence of the times in which the model was developed for use in the classroom, the 1960s and 1970s, it is not surprising that the objectives of Role Playing included preparing citizens to live responsibly and with integrity in a free, democratic, and diverse U.S. society.

Should teachers give their opinions of actions taken during role plays? Certainly. As with much of teaching, however, timing is everything. Your opinions, considered in concert with your rationale for holding them, will be an important dimension in Role Playing sessions. Given the structure of Role Playing, offering your views on a level playing field as a participant in the full-group discussions will be more effective than presenting your views immediately as "the lesson to be learned" for that day.

Mr. Liben began the first discussion by asking his students to analyze the players' motivations and the possible effects of their actions. He also modeled active listening by paraphrasing points made during the discussion. He hopes this paraphrasing of student ideas will help underscore the importance of understanding others' thoughts and feelings that surface during the discussions. A major goal of Role Playing is helping students see that all behavior is based on individual values or the values of a social group with which we readily identify. Neither individual nor group behavior occurs in a vacuum. All our actions and reactions in response to the world rest on our conceptions of what is valuable, right, and good. Any response we have to our environment and to one another can be analyzed to reveal what it says about our commitments and concerns as individuals. The teachers demonstrated this connection between actions and values when they asked what Noemi's suggestion to enlist a teacher's help said about her character.

Revising the Scene With New Players

Students will experience aha! moments as a result of observing the first scene. Then it is time to explore alternative solutions to the problem. Ask which of your students has another idea about how the situation might be addressed. Out of a number of possible solutions, choose another one to advance the role play into unexplored territory.

At this point, other players are selected from the students who have proposed new solutions, as Mr. Liben did by choosing Danny and Vanessa. You will need to help these new players set their scene by asking these questions:

Where are you?

What are you doing as the scene begins?

What will you need to say to show how your solution works?

What will you need to do to show how your solution works?

These questions or similar ones, repeated as each new role play begins, help keep the players and the observers focused on the next role play.

Stopping Action Again for Discussion and Evaluation

As you observe alternative scenes, look for shifts in characters' responses, evidence of how these new responses reflect characters' values, and clues to different consequences that are implied or shown directly. Your observations will provide you with appropriate places to stop the action. Depending on the time you have available, you may work through several alternative solution cycles. Remember that the follow-up discussions to each role play are crucial to student learning and should not be shortchanged.

Generalizing About the Experiences

The final reflective task in a Role Playing session is to guide the students in deciding what they learned as a result of the role play. You might ask your students to judge which solution seemed to be the best one and why that was so. Shaftel and Shaftel (1967a) suggest these questions to help your students with this process of generalization:

Which of the solutions to this problem do you think is best?

Why is it best?

For whom is it best?

Who will be unhappy with this solution?

Table 10.2 The Role Playing Cycle

Stage	Teacher's Tasks	Students' Tasks	Notes
Warming up the class	Provide verbal and physical warm-up activities—exercises, theater games, etc.	Participate	Warm-up requires only a brief time but is essential for preparing students to contribute.
Choosing the first set of participants	Chooses student volunteers who will most likely get the role play session off to a good start.	Volunteer	The combination of student volunteers and teacher choice of participants will likely get the role play off to a good start.
Establishing the problem, characters, and setting	Reviews reason for the role play, questions students about the setting and the characters	Answer the teacher's questions	Make sure that the problem you wish to focus on is clearly defined by the answers to these questions.
Preparing the observers	Asks a specific question or directs the observers to watch or listen for something specific during the role play	Observe with teacher's prompt in mind	Narrowing the focus of the observation is important so that the discussions can center on the problem at hand.
Role playing the first scene	Gives the signal for the players to begin Allows the first role play to continue until the problem situation has been established or until the first solution has been provided	Play the first scene to get the role play session underway Observers watch the role pay	Make sure that the players are clear about the situation and the observers know what to look for in the role play.
Stopping action for discussion and evaluation	Discusses the viability of the first solution	Participate in the discussion	Coach the observers in appropriate comments.
Revising scene with new players	Chooses new players and sets up the next role play	Volunteer to role-play the next solution Watch the role play	Make sure that the players are clear about the situation and the observers know what to look for in the role play.
Stopping action again for discussion and evaluation	Allows the next role play to continue until the next solution has been provided. Discusses the viability of the new solution played by the participants	Participate in the discussion	Remind the observers about appropriate comments.
Repeated revising and stopping action for discussion as necessary		Participate in full-group discussion	Involve as many students as possible in the discussion
Generalizing about the experiences	Facilitates full-group discussion Asks such questions as, Which of the solutions to this problem do you think is best and why? Who will be happy and who will be unhappy with these solutions? How do you choose if you can't make everybody happy?		

SOURCE: Adapted from Shaftel & Shaftel, 1967a.

How do you choose if you can't make everybody happy?

If you were _____ (a person in the scene), how would you choose?

If you were _____ (another person in the scene), how would you choose?

Expect your best questions to arise out of the role play discussion itself.

For another kind of generalizing activity, ask students how they might describe the "big ideas" that emerged in the session. You can ask them directly what they learned as a result of the Role Playing session. Ms. Meredith and Mr. Liben asked their students for the "headlines" of today's class. The class agreed that outbursts of temper may jeopardize their opportunities on the field.

The richness of discussion intervals throughout a role play and the wrap-up generalizing discussion determine the success of the session. If students' behavior changes over time in a positive way as a result of the critical thinking generated through role playing, discussions, and generalizing, then the experience has definitely been worthwhile.

Themes for Role Playing in Social Studies and Literature

Creative classroom teachers have adapted Role Playing for exploring academic content in social studies and language arts (Shaftel & Shaftel, 1967b). Some topics that serve as excellent material for real-life role plays can also be explored in the context of a historical era or event or of character motivation in literature. Issues of honesty, fair-mindedness, revenge, rules, self-acceptance, prejudice, rejection, integrity in friendship, responsibility to the self and to the group, and cooperation are perennial themes that resonate in students' personal lives at both elementary and secondary levels (Shaftel & Shaftel, 1967a).

The improvisational nature of Role Playing allows students to explore ways in which both famous and everyday people reacted or might have reacted in moments of historic significance. Preludes to historic moments or situations can also provide topics for role plays. For example, what conversations did Harriet Tubman have with abolitionists as she described how the Underground Railroad would be run? What dialogues might have occurred between Martin Luther King, Jr., and his wife, Coretta Scott King, on the eve of the March on Washington? What conversations might have transpired at the dinner table of Neil Armstrong's family as he was deciding what to say as he took the first steps on the moon? Multiple role play cycles allow the players and observers to reassess and revise their responses to what actually happened and what might have been.

In studies of novels or plays, role plays can be used to create scenes that do not exist in the actual work. What might have been said between Scout and Boo Radley on the porch swing at the end of the film version of *To Kill a Mockingbird?* In *Because of Winn-Dixie*, what might Opal say to her mother if she meets her when she is a teenager? Providing creative opportunities to use Role Playing deepens students' understanding of characters and situations, as well as curiosity about the author's intentions. The stop-action feature of Role Playing allows students to envision, perform, and analyze choices made by the players in a role.

Case Study 10.2: Fourth Grade, the Tattletale Problem

Ms. Hazekamp and Mrs. Abraham have team taught fourth grade for many years in a highly diverse elementary school. While they find the fourth-grade curriculum exciting to teach, this age group typically goes through social difficulties that try the teachers' patience. The tattletale issue has become especially problematic this semester. While they realize that this is a problem in most elementary school classrooms and generally needs to be addressed each school year, the two teachers have found that this year their students are particularly interested in everyone else's business, and especially the transgressions of others. Last week was particularly aggravating for the teachers.

At the beginning of every school year, Ms. Hazekamp and Mrs. Abraham model appropriate behaviors such as lining up in the classroom, walking to and from their specials or the library, and of course, fire drill procedures. The children enjoy their teachers' antics as they model silly behaviors that are clearly not appropriate in school situations. (Fire drill behaviors are modeled more seriously.) However, these teachers believe the class's increasing tattletale problem is best addressed with a more formal, problem-solving approach. Many of their students remember how to role play because they used it in class to help solve their difficulties sharing supplies last year. Mrs. Abraham begins.

Mrs. Abraham:	Yesterday things got very out of hand. Who can tell me why Ms. Hazekamp and I were so angry in the afternoon? Ben?
Ben:	We had a team meeting before the end of the school day. You told us that it had been one of the most difficult weeks of the whole school year. You wanted us to think about our tattling and be ready to talk about it today.
Mrs. Abraham:	How many of you have had students tattle on you this week? (*Many hands are raised.*) What do tattletales sometimes tell their teachers about other students? What are the kinds of things students will tattle about? Please don't use anyone's name. We don't want this team meeting to be another episode of tattling. Ms. Hazekamp will write your ideas on the chalkboard. Jay?
Jay:	Copying someone's work.
Mrs. Abraham:	Another tattle? Patrick?

Patrick:	Taking too much of something.
Mrs. Abraham:	Carrie?
Carrie:	Fooling around during silent reading time.
Mrs. Abraham:	OK. Another idea? Brad?
Brad:	Cutting in line in the hallway.
Ms. Hazekamp:	Mrs. Abraham, I think we have more than enough to work with today. Now we need to work out solutions to some of these problems so that they don't always end in tattling. Brad is right. We did have a lot of trouble this week with people cutting in line on the way to lunch or the library. Anywhere else? Marianna?
Marianna:	The recess line. Some people want to cut to the front of the line so they can race to their favorite play area first.
Ms. Hazekamp:	Let's not jump to any reasons just yet. Mrs. Abraham, would you like to set up our first role play?
Mrs. Abraham:	Sure. We need two players. One player needs to be a person who is trying to cut into the line. The other player is the person who is angry about this. Let's have the role play take place after the class visit to the library. You are in line outside the door waiting for us. Who would like to role play first? Alli and Scott? Alli, why don't you play the person who is second in the recess line. Scott, try to cut in line, and see how Alli responds to you. (*Alli is standing in line. Scott walks up from behind and tries to take the place in line in front of her.*)
Alli:	Ms. Hazekamp, should I tattle on Scott?
Ms. Hazekamp:	We'll tell you when to stop the scene. Right now, just do and say what you might under these circumstances. Here we go.
Scott:	This is my spot behind Jacob.
Alli:	No it isn't, Scott. You are somewhere back in the line with Brian.
Scott:	I needed a drink of water. That is why I am late lining up. This is my spot, Alli.
Alli:	Scott, you always try to do this. You always try to cut into the line, and you always pick on the girls.
Scott:	That is so not true, Alli. You are always so whiny. Mrs. Abraham and Ms. Hazekamp don't like it when you are whiny.

Alli:	Well, I'm not going to push you out of line, because then I'll get into trouble, but as soon as the teachers come out of the library, I am going to tell them what you did.
Mrs. Abraham:	OK. Let's stop for now. Good job. Did Alli and Scott set up this problem well? Did they leave anything out? Karyl?
Karyl:	Alli didn't say anything to you or Ms. Abraham yet about Scott's tattling.
Ms. Hazekamp.	Remember, we want to practice some ideas that will help you solve these problems before someone tattles. What do Mrs. Abraham and I usually say when someone tattles? Nicole?
Nicole:	Work it out yourselves.
Mrs. Abraham:	Right. Good job, you two. Let's have another two players set this scene up again, but this time we want the players to try to work this out before one of them comes to the teachers. Nicki and Sandy?
Sandy:	Do we need to say those same words exactly?
Mrs. Abraham:	No, not exactly, but play the scene in a similar way. It is OK to change the words. Start when you are ready.
Nicki:	(*moves right in front of Sandy*) Sandy, you are in my way.
Sandy:	(*moves in front of Nicki*) This is my place, Nicki. Your place in line is back there. I remember when Ms. Hazekamp called our names before we left the classroom. We are supposed to be in the same places now.
Nicki:	I wanted some water and that made me late.
Sandy:	Nicki, you and Zoe do this every day. You always try to cut into the line, and you always pick on me and Anisa.
Nicki:	Uh-uh. Stop whining. Mrs. Abraham and Ms. Hazekamp don't like it when we whine.
Sandy:	I am going to tell on you. You could have waited to get back to the classroom for a drink of water.
Ms. Hazekamp:	Now wait, Sandy. At this point, you need to try another idea besides saying right away that you will tell on Nicki. What else might you say to her that could help solve the problem? The teachers will be out of the library soon.
Sandy:	(*She pauses*) Ms. Hazekamp, this is hard. I just want her to stop cutting.
Ms. Hazekamp:	That is why we are role playing today. What else might you say?

Sandy:	Well, if Manuel and Victoria are behind me, and Ben was in front of me as line leader, they would remember how our line began.
Mrs. Abraham:	Let's get those players up there with you. Ben will be the line leader, and Manuel and Victoria stand behind Sandy. You two can have your own quiet conversation in line. OK, Sandy, what are you going to say?
Ben:	Wait, Mrs. A. What do I do?
Mrs. Abraham:	What do you usually do when you are standing in line—especially when you are a line leader?
Ben:	I think about recess—after I think about lunch.
Mrs. Abraham:	Then you don't have to do or say anything yet. We'll see how you are put into the scene by our players. Are we ready to continue? (*They nod.*)
Sandy:	Nicki, let's ask Manuel and Victoria who was the line leader in front of me when we left the classroom. Manuel, do you remember who was in front of me when we walked to the library?
Manuel:	(*Groans*) Not again, Sandy. (*The class laughs.*) Yeah, I remember that you were right behind Ben. You made a big deal about it . . . again. (*The class laughs, including Sandy.*)
Sandy:	Still, Nicki wasn't in front of me. Am I right, Victoria?
Victoria:	Yes, Sandy. You are right.
Sandy:	Ben, are you listening?
Ben:	(*He turns to face Sandy*) What? What?
Sandy:	Weren't you listening?
Ben:	No, I wasn't. (*The class laughs again.*)
Sandy:	Do you remember who walked after you in line to the library?
Ben:	Yes, I do. It was you, Sandy. You were taking big steps, and you stepped on the heel of my shoe. You said you didn't do it on purpose. I had to take it off in the library and retie the laces.
Sandy:	See, Nicki, you weren't in line after Ben. Everyone remembers that I was.
Nicki:	OK . . . OK. I'll try to find where I was in line. (*She moves to the back of a long imaginary line of students.*)
Ms. Hazekamp:	Stop! Excellent solution! Did anyone call anyone else a name?
Class:	No!

Ben:	Yeah, but she kept pestering us, Ms. Hazekamp.
Ms. Hazekamp:	Maybe a little, but did she threaten to tattle?
Class:	No!
Ms. Hazekamp:	Great! So, let's try another solution to the problem. Heather?
Heather:	Ms. Hazekamp, it shouldn't always be a girl who wants to tattle. The boys tattle, also.
Ms. Hazekamp:	That's true. How about one boy and one girl as players for the scene? Jason and Rosie. Jason, you need to be the student in line.
	(Jason and Rosie play out their version of the beginning of the scene. When they get to the place where Jason says that he is going to tattle, Rosie stops the action and addresses Mrs. Abraham.)
Rosie:	So, he can't push me out of line, right? And I can't push him out of line, either, right?
Mrs. Abraham:	Right. That is one of rules when we role play. OK, continue.
Rosie:	Jason, if the teachers see us fighting in the hallway, they'll be very angry at us, and I'm not going to move back in the line because I want to be closer to the line leader spot because it isn't fair that I have never, ever been the line leader this whole year . . . so there. *(She stands defiantly next to Jason in line.)* So, are you going to tattle on me, you tattletale? Everyone knows you are a big tattletale. *(Jason looks distraught)*
Mrs. Abraham:	*(in a quiet voice)* Remember that this is just a role play. Jason, what will you say next?
Jason:	*(pauses for a few moments)* Rosie, I don't know who has been the line leader this year and who hasn't. I haven't had my turn yet, either. I am sure that the teachers have a list, and someone will be at the beginning of the list and someone will be at the bottom. Maybe we are just at the bottom. It isn't fair for you to push away anyone in line because it isn't our fault you haven't been the line leader.
Rosie:	But I get so mad. No one ever sees me first in my class. The teachers and students in the hallways always notice who the line leader is, and it is never me.
Jason:	Listen, hurry up and find your real place in line now. Sometime today we can ask one of the teachers which one of us will be line leader first, you or me. If I am supposed to be first, you can have my week if it is OK with them. *(Rosie sadly nods and walks to where the back of the line might be.)*

Mrs. Abraham: Wow! Jason never threatened to tattle, and Rosie agreed to move back to her place in line. This is what we call a compromise. Both Jason and Rosie got something that they wanted. Do you think Ms. Hazekamp or I would agree to Jason's plan? Anthony?

Anthony: I think so. But I think we would all like to know how you put our names in order to be line leaders.

Mrs. Abraham: Ms. Hazekamp, do you want to tell them how we do that?

Ms. Hazekamp: Sure. At the beginning of the year, we take your name cards before we tape them to your desks, and we shuffle them just like we might when we play a game of Crazy Eights. Then we record them in order from the top card down. We shuffle again to decide who will be the Star Student each week. Do you think that is fair? (*The students nod.*)

Mrs. Abraham: You all did an excellent job today. The players found solutions that worked out well without any tattling, and the observers paid careful attention to what was happening in each scene. Those of you who are new to our team this year know a little more about how we learn to solve problems in our class. Ms. Hazekamp and I will expect all of you to think more carefully about what you say and what you do about tattling from now on. On Monday, we will finish our discussion about your Role Playing work today and what we have learned about tattling.

Case Study 10.2: Post-Lesson Reflection

Ms. Hazekamp and Mrs. Abraham are pleased that the fourth graders who asked to be players today remembered most of the rules for Role Playing. After this lesson, they wonder whether they should have reviewed the steps of Role Playing before jumping into today's work. Did they make an emotional decision based on how cranky they increasingly were throughout the course of the week, or did they sense their students were ready to go right to work this afternoon? After the fact, they also realize that they did not take time to warm up the class before today's role plays. Ordinarily, they use both these stages in Role Playing. In any case, they believe today's role plays were very productive for everyone.

The solutions the players came up with worked out well. Mrs. Abraham mentions that Nicki bordered on the sarcastic at times during her role play. When the teachers reviewed what was said in that role play, they tried to decide whether those same words could have been said in a manner that was neither sarcastic nor whiny. They didn't want to call Nicki on this during the role play because her solution did work, and they couldn't be sure what her player's intention was during the role play. Not being sure, they decide to talk about this point the next time the class role plays. They will tell the students, "What you say is important, but how you say it is equally important. Voice and mannerisms count when you are trying to solve a problem."

Even though it was not their intention, humor did creep into the role plays. Today, the jokes and reactions made by the students did not compromise the purpose of Role Playing. If they had, the teachers might have addressed the distractions in the moment, but everyone stayed on task today.

Mrs. Abraham and Ms. Hazekamp's first hope is that they will not have to revisit tattling again this year. Because the day was coming to a close, the class did not have time to discuss which solution was the most effective or how the students might start thinking more generally about tattling. The teachers decide that they clearly prefer how Jason addressed the problem in the last role play. His solution provided a compromise that addressed the feelings of both players, even if Rosie ended the role play less happy than she might have been. Mrs. Abraham and Ms. Hazekamp realize that fairness is a very big issue with third and fourth graders, and they often weigh everything that is said and done in class and on the playground. Sandy needed to feel that the problem was solved in a fair way, which, for her, required testimony from the other players.

Mrs. Abraham and Ms. Hazekamp hope that from now on, their students will work harder toward solving their real-life problems effectively on their own. The teachers decide to bring this issue up again during their Monday morning meeting, praising the students for their Friday role plays and stating their expectations for the week in regard to tattling. Both teachers believe their students showed their true colors.

Brief Background of Role Playing

Role Playing was developed in the 1940s by Hendry, Lippitt, & Zander (1947) to use "problem stories" to help people learn to cope with difficult interpersonal relationships. Shaftel and Shaftel, a husband-and-wife team of psychologists, modified the format for Role Playing, and in the 1960s they introduced the model to educators to teach students "ethical behavior" (Shaftel & Shaftel, 1952, 1967a). The Shaftels published a number of books that codified a series of steps to help teachers facilitate Role Playing in classrooms (1967a, 1967b, 1967c, 1976, 1982). Similar Role Playing procedures have been described by others (Chesler & Fox, 1966). This chapter relies primarily on the Shaftel and Shaftel format. Role Playing provides reality practice for students to experiment with various reactions, behaviors, and approaches to social problems (1967a). As a result of their Role Playing experiences, students come to understand that behaviors are chosen by individuals and that values and beliefs inform their actions.

Many teachers believe that Role Playing is synonymous with students doing simulations or some form of creative drama. As a formal model of teaching, this is not the case. However, all the models of teaching can be modified creatively to meet teachers' objectives and students' needs. The three sections below view Role Playing as a model of teaching for social problem solving.

Role Playing and Research on Teaching

Research in the last half of the 20th century demonstrated in several ways the positive effects of Role Playing in K–12 classrooms. As early as the late 1940s and early 1950s, Role Playing was seen to alleviate social tensions among classroom cliques. Providing time for Role Playing experiences for students also helped teachers establish a comfortable classroom atmosphere and promote academic achievement (Lippitt, 1949–1950; Trow, 1950; Jensen, 1955; Crosby, 1963).

In the course of their research in 1953, Daley and Cain requested permission to introduce Role Playing to a group of cognitively impaired adolescent students. Initially, the teacher was skeptical that her students could achieve the attention span needed to grasp the problem presented to them, comment on the situation and characters, and then offer solutions. She underestimated their attention span, their level of interest, and their willingness to engage in problem solving. Her students' response to Role Playing measured up to the responses of adolescents without impairments. Daley and Cain attributed the students' success to the fact that they had also experienced elements of the problem situation and could empathize with the characters (Shaftel & Shaftel, 1967a).

Moser (1975) found that Role Playing affected students' **locus of control** in a positive way. Positive locus of control expectancy means that as a result of their Role Playing, the students were likely to see that things happened to them as a result of their own actions and not because they were lucky or profited from the actions of others. Role Playing helped them experience how their actions affected themselves and others in difficult situations.

Swink and Buchanan (1984) also analyzed the effects of Role Playing on students' perceptions of the power of their own actions. Swink and Buchanan demonstrated that the discussion intervals in the Role Playing procedure were the determining factor in the beliefs students' held about their own efficacy. Discussion intervals foster both the safe environment and the cognitive stimulation necessary for students to have significant discovery moments about their behavior and its effect on others. Swink and Buchanan also found that Role Playing that focused on creative play alone did not promote students' sense of self-efficacy or student self-knowledge.

The overall effectiveness of Role Playing in promoting successful interpersonal problem solving led business and industry communities to use the model in corporate managerial training. By the 1960s, when education discovered the uses and benefits of Role Playing, the business community and the mental health professions had been using the model in their fields for some time and with much success. It is still used in these professions in a variety of ways. Currently manuals, videos, and workshops explore the value of Role Playing in improving interpersonal relationships among colleagues and between labor and management (Shaw, Corsini, Blake, & Mouton, 1980).

Role Playing and Learning Theory

The humanist movement in education took its lead from the human potential movement in psychology, which came of age in the 1960s. As its title implies, the goals of the human potential movement were to establish and maintain a society that promoted individual freedom and nourished the creative potential in everyone. Rather than focus solely on students' mastery of academic content, humanism advocates that schools educate "the whole child," the affective, physical, and cognitive lives of students. In the classroom, humanism emphasizes the affective development of students: their feelings, values, attitudes, beliefs, self-esteem, relationships with others, and relationship to society.

These goals of humanism also relate directly to Howard Gardner's ideas about two of the multiple intelligences (Gardner, 2000). The **interpersonal intelligence** is the ability to interact well with others under a variety of circumstances, both pleasant and unpleasant. The **intrapersonal intelligence** is the ability to reflect on one's own thoughts, feelings, and emotions. Given the structure and dynamics of Role Playing, students are able to display and strengthen both their interpersonal and intrapersonal intelligences.

Several assumptions of humanism relate directly to the classroom: Individuals are capable of making autonomous choices about their education; human development is unlimited; self-concept affects human development; humans are drawn toward personal development; and individuals are responsible to others as well as to themselves (Elias & Merriam, 1980). Role Playing is consistent with each of these humanist assumptions. To believe in the efficacy of Role Playing as a tool for social problem solving is to believe that human beings are capable of change. Role Playing helps students make responsible autonomous choices because it provides a forum for exploring multiple ways of acting and reacting in a given situation. Successive role plays and discussion intervals provide students with guided experiences in observing individuals as they create solutions to social problems—solutions that will benefit all stakeholders, not just themselves. The last stage in the cycle, generalizing, helps students view the outcome of role plays and discussions in a larger social context. These discussions can help students understand and apply their role play experiences to their everyday lives and growing self-awareness.

Significant learning about oneself is apt to take place in the context of learning experiences (such as Role Playing) that actively involve both the intellect and the emotions. Students achieve a greater measure of self-awareness and ultimately self-control as they hear the motivations of characters, observe the consequences of their actions, and have the opportunity to reflect on their own motivations and values in similar situations. Role Playing sessions that are facilitated well by teachers can help reveal students' emotional and social progress over time. This sense of personal accomplishment will affect their self-esteem in a positive way. These are goals of humanism that are furthered by Role Playing.

Role Playing and Philosophies of Curriculum and Instruction

Role Playing reflects the self-actualization philosophy of curriculum and instruction. Major figures of humanism are associated with the self-actualization philosophy, including psychologists Carl Rogers and Abraham Maslow. Role Playing is aligned with several of Carl Rogers's educational priorities (1969). As you read in

The self-reflection that occurs in discussion intervals and generalizing stages of Role Playing provides support for students' affective and cognitive development.

Chapter 2, Rogers believed that students will thrive only when a climate of trust has been established in the classroom. The success of Role Playing depends on students feeling comfortable enough to be vulnerable to others when they participate as players. They must know that their efforts as players will be regarded in terms of the appropriateness of their solutions and not the quality of their acting abilities. They also need to know that their contributions as observers will be met with respect, even if their ideas differ from their classmates'. These guiding principles of Role Playing help strengthen students' positive self-esteem as they experience being valuable members of their classroom community.

Teachers who are skilled in facilitating the interval and final discussions in the Role Playing cycle will further students' understanding that there are emotional as well as intellectual learning processes. The teacher's bird's-eye view of students' emotional growth can be communicated to the students over the course of the school year. Their personal self-reflection involved in the generalizing stage of the

Role Playing cycle will provide students with significant touchstones in their continual self-discovery or, using Maslow's term, self-actualization.

Several of Carl Rogers's ideas are mirrored in Abraham Maslow's hierarchy of needs (1968), several of which are addressed in Role Playing. As you read in Chapter 2, Maslow believed that students' deficiency needs must be addressed before learning can occur. The structure and ground rules of Role Playing can be said to focus on two of the four deficiency needs: safety and esteem. When teachers have created a trusting climate, students feel that they are not threatened in their classrooms. During Role Playing discussions, students should know that what they have to offer will be valued by their peers. Maslow believed that once deficiency needs are met, people can turn to being needs as lifetime endeavors that lead them toward self-actualization. Role Playing promotes students' exploration and discovery of their own values. Opportunities for students to explore their values relate directly to their cognitive needs, one of the being needs in Maslow's hierarchy.

Technology and Role Playing

Technology can be integrated into Role Playing lessons and activities in two major ways. Role plays can illustrate how individuals and groups contend with the "social, ethical, and human issues" connected to the use of technology (National Educational Technology [NET] Performance Indicators and Standards for Students 2; International Society for Technology in Education, 2000).* Here are a few examples:

Freedom of speech issues in a democracy

Fair use of commercial software

Opinions about and uses of violent software

Responsible use of the Internet

Creation of Web sites that mislead the public

Protection of minors from unsavory and inappropriate Web sites

Uses and misuses of blogs and chat rooms

Misuse of videophones

Opinions differ about these emerging issues, and Role Playing can provide an added dimension to the typical class discussion of these controversies. The model may also permit students who have been reticent in class discussions to contribute their ideas "in role."

---

*National Educational Technology Standards for Students: Connecting Curriculum and Technology by ISTE. Copyright © 2000 by International Society for Technology in Education (ISTE), 800–336–5191 (US & Canada) or 541–302–3777 (Int'l), iste@iste.org, www.iste.org. All rights reserved. Reproduced with permission of ISTE via Copyright Clearance Center. Reprint permission does not constitute endorsement by ISTE.

Students can also use technology to create products that illustrate role play solutions for situations that confront school-age children and adolescents: honesty, bullying, cheating on examinations, stealing, plagiarism, fighting, tattling, not sharing class materials, and moral dilemmas similar to those developed by Lawrence Kohlberg (1963).

Various media can be used to create oral and written text and visuals illustrating these solutions. Audiotapes can be developed for use at listening centers where students respond in writing to characters' interactions in problematic situations. Digital cameras can be used to illustrate appropriate and inappropriate body language, facial expressions, and gestures in scenario-specific assignments. Video, iMovie, or CD-ROM productions of role plays can be created for class evaluation. These same products can be given to students in other classes at different grade levels as they learn the techniques of the Role Playing model. Classes can also create their own Web sites that illustrate students' social problem-solving techniques and experiences through Role Playing. This feature can also be added to existing Web sites.

Role Playing can be used to support the following NET Standards and Performance Indicators:

GRADES PK–2

NET Standard 3: Technology Productivity Tools

NET Standard 4: Technology Communication Tools

NET Standard 5: Technology Research Tools

NET Standard 6: Technology Problem-Solving and Decision-Making Tools Performance Indicator 9: Use technology resources (e.g., puzzles, logical thinking programs, writing tools, digital cameras, drawing tools) for problem solving, communication, and illustration of thoughts, ideas, and stories.

Role Playing Extension

Using a digital camera, young children can develop scenes to illustrate the sequence of events in an age-appropriate social problem and assemble them in the style of a cartoon strip. In addition, a number of photos can be composed to reflect a variety of solutions to a problem. Word processing programs can be used to write text—if desired—to accompany the cartoon strip.

GRADES 3–5

NET Standard 3: Technology Productivity Tools

Performance Indicator 5: Use technology tools (e.g., multimedia authoring, presentation, Web tools, digital cameras, scanners) for individual and collaborative writing, communication, and publication activities to create knowledge products for audiences inside and outside the classroom.

Role Playing Extension

Students can collaboratively write books that illustrate characters in novels, their solutions to problems presented in the novels, and alternatives to those solutions. These books can be illustrated using digital cameras or copyright-free pictures found on the Internet, in magazines, or in other print sources.

GRADES 6–8

NET Standard 4: Technology Communication Tools

NET Standard 5: Technology Research Tools

Performance Indicator 7: Collaborate with peers, experts, and others using telecommunications and collaborative tools to investigate curriculum-related problems, issues, and information and to develop solutions or products for audiences inside and outside the classroom.

Role Playing Extension

In small groups, students can identify crisis situations in social studies in which alternative outcomes could have altered the course of history. They can explore these situations, role-play the problem, and develop a variety of solutions and their possible consequences. Using word processing programs, they can write plays or narratives that come directly from their experimentation. Alternative solutions and their consequences could be illustrated using digital cameras or Internet resources. Made into a handbook, these products could be used in other teachers' sections of the same class.

GRADES 9–12

NET Standard 4: Technology Communication Tools

NET Standard 5: Technology Research Tools

NET Standard 6: Technology Problem-Solving and Decision-Making Tools

Performance Indicator 10: Collaborate with peers, experts, and others to contribute to a content-related knowledge base by using technology to compile, synthesize, produce, and disseminate information, models, and other creative works.

Role Playing Extension

In small groups using Role Playing cycles, students can create videos that explore alternate solutions and consequences of crises in U.S. and world studies. The videos can be designed to be used as lesson material for upper elementary students and their teachers. Each videotape would include narration that sets up each situation and would provide question prompts to be used in the lessons. Print materials to accompany these videotaped role plays can also be designed.

Role Playing, Content Standards, and Benchmarks

Role playing can be used creatively with academic content in several strands of the social studies and language arts curriculum. The content standards and benchmarks provided below in each subject, specific strand, and level of schooling apply to any grade level in the social studies and literature content in the language arts. Some of the examples from the *Michigan Curriculum Framework* (Michigan Department of Education, 1996) below show the progression of one benchmark throughout the four levels of schooling: early elementary, later elementary, middle school, and high school.[*]

Social Studies—History

CONTENT STANDARD 4: All students will evaluate key decisions made at critical turning points in history by assessing their implications and long-term consequences.

Early Elementary Benchmark: Recall situations in their lives that required decisions and evaluate their decisions in light of their consequences.

Possibilities for Role Playing

Classmates at school wanting to copy work during tests

Leaving homework in a brother's room by accident and not having permission to go into his room

---

Later Elementary Benchmark: Select decisions made to solve past problems and evaluate those decisions in terms of ethical considerations, the interests of those affected by the decisions, and the short- and long-term consequences of those decisions.

Possibilities for Role Playing

Needing a friendship break from a classmate who continually belittles another student

Knowing that out of need, a classmate has stolen lunch money from the teacher's desk

---

[*]Excerpts from the *Michigan Curriculum Framework* are reprinted with permission of the Michigan Department of Education.

> **Middle School Benchmark:** Select historic decisions and evaluate them in light of core democratic values and resulting costs and benefits as viewed from a variety of perspectives.

Possibilities for Role Playing

Family members deciding whether to allow their home to be part of the Underground Railroad during the Civil War

> **High School Benchmark:** Identify major decisions in the history of Michigan and the United States since the era of Reconstruction, analyze contemporary factors contributing to the decisions, and consider alternative courses of action.

Possibilities for Role Playing

Harry Truman in discussion about dropping the atomic bomb on Japan

Franklin D. Roosevelt's decision to intern Japanese Americans during WWII

Lyndon Johnson's decision not to run for a second term as president

---

Language Arts—Depth of Understanding

CONTENT STANDARD 9: All students will demonstrate understanding of the complexity of enduring issues and recurring problems by making connections and generating themes within and across texts.

Early Elementary Benchmark: Explore and reflect on universal themes and substantive issues from oral, visual, and written texts. Examples include new friendships and life in the neighborhood.

Later Elementary Benchmark: Explore and reflect on universal themes and substantive issues from oral, visual, and written texts. Examples include exploration, discovery, and formation of personal relationships.

Middle School Benchmark: Explore and reflect on universal themes and substantive issues from oral, visual, and written texts. Examples include coming of age, rights and responsibilities, group and individual roles, conflict and cooperation, creativity and resourcefulness.

High School Benchmark: Explore and reflect on universal themes and substantive issues from oral, visual, and written texts. Examples include human interaction with the environment, conflict and change, relationships with others, and self-discovery.

Possibilities for Role Playing for Each Level of Benchmark

Dialogues between students and characters in books based on situations that students identify

Dialogues between characters in two different books as they might talk about a shared dilemma

Why Choose Role Playing?

1. Can you identify specific group interpersonal challenges students face in the classroom, before or after school, during recreational or athletic events, or on the playground?

2. Can you identify particular social problems that prevent students from fully engaging in their studies?

3. Have you observed situations in which you believe students might make better choices if they had the opportunity to rethink their actions and reactions?

4. Are issues of fairness, cheating, teasing, or selfishness affecting how well you are able to conduct class periods?

5. Does the content you teach include situations in fiction in which characters could have made different choices that would have altered the plot?

6. Does the content you teach include situations in history in which characters could have made different choices that would have altered the plot?

Summary

Role Playing is a model of teaching that provides students with practice opportunities to explore interpersonal relationships and that helps prepare students to make wise choices in difficult circumstances. Eventually, real-life performances of appropriate social behaviors based on strong, positive values can result from Role Playing experiences.

During a typical role play, a relevant problem is identified, and players are chosen to act out the situation and provide a possible solution. The observers then discuss the relative merit of the solution. The values and intentions revealed by the role players' actions are brought to light through these exchanges. Alternate solutions are suggested, briefly discussed, role-played, and then analyzed. The cycle of enacting multiple solutions and reflecting on their viability culminates in a generalizing experience. At the end of the role play session, all the participants discuss what they have learned and how they might best behave in similar situations.

Role Playing has been found to foster a positive classroom climate and improve students' intrapersonal and interpersonal skills. When applied to academic content in the social studies and language arts, Role Playing can be used creatively to bring concepts, events, and characters to life.

Putting It Together

1. Identify content standards and benchmarks from your state or district curriculum that include, explicitly or implicitly, issues of interpersonal conflict.

2. Using your knowledge of educational psychology and child development, choose a grade level and identify age-appropriate issues that might be explored in a role play or related series of role plays.

3. Choose a character from your favorite historical period and identify a moment of decision or crisis that might be explored in a two-character role play.

4. Choose a character from a favorite novel for students at any grade level. Identify a personal situation from the novel that can form the basis of a two-character role play.

Student Study Site

The Companion Web site for *Models of Teaching: Connecting Student Learning With Standards*
www.sagepub.com/delloliostudy

Visit the Web-based student study site to enhance your understanding of the book content and discover additional resources that will take your learning one step further. You can enhance your understanding by using the comprehensive Study Guide, which includes chapter learning objectives, flash cards, practice tests, and more. You'll find special features, such as the links to standards from U.S. States and associated activities, Learning from Journal Articles, Field Experience worksheets, Learning from Case Studies, and PRAXIS resources.

References

Chesler, M., & Fox, R. (1966). *Role playing methods in the classroom.* Chicago: Science Research Associates.

Crosby, M. (1963, February). A portrait of blight. *Educational Leadership, 20,* 300–304.

Daly, F., & Cain, L. (1953, October). Mentally retarded students in California secondary schools. Bulletin of the *California State Department of Education, 22*(7) 19–179.

Elias, J. L., & Merriam, S. (1980). *Philosophical foundations of adult education.* Malabar, FL: Krieger.

Gardner, H. (2000). *Intelligence reframed: Multiple intelligences for the 21st century.* New York: Basic Books.

Hendry, C. E., Lippitt, R., & Zander, A. (1947). *Reality practice as educational method.* Psychodrama Monograph 9. New York: Beacon House.

International Society for Technology in Education. (2000). *National educational technology standards for students: Connecting curriculum and technology.* Washington, DC: Author in collaboration with the U.S. Department of Education.

Jensen, G. E. (1955). The social structure of the classroom group: An observational framework, *Journal of Educational Psychology, 46,* 362–374.

Johnson, D., Johnson, R., & Holubec, E. J. (1994). *The new circles of learning.* Alexandria, VA: Association for Supervision and Curriculum Development.

Kohlberg, L. (1963). The development of children's orientations toward moral order: Sequence in the development of moral thought. *Vita Humana, 6,* 11–33.

Lippitt, R. (1949–50). Human dynamics in the classroom, *Journal of Social Issues, II*(2, 5-6), 31–41.

Maslow, A. (1968). *Toward a psychology of being.* New York: Wiley.

Michigan Department of Education. (1996). *Michigan curriculum framework.* Lansing: Author.

Moser, A. J. (1975). Structured group interaction. *Journal of Contemporary Psychotherapy, 7,* 23–28.

Rogers, C. R. (1969). *Freedom to learn: A view of what education might become.* New York: Merrill.

Shaftel, F., & Shaftel, G. (1967a). *Role playing for social values: Decision making in the social studies.* Englewood Cliffs, NJ: Prentice-Hall.

Shaftel, F., & Shaftel, G. (1967b). *Role playing in the curriculum.* Englewood Cliffs, NJ: Prentice Hall.

Shaftel, F., & Shaftel, G. (1967c). *Words and actions: Role playing photo problems for young children.* New York: Holt, Rinehart & Winston.

Shaftel, F., & Shaftel, G. (1976). *Values in action.* Minneapolis, MN: Winston House.

Shaftel, F., & Shaftel, G. (1982). *Role playing in the classroom.* Englewood Cliffs, NJ: Prentice Hall.

Shaftel, G. A. (1952). *Role playing the problem story: An approach to human relations in the classroom.* New York: National Conference of Christians and Jews.

Shaw, M. E., Corsini, R. J., Blake, R. R., & Mouton, J. S. (1980). *Role playing: A practical guide for group facilitators.* San Diego, CA: University Associates.

Stock, G. (2004). *The kids' book of questions revised for the 21st century.* New York: Workman.

Swink, D., & Buchanan, D. R. (1984). The effects of sociodramatic goal-oriented role play and non-goal-oriented role play on locus of control. *Journal of Clinical Psychology, 40*(5), 1178–1183.

Trow, W. C. (1950). *Educational psychology* (2nd ed.). Boston: Houghton-Mifflin.

chapter 11

Inquiry-Based Learning

When was the last time you had an aha! moment? Aha! moments occur when something surprising is revealed to you or you find the answer to an intriguing problem that has puzzled you for some time. Many of our most vivid ahas happened during our childhoods. After much trial and error, we may have finally figured out just when to run into the circling rope when it was our turn to jump. Some of us may have had similar moments when we realized how to use a knight to our best advantage in a chess game, found a preferred way to begin a jigsaw puzzle, or "discovered" geometry in a game of caroms. These experiences are powerful for us because we are the discoverers. The aha! moment is ours alone.

Educators have long promoted learning that occurs through students' direct experiences. In *Experience and Education,* John Dewey states that students learn best when they are engaged in purposeful experiences that give life to concepts, procedures, and perspectives (1933). Jerome Bruner elaborated on this approach to instruction when he coined the phrase **discovery learning** (1961). Discovery learning, **Inquiry-Based Learning**, and **problem-based learning** all describe students' experiences as they grapple with a question or problem, engage in a systematic procedure to solve that problem, and communicate what they discover to others. These hands-on experiences provide the aha! moments students will remember.

Most states use the term *inquiry* or *inquiry and research* in content standards, benchmarks, and grade-level expectations. In some state curriculum documents, there is a separate inquiry strand in science and social studies; in other state documents, the inquiry and research objectives are embedded in the benchmarks for each academic discipline.

Like other models of teaching presented in this book, Inquiry-Based Learning may take place in just one class period. However, Inquiry-Based Learning may also extend over a number of class periods or over the course of several weeks in an instructional unit. In this chapter we will take a look at Inquiry-Based Learning structured for a single class session as well as for an extended investigation. Case Study 11.1 illustrates an inquiry-based lesson that takes place in a single class session.

Case Study 11.1: Middle School, Science

Mr. Zwart is an experienced middle school science teacher in a small rural school district. He has taught science at this level for 20 years, but this is his first year at this school. Class periods here are only 45 minutes long. He has found that he needs to plan carefully so that his science labs, which must include time for cleanup, will end on time. Currently Mr. Zwart is teaching a unit on matter and energy, and today he will be leading his students through an experiment involving density. He knows these students have not had a great deal of experience using the **scientific method**. However, they are becoming more able to form hypotheses, observe and record data, and apply what they learn to new situations. He is hoping that his students will enjoy today's inquiry lesson. The subject of this experiment should engage their interest.

While this lesson reinforces a number of content standards and benchmarks in science, today's lesson focuses on one content standard. Mr. Zwart's long-term objective for this unit is stated in exactly the same way as the middle school benchmark for matter and energy:

The learner will describe and compare objects in terms of mass, volume, and density.

Here is his lesson objective for today:

The learner will use the scientific method to determine why cans of soda sink or float when immersed in water and will describe the density of the soda in each can.

This is Mr. Zwart's last period of the day. He has already taught this lesson twice, and he has managed throughout the day to keep his materials organized for each new class. Students are in groups of four or five today. When he first started teaching, Mr. Zwart performed the demonstrations for his class experiments while his students watched. Over the past 15 years, he has become committed to student exploration in his classroom, and he has acquired materials so that every group can run its experiments independently.

On the easel by his classroom door, Mr. Zwart has posted a list of group members for today's class and indicated where each group should sit. Each table is covered with a bath towel. On top are a small aquarium that is three-fourths filled with water, a can of regular soda, and a can of diet soda. Each student has a clipboard with observation sheets attached. So that he can explain what they will be doing during their experiment, Mr. Zwart also has these items on his table in the front of the class. Students begin to enter the classroom. They are surprised to see cans of soda at their tables.

Mr. Zwart: Please take your seats. Today we are going to be doing an experiment using the two soda cans you have on your tables. Our experiment also involves water in the aquariums. The two previous classes were considerate enough to keep their tables dry for the next class. Even though you are my last class of the day, we will still be cleaning up together, and I expect you to work at your tables as real scientists would work: carefully and cautiously.

For the last few weeks, we have been talking in class about the scientific method. You know that scientists have a series of stages in their experiments. Before they begin experimenting, what must happen? I know you all know this. Sarah?

Sarah: They have to know what they want to do?

Mr. Zwart: Sarah, you're so close. How have we been phrasing that first step in class? Sandy?

Sandy: They develop a question. There is something they want to investigate, and they write a very specific question.

Mr. Zwart: OK. I'll write that first step on the board. (*He writes.*)

1. Develop a question.

What happens next? Bruce?

Bruce: They decide what they think will happen, what they think they will find out.

Mr. Zwart: And what do we call that? Amy?

Amy: A hypothesis.

Mr. Zwart: Yes. I'll write that on the board, as well. I am going to use the word *generate*, which is the word I have been using this week. *Generate* means to make or create. (*He writes*.)

1. Develop a question.
2. Generate a hypothesis.

Mr. Zwart: So how do we go about finding the answers to our question? Can we just mess around and hope we get it right? What do we have to do next? Lorna?

Lorna: We design an experiment. We did that at the beginning of the year with the mealworms, remember?

Mr. Zwart: Right. You all decided what you wanted to find out about your mealworm and then you made a hypothesis. You designed an experiment that you could repeat to test your hypotheses and to see if your data were collected correctly. Let me put this next step on the board. (*He writes*.)

1. Develop a question.
2. Generate a hypothesis.
3. Develop an experimental design.

Today we will all be working with the same question and experimental design. While you will be working in groups, as individual scientists you will still be able to generate your own hypothesis. While we are conducting our experiment, what is important that we do at all times? Al?

Al: Well, we have to watch what happens.

Georgie: Al, in this class, we observe.

Al: OK, right. In this class we observe. But we also have to write down everything we see in an organized way.

Mr. Zwart: Al, why do we need to be so well organized as we do our observations and write them down?

Al: Well . . . we all have to write what we see down in the same ways so that we can compare our observations with everyone in the class.

Mr. Zwart: Does anyone remember what we call the information we write down? I bet you also use this word in math class. Mattie?

Mattie: We call it data, and we say that we collect it. We collect data.

Mr. Zwart: That's right. I'll write this on the board, too. (*He writes*.)

1. Develop a question.
2. Generate a hypothesis.

3. Develop an experimental design.

4. Collect and record data.

Remember, we use the word *record* when we talk about writing down our observations.

Let's begin our investigation for today. There are other steps in the scientific method, but we'll get to those later. You have two cans of soda at each table—regular soda and diet soda. The question for today is this: What will happen if we immerse both of these unopened cans of soda in the aquarium?

Before you make your hypotheses, observe your two cans of soda very closely with your group members. On your Soda Can Experiment Worksheet, you will find our question at the top. In the space below, work with your group members to describe each can as thoroughly as possible. Once you have listed as many details as you can about your two cans, you will be ready to make your own hypothesis. Your hypothesis does not need to be the same as your colleagues'; it should be your own.

Here is our experimental design. I've written it on the chart, but you also have a copy at your tables.

- Immerse each can in the aquarium one at a time.
- Leave both cans in the aquarium.
- Observe what happens to each can.
- Record your observations.
- Draw a picture of the aquarium with both cans in it, and label each can.
- Remove both cans, and repeat the experiment two more times.
- Indicate on your worksheet whether you obtained the same results each time you performed the experiment.
- Have one person from your group come up to the chart and record your data.
- In your group, discuss why you think your experiment turned out as it did.
- Record your thoughts in the bottom section of the worksheet.

Mr. Zwart checks his students' understanding of the experimental design before he gives the signal for them to begin. They will be using the worksheet (Table 11.1) to record their observations and findings for each step of their investigation. He reminds them that they have only 25 minutes to accomplish all the steps on their worksheet, as the class needs to discuss the findings. He asks that each group appoint one student as timekeeper.

As Mr. Zwart moves from table to table in his classroom, he asks questions about his students' progress and what they are discovering. When he does inquiry-based teaching in his class, he knows that it is important to answer students' questions with other questions rather than to give them answers. The point of these investigations is for the students to find the answers rather than for the teacher to teach the lesson directly.

Table 11.1	Soda Can Experiment Worksheet

Group Members

_____   _____

_____   _____

_____

This is our question for today's experiment:
What will happen if we place both of these unopened cans of soda into the aquarium?

This is what we notice about our two unopened cans of soda:
Regular Soda   Diet Soda

This is my hypothesis:

This is why I think my hypothesis may be correct:

This is what we observed:
Trial 1

This is a picture of what we saw:

This is what we observed in our next two trials:
Trial 2   Trial 3

This is our explanation of what we observed:

Students record as many things about their soda cans as they are able to find, both similarities and differences. Some of the groups decide to split in two and have each pair or trio take notes on separate cans, and then they will compare what they found. Other groups decide to look over both cans together. One group decides to compare and contrast their two cans of soda using a Venn diagram. They decide to do this on a separate sheet of paper. These are some of the details the groups wrote down about each can:

Regular Soda	Diet Soda
Similar can design	Similar can design
Different color scheme	Different color scheme
11.5 oz. can	11.5 oz. can
Number of servings—1	Number of servings—1
Calories—110	Calories—0
40 grams of sugar	aspartame

Once the groups have recorded everything they notice about the two cans, they individually write down what they think will happen when they place each can in the aquarium. In addition, they each have to explain why they think their hypothesis is correct. Most of the students write that they think both cans will sink to the bottom. One student is sure that both cans will float. They back up their hypotheses with statements like these:

The two cans are shaped the same way, so I think they will both float or both sink.

The cans are both full of soda, and soda pop is always fizzy when we open the can, whether it is diet or regular. Both cans will float because of the bubbles.

The cans weigh the same, so they will both sink. The cans are not full of air. If they were, they might both float.

None of the students made the hypothesis that will be shown to be the correct one: the regular soda will sink, and the diet soda will float.

The students are all ready for their first trial. Once both cans are in the aquariums, students are visibly and audibly surprised at what they see, and they look around at the other tables to see if everyone's first trial turned out the same. A couple of students start to ask their friends across the room if any of them had guessed correctly. Mr. Zwart reminds them that time is running out, and they still have two more trials. They quickly write down what they observed, draw the outcome of their first observation, and begin their last two trials. Each group sends someone to the front of the classroom to enter their data on the class chart (Table 11.2). When they return to their tables, the groups spend a few minutes discussing why they think the diet soda floated while the regular soda sank to the bottom of the aquarium. Here are some of the reasons they came up with as they talked:

We think the diet soda floated because it has fewer calories.

We think the regular soda was made at a different factory, and the materials used on the cans are different.

One of the cans is a darker color, and it may weigh more when they put the soda in the can.

| Table 11.2 | Data Recording Table: Sink or Float? |

	Regular soda			**Diet soda**		
Table A	#1	#2	#3	#1	#2	#3
Table B	#1	#2	#3	#1	#2	#3
Table C	#1	#2	#3	#1	#2	#3
Table D	#1	#2	#3	#1	#2	#3
Table E	#1	#2	#3	#1	#2	#3

Mr. Zwart is ready for his full-group discussion:

Mr. Zwart: So, this is where we have gotten so far. Now we need to add our next step. (*He writes.*)

1. Develop a question.
2. Generate a hypothesis.
3. Develop an experimental design.
4. Collect and record data.
5. Analyze the data.

But before we analyze why our experiment turned out the way it did, let's hear what some of your hypotheses were before you began your second and third trials.

Students begin to share what they thought would happen when each can was submerged in the aquariums. After each one, Mr. Zwart asks how many other students shared the same hypothesis, and then he asks for something new, something no one has mentioned yet.

Mr. Zwart: Even though you came up with different hypotheses, every group found that the regular cans of soda stayed at the bottom of the aquarium, but the diet sodas floated to the top. Let's hear how groups explained what they observed.

Mr. Zwart's students share their reasoning behind the outcome of their experiment. He writes each reason on an easel in the front of the room so that the reasons can all be seen at once.

Mr. Zwart: Is the volume the same in each can of soda? Barbara?

Barbara: Well, yes. Each can holds 11.5 oz. of soda pop.

Mr. Zwart: We have been talking about density in class. Is there anything different in the cans of soda that might make one of them more or less dense? Talk about that for a couple of minutes in your groups. (*He waits a few minutes.*)

Ev: Mr. Z., we have it! We have it!

Mr. Zwart: Hold on, Ev. What about the rest of the groups? Any ideas? Only Cheryl's group?

Cheryl: Well . . . we think so, but we'd rather hear something from Ev's group first.

Ev: OK. We think that the regular can of soda is heavier and stayed at the bottom of the aquarium because it has sugar in it to make it sweet. Lots of sugar.

Mr. Zwart: What about your group, Cheryl? Did you come up with the same idea or a different one?

Cheryl: We had the same kind of idea. Pretty much. We said that the diet sweeteners you can get in packets in the restaurants, you know, the pink, yellow, and blue packets, they are a lot lighter in your hand than the white packets of sugar. You can shake the sugar in the sugar packets so that it falls to the bottom, and you can feel how grainy it is. The diet sweeteners, they are flatter and slide around in their packets, but you can't really feel or hear them in the same way. We've never looked at how much they weigh, though.

Mr. Zwart: You may not realize just how much sugar or high-fructose corn syrup is put into one can of regular soda to make it sweet. About 40 grams of sugar are in each can. Lots of sugar dissolved in water and high-fructose corn syrup are both very dense substances. (*He draws Figure 11.1 on the board.*)

The diet sweeteners, whether they come in any color packet, are a lot sweeter, and less is needed to make the soda sweet. (*He draws Figure 11.2 on the board.*)

Figure 11.1

Figure 11.2

Even though the volume of the cans is the same, 11.5 oz. (*He uses the chalk to outline the shapes of the cans for emphasis*), the masses are different as a result of the sweetener being used.

Does our aquarium water have sugar dissolved to make it sweet? Victoria?

Victoria: Well, you didn't say it didn't, but I suppose it is plain water.

Mr. Zwart: So why did the regular soda can sink? Talk this over with your neighbor. (*He pauses for several moments*.) So, what do you think? Mattie?

Mattie: If the regular soda has sugar dissolved in it and the aquarium water does not, then the regular soda weighs more than the water in the aquarium, so it will sink right away. Which is what we saw.

Mr. Zwart: Does anyone agree or disagree? Then why did the diet can float? Brenda?

Brenda: Well, if the aquarium water and the can of diet soda have the same density, the can won't sink.

Mr. Zwart: I am going to leave these possibilities up in the air. We'll think about them more tomorrow. This was a great discussion. You are really getting the knack of scientific analysis. I was hoping to get to continue our discussion about density today, but everything you had to say during this class was important.

We are running out of time. I want you to answer this question in your science journals tonight: What do you think will happen if we slowly pour corn oil into the water? Will the two cans sink or float, and why? This is for class tomorrow, so don't try the experiment at home tonight!

Case Study 11.1: Post-Lesson Reflection

Overall, Mr. Zwart was pleased with today's class. He is always concerned that his 45-minute periods are not long enough for meaningful exploration and discussion. While he understands that not every science lesson can be inquiry-based, he also knows that these students have not internalized the scientific method, because they have had few occasions to put it into practice. His students will require repeated opportunities to engage in structured explorations.

Mr. Zwart thinks that the next time he teaches this lesson, he may ask the students to do a "quick write" first. For example, all students would have participated silently had they been asked to write down the stages of the scientific method before he began. Everyone would need to think about the quick-write question, not just the students who had their hands up first.

Mr. Zwart has noticed there is a hesitancy among some students that makes them participate less than others in the full-group discussions. He considers who tends to be quieter and when. All the students work well together in small groups. Perhaps their participation in full-group discussions during inquiry lessons is less important. However, Mr. Zwart believes the concept development that takes place during the final class discussions is integral to his students' understanding. He will keep an eye on these students with the hope that he can elicit an individual response from each of them soon.

Mr. Zwart was especially pleased today at how much better his students were today at articulating the rationale for their hypotheses. At the very beginning of the year, many students would answer "I just think so" when asked for the reasoning behind their hypotheses.

In earlier investigations this year, many of Mr. Zwart's students wanted to do each of their trials differently. They thought it was fun, and they believed they were learning more by coming up with new ideas each time. He is relieved that they finally understand the scientific importance of repeating their experiments in exactly the same way for each trial. The mealworm experiments provided a good way to introduce the concept of variables, which he taught using Direct Instruction. The issue of variables did not arise in today's lessons. He is looking forward to reviewing the designs for their science fair projects this spring. The project designs will give him a solid individual assessment of their understanding of the cognitive process skills that have been one focus of their work this year.

Today's experiment was an effective prelude to students' understanding of the power of discrepant events. Mr. Zwart's students assumed that because the soda cans were the same size, they would weigh the same. They assumed this because there is no discernable difference in weight when the cans are held. He wants his students to know the importance of applying the scientific method precisely. They must be aware of their assumptions as they approach many intellectual tasks, not just those in science. Tomorrow Mr. Zwart will end his discussion by introducing the concept of discrepant events explicitly and having his students discuss its importance in their role as budding scientists.

While some of the observations made by students today were relevant, some were not. For example, students' observations about the colors of the soda cans were not important ones in this experiment. However, Mr. Zwart does not believe he should design a separate lesson around the comparative relevancy of observations. This topic may come up in discussions of individual experiments, and in that context it would be appropriate.

In his reflections, Mr. Zwart returns to his original question of comparing hands-on science lessons and teacher-demonstration lessons. He could easily have done today's demonstration by himself; the outcome would have been the same, and he would have been able to move into concepts of density more quickly. However, this class needs repeated opportunities with systematic inquiry, and the lesson provided a relatively easy experience. Earlier in the week, he had decided to do the second phase of this experiment tomorrow by himself. Removing the solution of corn oil and water from each table aquarium between classes would be problematic. He can rotate two aquariums tomorrow, one to use with the corn oil while the other one soaks in the sink. Even if he had the time to prepare the aquariums for each new section tomorrow, working with corn oil poses too many opportunities for unintended disaster. He's going to keep it simple.

Structuring Inquiry-Based Learning Experiences

Inquiry-Based Learning experiences can take place in a single lesson or over the course of several lessons or even several weeks. An entire unit can be organized around a number of related questions. Most state and district science curriculums require that students use the scientific method independently to carry out experiments and eventually to design their own. To meet these content standards, students must demonstrate competence in using the stages of the scientific method in a prescribed order. Table 11.3 presents a summary of the stages, which are discussed below.

Developing a Question

All Inquiry-Based Learning, whether the content is science, social studies, or math, begins with a question. Questions in these content areas may be contained in the district or state curriculum. Inquiry-Based Learning experiences will be successful only when questions have been phrased clearly and when students can discover answers through either hands-on experiences, traditional library research, or electronic research. State curriculum documents often include "real world contexts" as part of the math, science, and social studies curriculums. This feature helps make each inquiry experience relevant to students' daily lives.

Some districts provide sets of materials that contain all that is needed for instructional units—lesson outlines, supplies, workbooks, and so forth. In some cases, teachers develop their own inquiry experiences from the curriculum they are required to teach. Working directly from the benchmarks or grade-level expectations, teachers frame questions that will guide the development of lessons. If the objective is for students to demonstrate their competence in inquiry skills such as data collection, observation, using research sources, and so on, teachers may be able to provide students with the opportunity to choose their own topics for investigation. Unfortunately, because of time constraints and grade-level curriculum that must be covered, this opportunity arises infrequently in K–12 education, and usually only for science fairs.

Generating a Hypothesis

In the scientific method, students bring their prior knowledge and understanding to bear on the question by predicting answers at the beginning of the inquiry. This is called *generating a hypothesis*. For the very youngest children, *guess* is frequently used instead of *hypothesis*, but by second grade, children can usually handle the formal term. You can simply ask them how they would answer the question, given what they know about the topic.

Sometimes the question that teachers ask at the beginning of an inquiry centers on a discrepant event that contradicts a concept students previously held. Students' beliefs about the validity of their own prior knowledge will often prompt hypotheses very quickly. For example, a kindergarten teacher may ask students what they think plants need in order to survive. While most children are familiar with family members watering the plants in their homes or the effect of rain on grass and flowers, they may be unaware of the central importance of light for plant growth. Throughout the course of their investigations as they watch plants grow under different circumstances, the students will find discrepancies between what they thought to be true (the hypotheses they generated) and what is actually true about plant development. In this example, Inquiry-Based Learning can result in kindergarten students' "discovering" photosynthesis.

Often teachers will ask their students to verbalize or write a rationale for the hypotheses they have made. Students will return to these hypotheses and rationales at the end of the lesson to compare their initial ideas with what they discovered through their investigations. This compare-and-contrast activity provides scaffolding for students' metacognition, their thinking about their thinking.

Developing an Experimental Design

A viable experimental design is one that can test hypotheses and helps students construct knowledge. The results of a clearly defined procedure in an experiment should help students answer the original question. Many districts use science kits in which each experiment has already been designed, the procedures are written in teacher's manuals and student workbooks, and all required materials are provided.

Even when teachers are provided with prescribed investigations that go with units, they may still have some flexibility in developing additional lessons based on students' needs. For example, middle school science curriculums frequently emphasize the skills required to design and conduct experiments. Some groups of students may be conversant with multiple variables while others may need explicit instruction in working with more than one variable. Therefore, you may need to teach directly about any of these topics: defining variables, describing their function in scientific investigations, determining significant variables in a particular experiment, developing workable systems for using multiple variables, and recording data efficiently and effectively.

Alternatively, a teacher might structure a science inquiry in which the objective for the students is to construct a scientific concept. For example, students may be asked to find out as much as they can about pendulum swings. What statements can they make that they can prove to be true when given materials to build a pendulum and experiment with its action? Given a ball of string, various weights, a clearly defined question, and an extended period of time, students can construct the concept of *variable* through investigation. They may name the concept *modifications*, *different ideas*, *tries*, or *changes* in their experiments. When the students have presented their findings to the class, the teacher can then introduce the term *variable*.

Teachers may also provide students with hypotheses and opportunities to develop their own experiments to test them. In this case, the teacher's objective is to have students analyze what factors are necessary to prove hypotheses true or false, sequence a series of steps to structure their investigation, and then proceed. When students design their own experiments, they are working in the highest levels of Bloom's cognitive taxonomy.

These instructional decisions will be influenced by the amount of time teachers have to complete a unit and by the extent to which the content of the unit will be evaluated on standardized grade-level tests.

Collecting and Recording Data

Collecting and recording data are integral to the success of all Inquiry-Based Learning. Students must be responsible for collecting relevant data that will help them answer their questions. Data can be collected through hands-on experimentation; observation; working with primary sources, such as face-to-face interviews, surveys, or questionnaires; or traditional library or electronic research. Data collection may happen during one class period or over the course of several days or weeks. If you want data to be recorded in a specific way, you must make that way clear to students through explanation and modeling. For example, data that comes in numbers or figures might best be recorded in a table or retrieval chart such as the one Mr. Zwart's students used in Case Study 11.1. Once they are experienced in recording data in the ways you have instructed, you may want students to try their hand at designing appropriate methods of recording data. One criterion you should ask them to meet is that the information be accessible to others.

Analyzing Data

As an intellectual activity, the process of data analysis also moves the students into higher levels of Bloom's cognitive taxonomy. Once all the data have been collected, it is time for students, either in small groups or alone, to begin thinking about what the information means. Data analysis might begin with the questions, What did you find out? and What were your discoveries during the investigation? Then students can address a series of specific questions that relate to the particular experiment.

In the next important part of data analysis, students look for relationships or discernible patterns in the data. Teachers can model the data analysis process by using

Students' hands-on observation, data recording, and analysis experiences provide them with opportunities to work as scientists, regardless of their grade level.

the think aloud method. When the teacher's thinking is transparent, students begin to see how their minds must work when they try to make sense of the information they have collected. Teachers also need to model stating why they think their analyses are true. When teachers model statements that begin with "I can see this because . . . ," "I know this because . . . ," "This information shows that . . . ," or "This evidence supports my thinking because . . . ," they are helping scaffold students' reasoning. Students must learn how to explain their reasoning clearly to support the validity of their analyses.

Reaching Conclusions, Forming and Extending Generalizations

Once students have analyzed the data and answered their inquiry question, the teacher needs to move them to deeper levels of understanding. At this final stage of the investigation, students must compare their results to the hypothesis they made at the beginning. If their hypothesis turned out to be correct, why do they think it did so? If their hypothesis was incorrect, what misconceptions were proven wrong by the experiment?

Students must also be provided with multiple opportunities to move beyond answering the original question by explaining why their results are important. Sometimes this is called the *So what? question*. In the real world, with a particular set

Table 11.3   Stages of the Scientific Method

Stage	Teacher's Tasks	Students' Tasks	Notes
1. Developing a question	Models working with given questions and developing original questions	Work with given questions eventually develop their own questions	Teacher uses think-aloud procedure
2. Generating a hypothesis	Models	Work with given hypotheses and develop their own hypotheses	Teacher uses think-aloud procedure
3. Developing an experimental design	Models experimental designs for both qualitative and qualitative studies	Work with given designs and eventually develop their own designs	Teacher uses think-aloud procedure, provides multiple examples
4. Collecting and recording data	Models	Work with given systems for collecting and recording data and eventually develop their own systems	Teacher uses think-aloud procedure, provides multiple examples
5. Analyzing data	Models analyzing both quantitative and qualitative data	Analyze given data Analyze their own data	Teacher uses think-aloud procedure, provides multiple examples
6. Reaching conclusions, forming and extending generalizations	Models	Reach conclusions, form and extend generalizations of given data Reach conclusions, form and extend generalizations of their own data	Teacher uses think-aloud procedure, provides multiple examples
7. Communicating results	Models multiple ways of communicating results of both quantitative and qualitative studies	Communicate results of quantitative and qualitative studies using given data Eventually communicate results of their own quantitative and qualitative data	Teacher uses think-aloud procedure, provides multiple examples

of circumstances, would the results of their experiment be valuable? Why or why not? Would their discoveries be helpful, if not indispensable, in any other real-world situations? Can they make any generalizations as a result of their findings? For example, will the results and analysis of their experiments in composting affect how cafeteria waste could be used at school?

Students will begin to formulate their own follow-up questions for additional research if the inquiries have been intrinsically interesting and relevant to them. They may have ideas for further experimentation. What else would they like to know as a result of their findings? Inquiry-Based Learning works as a catalyst for extending investigations. It also demonstrates how scientists go about their work—with curiosity, conjecture, and connections.

Communicating Results

The final step in any inquiry is for students to communicate what they have learned to others. This communication can be accomplished in any combination of written formats, such as reports, PowerPoint presentations, tables, or charts, depending on the nature of the inquiry and the form of the data that students have collected. A number of computer software programs create these products. Students can give oral presentations that describe their process and their findings, as well. Depending on the teacher's objective, it may be appropriate for students to decide how to communicate what they have learned to others. Whether students' investigations or experiments were in science, math, or social studies, this stage of the scientific process can be connected to both oral and written language arts standards.

We can describe inquiry experiences as being **guided** or **unguided** by the teacher; **open** or **closed** by design; and **descriptive**, **classificatory**, or **explanatory** by purpose. Each step of the formal scientific method is used to structure some Inquiry-Based Learning experiences but not others. Brief descriptions of these modifications of the scientific method can be found in the Appendix, "Purposes of Inquiry-Based Learning."

Case Study 11.2: Third Grade, Inquiry-Based Units

Like the other models of teaching presented in this book, an Inquiry-Based Learning experience can take place in just one instructional period. However, Inquiry-Based Learning may also extend over a number of class periods or over the course of several weeks. In the next case study, students will be asked to think inductively and arrive at possible answers based on their observations and discoveries. This extended case study will provide you with a view of developing a progressive Inquiry-Based Learning experience in one unit.

Designing the Inquiry: State and Local Mandates and Teacher Choices

Mrs. Munoa, who has been teaching third grade for 10 years, is teaching for the first time in a year-round school. She wants to broaden her students' understanding and appreciation of systematic inquiry as they study a unit on global climate zones. Mrs. Munoa hopes that a high level of student engagement will help her students stay motivated as their school year moves into the summer months. Toward this end, she has incorporated several models of teaching to keep her classroom lively.

Mrs. Munoa has examined her state's benchmarks and third-grade expectations. In her research, she found a number of benchmarks related to the study of global regions. This case study will highlight lessons related to this elementary science benchmark, which also serves as her long-term objective:

The learner will describe weather conditions and climate (desert, hot and dry; continental, seasonal; tropical, hot and moist; and polar, cold)

Key Lessons in Extended Inquiries

Several of Mrs. Munoa's lessons for this unit are described below. Notice how she elicits her students' critical thinking skills through questioning.

1. The learner will predict the climate of four different cities around the world.

Mrs. Munoa tells her students that for the next few weeks, they will be researching what life is like in different cities around the world. In small groups, they will create a PowerPoint presentation that describes the places they have researched. Each project will be put on the school Web site. Mrs. Munoa refers to a large world map stapled to a bulletin board on the side of the classroom. On it, 24 cities have been marked with pushpins. These locations have been color coded—four push-pins in each of six different colors. The pins are spread out across the map. Four students are assigned to each color group. Mrs. Munoa begins her first lesson:

Mrs. Munoa: At some time during the school day, take a look at your pushpins and think about their location on the map. Individually in your journals, your job today is to predict what you think the typical climate will be for each of your cities in June, July, and August and why you think so. Remember that climate refers to the weather in one place over time. Don't share your ideas with anyone yet. I'll be reading your journals tonight to take a look at your predictions. Who remembers the scientific word we use to describe a guess or prediction we have made about something? Stephen?

Stephen: A hypothesis?

Mrs. Munoa: Right, and what word do we use to describe our reasons for believing something? Leo?

Leo: A rationale. Rationales give our reasons for things.

Mrs. Munoa: Yes. I am looking forward to reviewing your hypotheses—what each of you believes to be true about the climate of your locations—and your rationales, your reasons why.

2. In small groups, the learners will collect temperature data for their cities over five days, determine the most effective way to organize their data on a chart, and create the chart for display.

Mrs. Munoa's students are sitting in their groups. They have been asked to share some of their predictions about the climate in their four cities and explain why they believe they are correct. In some cases, students in the same group have similar ideas, but in other groups, students have disagreed. Mrs. Munoa is ready to move her class into the next stage of their inquiry. Once she has used her signal and gotten their attention, she begins the next part of the lesson:

Mrs. Munoa: So, how have we used the scientific method so far in answering our question? Gilberto?

Gilberto: We know what our question is, and we have made a hypothesis about each of our cities.

Mrs. Munoa: Great. Now we need to think about collecting data. You will first be checking the temperature of your four cities over the next five school days and recording all your data. What do you think is the best way for you to do this? Talk in your groups about ways you might accomplish this over the next few days.

Each group discusses the possibilities they had brainstormed. Everyone agrees that the Weather Channel and Internet weather sites would provide all the weather information they needed every day. Mrs. Munoa continues to describe their first assignment. They will also be responsible for designing a chart to keep track of their information. Their chart must be easy for everyone to read when they are working at their desks.

3. The learner will identify relationships among cities with a variety of daily temperatures, categorize cities with similar temperatures, and label groups of cities with common characteristics.

Ms. Munoa will be using inquiry experiences to help students construct concepts about climate zones, specifically that cities within the same latitude range usually have similar climates. After she reviewed their data, she posted the chart each group made. Mrs. Munoa instructed the students to make individual journal entries about their observations. She asked them to tell the class what patterns they saw as they reviewed the data from all six groups. She also wanted to know whether anyone thought some of the data seemed out of place as they analyzed the charts.

For two days, the six charts were posted in the classroom, and the groups were given time to compare and contrast the temperatures of their cities with the temperatures posted by the other groups. Today, Mrs. Munoa is beginning a series of learning experiences designed to help her students construct the concept that climate regions are usually determined by latitude. This question will be the focus of her students' work today:

Why do you think cities in different places around the world have the climate that they do?

Mrs. Munoa's students have been instructed to bring their science journals, group observations, and questions to the rug area.

Mrs. Munoa: What did you notice about the information recorded by our class? Lee?

Lee: Each city on the list was from a different continent and a different hemisphere. They were from all over the world.

Mrs. Munoa: Right. That was for a reason you'll figure out later. Andrew?

Andrew: We found that in each group, some cities had high temperatures, and some were low.

Mrs. Munoa: Can someone else from Andrew's group say more about that?

Amy: Well, when we watch the weather report at home, the weather announcer talks about our town and the towns around where we live. The temperatures are usually very close to one another—just about the same number. The temperatures for the cities in these groups were far apart from one another.

Mrs. Munoa: We can say that the cities in each group have very different temperatures. I'll write that on the board. What else can we say about the data on the charts? Robin?

Robin: Every day the temperatures for each city were a little different. They were never exactly the same every day.

Mrs. Munoa: How shall I record your comment? "Temperatures for each city differ from day to day"? (*She writes this on the board.*) Sam?

Sam: Almost every group had one city with temperatures in the 90s.

Mrs. Munoa: "High temperatures," then. (*She writes.*) Shari?

Shari: Each group had a city with very cold temperatures, although some were colder than others.

Mrs. Munoa: "Cold temperatures." (*She writes.*) Mark?

Mark: We were surprised to see that some temperatures were cold even though it is June.

Mrs. Munoa: "Cold temperatures in June." (*She writes.*) Kathleen?

Kathleen: Some cities had much hotter temperatures than we have in the summer.

Mrs. Munoa: "Very hot for June." (*She writes*.) Juan?

Juan: Some of the cities had the same temperatures, just about, that we had here last week.

Mrs. Munoa: Right. "Similar temperatures to our town's." (*She writes*.) Is there anything else anyone would like to mention?

At this point, Mrs. Munoa wants to facilitate the group's concept development by adapting the Inductive Model.

Mrs. Munoa: Can we begin to group the cities in some way? Let's begin with pairing two cities that you believe belong together. Andrew?

Andrew: Phoenix, Arizona, and Riyadh, Saudi Arabia, because they are both very hot places.

Mrs. Munoa: Andrew has gotten us started by grouping cities together that have similar temperatures. What other cities belong to this first group?

The students continue to group the cities according to like temperatures based on the five-day data. Their initial lists look like this:

A	B	C
Phoenix, Arizona	Narvik, Norway	Berlin, Germany
Riyadh, Saudi Arabia	Iqaluit, Canada	Brazzaville, Congo
Singapore	Murmansk, Russia	Beijing, China
Manaus, Brazil	Fairbanks, Alaska	Tokyo, Japan
Cairo, Egypt	Mawson, Antarctica	Toronto, Canada
Jakarta, Indonesia	Thule, Greenland	Budapest, Hungary
Alice Springs, Australia	Antofagosta, Chile	New York, New York
Manila, Philippines		
Miami, Florida		

Since the class decided to categorize their cities by temperature, they began to refer to lists A, B, and C as "Hot Cities," "Cold Cities," and "Cities with June Temperatures Like Ours."

When the time comes to explore the relationships among latitude, hemisphere, and climate, Mrs. Munoa needs to move her students' thinking beyond a focus on temperature alone.

Mrs. Munoa: Take a good look at the three lists on the board. Do you see any ways to further separate groups of these cities from one another? Zach?

Zach: In List A. My mom is in the Air Force, and she was stationed in Saudi Arabia. I know that Saudi Arabia is always hot and dry, but I also know that monsoons happen in Indonesia.

Mrs. Munoa: We studied monsoons in class. Can you remind us what a monsoon is, Zach?

Zach: Monsoons are very strong winds that bring rain to a place. You won't find a monsoon in Saudi Arabia, I know that! Those two places, Jakarta and Riyadh, could be on separate lists.

Mrs. Munoa: So, what criteria might we use to divide the cities on List A, then? Jon?

Jon: Well, dry and hot cities and wet and hot cities. My grandparents live in Arizona, and I know that it is very hot and dry there.

Mrs. Munoa: (*Begins to divide List A into two separate lists*) Does anyone else know something about the climate of these other cities in List A that might help us decide where to place them? In-Kyung?

In-Kyung: My grandparents now live in Miami Beach in Florida, and my mother complains about how humid it is when we visit there. It doesn't have monsoons, but I know they get hurricanes there.

Mrs. Munoa: There is a lot of precipitation in Miami and Jakarta—even though they are far away from one another. Any other changes to make?

The class decides to create List 1A and List 2A. Mrs. Munoa wonders whether the students go no further with the "hot and dry" and "hot and humid" division of List A because they are unfamiliar with the other cities. Rather than shift the class into a discussion of students' familiarity with the rest of the cities in Lists B and C, she chooses to move ahead with the lesson. So far, Mrs. Munoa's class has identified locations in four climate zones—tropical, desert, polar, and seasonal—although no zone has been given a name yet. She continues:

Mrs. Munoa: So what have we figured out today as we examined our data? Take a few minutes in your groups to write two sentences about our discoveries so far.

After several minutes of discussion, each of the six groups shares their sentences, and then the full class comes to a consensus on this summary statement:

Cities all over the world have different temperatures on the same day.

With this preparation in place, Mrs. Munoa explains the scope of the group research task, and she provides a detailed assignment sheet that outlines her exact expectations. These are the major components of the project:

Use a variety of sources (Internet, CD-ROM, books and journals, and other print sources) to locate information.

Describe the geographical features of the region surrounding each city.

Describe the typical climate of your cities and the regions in which they are located during the following months: June, September, December, and March.

Describe how people have adapted to the environment to meet their basic needs.

Each group is responsible for finding appropriate, reliable sources of information on their own. All Internet work will need to be done on school computers, which are equipped with filters.

4. The learner will describe the relationship of latitude lines to the Equator.

Mrs. Munoa's students can already identify the North and South Poles, the Equator, the seven continents, and the 50 states. During the first part of this lesson on latitude lines, she will teach directly about the Tropics of Cancer and Capricorn and the Arctic and Antarctic Circles. In the second part of the lesson, she will be asking questions to help her students discover climate relationships. She asks them to look closely at their desktop maps. Instead of pointing out that the Equator is at 0 degrees, with the latitude lines north and south increasing in degrees as they move away from the Equator, she asks questions like these:

How are each latitude line including the Equator and the Tropics labeled?

What do you notice about the changes in the numbers?

Why do you think the Equator was chosen to be labeled as 0 degrees?

How might we write the differences between latitudes above and below the Equator?

What do you think might be the significance of the names *Tropic of Cancer* and *Tropic of Capricorn*?

What do you notice about the distances between each latitude line on your maps?

In a later lesson, a similar list of questions will prompt discussion of the Prime Meridian.

5. The learner will compare and contrast six different cities around the world in terms of continent, hemisphere, coordinates, and average year-round temperatures.

Today's lesson will help Mrs. Munoa's students understand that locations with similar latitudes will have similar climates. To prepare the entire class for this discussion, she asks that each group member take responsibility for one of the group's assigned cities. She has prepared a retrieval chart and a set of questions from their research (shown in Table 11.4) that must be answered about each city. This afternoon, students will participate in a modified Jigsaw to share one of their city's locations and climates with students from other groups. Mrs. Munoa has formed four new groups of six students each for the Jigsaw.

After this activity, Mrs. Munoa gives her students a movement break, then asks them to bring their pencils, lapboards, and desk maps to the rug. She asks that a representative from each group come up to the large world map, place a small adhesive note next to the location of each of their cities, then call out their average June temperatures. On a recording sheet with all 24 cities listed in alphabetical order, the students will record the average June temperature of each of the 24 cities on their desk maps. Once the average June

Table 11.4 City Data

My City

City/country	1	2	3	4	5	6
Continent						
Hemisphere						
Coordinates						
June average temperature						
September average temperature						
December average temperature						
March average temperature						

1. What are the similarities in your cities?

2. What are the differences in your cities?

3. What are your observations after sharing your information?

4. What is the most important piece of information you would like to share with the full group?

---

temperatures are recorded for each city, she asks the students to observe the map data carefully to see if they can see any patterns. They should feel free to converse with their neighbor. After a few minutes, she asks for their attention again.

Mrs. Munoa: Any observations? Ashley?

Ashley: Right away we saw that the "top row" of cities all have low temperatures. Those cities at the top of the map. They are all in the 40s.

Mrs. Munoa: How can we describe where those cities are located? James?

James: They are all close to the North Pole. The North Pole is at the very top of the map. But my group had Mawson in the Antarctic as one of our places, and it has the lowest temperature of all—4 degrees. That is the very, very coldest.

Mrs. Munoa: What can we say about the location of Mawson, then? Talk this over with your neighbor. (*She waits.*) How many of you think you know? Ah, many hands on this one. Sammie?

Sammie: Mawson is at the South Pole. The coldest places we looked at were all near one of the poles—most of them near the North Pole.

Mrs. Munoa's students began this unit with knowledge of the location of the poles. Earlier in the week, she had identified both the Arctic and the Antarctic Circles for her students, but she introduced them as lines of latitude without referring to their relationship to climate. Now the class discusses how the poles receive the least direct rays of the sun, and they are always the coldest places on the planet. Mrs. Munoa identifies the Arctic and Antarctic Circles as being the boundaries of the polar climate zones.

Next she asks her students what observations they have made about the other locations. Esme says that there are too many other cities. She and Sy think that the class should put the rest of them in order of their temperature. Maybe they should all be put in order. The students agree and list each city on the board according to temperature. They decide to begin with the cities in the polar region. Once the list is complete, Mrs. Munoa gives them a few more moments to consider the data and the map.

The class notices that a band of cities has temperatures in the 80s and 90s. When asked why this might be so, the students notice that these locations are closer to the Equator. Mrs. Munoa says that typically, the closer to the Equator, the hotter the temperature. Locations between the Tropic of Cancer and the Tropic of Capricorn are said to be in the tropical climate zone.

The groups that are researching Cairo, Phoenix, Miami, and Riyadh mention that these cities are all 30 or more degrees above the equator, but they still have the hottest temperatures. Mrs. Munoa says that in their research, they need to find out why each city has the climate it does. Generalizations about climate always have exceptions to the rules. For example, elevation and position near a large body of water can affect the climate in just one location of a region. Mrs. Munoa closes this lesson by saying that the cities not discussed today will be examined tomorrow.

6. The learner will describe the locations of global climate zones: Polar (Arctic Circle to the North Pole and Antarctic Circle to the South Pole), Tropic (latitudes between the Tropics of Cancer and Capricorn), and Temperate (the two areas between the Tropic of Cancer and the Arctic Circle and the Tropic of Capricorn and the Antarctic Circle).

During social studies time the following day, students share their information about the year-round climate of cities with average June temperatures in the 60s and 70s. Through Mrs. Munoa's skilled questioning, students come to realize that these cities lie in what we call a temperate climate zone—more informally called a seasonal climate zone. The students' own state lies in the temperate zone, so they all understand what that means.

Mrs. Munoa then asks what the Antofagosta and Alice Springs groups have to say about the reason for the climate of their city. Students from these groups mention that both of these cities are almost exactly on the Tropic of Capricorn—the beginning of the seasonal climate zone in the southern hemisphere. In their research, they found out that the seasons are reversed south of the Equator. This accounts for the average June temperatures being colder than those of counterpart cities in the northern hemisphere.

When the class is shown the location of Stanley, on the Falkland Islands, and Melbourne, Australia, and are asked what they think the June temperatures might be, they agree that those temperatures would probably be much colder than those of Antofagosta and Alice Springs because Stanley and Melbourne are closer to the South Pole. The Mawson group reminds the class that the average June temperature there is only 4 degrees. Mrs. Munoa states that in upcoming science lessons over the next few days, the students will be learning more about the reasons for seasonal differences in climate in the northern and southern hemispheres, as well as the effects of altitude and bodies of water on climate. She asks that the class write summary statements about climate zones on Earth. They come to consensus on these statements:

Locations in the polar regions are the coldest on the planet.

Locations near the equator usually have the hottest temperatures.

Locations between the Tropic of Cancer and the Arctic Circle and the Tropic of Capricorn and the Antarctic Circle have seasonal climates that change every few months.

Next week, the class will be focusing in greater detail on longitude lines, with specific emphasis on the Prime Meridian, the International Date Line, and the organization of time zones.

Case Study 11.2: Post-Lesson Reflection

Over the course of the year, Mrs. Munoa's students have engaged in single-period investigations in science, math, and social studies, but they have never had the experience of using their inquiry skills over an extended period of time. When she first planned this unit, she outlined her ideas and then identified the number of content standards, inquiry skills, and technology standards that were addressed in her first draft. She found that her initial ideas were an excellent fit for the content she was required to teach.

Mrs. Munoa sees that her students are becoming increasingly conversant with the stages of the scientific method. They responded to her requests to make predictions based on their inquiry question; provide rationales for their hypotheses; and collect, record, analyze, and communicate data to one another. As a result of their fluency in these skills, Mrs. Munoa could concentrate on her questioning strategies during lessons. When she reviewed her plans after each lesson, she saw that most of the questions she had anticipated using were appropriate. She did have to come up with some spontaneous questions based on students' comments, but that is to be expected in any inquiry lesson.

As a result of her lesson designs, Mrs. Munoa was able to assess her students' full-group work, small-group projects, and individual journal responses. She was especially pleased that students were able to analyze class data to discern patterns. Her third graders worked together inductively to construct the concept of global climate zones. Not only were they able to make the connections she was hoping for regarding latitude lines and climate, but they went further than expected in the last lesson described. Students mentioned that their research revealed seasons in the southern hemisphere to be the opposite of those in the northern hemisphere—something she was going to address using Direct Instruction in a later lesson.

One question Mrs. Munoa has asked herself from time to time concerns the structure of her journal assignments across the curriculum. She wonders how often she should give students the freedom to write about a lesson or experience as they please and when it is best to require them to answer specific questions. Unsurprisingly, she found that some students thrive when they are allowed freedom, but other students require structure. She wonders whether she should give her students this choice, or whether she should work to help the latter group become more comfortable with more freedom. When she considers these assignments, she can see that science journals require a uniform structure so that the data and observations can easily be compared and analyzed. In social studies and math, the format of the journal entries may depend on the lesson objective.

Mrs. Munoa was pleased that she has been able to incorporate a number of models of teaching as this unit has progressed. In the context of the inquiry, she was able to include modified Jigsaw, Inductive Model, and Direct Instruction lessons appropriately and effectively.

Brief Background of Inquiry-Based Learning

Inquiry learning in the social studies began in the 1880s with the use of primary sources to develop historical accounts of events (Hertzberg, 1971). The source method prevailed until the 1930s, when social studies instruction turned to focus on issues relevant to students' lives.

The use of inquiry models of teaching that incorporate the scientific method has a dramatic history in the United States. A number of curriculums were developed in the 1960s and 1970s as a result of the Cold War space race. The complacency of the traditional K–12 curriculum and methods of instruction in the United States came into question once the Soviet Union launched *Sputnik*, the first satellite to orbit the Earth, in 1957 (Bulkeley, 1991). The government was concerned that U.S. school children would continually lag behind Soviet children if curriculum and instruction in this country were not revised significantly, especially in the sciences. During the next decade, the National Science Foundation funded curriculum development programs primarily in science education, but also in social studies and math.

Collaborative inquiry experiences help prepare students for their individual investigations.

In 1961 the Education Policy Commission advocated that "ten rational powers" be embedded in inquiry models of teaching: recalling and imagining; classifying and generalizing; comparing and evaluating; analyzing and synthesizing; and deducing and inferring (Krajcik, Mamlok, & Hug, 2001). Curricular programs developed during this time were responsive to this request. These programs have distinguishing attributes, and each of them relates to the formal scientific method in different ways: Elementary Science Study, Biological Sciences Curriculum Study, Science Curriculum Improvement Study, Michigan Social Science Curriculum Project and Physical Science Study Committee, Harvard Project Physics, Chemical Bond Approach, and Chemical Education Materials Study. All programs were field-tested in classrooms, and professional development was provided for teachers (Krajcik, et al., 2001).

However, in the 1970s, as these programs were being evaluated, dissatisfaction with their focus on process skills and the amount of classroom time their investigations required became widespread. For example, many critics believed that the high school curriculum in science was too demanding, the programs were no more popular than traditional science programs and had little relevance to students' everyday lives, and the programs did not produce more scientists (Krajcik, et al., 2001). However, while many of the specific programs in science developed during this period are no longer in use in their original forms, their influence on curriculum and instruction can be seen today in educational materials such as the Battle Creek Math and Science Center program (Battle Creek Area Math and Science Center, 2006).

The return to an emphasis on inquiry-based social studies also occurred during the post-*Sputnik* era. It was believed that students would best understand concepts in social studies by doing the work of social scientists (Thornton, 2001). Jerome Bruner's Man: A Course of Study (MACOS; Bruner, 1966) gave upper elementary students a grasp of social science concepts through experiences designed to replicate the work of anthropologists. The major philosophical question posed by the MACOS curriculum was "What does it mean to be human?" The development of critical thinking skills through inquiry was a primary focus of MACOS. Rather than being presented via traditional instruction, these experiences were discovery based. In spite of extensive professional development opportunities, teachers did not feel equipped to make radical changes in the ways they had taught social studies over the years. In its move away from traditional curriculum and instruction in the social studies, MACOS proved to be too controversial for its time (Thornton, 2001). In another effort at reforming social studies education using inquiry, the Amherst Project, which lasted from 1961 to 1971, developed high school curriculums that originally addressed traditional topics in U.S. history. Later this curriculum came to include topics socially relevant to the time, such as the Civil Rights struggle and the antiwar movement (Kline, 1974).

Inquiry learning reemerged in science curriculums in the 1990s. In contrast to the programs developed in the 1960s, these programs focused on student collaboration; inquiry experiences that are relevant to students' lives; authentic, multiple forms of assessment; and the integration of current technology (Krajcik, et al., 2001). Another major difference between science inquiry programs of the 1960s and those of the 1990s are their ultimate goals. In the 1960s, the major goals of curriculum reform were to create scientists and ensure the United States' continued dominance in the sciences. In the 1990s, scientific literacy was seen to be essential for all citizens, not just an elite few (Krajcik, et al., 2001). However, with the international outsourcing of many 21st-century jobs requiring advanced skills in math, science, and technology, many post-*Sputnik* concerns have come full circle. Our concerns now are twofold: How can our schools prepare future scientists to be producers of knowledge, and how can we best educate the general U.S. populous to be scientifically literate?

Inquiry-Based Learning and Research on Teaching

Regardless of your views of the No Child Left Behind Act and other federal and state initiatives that may arise in the near future, the opportunity to implement inquiry as a staple of teaching in K–12 schools is uncertain. In an age of federal and state legislation that increasingly evaluates student progress on the basis of standardized test scores, the time required to use inquiry in our classrooms may soon become a luxury. However, students' understanding of the major concepts in mathematics and the social and natural sciences, their positive attitudes about learning these disciplines, their skills in cognitive processes and systematic investigation, and their ability to analyze and evaluate the global impact of social and scientific progress are dependent on their substantive experiences with inquiry learning in school. It is also imperative that teachers have a deep understanding of the content they will be teaching as they learn to use inquiry in their classrooms. Teachers must be given adequate preparation in the content areas, instruction in the models of inquiry, opportunities to use these models, and support as they implement them.

What do we know specifically about the effects of Inquiry-Based Learning on students' learning? Traditional methods of lecture and lab experiences have not been shown to be more effective than inquiry methods in science classrooms (Schrenker, 1976). In fact, studies demonstrated that students' achievement in the sciences, as well as their positive attitude toward the sciences, increased with the programs developed in the 1960s. These benefits of the inquiry approach in science applied to students in both elementary and secondary classrooms (Bredderman, 1981, 1983; Shymansky, Kyle, & Alport, 1983; Shymansky, Hedges, & Woodworth, 1990).

Through the process of inquiry, students become conversant with the scientific method as it can be applied to the natural and social sciences, and they learn and retain scientific concepts (El-Nemr, 1979; Bredderman, 1981, 1983). Students also exhibit a deeper understanding of science concepts, superior abilities in higher-order thinking skills, and a higher level of creativity through experiences in inquiry (Schrenker, 1976). Studies directly related to the "learning cycle" described by Karplus and Their (1967) are included in this body of research investigating the use of inquiry in the science classroom. Robert Karplus worked on the Science Curriculum Improvement Study team, which researched how children developed reasoning skills and conceptual understanding in science. Karplus and Their's original learning cycle was a three-step model: exploration, concept invention, and application. An expanded, five-stage learning cycle now includes engaging, exploring, explaining, elaborating, and evaluating in the structure of inquiry experiences (Trowbridge & Brybee, 2000). The various stages of the scientific method, as well as the different formats for inquiry, are aligned with each of the learning cycle models in different ways and different measures.

Inquiry-Based Learning and Constructivism

John Dewey said that learning is the sum of action plus reflection (1933). When students are involved in learning through inquiry, they are provided with opportunities to act in systematic ways in response to engaging questions. They act by participating in Inquiry-Based Learning, and then they reflect on what they have seen and made sense of during the course of their investigations. Dewey believed that learning involves

> (1) a state of doubt, hesitation, perplexity, mental difficulty, in which thinking originates, and (2) an act of searching, hunting, inquiring, to find material that resolve the doubt, settle and dispose of the perplexity. (p. 12)

This process is a hallmark of constructivist learning theory. Students assemble their understanding of information, concepts, and principles through multiple experiences with hands-on explorations (Brooks & Brooks, 1993). As part of this process, they must think about what they have learned, how they have learned it, and what that learning might mean in a real-world context.

Learning experiences based on constructivist theory often challenge students' ideas about the world. Instead of collecting new information to add to their existing schemas, which Piaget calls assimilation, constructivist learning experiences challenge students' previously held knowledge and beliefs. During constructivist learning experiences, students will encounter new knowledge and must rearrange their schema by accommodating what has been discovered through their inquiries (Piaget, 1960; Ginsberg & Opper, 1969). Their schemas will rearrange as their thoughts, beliefs, and attitudes change.

What is even more important is that in the absence of rich experiences in inquiry in the natural and social sciences, students will remain consumers of knowledge in those disciplines. A steady diet of Direct Instruction, which is based on behaviorist learning theory, will continually focus students' attention on the past, on what has already been discovered by others. Inquiry experiences based on constructivist learning theory will provide them with the tools to move into the future as producers of knowledge.

Direct Instruction is a relatively easy model of teaching in which to gain competence as a beginning teacher. Driven by statements, Direct Instruction lessons are developed in a straightforward manner, the outcomes of lessons are told to the students at the beginning of each lesson, and the teacher directs each lesson toward those outcomes. For both students and teachers, Direct Instruction is a "tidy" experience. Inquiry lessons are driven by questions, and the eventual outcome of each experience will unfold only as a result of the process. While Inquiry-Based Learning will be planned around objectives, the paths taken to reach those objectives may be circuitous at best and sometimes unavoidably messy. Skill in using models of teaching that are grounded in constructivist theory, such as Concept Attainment, the Inductive Model, or any model of Inquiry-Based Learning, takes considerable study, practice, and perseverance—opportunities for teachers to learn through "action plus reflection."

Inquiry-Based Learning and Cognitive Processing

Inquiry-Based Learning is, by definition, aligned with the cognitive processing philosophy of curriculum and instruction. In the cognitive processing philosophy, academic content and inquiry skills play in counterpoint. Inquiry skills are used to reveal knowledge, and that knowledge is best understood in meaningful ways as a result of students' hands-on experiences. The "ten rational powers" suggested by the Education Policy Commission in 1961 (Krajcik, et al., 2001) could be said to provide structure for a "cognitive curriculum" for K–12 students. Lessons that require recalling, imagining, classifying, generalizing, comparing, evaluating, analyzing, synthesizing, deducing, and inferring can be designed across the curriculum. Creative teachers can incorporate these cognitive process skills in many learning experiences, whether or not they are explicitly called for in the governing content standards and benchmarks.

The various ways to design Inquiry-Based Learning experiences make it an especially versatile model in school. Open or closed, guided or unguided inquiry experiences will all involve cognitive processing skills, but in different ways, in different measures, and for different purposes.

Technology and Inquiry-Based Learning

The Inquiry-Based Learning model is especially suited to integrating technology into lessons and units of study. Various types of technology are clearly seen as tools for inquiry in every discipline and in nearly every career or form of employment. Students' abilities in inquiry using technology can begin in the early childhood years and progress through high school.

Internet resources will continue to be a major component of research in schools from now on. Developmentally appropriate Web sites can now be found on many topics for students at all reading levels. While they were required to use multiple resources for researching their cities, Mrs. Munoa's students used the Internet extensively as they put together their projects. If classrooms are equipped with Smart Boards, teachers can model the research process, note taking, and data organization. The screens that the teacher creates can be saved and duplicated for students. Software or Web sites that provide an array of graphic organizers can be useful as students collect various kinds of data and organize their information for presentation.

Mrs. Munoa's students' increasing sophistication in their use of PowerPoint will soon include incorporating various media into their presentation. Data or information for class or individual surveys can be recorded via audiotape, videotape, CD-ROMs, or digital camera, depending on the nature of the inquiry. These media can all be used in students' upcoming PowerPoint presentations. The next step for students doing inquiry-based assignments may be to create movies to demonstrate what they have learned as a result of their research.

Inquiry-Based Learning can support the following National Educational Technology (NET) Standards for Students (International Society for Technology in Education, 2000) at each grade level:[*]

GRADES PK–2

NET Standard 1: Basic operations and concepts

Performance Indicator 3: Communicate about technology using developmentally appropriate and accurate terminology.

Performance Indicator 4: Use developmentally appropriate multimedia resources to support learning.

Performance Indicator 7: Use input devices to successfully operate computers, VCRs, audiotapes, and other technologies.

Inquiry Extension

Students in early childhood programs can use the computer to do simple research on topics related to their science or social studies curriculum. First graders can create PowerPoint projects that present their research.

National Educational Technology Standards for Students: Connecting Curriculum and Technology by ISTE. Copyright © 2000 by International Society for Technology in Education (ISTE), 800–336–5191 (US &Canada) or 541–302–3777 (Int'l), iste@iste.org, www.iste.org. All rights reserved. Reproduced with permission of ISTE via Copyright Clearance Center. Reprint permission does not constitute endorsement by ISTE.

GRADES 3–5

NET Standard 4: Technology Communication Tools

NET Standard 5: Technology Research Tools

Performance Indicator 7: Use telecommunication and online resources to participate in collaborative problem-solving activities for the purposes of developing solutions or products for audiences inside and outside the classroom.

Inquiry Extension

Establish ties with sister classrooms in various parts of the United States or across the globe. Students can become involved in a collaborative inquiry with international students that will be facilitated online or through telecommunications.

GRADES 6–8

NET Standard 3: Technology productivity tools

NET Standard 5: Technology research tools

Performance Indicator 4: Use content-specific tools, software, and simulations to support learning and research.

Inquiry Extension

Provide students with an experience in unguided inquiry in the next science unit. In the course of their investigations, students will be responsible for identifying, evaluating, and using technology that will support their learning.

GRADES 9–12

NET Standard 2: Social, ethical, and human issues

Performance Indicator 3: Analyze advantages and disadvantages of widespread use and reliance on technology in the workplace and in society as a whole.

Inquiry Extension

High school students can do individual or group research projects examining the effects of technology on a particular U.S. industry. The project will document how technology in that industry has developed over time, the advantages and disadvantages for the industry itself, and the advantages and disadvantages for U.S. families.

Inquiry-Based Learning, Content Standards, and Benchmarks

Inquiry-Based Learning promotes students' understanding of key concepts, principles, and laws in the sciences, properties in mathematics, and concepts and generalizations in the social studies. Problem solving in each of these disciplines can be structured as inquiry by incorporating the stages of the scientific method. As you review the standards, benchmarks, or grade-level expectations in your state, consider how you might use the models of inquiry from the *Michigan Curriculum Framework* (Michigan Department of Education, 1996).*

Science—Constructing New Scientific and Personal Knowledge

CONTENT STANDARD 1: All students will ask questions that help them learn about the world; design and conduct investigations using appropriate methodology and technology; learn from books and other sources of information; communicate their findings using appropriate technology; and reconstruct previously learned knowledge.

Middle School Benchmark: Design and conduct simple investigations.

This content standard and accompanying benchmark will be addressed whenever any of the inquiry models are used in the science classroom.

Social Studies—Economics

CONTENT STANDARD 4: All students will explain how a free market economic system works, as well as other economic systems, to coordinate and facilitate the exchange, production, distribution, and consumption of goods and services.

Elementary Benchmark: Describe how the choices they make impact business decisions.

Students can predict which of five types of books will be the one most purchased at the book fair (animal, sports, comic book, science, sticker), then determine how the book fair organizers will order similar books the following year.

Inquiry

CONTENT STANDARD 2: All students will conduct investigations by formulating a clear statement of a question, gathering and organizing information from a variety of sources, analyzing and interpreting information, formulating and testing hypotheses, reporting results both orally and in writing, and making use of appropriate technology.

High School Benchmark: Conduct an investigation prompted by a social science question and compare alternative interpretations of their findings.

---

*Excerpts from the *Michigan Curriculum Framework* are reprinted with permission of the Michigan Department of Education.

Students can predict how individual U.S. Supreme Court justices will vote on an upcoming case based on an analysis of their previous judicial decisions.

Math—Data Analysis and Statistics

CONTENT STANDARD 3: Students will draw defensible inferences about unknown outcomes, make predictions, and identify the degree of confidence they have in their predictions.

Elementary Benchmark: Make and test hypotheses. Conduct surveys, samplings and experiments to solve problems and answer questions of interest to them.

Students can predict, survey, record, interpret, and communicate data from a survey of 20 students in various grade levels to determine their favorite flavors of ice cream.

Why Choose Inquiry-Based Learning?

1. Does your state or school district have benchmarks or grade-level expectations that explicitly require an inquiry-based approach?

2. Are there topics or lessons that require data collection or analysis or both?

3. Are there topics or concepts in your benchmarks or grade-level expectations that are not explicitly identified with Inquiry-Based Learning in the documents but that can be organized around questions?

4. Have you found that your students need greater opportunity to work on process skills (observation, analysis, comparison, evaluation, etc.)?

Summary

Inquiry-Based Learning experiences at every grade level will be found across the curriculum in district and state documents. Inquiry lessons can be designed around the stages of the scientific method; however, less-structured inquiries can also provide students with discovery experiences. Inquiry-Based Learning can be developed as single-lesson experiences or as extended instructional units. In any Inquiry-Based Learning experience, students are asked to develop hypotheses in response to questions; observe, collect, record, and analyze data; and communicate their results to others. One eventual goal of Inquiry-Based Learning is that students will develop their own investigations.

The use of technology in Inquiry-Based Learning experiences in any area of the curriculum will transfer to all other areas of the curriculum. Designing and facilitating inquiry-based experiences takes patience, commitment to the process, and faith in students' developing skills as independent learners. The flexibility in designing Inquiry-Based Learning experiences makes them especially suitable models for teachers to have in their repertoire.

Putting It Together

1. Find "describe, classify, and explain" benchmarks or grade-level expectations in each of the four core curriculum areas in your state's curriculum document.

2. Choose one of the benchmarks or grade-level expectations you have identified. Search online for lessons that use an inquiry approach. Evaluate the outline of one lesson plan. What components of the lesson are solid? Which components of the lesson would you strengthen to improve the students' inquiry experience?

3. Choose one strand of science, such as biology. Using a textbook series, trace the development of one unit topic. For example, locate when plants are first introduced and note successive inquiry experiences over the course of the K–12 curriculum.

4. In either elementary, middle, or high school science or social studies texts, locate inquiry experiences in each of the strands.

5. Choose one critical thinking skill, such as analysis. In one textbook from either a science or a social studies series, trace the development of that critical thinking skill throughout the course of the school year.

Student Study Site

The Companion Web site for *Models of Teaching: Connecting Student Learning With Standards*
www.sagepub.com/delloliostudy

Visit the Web-based student study site to enhance your understanding of the book content and discover additional resources that will take your learning one step further. You can enhance your understanding by using the comprehensive Study Guide, which includes chapter learning objectives, flash cards, practice tests, and more. You'll find special features, such as the links to standards from U.S. States and associated activities, Learning from Journal Articles, Field Experience worksheets, Learning from Case Studies, and PRAXIS resources.

References

Battle Creek Area Math and Science Center. Battle Creek, MI. Retrieved May 31, 2006, from www.bcmsc.k12.mi.us/

Bredderman, T. (1981). *Elementary school process curricula: A meta-analysis.* (ERIC Document Reproduction Service No. ED 170–333)

Bredderman, T. (1983). Effects of activity-based elementary science on student outcomes: A quantitative synthesis. *Review of Educational Research, 53*(4), 499–518.

Brooks, J. G., & Brooks, M. G. (1993). *In search of understanding: The case for constructivist classrooms.* Alexandria, VA: Association for Supervision and Curriculum Development.

Bruner, J. (1961). The act of discovery. *Harvard Educational Review, 31*(1), 21–32.

Bruner, J. (1966). *Toward a theory of instruction* [including Man: A course of study, Chapter 4, pp. 73–101]. New York: Norton.

Bulkeley, R. (1991). *The Sputniks crisis and early United States space policy: A critique of the historiography of space.* Bloomington: Indiana University Press.

Dewey, J. (1933). *How we think: A restatement of the relation of reflective thinking to the educative process.* Chicago: D.C. Heath.

El-Nemr, M. A. (1979). *Meta-analysis of the outcomes of teaching biology as inquiry.* Boulder: University of Colorado.

Ginsberg, H., & Opper, S. (1969). *Piaget's theory of intellectual development.* New York: Prentice Hall.

Hertzberg, H. (1971). *Historical parallels for the Sixties and Seventies: Primary sources and core curriculum revisited.* Boulder, CO: Social Science Education Consortium.

International Society for Technology in Education. (2000). *National educational technology standards for students: Connecting curriculum and technology.* Washington, DC: Author in collaboration with the U.S. Department of Education.

Karplus, R., & Their, H. (1967). *A new look at elementary school science.* Chicago: Rand McNally.

Kline, W. A. (1974). *The "Amherst Project:" A case study of a federally sponsored curriculum project.* Unpublished doctoral dissertation, Stanford University, Stanford, California.

Krajcik, J., Mamlok, R., & Hug, B. (2001). Modern content and the enterprise of science education in the twentieth century. In L. Corno (Ed.), *Education across a century: The centennial volume.* Chicago: University of Chicago Press.

Michigan Department of Education. (1996). *Michigan curriculum framework*. Lansing: Author.

Piaget, J. (1960). *The child's conception of the world*. Atlantic Highlands, NJ: Humanities Press.

Schrenker, G. (1976). *The effects of an inquiry-development program on elementary school-children's science learning*. Unpublished doctoral dissertation, New York University.

Shymansky, J. A., Hedges, L. V., & Woodworth, G. (1990). A reassessment of inquiry-based science curricula of the 1960s on student performance. *Journal of Research in Science Teaching, 27*, 127–144.

Shymansky, J. A., Kyle, W. C., & Alport, J. M. (1983, May). The effects of new science curricula on student performance. *Journal of Research in Science Teaching, 20*, 387–404.

Thornton, S. J. (2001). Legitimacy in the social studies curriculum. In L. Corno (Ed.), *Education across a century: The centennial volume* (pp. 185–205). Chicago: University of Chicago Press.

Trowbridge, L., & Brybee, R. (2000). *Teaching secondary school science* (7th ed.). Columbus, OH: Merrill/Prentice Hall.

chapter 12

Synectics

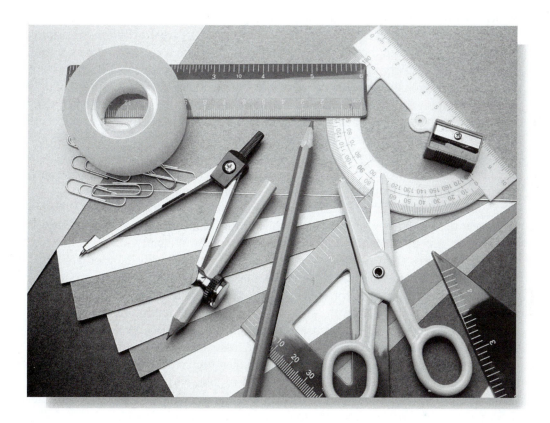

Recently I (T. D.) was walking in a small downtown area with my two young children when they both began yelling, "Hot lava, Daddy! Watch out! Your feet are burning!" After a few moments of confusion and asking questions, I began to understand a new activity they had created. It seems they had determined that the patterned brick sidewalk represented something new to them. The horizontally laid bricks were the "lava" and the vertically laid bricks that formed a large border around the lava were safe areas for walking. Sensing the danger I was now in, I jumped to the bricks on the border and remained on them as we made our way to our destination.

As I reflected on this incident recently, I marveled at the creativity of young children—their ability to transform the commonplace into settings for adventure, their ability to see what I could not. I was also reminded of the freshness with which my former first-grade students could approach the many tasks of daily life in a classroom setting versus the unwillingness of my former fifth graders and middle school students to stray from the tried and true. First graders turned their drawings into adventurous stories of giant flying bugs, while older students more often wrote uninspired and formulaic compositions about such things as their last football game. I struggled to promote creative thinking in my older students. It seemed that they feared thinking differently—or perhaps the accepted rituals and routines through which we often lead our lives had already trained creativity out of them. Sadly, a belief in our creative abilities begins to decline, for most of us, early in childhood (Lizotte, 1998). We begin to see the sidewalk pattern as only bricks for a walking path.

A lack of creativity in our students, or at least their perception of it, makes our work as teachers challenging. So much of what we do in any subject requires not only analytic thinking but also the ability to think creatively—using invention, artistic vision, or the many other ways we might think of creativity in such school subjects as science and writing. So often we hear our students lament, "I can't do that. I'm just not creative," whether they are talking about art, writing, a problem-solving task in social studies, or any other area of the curriculum. We are challenged to develop each student's creative potential as a companion to more rationalist ways of thinking.

Synectics is a model for developing students' creative thinking capacity. Although originally designed for group problem solving for adults in the work world, it was adapted for use by students in classroom situations by William Gordon (Joyce and Weil, 1996) more than 40 years ago and explored and modified by others since. Synectics uses metaphor and analogy to make the creative process explicit for students through strategies for *exploring the unfamiliar* and *creating something new*. In this chapter, we will focus on the strategy for creating something new. It should be noted here that Synectics can be used in virtually any content area. For purposes of illustration, we have chosen the area of writing instruction for the first case study.

As you read it, notice how the teacher makes the creative process clear to the students. Think about how students are asked to take on the fundamental parts of the procedures so that they can ultimately use them independently. Last, consider how the cognitive processing philosophy coincides with this model.

Case Study 12.1: Middle School, Writing

Mrs. Stich teaches language arts courses in a midsize suburban school district. She has been a teacher in the district's middle school for five years. Her class of sixth graders has been focusing on writing skills for several weeks. They have worked with expository texts and have lately been considering narrative texts. As she observed their early efforts at creating characters and settings for their stories, she noted a widespread inability to creatively express these components. For example, characters were commonly described only as *fun* or *sad*. Settings were described with such common adjectives as *sunny* and *nice*. Mrs. Stich began considering how to encourage more creative thinking among her students. She wants them to explore ways to provide characters and settings with more texture and feeling.

Initially Mrs. Stich tried doing a brainstorming session with her students to come up with as many descriptive adjectives and adverbs as possible. The students created a considerable list. She also encouraged them to use a thesaurus for variations of terms. At first this approach seemed helpful. The students began to use more variety in their word choices. However, students continued to use one-word descriptors, and the absence of texture and feeling continued.

Mrs. Stich decided to try using the Synectics model that she had learned during a recent summer course of graduate study. She knew this model could be applied in writing and in other areas.

As Mrs. Stich considered the use of Synectics, she also revisited the content standards and benchmarks for the language arts adopted by her state's board of education. She believed that this model would assist her students in meeting these goals, particularly one that stated that students should be able to "Identify and use aspects of the craft of the speaker, writer, and illustrator to formulate and express their ideas artistically. Examples include color and composition, flashback, multidimensional characters, pacing, appropriate use of details, strong verbs, language that inspires, and effective leads" (Michigan Department of Education, 1996, p. 17).

In this lesson, Mrs. Stich will introduce her class to the Synectics model. She will begin by involving them in stretching exercises—simple activities that help learners explore the use of metaphor. For example, she will ask questions like the following: A house is like what kind of animal? or How is freedom like a jaguar? or Can you tell me what it feels like to be the jaguar? After this short period of warm-up, Mrs. Stich will begin the lesson using a recent story draft (reproduced in Figure 12.1) by one student, Rachel. Rachel has been struggling to spice up her writing and has agreed to let Mrs. Stich use her writing as a sample for this exercise. Mrs. Stich has made an overhead of the portion of Rachel's writing to be used for this lesson. Here is her lesson objective for today:

The learner will understand and use the structure of the Synectics model to describe the setting of a story.

Figure 12.1 Rachel's Story

Jack sat in his office. It was a small cubicle connected to other cubicles that looked the same—except for the personal pictures of family and friends that people had put on the walls. It was hot and stuffy. The air-conditioning had stopped working that morning. He could hear telephones ringing in the other cubes and people talking. It was such a small office that he could roll around on his chair and get to the files and his computer without having to ever stand up. That's what everyone seemed to do there. He could always hear squeaky chairs rolling around. Jack hated his office.

Mrs. Stich: Now that we have had some time to get warmed up a bit and reminded about how metaphors work, I would like us to do two things with the rest of our time today. Many of you have been telling me that you are having some trouble thinking of creative ways to describe your characters and the settings in your stories. In fact, many of you have said that you just don't think you are very creative. I know what you mean because sometimes I feel the same way. But today, I want to introduce you to something called Synectics. It's a way to help us all think more creatively by using metaphors. It has really helped me since I learned about it and started using it last summer. Rachel has volunteered a part of one of her drafts for our work today. (*She places the overlay with the section of Rachel's writing on the overhead projector.*) We'll use it to give her the help she wants and to learn the Synectics model at the same time. I'd like you take a minute to read this paragraph from Rachel's draft to yourselves. (*She pauses for a few moments to allow for the reading.*) Rachel, could you please explain to everyone what you see as the problem in your writing?

Rachel: To be honest, I think that my description is boring. I can't find the words to show how this office is really an awful place to be. You know, my dad works in an office like this, and he doesn't mind it at all. Right now, this could be my dad in his office, except for the part where I say that Jack hates his office. I want this description to really show how my character feels about the place and why.

Mrs. Stich: OK, thanks Rachel. Now we know what Rachel sees as the problem. She wants Jack's office to feel like a place he really hates. How could we describe it to get that effect for the reader?

Peter: Describe the walls as dark.

Ellis: The lights could be really dim.

Tess: Maybe his chair could be broken, too.

Max: It could be late at night and scary looking with cobwebs and stuff.

Mrs. Stich: These are engaging descriptions. Do you think that they would work for what you are trying to do, Rachel?

Rachel: Well, they make it sound more like a haunted house, and I want it to be normal and awful at the same time.

Mrs. Stich: Well, let's try to do what Synectics calls *creating something new*. The idea is to use different kinds of analogies to make something that we are familiar with seem sort of strange. I'll show you what I mean. First, let's make a direct analogy. Let's compare the office to something that is alive, anything that makes sense to you. (*As students begin to respond, she records their ideas on a blank overlay.*)

Tess: How about a person?

Peter: No, that wouldn't work because. . . .

Mrs. Stich: Let's just give our ideas here. It's important for everyone to have a chance to share, and we can talk about these ideas later.

Yooyeun: It could be a flower, like a daffodil.

Ellis: Or maybe a weed, like a dandelion.

Maria: I would compare it to an insect, like a bee. A hornet that's angry.

Peter: I think it could be an amoeba—like the ones we saw in science yesterday.

Mrs. Stich: I think that your ideas give us some good analogies to start with. When we are using the Synectics strategy of making something new, we want to create a distance between our original object and the analogy we pick for it. In other words, the most unusual analogy might work best because it gives you such a new way of looking at something. Now let's pick one that would really surprise you, maybe because it's so different or interesting.

The students discuss the options Mrs. Stich has listed on the overhead and quickly decide that they like the analogy of an amoeba because it is such an unusual comparison.

Mrs. Stich: OK, now let's talk about how an amoeba lives.

Ellis: Usually they're found in stagnant water, and they eat the gross stuff floating around.

Tess: Sometimes they live inside other animals and eat even grosser stuff.

Peter: They float around in the water.

Rachel: They have a thing like a brain. It's called the nucleus, I think, and it tells the other parts what to do, kind of like a human brain.

Maria: I think they can change shape too.

Victor: It is only one tiny cell that you have to use a microscope to see, but it also has all these strange little parts.

Yooyeun: They have these things that kind of stick out like fingers. They're called pods or something, and I think that's how they get food, by surrounding it with their pods.

Mrs. Stich: OK, now here's the next part. We need to take what we know about amoebas and become an amoeba. In Synectics they call this *making a personal analogy*. Tell me what it feels like to be an amoeba! (*As the students respond, she writes the descriptive words on the overhead.*)

Tess: It stinks!

Mrs. Stich: That's a powerful word, Tess. I'd like you to rephrase it, though, so that you are the amoeba telling us how you feel. You could also add something that explains why you feel this way.

Tess: OK. I feel stinky because I live in swamp water.

Yooyeun: I feel free because I can move around in the water.

Peter: I am really small, and no one really cares about me.

Ellis: I feel like I'm the same as everyone else because we all look just about the same.

Maria: I feel hungry because I spend most of my time floating around looking for food.

Tess: I am powerful because I can eat things that are smaller than me in the pond.

Victor: I get to be different from all other amoebas because I can change my shape whenever I want to.

Jenna: I feel like a weakling because I am so small. Anyone could eat me.

Mrs. Stich: It's tough to imagine what it would be like to be an amoeba, but you've done a really clever job of it! By now, some of you might be wondering why we're talking about amoebas and how that will help us describe the setting of Rachel's story. I just want to ask you to hang in there until we get to the end of this session. I think that it will make more sense to you at that point. Now I'd like you to look at the words I've listed on the overhead. See if you can match up words that seem to be opposites of each other or seem to fight with each other. (*On the board she has listed the following words and phrases: stinky, free, small, hungry, powerful, the same, different, weakling.*)

Ellis: How about *powerful* and *weakling*? They are kind of like opposites.

Tess: Oh, and *the same* and *different* would work too.

Mrs. Stich: Are there any others that we should consider? (*The students indicate that there are no other matches that meet her criteria.*) OK, now let's look at the two we have. Which of these strikes you as the most different combination?

Carolyn: Well, I think that *same* and *different* are used a lot, but if you put *powerful* and *weakling* together, that's a really strange way to mix words. You know, like a powerful weakling!

Mrs. Stich: Can everyone agree that *powerful weakling* is the more engaging combination? (*Lots of bobbing heads and muffled agreement.*) In Synectics, this is called a *compressed conflict*, taking two words that don't seem to go together, that seem to be in conflict with each other, and putting them together as a description of something.

Peter: Do you mean any words that are opposites?

Mrs. Stich: Yes, they could be opposites or words that challenge each other. Next, let's think about things that we could describe as being powerful weaklings. I'd like you to think of another direct analogy with things that are not alive. Who can think of a nonliving thing that is powerful and a weakling?

Max: Hey, how about a hornet's nest? We had one at home, and it looked really powerful, but when my dad sprayed it with hornet poison, it just fell apart and looked like a bunch of mud, and there weren't any hornets in it.

Ellis: An eggshell because you can't break it by squeezing it, but you can crack it really easily.

Peter: Or it could be an egg carton with eggs in it.

Rachel: The *Titanic*!

Yooyeun: A firework, like the kind they shoot on the Fourth of July!

Maria: Scaffolding, you know, the pipes they put up around new buildings to hold them up. The ones around the new store by my house just fell down yesterday because of the wind.

Tess: Or a racecar. You know how they sound loud and powerful, but if they hit something, they fall apart!

Max: I think a mirror would be good. It is strong but can also crack easily.

Mrs. Stich: Now let's look at the ones we have talked about so far. Which ones would make the most fascinating direct analogy, a comparison of two unlike things, with the office that Jack works at in Rachel's story? Remember that Rachel wants to show that Jack doesn't like the office.

She places the story excerpt on the overhead, and the students begin to discuss possible selections. Eventually they decide that the analogy with a mirror has the most potential.

Mrs. Stich: Let's try to give Rachel a few suggestions using the analogy of a mirror to describe the office Jack works in.

Ellis: Well, Rachel said that each office looked the same, kind of like if Jack was looking in a mirror and everything was like a reflection.

Max: The noise he hears could be like that awful sound you hear when you scrape something sharp against a mirror, like another piece of glass or another mirror.

Peter: Or maybe even the sound of a breaking mirror.

Carolyn: Maybe she could also show how hot and stuffy it is by comparing it to the way a bathroom mirror gets all steamed up when you are taking a shower.

Mrs. Stich: These are some fine suggestions for Rachel. I am sure they will help her in her new drafts of this story. I hope that as we continue to learn about Synectics as a way to think about things differently, it will also help the rest of us! Today you might even want to go through the drafts in your notebook and circle some settings that might be improved using Synectics.

The lesson ends as students are dismissed to go work on their writing.

Rachel returns to her own story with new ideas and energy. She can take the familiar setting of an office and create something new through the use of the mirror analogy. Rachel's next draft (see Figure 12.2) reflects her experiences with the Synectics model. In the next lesson, Mrs. Stich let Rachel show her changes, which everyone appreciated.

Figure 12.2 **Rachel's New Draft**

Slowly Jack walked toward his office cubicle. He felt like he was walking through a hall of mirrors—each office an identical reflection of the others. Only the picture of his family on the gray walls told him which one was his. He sat down in his chair. As he turned on his computer, he noticed the screen had a thin layer of moisture. The air was hot and humid. The air-conditioning had probably stopped working again, and who knew how long it would take to get it fixed this time. It would be another long day with his clothes sticking to his body. In the background he could hear what sounded to him like glass scraping against glass. It was the annoying sound of telephones and squeaky chairs in the cubicles all around him. Jack hated his office.

Case Study 12.1: Post-Lesson Reflection

Mrs. Stich felt that this introduction to the Synectics model was effective. At each stage of the lesson, she was able to embed the structure and the language of the model while working on a real issue of writing. This allowed her to teach the model and had the added benefit of providing her students with the opportunity to see its relevance to their own writing efforts. The students' abilities to use the model to create a new way to approach the setting of Rachel's story worked well. Mrs. Stich felt that her lesson objective had been met.

In this lesson, Mrs. Stich provided the structure and informal definitions for terms such as *compressed conflict*. She wants her students to eventually use the language of the Synectics model that she has introduced. She knows her students will need some experience with the model before they can use the terminology and structure comfortably and independently (Land, 1995). She plans to have them use Synectics in more group writing experiences, as well as in other areas of the curriculum, both to gain fluency with the model and to see its applications to tasks besides writing.

Mrs. Stich also used this lesson to help foster a climate that would enhance creative thinking and expression among her students. To do so, she invited and supported all responses without judgment (Wald & Weil, 1974; Soriano de Alencar, 1993; Weaver & Prince, 1990). From past experience, Mrs. Stich had learned that immediate critiques of ideas being put forth resulted in students' becoming defensive or worse: withdrawing from the discussion altogether. Early in the lesson, when Peter began to tell Tess that her idea of comparing the office to a person would not work, Mrs. Stich directed the conversation back to idea generation and reminded the students of the importance of accepting all ideas.

Mrs. Stich also had some broader goals in mind for this lesson. In particular, she wanted to encourage and increase the active participation of her students in the lesson activities. She often noted that a few of her students contributed significantly, while others seemed disengaged—waiting for the class period to end. She was pleased to see that a number of students who fit the latter category contributed ideas in this session. In fact, most of her students seemed to be having a lot of fun inventing analogies and connecting at an emotional level to such things as amoebas. This was a benefit she had not fully anticipated but welcomed warmly.

Another broad goal was to help her students see that creativity was not something people either possess or don't. Rather, she wants her students to know that everyone has creative thinking capacities and that these capacities can be nurtured using the Synectics model. She wants them to see that creativity goes beyond artistic expressions like drawing and painting (their most common ways of defining creativity). By seeing the setting of Rachel's story in a new way, they are creating or inventing. She hopes that the continued use of the model will help them recognize, nurture, and explore their creative potential.

Perhaps most important, Mrs. Stich saw Rachel return to her draft with enthusiasm and direction for her writing effort. Rachel's resulting draft showed a new way of considering her topic. Both Rachel and Mrs. Stich believed Rachel's second draft to be an improvement. Synectics more effectively conveyed the tone that Rachel had envisioned but was unable to convey.

The Stages or Structure of Synectics

The Synectics model contains seven steps or exercises, summarized in Figure 12.3. This structure is rooted in the original work of William Gordon (1961). It also reflects the work of Wald and Weil (1974), as well as the more contemporary efforts of Joyce and Weil (1996).

Stretching Exercises

The students in Mrs. Stich's class were new to the Synectics model. Because they were relatively inexperienced in using the metaphors and analogies, she gave them a series of **stretching exercises** for practice before beginning the actual model. Stretching exercises involve asking questions that help students explore the different kinds of analogies used in the Synectics model: direct analogy, personal analogy, and compressed conflict (Joyce & Weil, 1996).

To provide practice making direct analogies, Mrs. Stich asked the students to describe how a house is like an animal and how freedom is like a jaguar. The direct analogy requires students to compare two different objects or ideas. Kawenski (1991) suggests that using things in the natural world is helpful because students are familiar with them. In addition, it is often helpful to compare living and nonliving things because these comparisons tend to create more distance from the object at

As students do the work of brainstorming, it is helpful for the teacher to record the information. Students can focus on creating, and the recorded information is available for use at a later time.

hand. This conceptual distance promotes opportunities for invention—seeing things from a new and different perspective.

As your students become more comfortable with the Synectics model, it may not be necessary to use stretching exercises to open lessons. Once students demonstrate expertise in making and applying analogies, you may choose to begin the lesson with a description of the condition or problem to be addressed (Wald & Weil, 1974).

Description of the Present Condition or Problem

Initially, you and your students will want to determine a specific problem or condition to be addressed. In Case Study 12.1, Rachel wanted her description of Jack's office to convey his negative feelings about being there. The issue could just as easily be how to conceptualize democracy or breathe life into a mathematical theorem. Regardless of the issue, clarity is essential. Initially you may want to guide students by naming the condition or problem. As they become more fluent with the model, however, you might want your students to propose the problem. Either way, it is essential to be sure that everyone involved understands the problem or condition.

Once the issue to be addressed has been identified and clarified, you will want to guard against premature attempts at a resolution. Sometimes students will want to

Figure 12.3 Synectics Structure for Creating Something New

Stretching exercises (optional): Mrs. Stich explored the use of metaphors with such questions as How is freedom like a jaguar? to warm up the class for the lesson.

Description of the present condition or problem: Mrs. Stich and Rachel described the problem related to her setting. Rachel wanted it to be more descriptive.

Make a direct analogy: The class offered analogies of the office to something that is alive, an amoeba. They explored what they knew about amoebas.

Personal analogy: Mrs. Stich asked them to become amoebas and describe what they felt like.

Compressed conflict: The students looked at the words they had used to describe their feelings as amoebas and paired words that seemed to be in conflict in some way, such as *powerful* and *weakling*.

Direct analogy based on the compressed conflict: Mrs. Stich asked the students to create another direct analogy with a nonliving thing, using the compressed conflict of *powerful weakling*. A mirror was suggested.

Reexamination of the original task: The students returned to the original problem of describing Jack's office. By making a final analogy between the office and a mirror, they created a new way of looking at the setting.

SOURCE: Adapted from Wald & Weil, 1974; Joyce & Weil, 1996.

resolve the problem with the first analogies that are offered, perhaps because they are uncomfortable with metaphorical work or have become accustomed to quick solutions. In other cases, students new to Synectics may not fully appreciate the need to go through all the steps in the model. You may simply have to ask them to "hang in there" until the end of the lesson, as Mrs. Stich did when the students were discussing the amoeba analogy. Premature resolution of the task precludes the opportunity to fully develop the conceptual distance so critical to the creative process (Wald & Weil, 1974). Students should also understand that at the end of the session, they can return to any idea that was brought forth but that completing the session and exploring all ideas are essential.

Synectics also allows you to address individual issues in a group situation. Mrs. Stich elected to have all the students work on Rachel's issue. However, she might just as easily have had all the students select a setting from their own writing and then work on their own ideas. In this case, rather than having everyone contribute to each other's ideas, you might have students write down their own analogies and compressed conflicts as you walk them through the structure. They can still share their thinking about their own work with others. Mrs. Stich believed that all her students would benefit from the exercise and that her students would gain more familiarity with the model if they worked together on one example. The implementation of the Synectics model is flexible and responsive to your professional judgment about your goals and setting.

Once the problem or task has been clarified, students begin the process of selecting a direct analogy.

Direct Analogy

A **direct analogy** is the comparison (not contrast) of two unlike things (Wald & Weil, 1974). In Case Study 12.1, Mrs. Stich suggested comparing the office to something living to increase conceptual distance. Her students compared the office to a person, a daffodil, a dandelion, a hornet, and an amoeba, all of which she listed on the overhead.

Sometimes it may be helpful to have students discuss or describe their choices as they offer them. At other times, you may want to save this discussion for later, when all ideas have been solicited. Having conversation about the analogies may invite criticism, which is not helpful, as some students may fear it and hold back their ideas rather than risk embarrassment. On the other hand, allowing students to say a few things about how they are making comparisons might spark ideas in students who are struggling to make analogies. The dynamics of the group you are working with may dictate your choice.

It will be an important part of your role to ensure a climate that is receptive and invites participation by all students, particularly if you hope to involve the more apathetic or fearful learners in your class. As Weaver and Prince (1990) argue and our collective experiences in classroom teaching confirm, a climate that strives to eliminate "discounts" (put-downs) is essential for the creative process. Mrs. Stich therefore redirected the conversation when Peter attempted to discount Tess's direct analogy of the office and a person. Mrs. Stich framed the conversation by noting that everyone's ideas were important and should be heard and that a discussion would follow. She trusted that Tess could see an analogy, even if Peter did not fully appreciate it.

After the direct analogies have been named, ask the students to select and focus on one of them. Ensure that students have sufficient understanding of the analogy to use it fully as they attempt to make personal analogies, that is, identify with the analogy by becoming it (Joyce & Weil, 1996, p. 241). It would be difficult to "become" an amoeba, for example, without a certain degree of understanding about the form and function of this one-celled animal. In Case Study 12.1, Mrs. Stich was fortunate because the idea of the amoeba analogy had come from her students' recent work in science class, and they had a fairly well developed understanding of amoebas. Using this understanding, the students were able to move on to the next phase.

Personal Analogy

In Synectics, the learner develops what Gordon and Poze (1979) refer to as an "empathic identification" (p. 2). In short, the learner becomes the object; in Case Study 12.1, the students "became" the amoeba. Joyce and Weil (1996), referencing William J.J. Gordon, describe this process as engaging in four levels of identification with the analogy, summarized in Figure 12.4. Each level allows the student to connect with the object or idea in a personal way.

Figure 12.4   Four Levels of Identification With an Analogy

1. First-person description of facts ("I feel hungry.")

2. First-person identification with emotion ("I feel free.")

3. Empathic identification with a living thing ("I feel like I'm the same as everyone else.")

4. Empathic identification with a nonliving thing ("[*As a piece of paper*] Everyone gets to write whatever they want on me without my permission.")

SOURCE: Adapted from Joyce & Weil, 1996.

For many students, creating a **personal analogy** may feel awkward or somewhat difficult initially. A stretching exercise may provide an opportunity for practice. We also suggest you give students your tacit approval to have fun in their identification with the analogy. Appreciative laughter at attempts to verbally become such things as an amoeba may help break the ice and allow students greater access to this form. You may want to model your own attempts first.

It is not possible to use all the levels of identification listed by Joyce and Weil. Only the first three in Figure 12.4 could be used with the analogy of the amoeba. You may want to model or promote the other types with stretching exercises, however, to discourage overreliance on any one.

As your students develop personal analogies, it will be important to list key words in a visible way on an overhead, chart paper, marker board, or Smart Board because in the next phase, the students will use them to construct compressed conflicts.

Compressed Conflict

A **compressed conflict**, according to Wald and Weil (1974), is a "two-word description in which the words seem to fight each other" (p. 11). Students may have some familiarity with compressed conflicts because they are found in everyday vocabulary (*working vacation*, *friendly fire*, etc.). Compressed conflicts are a way to begin seeing the original problem or condition from a unique perspective. They give the object or thing under consideration a kind of multifaceted depth or personality.

Compressed conflicts ultimately infuse the problem or condition with meaning. Land (1995) argues that "meaning is made possible through associations" (p. 2). For example, happiness is meaningful only when contrasted with sadness. Generosity is appreciated when contrasted with selfishness. In this manner, the compressed conflict deepens the learner's understanding of, and appreciation for, the final analogy drawn in the lesson.

It is not necessary to use all the terms generated in personal analogies when constructing the compressed conflict. Indeed, forcing words to fit together is not advised. In Case Study 12.1, the students found two examples that seemed to meet the criteria and then selected the one that struck them as most compelling: a powerful weakling.

Direct Analogy Based on the Compressed Conflict

In this phase, students use the compressed conflict they have selected to create another direct analogy (Joyce & Weil, 1996). In Case Study 12.1, the students offered a number of possible choices for a nonliving object based on the compressed conflict of a powerful weakling. The possibilities ranged from the *Titanic* to a mirror. Ultimately they decided that a mirror had the most interesting potential.

Again, as students propose analogies, it is important to foster an atmosphere of acceptance. Many of the analogies offered may not be a perfect fit with the compressed conflict, and it would be easy, but unproductive, for students to begin critiquing the contributions. You can inform your students that suggestions need not be perfect fits but ones that seem to fit in some way that they can describe.

The analogy that students select in this phase will be applied to the original problem or condition. Therefore, you may want to give them some direction in its selection. Mrs. Stich made it a student decision, but she provided them with some loose criteria: "Which one would make the most fascinating direct analogy . . . with the office that Jack works at in Rachel's story?"

Reexamination of the Original Task

Ultimately, students are asked to return to the problem or condition they identified at the start of the lesson. You will want to assist your students in considering how the final analogy sheds new light on the original task (Joyce & Weil, 1996). Typically, the analogy will be unique, having benefited from the Synectics model. Nearly always, it will be superior to what might have been generated if an analogy had simply been made at the beginning of the problem-solving activity.

Ask your students to consider how the very different objects in the final analogy can be compared or how they can be useful in the original task. In Case Study 12.1, the students came up with some powerful ways for Rachel to use the analogy of Jack's office and a mirror as she began to redraft her story—describing each office as an identical reflection of the others or comparing the sound of squeaky chairs to scraping something sharp on a mirror. Rachel's resulting draft was much improved. Perhaps even more important, she returned to her writing with fresh ideas, new enthusiasm, and a model for developing her own creativity.

We believe that students' increased awareness of their creativity is valuable, independent of the specific results of using the Synectics model. Increased awareness of their creativity has the potential to broaden their outlook in all their efforts with school content. Therefore, whether students use the ideas from a particular Synectics session is far less important than their new awareness of their capacity to create, invent, or discover, which has important implications for the way they approach tasks in the future.

Exploration of the Unfamiliar

Synectics includes more strategies than the one we have focused on here. Exploring the unfamiliar is another popular and widely used strategy contained in the model. According to Wald and Weil (1974), it is a very analytical strategy, and we chose to emphasize strategies for developing creativity (through creating conceptual distance) because they are less well known to teachers. If you wish to find out more about the strategy for exploring the unfamiliar, contact Synectics Education Systems, 121 Brattle St., Cambridge, MA 02138.

Case Study 12.2: High School, Science

Ms. Wisniewski (known to her students as "Ms. W." for obvious reasons) is a high school science teacher at a large urban high school. Her eleventh-grade students are working in small groups on a project she recently assigned. Each group must select a problem or issue that can be addressed using one of the areas of study they have completed during the semester. Their task is to determine the problem or issue and prepare a way to share their understanding of the topic with the class. In their presentation, they must demonstrate the information they learned and encourage class members to respond to the issue in some way. Ms. W. has told the students to consult with her over the next few weeks to discuss the way they will present their project.

Ms. W. wants her students to apply their understanding of science content to real-world issues and problems. She and the students have explored topics ranging from geological formations to the impact of acid rain on the human food chain. She has encouraged her students to think about ways some of these topics can be related to their own lives and believes this assignment will help them do that.

One group of students has already asked to meet with her. These students, Bridgeen, Oliver, Reagan, and Robert, want to focus on how to care for the Earth. They told Ms. W. that they have determined the content that they want to address and share with the class; however, they are struggling with ways to make the presentation engaging and visual for their audience. They have asked Ms. W. to assist them with some brainstorming for this segment of their assignment. Ms. W. does not yet know the specifics of their concerns, but she anticipates that an exercise using the Synectics model may be helpful. Because she wants to follow the students' lead initially, she has not determined a content-related objective for this lesson. She wants the students to use the Synectics model to tap into and enhance their own creativity. She and the students meet together to brainstorm.

Ms. W.: To get us started, why don't you tell me again what you are thinking about your topic and how we can work together to brainstorm some ways to give it the kind of interest you are hoping for in your presentation.

Bridgeen: OK. Our topic is caring for the Earth.

Robert: What we want to do is talk about how each of us can take care of the Earth in important ways. We want to share what we have learned about the impact of different kinds of pollutants on the environment.

Reagan: The angle we want to take is that the things each of us does really do impact the Earth. We've talked about how there are many things right at this school and in our neighborhoods that people do to pollute.

Oliver: Exactly. We were brainstorming things that people do right here that hurt the environment. Like when people throw their trash on the ground. All you have to do is look around this school, and you can see fast-food wrappers and things like that all over the place.

Robert: And we noticed that people sit in the parking lot with their cars running while they talk to their friends. That wastes gas. Plus the exhaust pollutes the air.

Ms. W.:   So, if I have this right, you want to share what you've learned in this class about the impact of pollution on the Earth, and your goal is to bring it to a local level by talking about things that happen right here—the things that all of us do that impact the Earth in a negative way. Is that right?

Reagan: Yes. But here's the problem. We don't want this to sound like one of those Earth Day things that people don't always pay much attention to.

Oliver: Right. We want them to see that all of us are part of the problem and that we really can do things every day to make a positive difference.

Bridgeen: So what we've been trying to do is come up with some way to show how what we do right here really impacts the Earth. We want to come up with something that will really help everyone identify with the Earth.

Reagan: Right. And how they can use what we've learned in this class to make a difference. We want them to really identify with the Earth and what we are all doing to it. Does that make sense?

Ms. W.:   It does. So it sounds to me like what you want to do is get them to connect with the environment, the Earth, right?

Robert: Exactly. And that's where we need help. We just can't think of a good way to help people connect. I guess we just aren't too creative!

Ms. W.:   Well, I don't think that's the case. I think one thing that might help is to use a kind of brainstorming activity that I've used before in class. Do you remember when we used the Synectics model earlier this year? (*They nod.*) I think that might help you come up with a new way to help people think of the Earth and how we treat it. How about if we do a Synectics exercise and see if that can help you?

Reagan: Sounds great. Anything will help at this point because we are really stuck.

Ms. W.:   OK. So this is the problem: How can we help people in this class identify with the Earth, our environment, right? (*They agree.*) Let's start by making a direct analogy with the Earth. Since the Earth contains so many living things, let's use nonliving things for our analogies. Any ideas will be good here. Since we are brainstorming, we don't want to discuss them yet or talk about whether they are good or not, OK? (*As the students offer ideas, Ms. W. types them into a computer attached to a Smart Board. She wants everyone to see the ideas and to eventually be able to manipulate them electronically.*)

Robert: How about a jacket?

Reagan: Or it could be a book filled with stories.

Bridgeen: Or a television, although I'm not really sure why.

Oliver: I think it could be a basketball because they are both round and get banged up by people a lot!

Ms. W.:   Those are very helpful. Now, what we want to do is create some distance between the analogy and the Earth itself. Sometimes the thing that is most odd or unusual works best because it gives us that space. It makes us look at the thing we're familiar with in a new way.

The students discuss the options they have generated and settle on the television, mostly because they wouldn't have thought of the Earth that way and think it's kind of interesting.

Ms. W.:   OK, next I think we should talk about what a television does.

Oliver: It brings all kinds of shows to your house.

Bridgeen: It has all these parts, like a picture tube, inside.

Reagan: Most of them have remote controls so that you can surf the channels really easily.

Oliver: You can learn from them, you know, like by watching the news or one of those educational stations. Or they can just bring you entertainment, like movies or sitcoms.

Ms. W.:   Good. Now here's what we need to do next. I want you to become a television. Tell me what you feel like. This is called making a personal analogy, by the way.

Robert: I feel abused. People just use me to entertain themselves, and sometimes I have to show these really stupid reality shows to them.

Reagan: I am proud of myself because I'm one of the most important parts of the house. People sit and watch me for hours at a time.

Oliver: I feel dirty. No one ever dusts me off and my glass has sticky handprints all over it.

Bridgeen: I am hot. I get turned on and then people just leave the room and I get left on for hours.

Oliver: I feel jealous. The lady who lives here won't let the kids turn me on at all, and all they do is read books now!

Reagan: I am controlling. I can get people to sit and watch me for hours and forget about everything else they were going to do.

Robert: I feel shiny, like a star, because everyone loves me, and they just love to watch me.

Ms. W.: Well, I would have thought that being a television would be a bit tricky, but you sure seem to be able to relate to it! I've listed on the Smart Board all the words you used to describe yourself as a television. Let's take a look at those words. (*The following words are listed on the board*: abused, proud, dirty, hot, jealous, controlling, *and* shiny.) What I want you to do next is match words, but the words you need to match are words that are opposites or at least seem to compete or fight with each other.

Reagan: How about abused and controlling? They aren't exactly opposites, but when you are abused, you don't feel like you are in control.

Oliver: OK, proud and jealous are kind of like that too. They aren't really opposites, but when you are proud, you feel important, and that can make people jealous sometimes.

Bridgeen: Dirty and shiny would work. When you are dirty, you aren't shiny, so they are like opposites.

Ms. W.: OK. Let's look at the ones we have. If we combine these words, which combination do you think is the most interesting or unusual?

Oliver: I think the weirdest one would be abused and controlling because you just don't think of those two words together when you're describing something.

After some discussion, all the students agree that this is their most interesting combination.

Ms. W.: OK. If you remember from when we did the Synectics exercise several weeks ago, this is called a compressed conflict. You put together two words that don't seem to go together, to describe something. Now, we want to make another direct analogy using these words. I'd like you to think about something that is living that could be described as controlling and abused.

Oliver: Well, no offense, but how about a teacher? They have a lot of control, but kids can be pretty abusive to them.

Ms. W.: None taken. (*Laughs*) Let's see if we can add some more.

Bridgeen: How about a mole? We had a lot of them in our yard last summer, and they sure did control my dad, but he abused them with traps and things because he said that they are pests.

Reagan: I think you could describe a family pet like that. You know, like a dog. They are controlling because you have to walk them and care for them, but sometimes they get abused when we don't pay enough attention to them, and they get left outside in the cold or they are by themselves all day.

Robert: I think a bear might work. When you see one, they are definitely in control, but people also shoot them, so they can be abused too.

Ms. W.: I've listed your suggestions here on the board. Which one do you think will make the most interesting comparison with the Earth or our environment?

After some discussion, they decide that comparing the Earth to a pet would be the most interesting.

Ms. W.: Now let's try to think how that might help you achieve the goal we started with. You said you want your audience to connect with the Earth. So how could we use the analogy of the Earth to a pet to make that happen?

Oliver: Well, here's what I'm thinking. Everyone loves their pets, right? So if we can get them to think of the Earth as their pet, we could make the point that if you want your pet to be healthy and love you, you need to take care of it. And the Earth is like that, too.

Bridgeen: Yeah, pets need clean water and air. Things that will keep them alive. You can't just ignore them.

Reagan: Maybe we could have all the kids in the class bring in a picture of their pets ahead of time, and we could make a PowerPoint presentation of them. Then maybe we could get some pictures from the humane society of abused pets and show what happens when you don't take care of animals. Well, if that wouldn't be too gross.

The students continue to brainstorm ways that the comparison of the Earth to a pet could be used to make their points about the importance of taking the care of the Earth. They feel that this is a comparison that their audience will be able to relate to and that they will be able to use to make their points about the impact of their personal behaviors on the environment.

Case Study 12.2: Post-Lesson Reflection ◆

Ms. W. was pleased with the way this session evolved. She believed that Synectics was a helpful way to assist her students. Indeed, this exercise was an excellent example of how Synectics can be used as a "group problem-solving approach" (Georgiou, 1994). As the group members worked together, they were able to use each other's strengths (p. 2). Together, the students were able to come up with the idea that comparing a pet (and pet care) to the Earth would help their audience connect with their topic in a more meaningful way.

This session also demonstrated the way Synectics can be modified as the situation and individuals require. For example, in the earlier case study, Mrs. Stich felt the need to do stretching exercises at the beginning of the lesson. Wald and Weil (1974) suggest that "stretching exercises are necessary only if the learners were not able to use a particular analogy" (p. 55). Ms. W. knew that her students had ample experience with analogies and metaphors, and she felt they could move straight into the model.

Ms. W. was also able to use the structure of Synectics to address her students' concerns that they lacked creativity. As noted earlier, students commonly have this perception of themselves in their high school years. Using this model, her students recognized their own creative abilities as they moved through the work with analogies. Ms. W. was particularly heartened because this exercise was done in a science class. High school students often have a perception of science as consisting only of facts and memorization activities.

Finally, this small-group lesson demonstrates the versatility of the Synectics model. As demonstrated here, Synectics procedures can be used with groups of all sizes, in a variety of content areas, and for multiple purposes. Ms. W. indicated that she had used the model before with the entire class, and she was able to use it with this small group of students as well. Synectics can be used with such diverse objectives as problem-solving in a science class and enhancing the setting of a story in a writing class. Its flexibility is one of the things that make it desirable.

Brief Background of Synectics

In the last several decades, many groups and organizations have focused on the issue of creativity and its development in individuals or groups (Soriano de Alencar, 1993). Synectics is one of the better-known models to emerge from this search.

The Synectics model was originally created by a design invention group. They recorded their own work sessions as they invented. From these recorded sessions came the beginnings of the Synectics model described here (Weaver & Prince, 1990). Synectics was initially used with corporate groups, and different forms of it have emerged over the years.

William J. J. Gordon and associates developed Synectics for classroom use in the 1960s. Since then, it has been used at grade levels from kindergarten through college and in subjects as diverse as apparel design and journalism. The form of the

Synectics is a versatile tool that can be used in groups of all sizes, as well as in both formal and informal settings.

Synectics model outlined in this chapter uses metaphor and analogy to enhance creative thinking (Wald & Weil, 1974; Joyce & Weil, 1996; Weaver & Prince, 1990).

The term *synectics* is most descriptive of the intentions of the model. It originated in Greek and means "the joining together of different and apparently irrelevant elements" (Gordon, 1961, p. 3). The Synectics model is based on the idea of putting analogies side by side so that comparisons of dissimilar things can be made. The ultimate goal is to create a kind of **conceptual distance** (a mental space between the individual and the subject) that allows us to look at something in a new way—such as seeing an office cubicle as similar to a mirror (Wald & Weil, 1974; Joyce & Weil, 1996). Teachers and students move through a series of exercises using analogies to create this distance. In the distance, creativity is nurtured as students invent new ways of seeing things or solving problems.

Synectics and Research on Teaching

From 1955 to the 1980s, as the Synectics model emerged, much of the literature focused on the development of the model itself. Researchers analyzed the factors that were consistent among groups charged with creating, inventing, or designing something. Attention was also given to applications in industrial and educational settings (Weaver & Prince, 1990). For example, in a review of the research on teaching models (Joyce, Showers, & Rolheiser-Bennett, 1987, p. 20), Synectics was highlighted as a model that not only met its goal of helping students generate ideas and solve problems but also promoted recall and retention of information from written passages—an unexpected benefit. More recently, the literature on Synectics in educational contexts has focused on its application to various groups of learners and its successful use and specific benefits in various content areas.

As mentioned earlier, Synectics has been used with learners of different ages and abilities. One good example comes from Meador (1994), who showed that the model can be used with children as young as kindergarten age. Meador's study was actually designed to show whether Synectics was particularly effective with gifted children. It concluded that "the training was beneficial for both gifted and nongifted students" (p. 69). In addition, Moeschl and Costello (1988) found that teachers using the Synectics model (as well as two other models) were "encouraged . . . in their task of involving the apathetic learners" (p. 79).

Much of the recent literature on Synectics highlights its use in various content areas. For example, Pollard and Schliefer (1990) demonstrate business education applications. Kawenski (1991) shows the model's effectiveness in an apparel design course, and Land (1995) discusses its use in a journalism class on feature writing. Moeschl and Costello (1988) describe a professional development opportunity for high school teachers that resulted in the use of Synectics in English, industrial arts, and science classes. The many mentions of Synectics in a variety of content areas suggest that it is a model with great flexibility.

Callison (1998) discussed how Synectics may be a way to combine critical and creative thinking, which could provide teachers with a way of engaging the multiple intelligences in classroom work. All students could be encouraged to enhance their creative capacities. In addition, Synectics could provide a way for students who are not dominant in the logical-mathematical ways of knowing, which many schools value, to demonstrate their understanding in a school setting.

Synectics and Learning Theory

Synectics represents a cognitive information processing perspective on learning theory, which emphasizes the way in which we "process information through attention, memory, thinking and other cognitive processes" (Santrock, 2001, p. 239). Students are regarded not as passive learners who focus on memorization but rather as learners actively involved in seeking, exploring, and making sense of the information around them. In applications of the Synectics model, your students will be doing exactly these tasks: investigating a problem by seeking and exploring alternative views and then sifting through them to organize and find sensible solutions (Joyce & Calhoun, 1996). In essence, this model will "generate creative thinking" (p. 9).

Also, as you assist your students with the Synectics model, you will be helping them develop metacognition, the awareness of their own thinking that is often discussed in information processing theory. In Synectics, the creative process is made explicit. Students are asked to create a cognitive distance between themselves and the subject. They both create and explore this distance using direct analogies, compressed conflicts, and so on. These names provide students with a conscious awareness of their mental processes. As the students internalize them, these terms and related processes can be deliberately used and applied in other settings.

Synectics and the Cognitive Processing Perspective on Curriculum

The Synectics model focuses on an intellectual process rather than specific subject matter. Consequently, it is highly compatible with the cognitive processing perspective on curriculum (Eisner & Vallance, 1974; Glatthorn & Jailall, 2000). Frequently, creativity is considered to be an inborn capacity that individuals either have or don't. However, Gordon and associates worked under the assumption that "By bringing the creative process to consciousness and by developing explicit aids to creativity, we can directly increase the creative capacity of both individuals and groups" (Joyce & Weil, 1996, p. 240). In short, we can learn to be creative.

For example, Mrs. Stich wanted to dispel her students' perceptions that they simply were not creative. As she involved them in the Synectics strategy of creating something new, she took care to explain the strategy itself to help the students develop an awareness of how this strategy could help them become immersed in and more fluent with the creative process. By working systematically with metaphors, they were creating.

The Synectics model is not limited to writing. It has broad application and can be transferred to a variety of situations, which is another feature of the cognitive processing orientation. Synectics can be used in social studies, science, math, and many other areas of the curriculum. More important, as students practice thinking creatively and using the Synectics strategies to do so, they will further develop their creative capacities. The Synectics model has been designed with enhancement of the intellectual process in mind.

Technology and Synectics

At least two uses of technology are evident when working with the Synectics model. First, the structure of Synectics can be illustrated for a small group or an entire class using a Smart Board as you work through a Synectics exercise. As Ms. W. worked with the students, she recorded their suggestions for analogies on her computer and projected them on the Board, which allowed all the students in the group to see what had been suggested. In addition, they could use the Smart Board to isolate or move suggestions around. The information is also preserved on the computer so that group members can return to it as needed or desired.

The second use of technology is related. If the Synectics exercise has been entered on the computer, students can use the computer to generate text (such as a story or a PowerPoint presentation) related to the original purpose for using the Synectics model. The computer serves as an archive for the information generated and a tool for continuing the work begun with the Synectics exercise. Rachel could continue her story and easily access the information generated about her setting, and the students in Ms. W.'s class could access the ideas they generated for connecting the care of pets with care for the environment.

The sampling of National Educational Technology (NET) Standards for Students (International Society for Technology in Education, 2000) listed below illustrates in a general manner how technology and the Synectics model could be connected.*

GRADES PK–2

NET Standard 1: Basic Operations and Concepts

NET Standard 3: Technology Productivity Tools

Performance Indicator 2: Use a variety of media and technology resources for directed and independent learning activities.

Synectics Extension

Use a Smart Board to work on making analogies. List open-ended sentences (e.g., A mole is like a _____) and have students generate responses. These can be displayed and preserved for future work. Illustrations can also be drawn on the board to emphasize the connection being made.

GRADES 3–5

NET Standard 3: Technology Productivity Tools

NET Standard 4: Technology Communication Tools

Performance Indicator 5: Use technology tools (e.g., multimedia authoring, presentation, Web tools, digital camera, scanners) for individual and collaborative writing, communication, and publishing activities to create knowledge products for audiences inside and outside the classroom.

Synectics Extension

While using the Synectics model with a practice exercise, the teacher and students can write together using a PC or a Smart Board. For example, as in Case Study 12.1, a story can be composed by a group for illustration purposes.

GRADES 6–8

NET Standard 3: Technology and Productivity Tools

NET Standard 6: Technology Problem-Solving and Decision-Making Tools

Performance Indicator 5: Apply productivity/multimedia tools and peripherals to support personal productivity, group collaboration, and learning through the curriculum.

---

*National Educational Technology Standards for Students: Connecting Curriculum and Technology by ISTE. Copyright © 2000 by International Society for Technology in Education (ISTE), 800–336–5191 (US & Canada) or 541–302–3777 (Int'l), iste@iste.org, www.iste.org. All rights reserved. Reproduced with permission of ISTE via Copyright Clearance Center. Reprint permission does not constitute endorsement by ISTE.

Synectics Extensions

If using Synectics to produce a content-related product (as in Case Study 12.2), PowerPoints of the final presentation could be made to share with other audiences.

Groups can be aided in their collaboration through the visual capabilities of a Smart Board, which allows all members of the group to see ideas as they are suggested and as they evolve.

GRADES 9–12

NET Standard 4: Technology Communication Tools

NET Standard 5: Technology Research Tools

Performance Indicator 8: Select and apply technology tools for research, information analysis, problem solving, and decision making in content learning.

Synectics Extensions

The Smart Board can be used to assist with problem solving during a Synectics exercise. Recording the information and suggestions of a group on the PC is efficient, and the Smart Board has the added feature of allowing all the group members to see the information simultaneously. Suggestions can then be analyzed by the group members throughout the session.

Recording information on a PC allows group members the flexibility of moving back and forth through the information as they move through the process and after the Synectics session.

Using a Smart Board, the teacher can highlight the details of a Synectics session to teach the structure itself so that the model can be learned for future applications.

Synectics, Content Standards, and Benchmarks

The Synectics model has broad applications to the content and benchmarks emphasized in school settings. Unlike some models we have discussed, it is not content specific. It can enhance creative thought processes and problem-solving functions that can be applied in nearly all school subjects. For example, developing a creative approach to understanding and applying concepts is important in science, social studies, and mathematics, even though these areas are often thought of as fact oriented. Consequently, the use of the Synectics model can be aligned with content standards and benchmarks in all areas of the curriculum, as well as standards that might specifically address and promote creative expression.

The example below focuses on an English language arts content standard and related benchmarks from the *Michigan Curriculum Framework* (Michigan Department of Education, 1996) that specifically address creative expression.*

English Language Arts

CONTENT STANDARD 8: All students will explore and use the characteristics of different types of texts, aesthetic elements, and mechanics—including text structure, figurative and descriptive language, spelling, punctuation, and grammar—to construct and convey meaning.

Early Elementary Benchmark: Identify and use aspects of the craft of the speaker, writer, and illustrator to formulate and express their ideas artistically. Examples include dialogue, characterization, conflict, organization, diction, color, and shape.

Later Elementary Benchmark: Identify and use aspects of the craft of the speaker, writer and illustrator to formulate and express their ideas artistically. Examples include intonation, hues, design, perspective, dialogue, characterization, metaphor, simile, and point of view.

Middle School Benchmark: Identify and use aspects of the craft of the speaker, writer, and illustrator to formulate and express their ideas artistically. Examples include color and composition, flashback, multidimensional characters, pacing, appropriate use of details, strong verbs, language that inspires, and effective leads.

High School Benchmark: Identify and use aspects of the craft of the speaker, writer, and illustrator to formulate and express their ideas artistically. Examples include imagery, irony, multiple points of view, complex dialogue, aesthetics, and persuasive techniques.

Why Choose Synectics?

1. Have you heard your students complain that they simply aren't creative? Do they regard artistic ability as the sole form of creativity, invention, or discovery? Could work with the Synectics model help them expand their views on creativity and allow them to consciously develop their own capacities?

2. Do you regard yourself as lacking in creativity? Would work with your students using this model provide you with an opportunity to develop your own creative or inventive capacities?

---

*Excerpts from the *Michigan Curriculum Framework* are reprinted with permission of the Michigan Department of Education.

3. Do some of your students resist participating in class discussions and activities? Could the Synectics model provide them with a way to begin or expand their participation?

4. Do your students tend to write about or view concepts in content areas with overused language or ideas? Could Synectics allow them to move beyond the tried and true?

Summary

Synectics is a classic model for developing the creative thinking capacities of students. The create-something-new form of Synectics allows teachers and students to use metaphorical language to promote invention and make the creative process explicit. In essence, it removes the mystique that often accompanies the issue of creativity and broadens the concept to include invention, discovery, and other ways of thinking about creativity in multiple fields and academic content areas.

In the Synectics model, the use of analogies and metaphors creates a conceptual distance. The learner steps back from the issue at hand by comparing dissimilar things, such as an office and a mirror. At the same time, the learner develops an emotional attachment by becoming the metaphor and describing its feelings. Both this distancing and the complementary emotional attachment allow the learner to return to the original condition or problem with new insights or perspectives. The learner creates something new.

Synectics is a flexible model, thus particularly helpful in school settings. It has been shown to be effective with learners at nearly all levels. It has demonstrated applications for multiple content areas. It can and has been altered to meet the needs of particular objectives and learning situations. Indeed, it is available in other forms that have not been fully explored here. Different configurations of groups, from whole-group to individualized instruction, can benefit from work with the Synectics model.

Synectics has been shown to be effective with all kinds of learners. Gifted and nongifted alike receive benefits. It also has the potential to appeal to uninvolved or apathetic learners and bring them into active participation. In addition, Synectics has been discussed as a way to promote the use of the multiple intelligences in classroom settings. Learners who demonstrate strengths in the more creative kinds of intelligence can continue to enhance their ability, while those who tend toward more rational ways of knowing can develop or increase their creative thinking capacity. At a time when we are learning more and more about the varying needs of students in classroom settings, Synectics holds much promise.

Putting It Together

1. Before trying out the Synectics model with your students, consider trying to create something new with a small group of friends as a kind of party-game activity. This will allow you to try out the structure and perhaps discover the enjoyment of using this model.

2. Review your district or state curriculum documents. Note how often the words *create*, *discover*, or *invent* are used to describe skills or dispositions that your students need to develop in various disciplines or content areas. Imagine how the Synectics model might be used to achieve these outcomes. (You might consider using this same process with the objectives that are listed in the teacher's guide for your textbook.)

3. Make a list of important concepts or objects you discuss in your content area—such as freedom, theorems, simple machines, and photosynthesis. Imagine a common problem or condition related to them. Using pencil and paper, apply the Synectics model to a few of these concepts and consider how you might use these exercises to deepen your students' understanding of the concept or object.

Student Study Site

The Companion Web site for *Models of Teaching: Connecting Student Learning* With Standards

www.sagepub.com/delloliostudy

Visit the Web-based student study site to enhance your understanding of the book content and discover additional resources that will take your learning one step further. You can enhance your understanding by using the comprehensive Study Guide, which includes chapter learning objectives, flash cards, practice tests, and more. You'll find special features, such as the links to standards from U.S. States and associated activities, Learning from Journal Articles, Field Experience worksheets, Learning from Case Studies, and PRAXIS resources.

References

Callison, D. (1998). Creative thinking. *School Library Media Activities Monthly, 15*(4), 41–47.

Eisner, E., & Vallance, E. (1974). *Conflicting conceptions of the curriculum*. Berkeley, CA: McCutchan.

Georgiou, S. N. (1994). Synectics: A problem-solving tool for educational leaders. *International Journal of Educational Management, 8*(2), 5–10.

Glatthorn, A. A., & Jailall, J. (2000). Curriculum for the new millennium. In R. S. Brandt (Ed.), *Education in a new era* (pp. 97–121). Alexandria, VA: Association for Supervision and Curriculum Development.

Gordon, W. J. J. (1961). *Synectics: The development of creative capacity*. New York: Harper & Row.

Gordon, W. J. J., & Poze, T. (1979). *The new metaphorical way of learning & knowing*. Cambridge, MA: SES Associates.

International Society for Technology in Education. (2000). *National educational technology standards for students: Connecting curriculum and technology*. Washington, DC: Author in collaboration with the U.S. Department of Education.

Joyce, B. R., & Calhoun, E. F. (1996). *Creating learning experiences: The role of instructional theory and research* (Report No. SP037102). Washington DC: Office of Educational Research and Improvement. (ERIC Document Reproduction Service No. ED 403242)

Joyce, B. R., Showers, B., & Rolheiser-Bennett, C. (1987). Staff development and student learning: A synthesis of research on models of teaching. *Educational Leadership, 45*(2), 11–23.

Joyce, B. R., & Weil, M. (1996). *Models of teaching.* Boston: Allyn & Bacon.

Kawenski, M. (1991). Encouraging creativity in design. *Journal of Creative Behavior, 25*(3), 263–266.

Land, F. M. (1995). Awakening the right brain in feature writing. *Journalism and Mass Communication Educator, 50*(3), 52–60.

Lizotte, K. (1998). A creative state of mind. *Management Review, 87*(5), 15–17.

Meador, K. S. (1994). The effect of Synectics training on gifted and nongifted kindergarten students. *Journal for the Education of the Gifted, 18*(1), 55–73.

Michigan Department of Education. (1996). *Michigan curriculum framework.* Lansing: Author.

Moeschl, S. H., & Costello, R. W. (1988). Using Joyce/Showers teaching models in the high school classroom. *ERIC Clearinghouse, 62*, 77–80.

Pollard, C. J., & Schliefer, J. M. (1990). Challenging complacency: Dynamic teaching models. *Business Education Forum, 45*, 16–18.

Santrock, J. W. (2001). *Educational psychology.* New York: McGraw-Hill.

Soriano de Alencar, E. M. L. (1993). Thinking in the future: The need to promote creativity in the educational context. *Gifted Education International, 9*(2), 93–96.

Wald, R., & Weil, M. (1974). (D. H. Flood, Ed.) *Synectics instructional system: Theory, demonstration, experience, peer teaching, application with children.* New York: Teacher Corps, Teachers College.

Weaver, W. T., & Prince, G. M. (1990). Synectics: Its potential for education. *Phi Delta Kappan, 71*, 378–388.

chapter 13

Advance Organizers

This past spring my wife and I (T. D.) spent a few hours walking around our yard with a landscape architect who was helping us develop a plan for gardens and a deck addition at the back of our house. Our yard has lots of beautiful plants, but we were looking for a plan that would help us have the kinds of gardens we have seen on all the popular home makeover shows on television! In many ways, I was just along for the ride. Although I love working outside in the garden and appreciate a beautiful garden when I see one, my knowledge of plants is limited. My wife and the landscape architect walked around the yard pointing at plants, naming them, and talking about their features—leaf formations, blooming periods, growth patterns, and ability to thrive in a variety of environmental conditions. Given that it was early spring and almost none of the plants had flowers or were more than a few inches out of the ground, I was even more impressed than usual. I spent most of the time saying things like "What's that one called again?" "What does that one look like?" and "Is that a coneflower or a daisy? I never can tell the difference!"

It was clear to me from this experience that my wife and the landscape architect have a deeper understanding of botany—the larger organizing scheme of plant life—than I do. For example, they can take the detail of a leaf configuration and use it to classify a plant and deduce its name. (Even more impressive, both of them can provide the Latin names for these plants!) You have probably had experiences in which the topic being discussed was complex, hierarchical, and part of a larger discipline, but because you understood the hierarchy, you could relate the new information to what you already knew. Connecting new information to prior knowledge made it possible to recall the new information when necessary. However, if your understanding of the bigger picture was limited, and consequently, you learned new pieces of information somewhat randomly, you had fewer ways to attach the new information, which made it difficult to recall at a later time.

This state of affairs represents a significant task for teachers. They must provide their students with large amounts of information in a way that helps the students understand, retain, and recall it. Most teachers know that this task requires fitting the information into a larger framework that can serve to organize it and allow multiple pathways for locating and retrieving it as needed.

Advance Organizers are a model for helping students organize information by connecting it to a larger cognitive structure that reflects the organization of the discipline itself. Developed by David Ausubel, Advance Organizers were a "practical implication of his theory of meaningful verbal learning" (Kirkman & Shaw, 1997, p. 3). Teachers consider the hierarchy of a subject as they plan lessons and prepare an advance organizer that outlines or introduces the more abstract or generalized structure of the subject (for example, what distinguishes a plant from an animal). The information presented in the lessons that follow is connected to this cognitive structure. (Photosynthesis is a process used by plants to produce carbohydrates by using light from the sun and chlorophyll. Plants use this process. Animals do not.)

As you read Case Study 13.1, consider how the teacher has developed the advance organizer, how it has been introduced to the students, and how it serves as a meaningful framework for understanding and retaining the specific information to be covered in the lessons that follow it. You may also want to consider how the academic rationalism perspective helps you understand this model and how the model itself can help you align your work with content standards and benchmarks.

Case Study 13.1: High School, Science

Ms. Wolters is an Earth sciences teacher in a large and urban high school. She has recently become concerned about two things she has heard from her colleagues. Some of her colleagues have said they feel a great deal of pressure to teach large amounts of scientific information to prepare students for the state-mandated testing. More important, they have said that when taking quizzes and tests, students just don't seem able to understand and recall the information taught. Ms. Wolters learned that these teachers have been preparing lists of vocabulary terms for students to memorize and then testing them on the terms. Students have had difficulty applying the terms and recalling their meanings.

As Ms. Wolters considered the concerns of her colleagues, she thought back to some of the science courses at the small college she attended. It occurred to her that what had made one of the courses so helpful was the instructor's ability to help her see the bigger picture of the discipline. This allowed her to connect the small bits of information she was learning to the major questions and issues of the discipline. She recalled gaining a good command of the information, and her ability to retain and recall it improved remarkably. She contrasted this with her college chemistry class, which primarily involved memorizing terms and formulas. She had little doubt which class had been the better learning experience.

Ms. Wolters decided to try to resolve the concerns her colleagues had expressed by making use of an advance organizer for the next segment of her Earth sciences course for tenth-grade students. She had recently become familiar with the structure and use of advance organizers and believed they would help her students understand and retain necessary information by connecting it to the larger structure of the content.

Ms. Wolters began by creating a hierarchy for the subject and information to be taught. One of her state's content standards and benchmarks dealt with the geosphere in general and recycling in particular (Michigan Department of Education, 1996, pp. 88–90). As Ms. Wolters wondered what to use for her advance organizer for this topic and how to present it, she considered the details she was required to cover in this unit: specific information about the impact that recycling natural resources has on health, the economy, and the environment. The content included terms like *supply*, *demand*, *conservation*, *natural resources*, *solid matter*, and *economic impact*, as well as the concepts these terms represented. Ms. Wolters then tried to generalize this content to explore the larger concepts and issues that framed the details. Using reference books, the district-mandated textbook, and electronic searches, she began to make lists of questions that seemed to capture the structure of the larger discipline of the Earth sciences and the topic of the geosphere specifically. Ultimately, she settled on the following questions: Can the Earth continue to supply and produce consumable resources, or should alternatives be explored? What are the costs and benefits?

Having determined this general and abstract question, Ms. Wolters next began to consider the structure of the advance organizer itself. She decided to write a short passage about the debates over drilling for oil in the Alaskan tundra region. The students had studied the tundra in an earlier segment of the course and had briefly discussed a newspaper article about drilling for oil in the Arctic National Wildlife Refuge. She knew from the lack of focus and participation during this brief discussion that her students knew little about this issue in particular, and it could serve to generalize the content she needed to cover—how the decision to recycle the Earth's solid resources has costs and benefits.

After the students had read the passage she created, she planned to have a brief conversation that would explore the larger question, followed by a presentation on the specific content she wanted to help her students learn. They could then return periodically to the larger question as they considered the detailed information. She wrote the following objective for this lesson:

> The learner will use an advance organizer to explore the costs and benefits of recycling.

Ms. Wolters's advance organizer is shown in Table 13.1.

Table 13.1   Advance Organizer on the Tundra

The tundra region is one of the most fragile environments on the face of the Earth. Footprints made in the snow have been known to last for decades. The ground located under the tundra area in the Arctic National Wildlife Refuge in Alaska is known to be a repository of major oil reserves. Recently, debates have raged about drilling for oil in that area. Proponents argue that drilling will have a limited impact on the environment, that few people inhabit the area, and that the drilling will bolster local oil production and limit dependence on oil from other countries. They contend that as long as people in the United States continue to use oil at current rates, this drilling will be essential. On the other hand, opponents cite irreparable environmental damage and a lack of necessity for more oil production. They argue that the United States should emphasize the development of alternative sources of energy and the conservation of natural resources.

The debate on the proposed drilling in the Arctic National Wildlife Refuge illustrates a fundamental issue for all people in the United States. There are costs and benefits associated with finding and using natural resources. Do the benefits outweigh the costs, or vice versa? Consider this question as we spend the next several weeks learning about natural resources and their uses.

Ms. Wolters: Today we are going to start a new unit of study. It will last for the next several weeks. I have just passed out a passage that we are going to use to organize our studies. I'd like you to take a few minutes to read this passage to yourselves. (*All students read the passage. Afterwards, Ms. Wolters resumes the conversation with the students.*) I'd like to get your initial reactions to what you have read here.

Thea: This really bothers me. I mean, what are they thinking? We learned before that the tundra is really fragile, like it says here. Once you mess it up, it's not going to get fixed easily or maybe never. I am totally against this drilling.

Corry: Right. Besides what it will do to the Earth, think about all the animals that live in the tundra. What will the drilling do to the environment they live in? This could cause some of those animals to lose their habitat and die. I'm with Thea on this one.

Willie: Well, I don't want to see the environment wrecked any more than anybody, but I have to admit, I'm tired of high gas prices. I can barely afford to drive my car. So maybe I would be willing to give up some land so that we can have more oil and bring down the price of gas. Maybe the cost isn't too high if you figure out how much we need the gas.

Manuel: Besides that, I don't think it would hurt the animals that much. Alaska is a big state, and they could find other places to live. I'm with Willie. Let's go ahead and drill. It will be worth it.

Ms. Wolters: So here is what I have heard so far. Some of you think that the cost of damage to the environment and wildlife is too high. Others of you believe that the benefits of being able to have more oil to make gasoline for driving are worth the cost. Any other thoughts?

Carla: Well, I'd be willing to drive less or maybe carpool with friends more if I thought it would help us avoid this kind of damage. I just don't think it's right.

Vera: Yeah, but you know oil isn't just used for gas. Lots of the plastic things we use are made with stuff they get from oil, so it would take a lot of changes in the way we live if we didn't drill for more oil. I don't want to hurt animals or the environment, but I have to be honest too. I'm not sure I want to change the way I live over this. Maybe the cost is worth it.

Ms. Wolters: This is a big question, and I don't think we'll be able to address it fully today. As I mentioned to you earlier, we will be using it to organize our studies for the next several weeks. Here's what I mean. We are going to be talking about things like recycling natural resources and products that are made from them. We are also going to talk about the costs—only this time I mean in dollars and cents. We are also going to look at health issues related to our use and perhaps abuse of natural resources. And as we do all that, I'd like us to keep coming back to this passage and asking ourselves how the things we are learning fit with it. I also jotted down your initial reactions so that we can come back to those too. Now I'd like you to turn to page 276 in your textbook. In this section we are going to read about the production of plastic products and the roles of natural resources and recycling. Remember to keep asking yourself about the costs and benefits as you read this passage.

Ms. Wolters concludes this introduction to the advance organizer. For the lessons that follow, she has exercises and activities planned that will focus on the specifics of this unit. Most specifically, the students will read and learn about recycling, economics, supply and demand, and health issues related to use of these natural resources. She will display the advance organizer on a classroom chart and will direct students often to the way the information they are learning relates to the larger question of costs and benefits.

Case Study 13.1: Post-Lesson Reflection ————————————◆

Ms. Wolters was very pleased with the use of the advance organizer and how it will serve as a framework for her students as they explore detailed information on the use of the Earth's resources. She believes that the organizer and its introduction contained enough familiar information about the tundra that her students could connect with it. She also believes that it was abstract and general enough that it will serve as a scheme for their learning. Her goal was not to teach her students about the oil drilling debate in Alaska, but rather to use the question of costs and benefits to anchor their thinking about upcoming course information. She wanted the organizer to strike a balance between the familiar and detailed, on the one hand, and the abstract and general, on the other. She believes her advance organizer and her introduction of it met this requirement.

As she constructed the advance organizer, Ms. Wolters also tried to capture the larger issues and questions that organize and guide this particular field of study. Rather than starting there, she began with the more detailed information that was part of the curriculum to be covered and worked her way up the hierarchy.

In addition, Ms. Wolters wanted to make sure that the advance organizer did not just provide an overview of the subjects to be studied or an introduction of details that she planned to cover. Rather, she wanted this organizer to be and do what its name implies—provide her students an organizational framework for the facts, figures, other details, and vocabulary they will encounter in this unit of study. This is why she explicitly reminded them, as they began reading from their text, to "remember to keep asking yourself about the costs and benefits as you read this passage."

Finally, Ms. Wolters was also aware that simply having her students read the advance organizer would not serve her entire purpose. She knew that a discussion would be needed to teach the organizer itself and overtly help students see how it would be used in the future. Without this discussion, she feared her students might not use the advance organizer or understand its purpose. Returning to the organizer in the future will further help the students see how it can help them organize their thinking about the details of ongoing course activities.

Constructing Advance Organizers

Unlike many of the models that we have described in this text, the Advance Organizer model does not have prescribed stages or procedures. As discussed by Kirkman and Shaw (1997), "The specific construction of advance organizers will depend on subject matter, learners, and the desired learning outcome" (p. 5). However, some guidelines for the construction and use of advance organizers can be discussed. In addition, we will consider the roles of teachers and students as they use advance organizers.

Advance Organizers Defined

Although some have suggested that an operational definition of advance organizers does not exist, others seem more comfortable with the way that Ausubel defined them:

> appropriately relevant and inclusive introductory materials . . . introduced in advance of learning . . . and presented at a higher level of abstraction, generality, and inclusiveness than the information presented after it. The organizer serves to provide ideational scaffolding for the stable incorporation and retention of the more detailed and differentiated materials that follow. Thus, advance organizers are not the same as summaries or overviews, which comprise text at the same level of abstraction as the material to be learned, but rather are designed to bridge the gap between what the learner already knows and what he needs to know before he can successfully learn the task at hand. (Ausubel, 1968, as cited in Kirkman & Shaw, 1997, p. 3)

In some respects, Ausubel has defined advance organizers by saying what they are not: "summaries or overviews." As demonstrated in Case Study 13.1, Ms. Wolters did not introduce the topic of recycling and its impact on health, the economy, and the environment by presenting the students with a summary or overview of these topics. Rather, she selected the tundra and the debate about drilling for oil—a subject not to be included in the unit of study—for their ability "to provide ideational scaffolding for the stable incorporation and retention of the more detailed and differentiated materials that follow." There may be times when beginning a unit of study with an overview or summary of the information you will be tackling makes sense. However, that is not the purpose of an advance organizer as defined by Ausubel and others (Relan, 1991).

The heart of Ausubel's definition of an advance organizer is its ability to "provide ideational scaffolding." Ausubel believed that all content areas have a structure or hierarchy. The advance organizer helps students see the governing questions, issues, and propositions that are reflected in that hierarchy. If students understand the basic outlines of the structure, they are able to fill in the "cracks" appropriately and effectively with new and related information as it is presented to them.

In addition, an advance organizer serves as an introduction that is "presented at a higher level of abstraction, generality, and inclusiveness than the information presented after it." The students in Ms. Wolters's class were asked to consider the costs and benefits of drilling in the Arctic National Wildlife Refuge as a way to consider the larger question of the costs and benefits of the use of natural resources from the geosphere, the solid matter in the Earth. Ms. Wolters constructed the advance

Advance Organizers provide a structure or scaffolding that allows students to organize information about the subject under consideration.

organizer in a generalized fashion, allowing the students to use the larger question to frame their study of specific information. Her advance organizer fits well with Ausubel's call for the use of abstraction and generality.

In summary, an advance organizer may best be defined by what it does. It allows students to develop an understanding of the structure behind a subject or content area—the hierarchy. It introduces students to that structure at a general, abstract, and inclusive level. In short, it is a versatile instrument for helping students understand and recall information by seeing how it fits with the larger structure of the subject.

Ausubel's definition of advance organizers does not include strict operational guidelines for constructing them (Kenny, 1993). According to McEneany (1990), Ausubel did not always follow his own definition strictly when constructing advance organizers for his own research into their efficacy. Perhaps the key is flexibility and consideration of the learners and the content.

Types of Advance Organizers

According to Kirkman and Shaw (1997), there are two categories of advance organizers: **expository** and **comparative**. "Expository organizers function to provide the learner a conceptual framework for unfamiliar material, and comparative organizers are used when the knowledge to be acquired is relatively familiar to the learner" (pp. 3–4). Familiarity with the new material is key to determining which type of organizer you will want to use. The concepts that Ms. Wolters hoped her students would understand, about the geosphere in general and recycling in particular, were largely unfamiliar to them and called for the use of an expository organizer. You will want to use a comparative organizer when the subject is familiar—although not the same—to the learner. It helps the learner distinguish between familiar concepts or subjects.

An advance organizer, whether expository or comparative, can take many forms. Ms. Wolters used a **text-based advance organizer** with a short discussion. In Case Study 13.2, the teacher uses a **visual advance organizer**. Given his students' reading abilities, he wants to ensure that all his students can participate fully, so the use of enlarged photographs and discussion is sensible. Others have developed advance organizers that are strictly oral, and some have made use of videos and computer programs. When Ausubel developed the Advance Organizer model in the 1960s, many of the technologies that are currently available had not yet even been conceived. The range of formats for constructing your advance organizer is wide and adaptable.

Guidelines for Constructing an Advance Organizer

Constructing an advance organizer is the task of the teacher. The teacher determines the structure of the discipline, content, or subject to be mastered and then develops the organizer. Some guidelines for this process may be helpful. Kenny (1993) cites characteristics or guidelines proposed by Mayer (1979) when Mayer reinterpreted Ausubel's theory.

Table 13.2   Advance Organizer Guidelines

1. Short set of verbal or visual information.

2. Presented prior to learning a larger body of to-be-learned information.

3. Containing no specific content from the to-be-learned information.

4. Providing a means of generating the logical relationships among the elements in the to-be-learned information.

5. Influencing the learner's encoding process.

SOURCE: Mayer, 1979, as cited in Kenny, 1993, p. 3.

When constructing an advance organizer, keep the content short. Because the organizer serves to introduce and frame the information that is to follow, it need not be lengthy. The advance organizer text Ms. Wolters constructed was only a few paragraphs long. Its use and the conversation that followed were completed in a short time.

The advance organizer should not include any of the specific information that will be presented later. This is in keeping with the idea that the organizer itself should deal with the subject or content at a more abstract and general level. Ms. Wolters never mentioned recycling or the other specific concepts she intended to present—either in the text of her organizer or in the introductory discussion.

Finally, the advance organizer should be designed to allow learners to see the logical relationships between the structure of the discipline or subject and the information to be presented later. Such a design will also enhance opportunities for learners to both understand and recall the details presented later.

Procedures That May Facilitate the Use of an Advance Organizer

Some specific procedures may help your students use an advance organizer in an efficient and productive way.

1. Read a text-based advance organizer orally to your students.

Some researchers (Rinehart, Barksdale-Ladd, & Welker, 1991) found that the teacher's reading the text and discussing it with students improved students' recall of information.

2. Add visuals to your advance organizer.

Visuals can include drawings or photographs, or pictures by themselves can serve as the organizer. Researchers Chun and Plass (1996) had success with videos as advance organizers.

3. Use concept maps or other forms of graphic organizers as advance organizers.

Concept maps and graphic organizers are variations of advance organizers (Story, 1998). Often used throughout a unit of study, they can be designed by the teacher for use as an advance organizer. Willerman and Mac Harg (1991) found that the use of a concept map in this way had significant and positive results for their learners.

4. Teach the advance organizer and remind students to use it often.

Students must understand the purpose of the advance organizer. Once this is understood, it is most effectively used if students are reminded to connect their new learning to it. As stated by one group of researchers (Groller, Kender, & Honeyman, 1991), "Students need to be taught how to use, monitor, and evaluate their use of advance organizers in order to use these to their advantage" (p. 473).

Roles of Teachers and Students in Using an Advance Organizer

The general roles of teachers and their students are clear in both the construction and introduction of an advance organizer. Initially the teacher is at the center in both of these activities (Downing, 1994). The teacher alone constructs the advance organizer because the teacher has the necessary understanding of the discipline. The teacher is also able to determine the prior knowledge of the learners (Jackman & Swan, 1994).

However, students do have an important role when the advance organizer is being introduced. Although some teachers may elect to limit student participation in the presentation of the advance organizer, others do not (Downing, 1994). Indeed, in both of the case studies in this chapter, students were active participants, sharing ideas and understanding. We encourage you to find ways to actively engage students physically and intellectually as you introduce and use advance organizers.

As you read the case study below, look for the features of construction and use of advance organizers outlined in this section.

Case Study 13.2: First Grade, Social Studies

Mr. Brehm is a first-grade teacher in a rural elementary school that serves students from a surrounding agricultural community. This is his first year teaching, and he is eager to organize his new curriculum so that his students can connect what they are learning to larger themes rather than teach information in a more isolated and fact-driven manner. In using the textbooks and curriculum documents he has been given, he notes that one social studies content standard says "describe, compare and explain the locations and characteristics of economic activities, trade, political activities, migration, information flow, and the interrelationships among them" (Michigan Department of Education, 1996, p. 36). Specifically, the benchmarks for this grade level call for learning how neighborhoods or communities include housing, commerce, transportation, and communication systems, as well as their interrelationships with each other and the environment.

To meet the content standards and benchmarks, Mr. Brehm has decided to construct an advance organizer around a theme he has labeled "Our Neighborhoods." Next he looked at the larger issue of what constitutes a study of communities and how communities can be reflected in housing, commerce, communications, and transportation. For example, he knows that the students in his class are very familiar with the flat expanses of land surrounding the school, but he is not certain that they understand that the moderate climate, many nearby lakes, and access to highways and a large city nearby have all interacted to make their neighborhood an ideal setting for a farming community. It is this sense of community that is implied by the content standards for this grade level, and he wants to help the students use this larger idea of interdependence with the physical and social environment as a framework for their exploration of the housing, transportation, communication, and commerce patterns.

After much consideration, Mr. Brehm has decided to use photographs and illustrations for his advance organizer. He has found several photographs of animals and insects in their environments. Using animals and insects will allow him to use something that the students are familiar with, given that they have spent considerable time studying various animals and insects in their science unit, to consider the larger concept of communities as places that reflect interdependence between the environment and those who live there. The animal and insect photos will allow the students to talk about human issues abstractly as they discuss how animals and insects travel, use their environment for finding food, and develop their housing. Mr. Brehm's goal is not to teach about the animal environments but rather to use them in a general way to help the students organize the larger concepts related to a community. His intention is to use this advance organizer as a frame for the details his students will learn about their own neighborhood, as a community they live in. Mr. Brehm has the following objective for today's lesson:

The learner will use an Advance Organizer to discuss the concept of community.

The dialogue below illustrates how Mr. Brehm introduced this visual advance organizer at the beginning of his "Our Neighborhoods" theme.

Mr. Brehm: Today I want to show you some pictures I have of animals and insects and where they live. Let's look at this picture of bees and their nest. (*He shows them the large picture he has—a procedure he will use throughout this introduction to this advance organizer*.) Does it look like this nest is a home for one bee?

Steve: No, there's a whole bunch of bees living in that big nest. It looks just like the one that was in the tree at my house, and there were tons of bees living in it.

Mr. Brehm: Do you mean that all these bees can live in one nest? (*Children nod in agreement*.) Well, wouldn't they all bump into each other all the time? The nest isn't that big, and there are a lot of bees.

Courtney: Well, they must be able to hear each other because they sure do make a lot of noise. So maybe that's how they know how to get around each other.

Jamila: Yeah. I think they know how to talk to each other or something because one time my dad hit a nest with a stick, and all the bees came after him. It was like they were telling each other to come after him.

Mr. Brehm: Very interesting. I was wondering how they got this big nest to live in. Did they just borrow it, or did they make it?

Dave: Oh, they definitely make them. Last summer we kept getting hornets on our hammock, and my mom said it was because they were using the rope to make their nests. We had some big nests on our barn too.

Mr. Brehm: So how did they get the rope to their nests?

Dave: Well, I'm not sure, but I think that they carry them in their mouths while they fly.

Mr. Brehm: Well, let's take a look at another picture. (*He shows them a photo of a group of prairie dogs with their heads sticking out of holes in the ground.*)

Dakota: Oh, I know that one. Those are prairie dogs. Remember, we saw some of those at the zoo during our field trip last month?

Mr. Brehm: Yes, I do remember. Now what I'm wondering about is why all these prairie dogs live so close together. I mean, with all that land around them, don't you think they'd rather live by themselves or at least have a little more space?

Jorge: But Mr. Brehm, remember what that lady from the zoo said? She told us that prairie dogs protect each other. They make a warning noise if some other animal is around that is going to hurt them. So they live close to each other so that they can protect themselves.

Annie: And didn't she say that they share food with each other too? I'm not really sure about that, but I think that's what she said. But if they do, they'd want to be close together so that they can share.

Mr. Brehm: I've got another picture to show you. (*He shows them a picture of a group of monkeys. One is holding a baby and appears to be the mother. In front of her is another monkey that appears to be making a vicious face at another nearby monkey.*) What do you think is going on here?

Nancy: It looks like that one monkey is really mad at the other one. He has a pretty mean face.

Keegan: You know, I saw a show about monkeys on television once, and these two monkeys were fighting because the one monkey didn't want the other one near the girl monkey with their baby. My dad said that in the monkey world, they have a kind of rule that if you are a boy monkey, you can't go near someone else's wife and baby. But he did say that monkeys don't really get married like people do. Anyway, I think that might be why he's mad—because the other monkey broke the rule.

Mr. Brehm: So you are saying that even insects and animals might have rules for how they have to behave, like the rules we have here in our classroom?

Keegan: Well, they don't write them down or anything, but they seem to have them somehow.

Mr. Brehm: There's one more photograph I want to show you. (*He shows them a picture of a large ant hill covered with ants.*) What do you think all these ants are doing?

Lindsay:	It looks like they are working. Look at how some of them are carrying stuff. They look like movers or something carrying stuff into their house.
Megan:	Yeah, I was watching an ant hill with my friend one time and we saw them carrying stuff into their hill. It was little stuff, but it must have been heavy for them.
Mr. Brehm:	So you're saying that ants work. Do you think any of the stuff they are carrying is like furniture or something for their house? (*He laughs.*)
Jon:	No, but I saw some ants carrying little bits of sand one time and I think that they were building their house. Maybe that's what they are doing.
Mr. Brehm:	So you mean that they are using things around them to build their house? (*Jon nods.*) OK. Well, I have learned a lot from these pictures today. I learned how bees make houses, how monkeys follow rules, and how prairie dogs protect each other and maybe even share food with each other. It sounds to me like some of these animals live in neighborhoods, just like we do. Of course, our neighborhood has people living with each other. And I would like you to think with me for the next few weeks about how our neighborhood works like some of these animal and insect neighborhoods. For example, how do we talk with each other, protect each other, use the land to make food and houses, and things like that? When people work with each other, help each other, and play with each other, we call that a community. I want to spend a lot of time talking during the next few weeks about what makes our neighborhood a community. We'll use our animal and insect friends to help us along the way.

As the lesson ends, Mr. Brehm sends the students to assigned centers. Each center represents a dimension of communities that he wants them to understand. For example, one center has a telephone and tape-recorded instructions for practicing how to call various emergency numbers. Another center is a grocery store where students can make grocery lists and "purchase" needed items.

Mr. Brehm will engage the students in many activities over the next several weeks to teach them about the specific content related to community commerce, transportation, and other aspects listed in his curriculum. He will post the photographs and remind the students occasionally of the connections between what they are learning about human communities and what they learned from this organizer about the concept of community interactions and interdependence.

Case Study 13.2: Post-Lesson Reflection ◆

As a result of the use of his visual advance organizer and ensuing discussion, Mr. Brehm believes that his students have a framework for the concept of community, not just details without a unifying anchor. For example, as the students begin to learn about things like using a telephone to call 911 in an emergency situation, they will be able to connect this to the ideas introduced in the organizer—that community members have ways to protect each other and communicate. He believes that when his students learn the specific content of this unit, they will have a greater understanding of the content itself and better recall later because the information has been moved into long-term memory in a connected fashion, as a result of his use of this advance organizer.

When Mr. Brehm was developing this advance organizer, he was mindful of the fact that many of his students are emerging readers. As a result, he considered whether a text-based advance organizer would be the most accessible for all his students. He elected instead a visual organizer that could easily be used by all his students. He included discussion, both to ensure that all his students could benefit from the organizer and to teach the organizer itself.

Another issue that Mr. Brehm considered in developing his organizer was whether students would be passive or active as it was used. His goal was to involve students as actively as possible. He was aware that the use of advance organizers can be a receptive activity for students. He believed that the use of pictures and the ensuing discussion allowed him to structure the lesson in a manner that was **developmentally appropriate** for this group.

Brief Background of Advance Organizers

According to Kirkman and Shaw (1997), "the concept of advance organizers to facilitate learning was first introduced by Ausubel (1960) as a practical application of his theory of meaningful verbal learning" (p. 3). Ausubel and his associates conducted a number of studies to provide support for his theories and the use of advance organizers (Ausubel, 1960; Ausubel & Fitzgerald, 1961; Ausubel & Fitzgerald, 1962; Ausubel & Youssef, 1963; as cited in McEneany, 1990, and Kirkman & Shaw, 1997). Since their introduction more than 40 years ago, much has been written about advance organizers as a tool for helping students understand and recall information.

Advance Organizers and Research on Teaching

The research on the Advance Organizer model has been extensive and decidedly mixed. Some researchers (McEneany, 1990) have suggested that the use of advance organizers has either limited or no efficacy in promoting understanding of information or recall, and others (Ruthkosky & Dwyer, 1996; Relan, 1991) have pointed out that particular types of advance organizers (visual, etc.) have no or only limited effect. On the other hand, many researchers and practitioners (Rinehart et al., 1991; Lawton & Johnson, 1992; Chun & Plass, 1996; Willerman & Mac Harg, 1991) believe advance organizers are very effective.

The mixed bag of research findings may result from the ambiguity of Ausubel's definition of an advance organizer (Story, 1998). In short, it is difficult to assess and compare the results of studies based on dissimilar interpretations of Ausubel's theory (Clark & Bean, 1982, as cited in McEneany, 1990).

Among the favorable findings, Chun and Plass (1996) reported that the use of visual advance organizers "does aid in overall comprehension" (p. 503). Willerman and Mac Harg (1991) concluded that "the use of concept mapping as an advance organizer produces a significant increment in academic gain for the students in eighth grade physical science classes" (p. 708). Rinehart et al. (1991) stated that "an advanced organizer read orally by the teacher and followed with guided discussion significantly increased recall" (p. 325).

Finally, it is clear that more research will be needed to identify all the benefits of advance organizers and determine what components of an advance organizer may be less effective. However, we concur with the sentiments of Carol Story (1998) in the conclusion of her review of the research on advance organizers: "Instructional designers can feel confident that advance organizers are an important part of their instructional designs, that organizers are needed whatever the media of instruction, and that organizers themselves can be delivered by a variety of media" (p. 259).

Advance Organizers and Learning Theory

Ausubel's work on his theory of meaningful learning fits within the larger theoretical perspective of **information processing theory**, which metaphorically views human learning and memory as a computer. Information is entered, considered, sorted, and filed for later retrieval. Ausubel's theory of advance organizers can likely best be viewed using general models of human memory that roughly fit with this comparison to the functions of a computer.

In human memory models, all information begins in short-term memory. Information that is attended to moves briefly into the working memory. Small amounts of this data are moved into long-term memory through various processes, including meaningful learning. Relan (1991) describes this process as it relates to advance organizers:

> According to the theory of meaningful learning advanced by Ausubel, an advance organizer would enhance learning by establishing a hierarchical framework to anchor new, incoming information. Memory traces resulting from such learning would be firm and enduring, ensuring effective transfer into long-term memory. (p. 214)

As illustrated by Relan, then, the advance organizer provides the "hierarchical framework" for students so that they can move information into long-term memory efficiently and effectively and in a connected manner. This framework helps students understand the "big picture" and categorize new information accordingly. Without this organizing feature, new information can move into long-term memory, but retrieval or recall can be difficult or nearly impossible. According to information processing theory, it is the connections that are made with existing structures that provide the multiple pathways for use and retrieval of stored information. Advance organizers provide a vehicle for building the framework and supporting recall.

Advance Organizers and the Academic Rationalism Philosophy of Curriculum and Instruction

Advance organizers represent the academic rationalism perspective on curriculum articulated by Eisner and Vallance (1974). As discussed by Glatthorn and Jailall (2000), proponents of the academic rationalism philosophy "believe that understanding a discipline's concepts and syntax of inquiry should be the central goal of all curriculums" (p. 98). The advance organizer was designed with this orientation in mind. It promotes a discipline's "concepts and syntax" as a way for learners to organize their own thinking in hierarchal fashion.

Further evidence supporting the advance organizer as a representative of this orientation to curriculum is rooted in its historical placement. Ausubel published his early treatments of this topic in the early 1960s. Glatthorn and Jailall have labeled the conceptions of curriculum during this period as the "structure of the discipline curriculums" (2000, p. 102). Reflecting on the work of Bruner, they contend that "the structure of the disciplines should constitute the heart of curriculums; each discipline has its own concepts, theories, and ways of knowing" (pp. 102–103). It is clear that this belief is reflected in Ausubel's use of advance organizers as a way to operationalize the use of "concepts, theories, and ways of knowing" for guiding student learning.

In Case Study 13.1, Ms. Wolters tried to construct and introduce the advance organizer based on her understanding of the structure of the subject of the geosphere and its related components. She also emphasized "ways of knowing," as illustrated by the question she posed for student consideration: "Do the benefits outweigh the costs or vice versa?" Likewise, Mr. Brehm considered a central concept of communities as part of the larger subject of social studies as he constructed his advance organizer. Through his use of comparisons with insects and animals, he helped his students begin to explore the structures of this subject. In both cases, the academic rationalists' orientation to curriculum was clearly in evidence.

Technology and Advance Organizers

As the development and introduction of advance organizers are largely teacher-directed activities, one important use of technology would be researching the topics and disciplines that guide instructional activities and that are being introduced and framed by the organizer. Although it can be presumed that most secondary teachers will have a deep understanding of the discipline related to their content area, most elementary teachers are required to teach many content areas, even those that were not a major area of study in their teacher preparation experiences. For them especially, the ability to find Web sites and articles, as well as Web sites of groups that govern various fields (see Table 1.3), would be invaluable as they construct their advance organizers and develop learning activities.

Advance Organizers used with personal computers or other technology have much potential for enhancing student learning.

Similarly, an assortment of Web sites produce graphic organizers for teacher use. These graphic organizers can sometimes be used to construct actual advance organizers. The use of a concept map as an advance organizer could be facilitated here. Another option would be to use these graphic organizers as tools to outline and construct a map of the hierarchy of a discipline for use in designing both the advance organizer and the lessons that will follow.

There are applications of technology, with the use of advance organizers, that more directly involve students. However, just as advance organizers can sometimes be a receptive activity for learners, the incorporation of technology may be as well. For example, teachers can put their advance organizer on a computer and project it on a Smart Board or in a PowerPoint presentation format. This allows for easy organization, and the teacher can also easily incorporate video, pictures, and other kinds of visuals and graphics. More important, students will have easy visual access—the kind that is less easily achieved when the teacher holds up photographs or other graphics for a group of 30 students.

Finally, students can use technology to more actively interact with advance organizers. Some researchers and developers have explored the use of advance organizers with educational computer software (Kenny, 1993). These kinds of software can be used in support of a current area of study or as stand-alone activities on a variety of topics.

Listed below are samplings of National Educational Technology (NET) Standards for Students (International Society for Technology in Education, 2000) that illustrate how an advance organizer can be aligned with technology for student activities.[*]

GRADES PK–2

NET Standard 1: Basic Operations and Concepts

NET Standard 3: Technology and Productivity Tools

Performance Indicator2: Use a variety of media and technology resources for directed and independent learning activities.

Advance Organizer Extension

Using a Smart Board or PowerPoint, present the advance organizer to students as a group.

NET Standard 1: Basic Operations and Concepts

Performance Indicator 4: Use developmentally appropriate multimedia (e.g., interactive books, educational software, elementary multimedia encyclopedias) to support learning.

Advance Organizer Extension

Locate and provide students with computer software that uses advance organizers for subject organization.

GRADES 3–5

NET Standard 3: Technology and Productivity Tools

Performance Indicator 4: Use general purpose productivity tools and peripherals to support personal productivity, remediate skill deficits, and facilitate learning throughout the curriculum.

Advance Organizer Extension

Locate and provide students with computer software that uses advance organizers for subject organization.

---

[*]*National Educational Technology Standards for Students: Connecting Curriculum and Technology* by ISTE. Copyright © 2000 by International Society for Technology in Education (ISTE), 800–336–5191 (US &Canada) or 541–302–3777 (Int'l), iste@iste.org, www.iste.org. All rights reserved. Reproduced with permission of ISTE via Copyright Clearance Center. Reprint permission does not constitute endorsement by ISTE.

NET Standard 5: Technology Research Tools

NET Standard 6: Technology Problem-Solving and Decision-Making Tools

Performance Indicator 8: Use technology resources (e.g. calculators, data collection probes, videos, educational software) for problem-solving, self-directed learning, and extended-learning activities.

Advanced Organizer Extension

Allow and encourage students to use PCs as they explore information relative to a subject that has been introduced with an advance organizer. This could include using PCs in centers.

GRADES 6–8

NET Standard 3: Technology Productivity Tools

NET Standard 6: Technology Problem-Solving and Decision-Making Tools

Performance Indicator 5: Apply productivity/multimedia tools and peripherals to support personal productivity, group collaboration, and learning throughout the curriculum.

Advance Organizer Extension

Provide students with access to reference software (encyclopedias, etc.) and Web sites to research information related to the content being studied.

GRADES 9–12

NET Standard 4: Technology Communication Tools

NET Standard 5: Technology Research Tools

Performance Indicator 8: Select and apply technology tools for research, information analysis, problem solving, and decision making in content learning.

Advance Organizer Extensions

Provide students with access to reference software (encyclopedias, etc.) and Web sites to research information related to the content being studied.

Direct students to Web sites offered by various discipline-related organizations and assist them in observing the structure of the discipline via resources available on the Web site. In addition, help them explore the discipline's ways of knowing—as demonstrated by content or tools located on the Web site.

Advance Organizers, Content Standards, and Benchmarks

As a model designed to use the structure of disciplines, Advance Organizers can easily be connected to content standards across the curriculum. Indeed, many content standards and benchmarks are designed in a way that reflects the structure or major concepts of various subjects (Glatthorn & Jailall, 2000). Therefore, it can be said that by their very nature, standards and benchmarks are aligned with the aims of an advance organizer.

Content standards and benchmarks sometimes direct students to use the methods of inquiry of a specific discipline or subject in fairly explicit ways. The first example listed below illustrates this point using science. In addition, content standards can always be aligned with the specific content being studied. The second example below illustrates how one set of content standards and benchmarks is connected with the content of Ms. Wolter's Earth science lesson. All Standards and Benchmarks listed below are taken from the *Michigan Curriculum Framework* (Michigan Department of Education, 1996).*

Science

STRAND II, REFLECTING ON SCIENTIFIC KNOWLEDGE: CONTENT STANDARD 1: All students will analyze claims for their scientific merits and explain how scientists decide what constitutes scientific knowledge; how science is related to other ways of knowing; how science and technology affect our society; and how people of diverse cultures have contributed to and influenced developments in science.

Elementary Benchmark: Develop an awareness of the need for evidence in making decisions scientifically. (Key concepts: Data, evidence, sample, guess, opinion.)

Middle School Benchmark: Evaluate the strengths and weaknesses of claims, arguments or data. (Key concepts: Aspects of arguments such as data, evidence, sampling, alternate explanation, conclusion.)

High School Benchmark: Justify plans or explanations on a theoretical or empirical basis. (Key concepts: Aspects of logical argument, including evidence, fact, opinion, assumptions, claims, conclusions, observations.)

STRAND V, USING SCIENTIFIC KNOWLEDGE IN EARTH SCIENCE: CONTENT STANDARD 1: All students will describe the earth's surface; describe and explain how the earth's features change over time; and analyze effects of technology on the earth's surface and resources.

---

*Excerpts from the *Michigan Curriculum Framework* are reprinted with permission of the Michigan Department of Education.

Elementary Benchmark: Describe uses of materials taken from the earth. (Key concepts: Transportation—oil into gasoline. Building materials—sand into glass, ores into metals, gravel into concrete and asphalt. Energy—coal burned to produce electricity; uranium for nuclear power. Water—drinking, cleaning and cooling.)

Middle School Benchmark: Explain how technology changes the surface of the earth. (Key concepts: Types of human activities—surface mining, construction and urban development, farming, dams, landfills, restoring marsh lands, reclaiming spoiled lands.)

High School Benchmark: Explain how and why earth materials are conserved and recycled. (Key concepts: Valuable materials—minerals, metallic ores, iron, copper, aluminum, fuels. Types of resources—renewable, nonrenewable. Conservation, limits, recycling, costs for developing more remote supplies. Recycling processes—melting, shredding, dissolving. Tools: Satellite images and resource atlases.)

Why Choose Advance Organizers?

1. As you consider the amount of content to be taught in a unit or subject, would your students benefit from having a mental framework for organizing and connecting this information as a way to understand it and recall it at a later time?

2. Do your students repeatedly demonstrate difficulty recalling information they have read about a topic under study? Could an advance organizer help prepare them to be better consumers of the information as they connect new information from their readings to things they already know?

3. Are your students mentally engaged with understanding a topic and related information? Would the use of an advance organizer provide them with the kind of focus that might facilitate more engagement?

4. Do you want your students to see how information from a unit of study fits together or is connected in some way? Could an advance organizer help you accomplish this?

5. Would a central theme be a useful way for you to organize the information students need to learn? Could an advance organizer help you find the themes and larger questions of a discipline?

Summary

Developed by Ausubel, advance organizers have been shown to be effective in helping students understand and recall information by providing a framework that represents the hierarchy and major concepts of a discipline or subject. The advance organizer presents introductory information that students are able to use to build a cognitive structure or scaffold in which they can anchor information presented in the various learning activities that follow the presentation of the organizer.

Advance organizers can be used in all subject areas and with all ages of learners. They also can be constructed using visuals, graphics, text, and a variety of other media. As such, they are flexible tools for both student learning and teacher construction and use.

Putting It Together

1. Select a textbook or other reading that students will be using. Take one section or chapter. As you read it, jot down the details and main information that are included. When you are finished, consider how the information fits together. Jot down the larger theme or questions that connect the information. Consider how these themes or questions might help you construct an advance organizer.

2. Review your state's content standards and benchmarks for a content area of interest to you. Note how the standards organize the subject into larger segments that reflect the structure of that discipline.

3. As you explore your state's content standards for a subject of interest to you, consider how you might construct an advance organizer, using one of the subtopics that reflect the structure of that academic discipline.

4. As you develop a unit plan for a course or field experience, begin with an advance organizer. Determine which type would be the best match for your learners and the particular subject you are using: visual, graphic, expository, and so forth.

Student Study Site

The Companion Web site for *Models of Teaching: Connecting Student Learning With Standards*
www.sagepub.com/delloliostudy
Visit the Web-based student study site to enhance your understanding of the book content and discover additional resources that will take your learning one step further. You can enhance your understanding by using the comprehensive Study Guide, which includes

chapter learning objectives, flash cards, practice tests, and more. You'll find special features, such as the links to standards from U.S. States and associated activities, Learning from Journal Articles, Field Experience worksheets, Learning from Case Studies, and PRAXIS resources.

References

Chun, D. M., & Plass, J. L. (1996). Facilitating reading comprehension with multimedia. *System*, *24*(4), 503–519.

Downing, A. (1994). *An investigation of the advance organizer theory as an effective teaching model* (Report No. SP035546). Washington, DC: Office of Educational Research and Improvement. (ERIC Document Reproduction Service No. ED377150)

Glatthorn, A. A., & Jailall, J. (2000). Curriculum for the new millennium. In R. S. Brandt (Ed.), *Education in a new era* (pp. 97–121). Alexandria, VA: Association for Supervision and Curriculum Development.

Groller, K. L., Kender, J. P., & Honeyman, D. S. (1991). Does instruction on metacognitive strategies help high school students use advance organizers. *Journal of Reading*, *34*(6), 470–475.

International Society for Technology in Education. (2000). *National educational technology standards for students: Connecting curriculum and technology*. Washington, DC: Author in collaboration with the U.S. Department of Education.

Jackman, D. H., & Swan, M. K. (1994). *Alternative instructional models for IVN delivery*. Fargo: North Dakota State University.

Kenny, R. F. (1993). *The effectiveness of instructional orienting activities in computer-based instruction* (Report No. IR016328). Washington, DC: Office of Educational Research and Improvement. (ERIC Document Reproduction Service No. 362172)

Kirkman, G., & Shaw, E. L. (1997). *Effects of an oral advance organizer on immediate and delayed retention* (Report No. TM027960). Washington, DC: Office of Educational Research and Improvement. (ERIC Document Reproduction Service No. ED415263)

Lawton, J. T., & Johnson, A. (1992, Winter). Effects of advance organizer instruction on preschool children's learning of musical concepts. *Council for Research in Music Education Bulletin*, *111*, 35–48.

Mayer, R. E. (1979, Winter). Can advance organizers influence meaningful learning? *Review of Educational Research*, *49*, 371–383.

McEneany, J. M. (1990, Winter). Do advance organizers facilitate learning? Review of subsumption theory. *Journal of Research and Development in Education*, *23*, 89–96.

Michigan Department of Education. (1996). *Michigan curriculum framework*. Lansing: Author.

Relan, A. (1991). Effectiveness of a visual comparative advance organizer in teaching biology. *Research in Science and Technological Education, 9*(2), 213–222.

Rinehart, S. D., Barksdale-Ladd, M. A., & Welker, W. A. (1991). Effects of advance organizers on text recall by poor readers. *Journal of Reading, Writing, and Learning Disabilities International, 7*(4), 321–335.

Ruthkosky, K. O., & Dwyer, F. M. (1996). The effect of adding visualization and rehearsal strategies to advance organizers in facilitating long-term retention. *International Journal of Instructional Media, 23*(1), 31–40.

Story, C. M. (1998). What instructional designers need to know about advance organizers. *International Journal of Instructional Media, 25*(3), 253–261.

Willerman, M., & Mac Harg, R. A. (1991). The concept map as an advance organizer. *Journal of Research in Science Teaching, 28*(8), 705–712.

Developing Curriculum That Addresses Content Standards

In Part 3, consisting of Chapter 14, you will learn how to develop instructional units that address content standards and benchmarks for your subject or grade level. Chapter 14 begins by distinguishing curriculum and instruction and defines the various components of the curriculum. Using each of these components, the chapter will guide you through the step-by-step process of designing curriculum for both **single-subject** and **interdisciplinary units**.

In Part 2 you became familiar with 10 classic and contemporary models of teaching. Chapter 14 will provide you with more insight into the process of selecting specific models of teaching that address student needs as well as the particular demands of subject-area content. One distinctive section of Chapter 14 describes the process

of modifying instruction for students with special needs: those with learning disabilities, the gifted, or modifying teacher language for English language learners and native English speakers. Several practical suggestions are provided for each special-needs category, and these ideas can be tailored to complement various models of teaching. Chapter 14 also provides you with templates for evaluating the effectiveness of your instruction and curriculum design.

chapter 14

Developing Original Instructional Units Based on Standards, Benchmarks, and District Grade-Level Expectations

When was the first time you heard the term *curriculum* in a conversation? Were you listening to teachers talk with one another about "everything we have to cover this year?" Were you speaking to a high school guidance counselor about college entrance requirements? The counselor may have said that your high school curriculum was rigorous enough to earn the respect of selective colleges. Perhaps your parents are teachers. As your family prepared dinner one evening, you overheard your father remark that he cannot teach as creatively as he used to because of the new curriculum in his school district. You may have become familiar with the term *curriculum* only recently, in your education classes. These classes may be titled Secondary Science Methods and Curriculum, Curriculum and Instruction for Elementary Education, or Multicultural Early Childhood Curriculum. Curriculum is a central component of education, but there are several ways to define what it is.

What Is Curriculum?
What Is Instruction?

Apprenticeship of observation refers to what beginning teachers bring to their teacher education courses (Lortie, 1975). From your own experiences, you come to your teacher preparation program with a general understanding of what teaching should look like and sound like, what content should be taught, and when, all based on the "apprenticeship" you have experienced as a K–12 student yourself. Usually, teachers refer to the scope of knowledge in K–12 education as the **curriculum**. However, educators have also defined curriculum as broadly encompassing every experience a student has while in school, including interpersonal relationships, the environmental conditions of schools, and playground politics (Campbell & Caswell,1935); as focusing on inquiry-driven experiences that define the learner as a creator of knowledge (Tanner & Tanner, 2006); and as only the academic content of K–12 schooling (Good, 1973). As you read in Chapter 2, philosophies of education also play a role by promoting what should be taught to students and why. The self-actualization philosophy advocates that we educate the "whole child" by providing children opportunities to choose content on the basis of their interests. The social reconstructionist philosophy advocates that the curriculum should help students understand issues of social relevance and see themselves as agents for social change. The cognitive processing philosophy advocates that the development of critical thinking skills should be the anchor of the curriculum. Academic rationalists believe a classical curriculum is best for all students, not only the college bound. The technologist approach to curriculum is to break down material in systematic ways so that any content can be taught traditionally and assessed easily.

For some educators, **instruction** is considered a component of the curriculum. They believe that in addition to academic content, how we choose to teach students affects their perceptions about themselves as learners and their place as resourceful members of society. For example, if the instruction in a classroom is always teacher directed, students may underestimate their own abilities as effective, self-directed learners and problem solvers. When we provide learning experiences that require predicting, analyzing, discovering, or creating, we are giving students opportunities to work directly as scientists, mathematicians, or historians. While there is a close relationship between curriculum and instruction, educators generally discuss them as two distinct entities. In this text, we address curriculum and instruction separately as they relate to what content is taught (curriculum) and how it is taught (instruction). In this chapter, we will discuss the process of curriculum development, and this will be our working definition:

> Curriculum development addresses what should be taught; to whom; when; organized in what fashion; using what strategies; what personnel; what resources; which assessments and evaluations; and includes a professional, student-centered rationale for each decision. (Passow, 1987, adapted by Dell'Olio, 1995)

This practical definition can apply to any of the five philosophies of curriculum and instruction. Each component of curriculum development is included in this definition, as are instructional choices and teachers' intentions.

How does this definition of curriculum and instruction relate directly to teachers' work? Teachers must be deliberative about every decision they make in their practice. By deliberative, we mean that they must make all professional choices for specific, student-centered reasons. Deliberative teachers, who think analytically about their teaching and their students' learning, continually ask themselves questions about their yearlong curricular goals and each individual **instructional unit**. The following questions will help you create, teach, and evaluate your units:

1. What state and district standards must I address in my grade level, and why is this content important for students?

2. Who are the students in my class this year?

3. When will this unit or lesson take place?

4. How will this content be organized?

5. What models of teaching will best help my students learn this content?

6. What instructional modifications will my special-needs learners require?

7. What personnel and other resources do I have to support this unit?

8. How will student learning be assessed and then evaluated?

9. How will my effectiveness as a teacher be assessed and evaluated?

10. What is my professional rationale for each of these curricular decisions?

11. Once I have taught this lesson or unit once, what changes might be needed?

You will have opportunities to develop original instructional units that require your own creativity and organization. In some cases, teachers are required to follow instructional units that have been developed by district personnel—teachers and curriculum specialists. In other cases, school districts have purchased commercially prepared units of study, or they follow a textbook series aligned with their state benchmarks as their curriculum in each subject. In any of these situations, the questions above can be used as guideposts to examine each component of curriculum development.

State and District Content

The United States is the only industrialized country in the world without a national PK–12 curriculum. As you might guess, this is a topic of debate among politicians, educators, teacher educators, and parents. In this country, we have given the right to determine the specific content in K–12 schooling to individual states. Each state has subject-level experts, educators, and sometimes legislators who work together to develop the mandated state curriculum. States base some of these decisions in each academic area on recommendations from specialty program area organizations such as the International Reading Association or the National Council of Teachers of Mathematics. The influence of these organizations is one reason we have much agreement in state curriculum documents across the country. The design of your state's curriculum document may be formatted somewhat differently from other states', but there is likely to be a great deal of similarity in the content and organization of these documents. When school districts integrate content in specialized courses, the state content standards for each individual subject will be addressed. For example, when English and social studies are integrated into an American Studies class, the content taught will come directly from state language arts and social studies standards. States have content standards for all core academic areas—language arts, science, social studies, and math—and many states also have content standards for the arts, physical wellness, and technology.

Emphasizing the Relevance of the Curriculum

The relevance of much of the content we teach is evident. Textbooks and other instructional materials regularly include real-life applications of concepts and skills. For some topics, we may have to work to connect our students' lives to today's lesson. At some point in their K–12 schooling, when studying subjects that held no immediate interest for them, most students have asked, "When will I need to know this?" It can be a great temptation to tell students they will need to know the material "for next year," "for high school," "for the next standardized test," or for some other time in the future. Deliberative teachers think creatively to find some point of entry to jump-start student interest. The Internet is an instructional tool that can provide possibilities and direction for you. For example, many educational Web sites demonstrate how principles in math, chemistry, or physics work in our everyday lives, not just in laboratories. As teachers, we also want our students to enjoy learning for its own sake, for the intrinsic pleasure of discovering something new. Modeling how the life of the mind enriches our whole lives is a powerful aspect of teaching. Accomplished men and women in every field have spoken or written about the teachers who helped them learn to appreciate the world of ideas.

However, many of your students will desire to see concrete, everyday ways that the material you are asking them to master is significant to them. The obvious "relevance check" for many people is whether learning something new will help them in their work. It is also important that we help students connect what they are learning with the responsibilities and joys of family life now and in the future. Some content knowledge relates to leisure activities, such as when students participate in sports, engage in arts activities, or visit museums and exhibitions locally or when they travel. When we consider how content is meaningful to all aspects of our students' lives, we can begin by thinking about how it has been meaningful in our own lives.

Diversity in Your Classroom

By necessity, people in the United States have broadened their understanding of what it means to live in a diverse society. **Diversity** in the United States is now used as an umbrella phrase that acknowledges and encompasses differences in culture; ethnicity; religion; social class; physical, mental, and emotional exceptionality; gender; and sexual orientation. At school, a number of additional factors come into play. For example, family composition, birth order, multiple intelligence strengths, learning styles, and academic achievement all play a role in shaping what our students bring into our classrooms. None of these factors can be ignored or dismissed as unimportant by teachers. Diversity will be manifest in your classroom in different ways each year. One of your first responsibilities at the beginning of each school year is to assess the unique attributes that each student brings to your classroom.

Sequencing Instructional Units

The "when" question of our definition of curriculum refers to sequencing grade-level content, unit content, and individual lessons in a unit. Some states and school districts have mandated every grade-level course of study to the extent that the unit order is sequenced, and in some cases, lesson order, model of teaching, and assessments are also dictated. A district-wide math program may be this uniform because it is driven by a particular textbook series adopted by the state, one that is closely aligned with standardized tests. District teachers and specialists may also be asked to develop original instructional units, including very specific lesson sequencing, based on state standards. Districts may provide a **curriculum map**, a yearlong schedule that shows which units must be taught at what time during the school year, what specific grade-level objectives must be met, and the amount of time that will be spent on each unit.

Some units are dependent sequentially on others because they expand on students' knowledge and skills from previous units. For example, in a third-grade classroom, addition is usually reviewed and then extended toward the beginning of the school year, prior to introducing a unit on multiplication. This review is essential for students to understand new content. Similarly, history classes move chronologically so that a unit on the Revolutionary War in an American Studies class will precede, and support, a later unit on the Civil War. Some units may be sequenced at the teacher's discretion. This may be the case for geometry or measurement units that provide a welcome break from math units that focus on computation. In some units, teachers have discretion as to how lessons are sequenced. Often teachers at the same grade level plan together, but they plan loosely enough to provide flexibility for the way each unit plays out in their individual classrooms.

The most effective way to sequence lessons in a unit is to decide what students need to know and be able to do at the conclusion of the unit. You will need to state this in a **long-term objective**. Once the long-term objective is written, teachers sequence daily lesson objectives that move students from the beginning of the unit to that goal. This concept of using sequential objectives to guide curriculum planning toward a long-term objective was introduced by Ralph Tyler in the late 1940s (Tyler, 1949). Versions of this process, Tyler's Rational Model of curriculum development, have been used for decades. *Backward design*, a contemporary description of this concept, is popular with many educators today (Guskey, 2000; Popham, 2001; Smith, Smith, & DeLisi, 2001; Wiggins & McTighe, 1998). Writing long-term objectives requires some preparation, described in the next section.

Unit Organization

Instructional units can be developed in two ways, as single-subject units or as interdisciplinary units. Single-subject units focus on only one academic subject, such as math, language arts, science, or history. Interdisciplinary means that two or more subjects are addressed together in one unit. What we call *social studies* is actually an interdisciplinary subject in itself, consisting of history, geography, political science, and economics. Interdisciplinary instructional units should be developed only when the content of the subjects being integrated can be blended in ways that enrich both subjects but do not dilute the content or processes of any of the disciplines. However, before you can begin to create either single-subject or interdisciplinary units, you need to be able to write performance objectives that will guide your long-term planning and the development of each of your daily lessons.

Developing Long-Term Unit Performance Objectives and Daily Lesson Objectives

Professional educators need to understand the process of developing original curriculum so that they can analyze and adapt commercialized curriculum and textbook material to suit the needs of their particular students each year. Teachers also need to see the bigger picture, the **curriculum articulation**. This means they should understand how content in a subject is related among grade levels. For example, they should know, not just their own grade-level expectations, but when a concept is introduced and how it becomes increasingly challenging over time. Once you understand the articulation of your curriculum and where your standards, benchmarks, and objectives fall in the overall development of your subject, you need to write essential questions for your unit.

Developing Essential Questions

Before you write a long-term objective, you need to consider what **essential questions** will serve as the compass for your unit. Essential questions come directly from the content of the unit and guide students' learning. Through instruction and exploration, students will answer these questions in the course of the unit. Essential questions address the important ideas you will be studying, and you will continually return to them. Essential questions serve several purposes. First, they indicate the importance of the material to be covered in a unit. Besides the fact that the unit content is part of the grade-level curriculum, why is it intrinsically important in the first place? Why did it find a place in the curriculum? Second, the essential questions reflect the content you are required to address at your grade level. In most cases, this is the material that will appear on the state tests your students will be taking. Third, essential questions help focus your thinking as you consider learning experiences and specific models of teaching that will bring the unit content to life. Fourth, essential questions must motivate your students, help hold their interest, and help them see the relevance of the content to their lives. How has this material affected our world and the people in it? What meaning does it have for your students right now? Table 14.1 contains several examples of essential questions related to long-term objectives across the curriculum. For clarity, the essential questions are contrasted with questions that are nonessential.

Essential questions can provide a framework that reveals relationships among content standards, benchmarks, and grade-level objectives. They also help teachers write their long-term objectives, daily lesson objectives, and assessment choices.

Writing Long-Term Objectives

When developing curriculum, you begin by writing a **long-term objective**. You need to decide what your students should know and be able to do at the end of the unit. Let's say that you are an eighth-grade social studies teacher and you have five

Table 14.1   Nonessential and Essential Questions Across the Curriculum

What are the laws of thermodynamics? (nonessential question)

What causes the motion of objects? (essential question)

How do we write different forms of poetry: haiku, tanka, limerick, and free verse? (nonessential)

What are poems, and why are they so popular among children? (essential)

What was the geography of the Eastern coast when the first European settlers arrived? (nonessential)

In what ways did natural environments affect the first settlers in the New World, and in what ways did the first settlers have an effect on their environments? (essential)

How do we create bar, line, and circle graphs? (nonessential)

How do we pick the appropriate visual—bar graphs, line graphs, circle graphs, pictographs, tables, or charts—to communicate important information? (essential)

weeks to spend on the Civil War and Reconstruction eras. You must keep several things in mind:

Specific Content

In many states, the eighth-grade social studies content, for example, focuses solely on the United States during the 19th century. Your five-week unit on the Civil War and Reconstruction must address historical events from 1850 to 1877. What should your students know and understand about this important time in U.S. history? What specific facts, concepts, and generalizations in social studies should they carry into their next unit in history?

For another example, long-term math objectives in computation must provide more information than that the unit is about multiplication or fractions. Your long-term objective must state specific details about each operation or skill. For example:

The learner will subtract any two 4-digit numbers with regrouping in any column.

The learner will multiply any three mixed numbers with different denominators and will reduce the answer to the lowest terms.

Performance Verbs

Performance verbs describe how students will show you what they have learned throughout the unit. Verbs such as *know, understand,* or *appreciate* are not helpful to teachers because they do not allow us to assess what our students have learned as a result of the unit. What will the students *do* to show you that they know, understand, or appreciate something? What thinking skill is required for them to master specific content, and what process or product will demonstrate this mastery? In order to answer these questions, it is helpful to examine the three domains of learning.

The Domains of Learning

Performance objectives can be placed in one of three categories—those in the **cognitive domain,** which relates to thinking processes; those in the **affective domain**, which relates to values, attitudes, and emotions; and those in the **psychomotor domain**, which relates to fine and gross motor skills. Each of the domains has been organized into taxonomies—hierarchies of levels of complexity and student engagement. While several taxonomies have been developed for each of the domains, one in each domain seems to be most prevalent in teacher education, and these three are described below.

Cognitive Domain

As you discovered in Chapter 1, Benjamin Bloom, an educational evaluator, wanted to define and describe instructional objectives in a methodical way. In 1956 he and his associates developed a hierarchical taxonomy of critical thinking skills. Each of Bloom's six levels of critical thinking builds on the previous ones and encompasses and requires the thinking skills of the levels below it. Table 14.2 presents each level of Bloom's cognitive taxonomy, followed by an example of a performance objective for a unit with the Harry Potter novels (Rowling, 1998, 1999a, 1999b, 2000) as its content.

One caution is in order when you are working with the cognitive taxonomy. Although particular verbs are generally associated with specific levels of the taxonomy, you must always consider what is happening in the minds of the students before you assume they are working at one level or another. For example, this performance objective might be identified incorrectly as synthesis:

> Given ten nominative singular Russian nouns, the learner will write original sentences using the dative case.

While the task is to write original sentences, which you might associate with the synthesis level, students performing this objective are in fact working at the application level of Bloom's taxonomy. They need to apply their understanding of the dative case with nominative singular nouns; the emphasis in this objective is on grammar, not on writing elegant sentences.

Affective Domain

In 1964, David Krathwohl and his associates, including Benjamin Bloom, published a taxonomy of objectives in the affective domain. If we think of the cognitive domain as the "head" domain of learning, we can consider the affective domain as

Table 14.2   Objectives Using Bloom's Cognitive Levels in the Harry Potter Novels

Knowledge: the ability to state information or recite memorized information without necessarily understanding it

The learner will state the name of each Harry Potter book in order.

Comprehension: the ability to explain or summarize with understanding, but without the ability to apply the information to any other content or context

The learner will explain how and why Harry received the scar on his forehead.

Application: the ability to apply content knowledge and understanding to solve problems or to consider how a situation may relate to oneself personally

The learner will describe a time when he or she had to contend with bullies like Draco Malfoy and his friends.

Analysis: the ability to break something down into its component parts, to compare and contrast

The learner will analyze how the character of Ron Weasley develops over the course of the first four Harry Potter books.

Synthesis: the ability to create something new

The learner will write a different ending to *Harry Potter and the Chamber of Secrets* that will change the course of the books that follow.

Evaluation: the ability to evaluate between or among choices and provide a rationale for the choice made

The learner will decide whether Professor Snape or Lucius Malfoy is the more dangerous to Harry Potter at the end of *The Prisoner of Azkaban* and explain why.

the "heart" domain of learning. The affective domain includes the values, attitudes, emotions, and emotional responses of students. Table 14.3 presents the levels of Krathwohl's taxonomy and an example of a performance objective at each level.

Objectives in the affective domain are very difficult to assess. Earlier, we stated that the verbs *understand* or *appreciate* were not viable for objectives in the cognitive domain. While these and similar verbs, including *empathize*, *sympathize*, or *value*, clearly relate to the affective domain, they are not easy qualities to measure. Some educators argue that the affective domain cannot be assessed at all, and objectives written to measure and record these qualities in students reduce the essence of the affective domain to dry, if observable, student behaviors. This view is understandable. However, with renewed emphasis on character education in the public schools, we are increasingly seeing attempts at the fair and meaningful assessment of student behaviors in the affective domain. Whether or not you are an advocate of character education in the public schools, it is sobering to know that in 2005, more people looked up the word *integrity* than any other word in the online Merriam-Webster dictionary (Merriam-Webster OnLine, 2005).

| Table 14.3 | Performance Objectives in the Affective Domain |

Receiving: the ability to attend while others are expressing their points of view
   In a jigsaw group, the learner will listen and not interrupt when others are speaking.

Responding: the willingness to answer a call when needed—in interpersonal and social relationships and situations
   The learner will volunteer for extra cleanup responsibilities at least twice each semester.

Valuing: the willingness to express appreciation to others for their qualities and contributions
   In a journal entry, the learner will express appreciation for the contributions of five individual Asian-Americans to contemporary United States culture.

Organization: the willingness to make life-affirming choices by integrating new positive values into one's behavior
   The learner will choose nutritious food consistently in the school cafeteria and will record his or her choices over a two-week period.

Characterization by value or value complex: willingness to follow legal, ethical, or moral standards and to base personal decisions on these values with integrity
   The learner will follow school guidelines for the ethical and legal uses of technology.

Psychomotor Domain

With the exception of classes in physical education and dance, the psychomotor domain of learning has received less attention than the cognitive or affective domains. The emphasis of the psychomotor domain is on fine and gross motor skills of varying degrees of difficulty or dexterity. Anita Harrow's taxonomy, first published in 1972, is especially accessible to beginning teachers in physical education as well as in general education classrooms. Table 14.4 presents the psychomotor domain and gives examples of corresponding performance objectives.

Lessons that fall within the psychomotor domain are seen in the gym, on the playing field, or in dance classes. However, the psychomotor domain plays an integral role in mastering skills across the curriculum. For example, in math class, the correct use of measurement tools, protractors, and compasses are within the psychomotor domain, as are the perceptual abilities needed in the use of many manipulatives. In social studies class, locating coordinate points requires the integration of perceptual and fine motor abilities, as does the use of a scale given on a map legend. In the fine or performing arts, psychomotor skills in each level of the taxonomy can be seen in every class session or private lesson.

Specific Conditions

Are there any specific **conditions** that need to be included in the objective? Will your students need any particular materials, or are there circumstances that need to be in place for your students to complete their long-term objective?

| Table 14.4 | Performance Objectives in the Psychomotor Domain |

Reflex movements: to flex, to stretch, to extend, to shorten, to tense, to relax, to inhibit
  The learner will pull his or her hand away from a hot stimulus.

Basic fundamental movement: to crawl, to walk, to slide, to run, to reach
  The learner will run around a baseball diamond.

Perceptual abilities: to catch, to write, to bounce, to eat, to balance
  The learner will print each lower-case manuscript letter in Zaner-Bloser form.

Physical abilities: to improve, to increase, to stop, to start, to bend
  The learner will do 10 sit-ups properly and without assistance.

Skilled movements: to skip, to juggle, to skate, to throw a ball, to type, to perform the box step
  The learner will skip the width of the basketball court.

Nondiscursive communication: to make facial expressions, to make expressive body gestures, to dance skillfully with expression
  In a short choreographed dance, the learner will express sadness using low, medium, and high levels of space.

SOURCE: Adapted from *A Taxonomy of the Psychomotor Domain: A Guide for Developing Behavioral Objectives* by A. Harrow. Copyright © 1972 by Longman Publishing.

Here are some examples:

Given a world map and a list of five major cities in each of the four hemispheres, the learner will determine the coordinates of each city within a margin of 2 degrees in either latitude or longitude; label the Equator, Arctic and Antarctic Circles, Topics of Cancer and Capricorn, and Prime Meridian; and draw the boundaries of the global time zones.

Given a list of 20 works of literature (books, magazines, journals, encyclopedia volumes, newspapers, Web sites, and historical primary-source documents) written without capital letters or punctuation, the learner will rewrite the titles using the correct punctuation and style (italics, underlining, etc.).

If a condition phrase is part of an objective, it must be integral to students' successful performance, not extraneous. Some aspects of classroom life can be taken for granted. For example, it is not necessary to include the words in italics in the following instructional objectives: *After lessons on the parts of speech,* the learner will identify the part of speech of each word in a sentence; *After reading textbook chapters on plant anatomy, the life cycle of common plants, and the process of photosynthesis,* the learner will choose a plant and create an illustrated poster that describes the parts of a plant, the life cycle, and the process of photosynthesis. In these examples, the condition phrases are not needed. Some teachers regard the inclusion of a conditions phrase in their objectives as a matter of teacher style. Ask yourself whether the condition phrase is helpful to you as you work through an individual lesson or a unit.

Criteria

What **criteria** constitute a quality performance or product? Do your students merely need to accomplish a task, or is the quality of their product or performance important? In some cases, mastery of a long-term objective can be assessed and recorded using only a checklist. Knowledge or skill is either present in the student's behavior or it is absent, so a criteria phrase is unnecessary in the objective:

The learner will identify whether a letter is a vowel or a consonant.

In this example, students can either distinguish among vowels and consonants or they cannot.

Not all long-term objectives need a criteria phrase by virtue of the content or grade level, as in this example:

The learner will print his or her first and last name, full address, and telephone number.

However, a criteria phrase may be needed at the beginning or at the end of an objective to make it more specific or supply relevant information:

The learner will state the categories of plant and animal classification in the proper order: kingdom, phylum, class, order, family, genus, species.

In this case, the proper order of these terms is integral to the student's understanding of the content. This criteria phrase states how or to what extent the objective will be accomplished.

If you are giving a traditional test on computation, you may want to include a percentage to indicate students' levels of proficiency. Here is an example of a long-term objective for an upper-elementary unit on multiplication:

Using both the lattice method and the traditional algorithm, the learner will multiply any two 3-digit numbers with regrouping in any place to 90% accuracy.

A teacher using full-group instruction for this unit will need to decide the level of proficiency the class needs. While we hope that children will master an objective 100% of the time, it is not likely that they will always do so. Given this reality, a percentage criteria phrase helps the teacher decide whether to move the entire class to the next daily lesson objective or to differentiate instruction by creating small groups that can move at their own rate.

A long-term objective for an instructional unit on the Civil War could include a criteria phrase, but it would be qualitative rather than quantitative:

> The learner will describe the lives of four different people from the Civil War era with reference to their family roles, occupations, social status, political identification, effects of local geography on their experiences, effects of economic changes during this time, and personally significant facts or events.

The criteria that make up much of this long-term objective state what students need to include as they describe their characters. The content of the description constitutes the qualitative criteria.

As soon as you have written your long-term objective, you need to consider your formative and summative assessments. Sometimes your assessment choices change your long-term objective in some way. In addition to traditional tests, you may want to include something creative for your students' final projects. For example, you may be a social studies teacher on a team of eighth-grade teachers, and the language arts teacher is going to collaborate with you on a unit about the Civil War. There are many ways for students to demonstrate their knowledge of the content of this unit, such as posters, Web site creations, PowerPoint presentations, and individual or group projects. Together you and the language arts teacher decide that the students will write five simulated journal entries for each of four characters. At least one historical figure and three original characters living in different circumstances during the period must be included. Throughout the journal entries, these characters must refer to the relationships between political and personal events that are affecting their lives. This is your amended long-term objective:

> The learner will write five journal entries for each of four different people from the Civil War era—one historical and three fictional—with reference to family roles, occupations, social status, political identification, effects of local geography on their experiences, effects of economic changes during this time, and personally significant facts or events throughout the five entries.

Planning Initiating and Culminating Events

Once you have reviewed state and district curriculum on the Civil War and Reconstruction, written your long-term objective, and developed the essential questions, you will also plan initiating and culminating events for your unit. An **initiating event** can be a motivating learning experience or provide an overview of the unit to follow. As an initiating experience for the Civil War unit, options may be to show the film *Glory*, about African American soldiers who fought bravely for the Union army, or to have your students participate in a simulated nighttime journey on the underground railroad. A **culminating event** might be to invite theater or history students from a local college to come as characters from this period, speak about the

When teachers collaborate as they develop curriculum, their ideas and styles often complement each other's.

challenges in their lives, and answer students' questions. Initiating and culminating activities can provide meaningful "bookend" experiences for students.

Writing Daily Lesson Objectives

Your long-term objective provides you with a specific destination for students. You have stated your content and described how students will demonstrate what they have learned. Once your long-term objective is set, it is time to consider what **daily lesson objectives** will help the students reach their destination. You will need to consider your "itinerary": the direction of the unit and the stops along the way. You will also need to identify which concepts and skills will be new to your students and which concepts or skills they must review.

Daily lesson objectives share the same components as long-term objectives (specific content, performance verbs, condition and criteria phrases); however, each objective is usually the focus of a single lesson. Table 14.5 provides daily lesson objectives in several subjects.

One of the common mistakes beginning teachers make is to confuse a class activity with an objective. This is an important distinction. You may want your students to bake cookies or prepare international foods for the pure enjoyment of the activity. However, if these activities will be ways to reinforce grade-level content, your objective needs to be written to address that. If your idea for preparing food comes from a unit on measurement or the differences between the metric and the U.S. systems of measurements, then that is what should drive your objective:

| Table 14.5 | Daily Lesson Objectives Across the Curriculum |

The learner will compare and contrast the style and characteristics of Jane Austen and Charlotte Bronte.

The learner will compare and contrast three multicultural Cinderella tales using Venn diagrams.

The learner will describe and illustrate the stages of the water cycle.

In a journal entry, the learner will describe a time when he or she felt like Ira in *Ira Sleeps Over*.

The learner will convert common fractions into percentages to 90% accuracy.

The learner will describe the major consequences and cleanup procedures of oil spills.

The learner will write the positive, comparative, and superlative forms of regular adjectives.

The learner will serve a volleyball over the net successfully four times out of five attempts.

The learner will increase cookie recipe ingredients multiplying the given amounts by 2½.

The learner will convert dry and liquid measurements from the metric system to the U.S. system.

"Doing an experiment with different metals" in science or "doing a geometry exploration with circles" in math are not well-written lesson objectives. These phrases describe activities, but they do not state what is happening cognitively. Neither phrase indicates what specific thinking skill is at work in the minds of students as they experiment or what the outcome of the experimentation will be. These are objectives that are written specifically:

Given ten objects made from different materials, the learner will determine which are magnetic and which are not.

The learner will describe the relationship between the diameter and the circumference of circles.

It may be helpful to consider an activity as the "vehicle" for the objective. The activity provides the context in which the objective can be accomplished by the student. If you have any doubt that your lessons have been written with solid objectives, ask yourself, What is happening in the mind, heart, or body of the students during this lesson or as a result of this lesson?

Single-Subject Curriculum Development

When you develop an instructional unit that focuses on a single academic subject, you must first develop a long-term objective based on your state standards and grade-level objectives. This process is easily explained with examples from the math curriculum, but the process will be very similar across the curriculum.

This is one of the grade-level expectations for adding and subtracting whole numbers that appears in the *Michigan Curriculum Framework* for the third grade (Michigan Department of Education, 1996):

Add and subtract two numbers up to two digits with regrouping and up to four digits without regrouping.

Examples: 58   4597
          -39 -1352

While the grade-level expectation, as is, can serve as the long-term objective for this unit, the teacher may decide to alter it somewhat to include tasks that are important even though they are not stated directly in the grade-level expectation. For example:

The learner will add and subtract two numbers up to two digits with regrouping and up to four digits without regrouping, solve given word problems, and generate and solve original word problems.

Many teachers add the last component to long-term objectives of computation units to assess whether students can apply their understanding of the operations in the creation of their own sensible story problems.

In mathematics instruction, it is easy to ask, Why not just follow the textbook provided by the district to figure out daily lesson objectives that address grade-level expectations? You need to remember that textbooks do not always break down material to the degree needed for all children to succeed in the classroom. The math content on each two-page spread may be mastered by some children in one day, but many children will need this content broken down into several component parts. Each component may take these children more than one day to learn. When you begin with your standards or grade-level expectations rather than with your textbook, you take the desired outcome, your long-term objective, and break it down into component parts. These component parts should be the smallest amount of content that might be taught in individual lessons.

It may also be that your views of content organization differ from those of the textbook's authors. There is no one perfect way to develop a **continuum** of objectives in an instructional unit, even in a math unit. A continuum is the sequenced list of daily lesson objectives that takes the students from the beginning of the unit to the long-term objective. Sometimes how you choose to sequence objectives in a unit depends on your style of teaching. Other times, your view of the best organization of concepts or skill progression will be based on your understanding of your students' learning needs.

When you develop an original continuum of objectives for a unit, it is wise to look at the expectations of the previous grade levels. An understanding of the articulation of the curriculum will help you assess students' mastery levels before you begin each new unit. For example, in kindergarten, students are expected to add and subtract single-digit numbers using manipulatives to find solutions. In first grade, students are expected to find the sums and differences of two-digit numbers using basic math facts without regrouping. In second grade, they are expected to add and subtract two-digit numbers with regrouping and use the formal algorithm. You need to determine what lesson objectives will move your students from their addition and subtraction skills in kindergarten, first, and second grades to your long-term objective for third grade.

Later, you will be choosing landmark objectives to create a **pretest** and a **posttest** to assess what your students understand. The pre- and posttests will be written as mirror images of one another. The questions on each test will represent the landmark objectives (although the questions will not be identical). Your pretest will assess your students' knowledge at the beginning of the unit, and it will guide how you proceed with your instruction. Your posttest will provide you with data that will illustrate how much your students have learned as a result of the unit. It is best to begin your pre- and posttests with material that is familiar to your students. You do not need to include all the unit content in your pretest; a sample set of questions or equations will do. Often, teachers make use of pre- and posttests during parent conferences to demonstrate student progress.

Objectives in single-subject units such as math may be organized and sequenced according to conceptual progression. In a history unit, sequencing is always chronological; the passage of time is the essence of history. In a single-subject unit in geography, the organization of content may depend on the specific nature of the material. For example, map study may require sequential objectives based on increasingly difficult material, beginning with simple grid maps, then moving to more detailed political, physical, or product maps. A state-supported textbook series that addresses state content standards may define the exact sequencing of single-subject units in each grade level and across grade levels.

You will be affected by your district's commitment to either "covering" the curriculum or using the **mastery learning** approach. Some school districts insist that all grade-level curriculums be "covered": Each day, new material must be presented even if some students have not achieved mastery of previously taught material. Other districts support mastery learning, in which students move through the curriculum at their own rates. With mastery learning, students demonstrate competence in each new objective before moving on to the next. The advantage of "covering" the curriculum is that every student will be exposed in some measure to all the new content for their grade level, even if not all objectives are mastered. The advantage of mastery learning is that students will have a solid grasp of the material they are taught, even if fewer objectives are addressed.

Many teachers believe that full-group instruction in computational units in math does all students a disservice. Frequently, students who need more time to understand and apply their skills do not receive the amount of instruction and practice they need. Conversely, students who are ready to move at an accelerated pace can become bored when an instructional unit moves too slowly for them. In spite of its seeming contradictions, small-group instruction in some units facilitates students' reaching and often exceeding standards and grade-level expectations. The lower student-to-teacher ratio in small groups provides all students with more attention and personalized instruction. Given these benefits, some students are able to move more rapidly through the same sequence of objectives than they would with large-group instruction. Using small groups, teachers can **differentiate instruction** in a variety of ways: pacing, learning styles, need for manipulatives, and so on. Some groups may require individual lessons on every objective sequenced in your continuum; other groups may be able to take on two or more objectives in one lesson.

Interdisciplinary Curriculum Development

Interdisciplinary curriculum organization combines two or more subjects in a unit. Examples include a Westward Expansion unit that integrates the social studies, language arts, and science; a secondary-level class in American Studies that combines social studies and language arts; or an undergraduate degree in the classics that integrates history and the classical languages, Latin and Greek. In an interdisciplinary curriculum organization, the knowledge, methodology, and language of each discipline will be used to study topics, questions, and problems for which each of those disciplines has relevance. In the words of Heidi Hayes-Jacobs, "interdisciplinary (curriculum) does not stress delineations but linkages" among subjects (1989).

Advocates of interdisciplinary curriculum point out that in authentic situations, we rarely use one of the disciplines to the exclusion of others (Hayes-Jacobs, 1989; O'Neil, 2005; Taba, 1962; Tanner & Tanner, 2006). One of the strongest examples of this is the necessary integration of math and science when we solve authentic problems in medicine and engineering. Social studies and language arts are two subjects that are also natural pairings for curriculum integration. Most students in the United States have experienced interdisciplinary study in some measure if they participated in social studies classes rather than separate history or geography classes in their K–12 education.

Some have misgivings that K–12 students can learn the fundamental structures or main skills of inquiry with interdisciplinary curriculum (Ellis & Fouts, 1996; Gardner, 1999). Gardner is particularly concerned that early- and middle-elementary children cannot understand the uniqueness of individual disciplines if the nature, structure, and skills of each discipline are not taught directly and in isolation—at least initially. Jerome Bruner advocated that students at all levels of schooling learn to do the work of professionals in their disciplines (2004). For example, there is a difference between students' learning about history through traditional textbook-and-lecture methods and their doing the work of historians through document analysis.

A well-conceived and implemented interdisciplinary unit can provide these authentic learning experiences and address Gardner's uneasiness as well.

Another concern is that some teachers at the elementary level try to include subjects in interdisciplinary units inappropriately (Alleman & Brophy 1991; Ellis & Fouts, 1996). Not every unit can incorporate every subject in significant ways. It may be difficult to integrate math or science at the elementary level into many interdisciplinary units, for example. Alleman and Brophy are concerned that activities in interdisciplinary units are not always educationally significant. They believe that if an activity or lesson would be worthwhile, whether or not the curriculum is integrated, then it can be considered educationally sound. A related concern called the **potpourri effect** results when "weak or forced connections define an interdisciplinary unit" (Hayes-Jacobs, 1989). In these cases, there is no synergy; the whole interdisciplinary unit is not greater than the sum of its parts. The connections among the subjects are not meaningful intellectually, and the unit may not foster student understanding of the concepts in each individual subject. However, interdisciplinary units do engage student interest, and for that reason, a well-designed, purposeful, and motivating integration may be the most effective way to organize curriculum at all levels of schooling.

Planning the Interdisciplinary Unit

When you are planning an interdisciplinary unit, you address the same foundational concerns as you do for single-subject units. First, you state your unit topic, which tells your students what your unit is about. Second, develop several essential questions that will be answered throughout the course of the unit. Once you have determined your essential questions, write a long-term unit objective that states what your students should know and be able to do at the end of the unit. Let's take a more detailed look at each of those concerns as they relate to interdisciplinary units.

The Unit Topic

The first step in planning an interdisciplinary unit is to identify your **unit topic**. Earlier in this chapter, we looked at a unit on the Civil War and Reconstruction eras. The following are sample Michigan middle school social studies content standards and benchmarks (Michigan Department of Education, 1996) that would help structure this unit.

Social Studies

HISTORY—CONTENT STANDARD 2: All students will understand narratives about major eras of American and world history by identifying the people involved, describing the setting, and sequencing the events.

Middle School Benchmark 4: Use historical biographies to explain how events from the past affected the lives of individuals and how some individuals influenced the course of history.

CONTENT STANDARD 4: All students will make key decisions made at critical turning points in history by assessing their implications and long-term consequences.

Middle School Benchmark 1: Identify major decisions in the United States prior to the end of the era of Reconstruction, analyze contemporary factors contributing to the decisions, and consider alternative courses of action.

GEOGRAPHY—CONTENT STANDARD 1: All students will describe, compare, and explain the locations and characteristics of places, cultures, and settlements.

Middle School Benchmark 3: Explain why people live and work as they do in different regions.

ECONOMIC PERSPECTIVE—CONTENT STANDARD 2: All students will explain and demonstrate how businesses confront scarcity and choice when organizing, producing, and using resources when supplying the marketplace.

Middle School Benchmark 4: Examine the historical and contemporary role an industry has played and continues to play in a community.

INQUIRY—CONTENT STANDARD 1: All students will acquire information from books, maps, newspapers, data sets and other sources, organize and present the information in maps, graphs, charts, and timelines, interpret the meaning and significance of information, and use a variety of electronic technologies to assist in accessing and managing information.

Middle School Benchmark 2: Use traditional and electronic means to organize social science information and to make maps, graphs, and tables.

You may have noticed some direct connections to content standards and benchmarks in language arts. Earlier, we mentioned that for this unit, the social studies and language arts teachers would be working together. Below are sample language arts standards and benchmarks that relate directly to the content of this unit:

Language Arts

VOICE—CONTENT STANDARD 6: All students will learn to use information accurately and effectively and demonstrate their expressive abilities by creating oral, written, and visual texts that enlighten and engage an audience.

Middle School Benchmark 2: Demonstrate their ability to use different voices in oral and written communications to persuade, inform, entertain, and inspire their audiences.

GENRE AND CRAFT OF LANGUAGE—CONTENT STANDARD 8: All students will explore and use the characteristics of different types of texts, aesthetic elements, and mechanics—including text structure, figurative and descriptive language, spelling, punctuation, and grammar—to construct and convey meaning.

> **Middle School Benchmark 4:** Identify and use aspects and craft of the speaker, writer, and illustrator to formulate and express their ideas artistically. Examples include color and composition, flashback, multidimensional characters, pacing, appropriate use of details, strong verbs, language that inspires, and effective leads.

Essential Questions in Interdisciplinary Units

Now that you have stated your topic and identified content standards and benchmarks that might structure the unit, you need to develop the **essential questions** that will drive your unit. The following are provided as examples of questions that are not truly essential questions for a unit on the Civil War and Reconstruction era in U.S. history:

- What happened during the Civil War?
- What is the chronology of the major battles of the Civil War?
- Who were the major figures during the Civil War?

The answers to those questions will not give your students a substantive understanding of this era in U.S. history.

Here are some essential questions that would be appropriate for this unit on the Civil War and Reconstruction era in U.S. history:

- What were the various stakeholders' beliefs, positions, and commitments prior to the beginning of the Civil War?
- What were the human, economic, social, agricultural, and industrial costs of the Civil War?
- What contemporary social issues have their roots in the Civil War and Reconstruction era, and how do they affect your lives today?

Long-Term Objectives in Interdisciplinary Units

Next, ask yourself how your students will show you what they have learned in this unit. What is the new knowledge? What are the new skills? What will you ask them to do at the end of the unit that will demonstrate these things? You answer this question by writing a long-term objective that will summarize what students must know and the manner in which they will display this information. For their combined social studies and language arts unit, the two middle school teachers wrote this long-term objective (given earlier):

The learner will write five journal entries for each of four different people from the Civil War era—one historical and three fictional—with reference to family roles, occupations, social status, political identification, effects of local geography on their experiences, effects of economic changes during this time, and personally significant facts or events that occurred during the war and the Reconstruction.

Brainstorm Lesson Ideas

Once you have reviewed your standards and written your long-term objective, it is time to brainstorm lesson ideas across the curriculum. Many teachers like to use a web approach as they brainstorm ideas for lessons and learning experiences. In the center of a large piece of chart paper, write your unit topic. Around the center, list all the content areas you could include in your unit. Be specific as you organize the chart to record your ideas. For example, social studies is broken down into several strands that you will be addressing in this unit: history, geography, political science, economics, and inquiry. Language arts has four components—listening, speaking, reading, and writing—that will be the focus of several lessons in your unit. You may also consider integrating, with the help of specialists, other subjects or experiences. Consider the arts, physical education, and technology as separate categories on your web. Your web will look something like the one in Table 14.6.

Now you are ready to consider specific ideas for lessons, activities, and assignments across the curriculum. As you begin to brainstorm, try not to censor yourself. Be creative and enjoy the process. If you have a great idea, write it down even if you can think of immediate reasons why it might not work. Get all your ideas on the chart first. It is doubtful that you will be able to bring every idea to life, but at this point in developing your unit, think freely. The visual format of the web will help you see possible connections between and among subjects and will serve as a catalyst for additional ideas. As your web becomes more detailed, it will look something like Table 14.7.

Table 14.6 Interdisciplinary Unit Web Organization

Arts and Crafts	History	Listening	
Economics	Political Science	Films	
Geography			Speaking
	Civil War and Reconstruction Era		
Inquiry	Technology	Reading	
Physical Education *Skills Dance Sport*	Writing	Music	Science

Table 14.7 Initial Brainstorm for Interdisciplinary Unit

Arts and Crafts

2-dimensional
* drawings
* painting
3-dimensional
* model of slave quarters
* quilting

History

* 1850-1860
* 1860-1865
* 1865-1867
* persons
* places
* battles

Listening

* Civil War re-enactors (information)
  – Harriet Tubman, Jefferson Davis, Grant, Lee, etc.
* sounds from nature (day/night)

Economics
* N/S agriculture
* N/S industry

Political Science
"Union Party"
U.S. government structure
Confederate government structure

Films
* *Glory*
* Ken Burns' *The Civil War*
* *The Red Badge of Courage*

Geography
* N/S differences
* port cities
* RR lines
* N/S natural resources

Speaking
* memorized speeches
* reading journal entries aloud

Civil War and Reconstruction Era

Inquiry
* slavery
* abolitionists
* secession
* manners and etiquette
* role of Quakers

Technology
* Civil War technology
  – agricultural
  – communication
  – transporation
  – industrial
  – agricultural

Reading
* fiction
  – *The Red Badge of Courage*
* primary sources
(Digital Classroom Web site and commercial facsimiles)

Physical Education

Skills	Dance	Sports
* running	* social dances	* baseball
* crawling	* slave games and dances	

Writing
* fiction
  – stories
  – stimulated journals
  – newspaper articles
* nonfiction
  – travel writing
  – persuasive essays
  – research papers

Music
* folk songs

Science
* constellations
* regional climate
* medicine

Writing Specific Lesson Objectives

At this point in your interdisciplinary unit development, return to your standards, benchmarks, and grade-level objectives. Here are a few questions that will help you determine your progress so far:

- How do your long-term and lesson objectives reflect your state's curriculum?
- Do you need to make any adjustments to secure the alignment of your unit long-term objective with your state standards?
- How can you choose lesson content that meets your state curriculum and both the scope and focus of your unit?
- How can you phrase your daily lesson objectives so that each one will build your students' knowledge, skills, and understanding about this era of U.S. history?

Your daily lessons must embody the means for your students to complete everything you have described in your long-term unit objective. Here are a few possibilities that relate to sections of the web:

The learner will list, describe, compare, and contrast the natural resources found in the North and the South that were used to each region's advantage.

The learner will create a poster of the constellations of the northern sky and describe how the travelers on the Underground Railroad used them to make their way north.

The learner will write a three-paragraph editorial in the voice of an abolitionist or an advocate of secession.

Once you have written your objectives, you need to sequence your lessons.

When you reach this point, you may need to adjust the time you have allotted for each separate objective. What you initially believed would take only one class period for the students to accomplish may require an additional day or two. These adjustments are to be expected. You may also find that you need to insert a lesson that addresses content that you didn't consider when you first developed the unit or to change the sequence of your lessons to create a better flow. These changes are also not unusual, especially when you are teaching a unit for the first time.

Choosing Models of Teaching

A wide range of instructional possibilities is at your disposal when you plan for either single-subject or interdisciplinary units. The choices can be described as a spectrum, with lessons controlled by the teacher, such as direct instruction at one end, and increasingly indirect, open-ended lessons that focus on student exploration, such as the models of inquiry, at the other end. Models designed for either small-group or full-group instruction can be the most appropriate choice. The following considerations will help you to determine which model of teaching will best serve your students:

- Content concerns—the need to focus on the structure of the discipline
- Research considerations—the research base supporting the effectiveness of a given model in some subjects, such as math computation, specific literacy skills, reading skills, or the acquisition of social skills

- Critical thinking skill needs—inductive reasoning skills such as observation, inference, and analysis

- Standards-based concerns—grade-level expectations or curriculum articulation

- Motivation concerns—identifying the model that most engages student interest

Before you choose a model of teaching, you need to consider student needs, lesson content, the wording of your objective, the appropriateness of small- or full-group instruction, and the structure of the models that will best meet those needs. Once you are conversant with each of them, you can "play out" lessons as they might be developed using a variety of models. For example, which models of teaching might be used to teach the boiling and freezing points of water using both the Centigrade

Small heterogeneous group instruction provides teachers with opportunities to design lessons that are tailored to meet students' particular needs. These small groups allow for greater teacher-student interaction and let students work through the curriculum at their own rate.

Table 14.8   Sample Ideas for Modifying Instruction in the General Education Classroom

Adjusting the level of difficulty

> Selecting texts with less print on the page
> Audiotaping texts
> Providing study guides or visual organizers
> Providing manipulatives

Modifying students' work space

> Using partitions or portable carrels
> Reducing the size of the paper by folding or covering portions
> Keeping work spaces clear
> Seating the student closer to the teacher

Adjusting time

> Reducing the number of problems
> Increasing allotted time
> Setting a timer to pace work
> Checking with the student at frequent intervals

Testing adaptations

> Reading test to student
> Audiotaping test to allow for repeating question or instruction
> Previewing instructions for each section and having student repeat
> Requiring fewer problems in each section

Modifying teacher language for native English speakers

> Adding gestures to explanations
> Reducing the amount of teacher talk
> Using visual aids
> Asking students to turn and repeat directions to a partner

Adjusting the presentation of subject matter

> Providing notes or PowerPoint-screen handouts
> Preteaching lesson vocabulary
> Using a variety of visuals
> Highlighting text on the page

Adjusting instruction for the gifted

> Raising the level of difficulty
> Moving up the levels of Bloom's taxonomy
> Accelerating the pace of teacher instruction
> Providing for independent interdisciplinary projects that enrich classroom content

Modifying instruction for the ESL student

> Encouraging students to translate English into their native languages for some key lesson
> activities or assignments
> Encouraging students to speak and write about their lives
> Pairing ESL students with bilingual students
> Using evocative words as an explicit focus of lessons

and Fahrenheit scales? How would you develop a number of lessons for this objective using different models of teaching? What factors might help you choose the most effective one for your students?

If time is short, you might choose direct instruction to present the material in a straightforward manner. However, if you need to reinforce the stages of the scientific method as well as teach this content, you may prefer to use one of the models of inquiry even though inquiry lessons take more classroom time. Maximum student participation and small-group social skill building, as one major concern at the beginning of the school year, might also lead you to consider models of inquiry.

Modifying Instruction for Students With Special Needs

Whether or not they have been formally identified as special education students, students with special instructional needs are found in every classroom. Concerned teachers want all students to flourish in their classrooms. When you have identified a particular difficulty a student is struggling with, reflect on ways you can **modify instruction** to ensure that the student will be successful. It may take considerable trial and error to find adjustments or interventions that provide the right support to promote a student's learning. While it is important to collaborate with special education teachers, your first steps will be to do your own experimentation. When you speak with special educators, they will ask what strategies you have already tried and the eventual outcomes. Once special educators understand which instructional modifications you have tried, they can better suggest additional ideas for you. How can teachers begin to address students' special instructional needs? How do teachers think about modifying their instruction?

Instructional modifications can be placed into categories that define the nature of the changes. Table 14.8 lists some examples of modifications in a number of different categories. Examples of adaptations for gifted students and English as a Second Language (ESL) students are also provided. Each of the models of teaching provides both opportunities and challenges as teachers modify instruction for students. Your creativity will be the most important factor in adapting your instruction so that all students in your classroom are learning.

Special education district offices often have checklists to assist teachers in choosing appropriate instructional modifications for their students. Teachers are regularly required to collect data for a formal child study if their interventions to address students' specific instructional needs have not been successful. To determine whether a child should be evaluated for special education services, teachers need to address the requirements in **Child Study Team** documentation. While the specifics of district documents may vary, they will be similar in many respects. Tables 14.9 and 14.10 show sample Child Study Team pages that teachers must complete before a

Table 14.9 Sample Child Study Team Documentation A

Student's Name _____ Date _____

Teacher's Name _____

Please provide two samples of student work in each of these areas and describe the student's strengths and weaknesses in each one.

Subject	Strengths	Weaknesses
Reading		
Writing		
Spelling		
Oral language		
Social studies		
Science		
Physical wellness		
Behavior		

Table 14.10 Sample Child Study Team Documentation B

Student's Name _____ Date _____

Teacher's Name _____

Learning difficulty	Tried this modification	For how long	Results
1.			
2.			
3.			
4.			
5.			
6.			
7.			
8.			

student can be evaluated for special services. Once a student has been evaluated formally and it has been determined that the child requires special education, an **Individualized Education Program (IEP)** will be developed. As long as special services of any kind are required, general education classroom teachers will be supplied with an IEP, a blueprint of the child's instructional needs.

Personnel

While it is true that many hands make light work, it is also true that too many cooks spoil the broth. The deliberative teacher must ensure that when there are several adults in the classroom, everyone's time is being used productively and meaningfully. As you are developing curriculum, whether you are planning a unit or a lesson, you need to take stock of everyone who will be involved in each learning experience.

In many schools, paraprofessionals are available for all or part of the day. Paraprofessionals' time at school may be devoted to working with a specific program or activity. For example, they may do individual math performance assessments with students, conduct writing conferences, or help facilitate small-group work. Inquire about the kind of experience in education your paraprofessional has had. Many school districts provide classes or workshops for their paraprofessionals. You may also find that your paraprofessional is enrolled in a teacher education program for full certification. This information will help you decide the kind of responsibilities you can assign. When you know exactly what you can expect from a paraprofessional in your classroom, you can begin to think creatively about how best to use his or her time with your students.

Many school districts also have a well-organized network of parent volunteers who spend regular time in elementary classrooms. Teachers generally decide how parent time will be spent, and you may find that you can request parents with a specific ability or interest. Your parent volunteers may be interested in a particular academic subject, such as math, and they would like to work with students who need more instructional support in that area.

When a learning experience is enhanced by a field trip or a guest speaker, consider ahead of time how the experience will support your lesson objectives. While many museums, nature centers, or corporations have materials already developed for students at various grade levels, that is not always the case. Often people who lead tours or activities at such places are willing to tailor their presentations to your specific learning goals if they are given time to prepare. Guest speakers will also find it helpful if you provide guidance and information about what your students already know, what your current objectives are, and where the class will be headed in lessons to come. Again, preparation is a key element in ensuring that your students get the most benefit from these experiences.

Resources

When you begin to plan for an instructional unit, it is wise to find out whether your school district requires every teacher in your grade level to use certain materials. For example, class sets or small-group sets of books are generally provided by school districts. Math and science materials and equipment are typically supplied by the school districts, as well. In some cases, developmentally appropriate math manipulatives and grade-level science equipment are organized into kits that are rotated from teacher to teacher at school. Consumable materials—those that can be used only once, such as chemical substances or dissection materials—are also supplied by the district. Depending on the resources of the school district, some consumables, such as workbooks, are purchased for each student. In districts with slender financial resources, students are not allowed to write in their workbooks because the books need to be used over a number of years. It is important that you find out how you are expected to use any resources given to you.

Teachers may also be given the freedom to choose their own materials when they create new instructional units. Some districts are able to give teachers a budget each year to purchase equipment, materials, or supplies not routinely provided by the district. You will learn how to project ahead of time what supplies are used every year in your class.

If you are preparing a unit for the first time, you will want to identify additional resources. Libraries are always a good place to start. The breadth of information you find in school and community libraries will help you develop curriculum that is significant, relevant to students' lives, and engaging. In addition to print sources, media centers may have videos and computer software that are appropriate for your students. Your college or university may have a curriculum library or instructional materials center that inservice teachers also use. Too often, teachers will visit a local teachers' store to see what instructional materials are commercially available. Choose these materials carefully. Commercially prepared instructional materials may provide you with worksheets or craft ideas related to your unit, but they cannot substitute for the intellectual and creative work you must do to develop lessons that meet your students' specific needs.

Community resources may also enrich your students' learning. Specialized libraries such as state historical libraries, nature preserves, museums, hospitals, power plants, stores, firehouses, courthouses, and other government organizations can provide excellent study trip experiences and can, in many cases, serve as the organizing focus of an instructional unit. Many of these institutions have prepared materials for various grade levels that can be sent directly to you. These institutions can be the site or focus for service learning projects, as well. For career days at every level of K–12 schooling, parents are frequently asked to talk about their professions and what their daily work life is like. Sometimes they are also able to schedule visits to their work locations so that your students can experience what their jobs are like.

Time is another resource in the classroom. In some cases, teachers are told how much time to spend on subjects. For example, in some states a minimum number of hours per day must be spent on particular subjects in the elementary grades, usually language arts and mathematics. Elementary teachers are generally responsible for planning how much time students spend each day on subjects such as science and social studies. They also plan how many weeks to spend on a given instructional unit. In these cases, teachers can make flexible decisions about the time to spend on any one lesson or unit on the basis of the progress of the students.

Secondary teachers, with a specific amount of time for each period, do not have the luxury of flexible time enjoyed by elementary teachers. The length of class periods in secondary schools is the same for all subjects, and the administration decides that length of time. Periods lasting 40 to 50 minutes are the norm in secondary schools. Some secondary schools are organized into **block scheduling**, in which fewer class periods are held each day, but each class meets for a longer amount of time. If you are a secondary teacher at a school that has recently changed to block scheduling, you will need to decide how you will reconfigure your course material over longer class periods.

All beginning teachers need time to develop the ability to project accurately how much time students will need in any one lesson. Even experienced teachers need to adjust themselves to the rhythms of each new class. Deliberative teachers, whether beginners or veterans, think carefully through each lesson or learning experience and forecast how much time might be needed for each stage, and this step becomes a regular component of their lesson planning. Keeping track of your timing during your lessons will help you adjust your teaching appropriately. The more experienced you become, the easier it will be for you to accurately forecast how much time your students will need for a given lesson or unit. In all circumstances, time is a resource in the classroom and should be considered carefully.

Assessment and Evaluation of Student Learning

As you read in Chapter 3, reflective teachers assess and analyze their students' achievement on a daily basis. Assessment occurs when teachers gather information indicating what their students have learned. Teachers reflect on their students' learning before, during, and after instruction. Reflection after instruction is critical to developing appropriate lessons for the next day or for modifying existing plans. General impressions of lessons cannot determine student achievement in ways that are helpful to teachers. Specific evidence of student learning is required. Data from well-designed in-class tasks and appropriate assessment tools will clearly demonstrate how well students have understood concepts or mastered skills. These data can come in many forms: written narratives, problem sets, interviews, and lab reports, among many others. You are already familiar with types of assessment—what you might use, when, and why.

Assessing and Evaluating
Teacher Effectiveness

Reflective teachers also review their own practice in the classroom, and they do so continually. While the primary focus of teacher reflection is on authentic student understanding, teachers also need to analyze how and to what extent their teaching behaviors have supported or hindered student achievement. As reflective teachers analyze their performance in the classroom, they will ask themselves questions that relate to components of every lesson. These are sample questions that reflective teachers ask themselves after a lesson:

1. Had I thoroughly planned for this lesson?

2. Did I choose an appropriate model of teaching for this lesson?

3. Was this lesson well paced?

4. Were my explanations and directions clear?

5. Did I model tasks both visually and verbally to accommodate different learning styles?

6. Would tactile or kinesthetic experiences have improved student learning?

7. Were the instructional modifications for my special-needs students on target?

8. Did I maximize student participation throughout the lesson?

9. Did I thoroughly check for student understanding during the lesson?

10. Did I provide assessment opportunities and present the assessment criteria clearly?

11. Did my transitions in and out of the lesson help or hinder momentum?

12. Could any classroom or behavior management problems have been handled more effectively?

13. Did this lesson have a satisfying closure?

As they analyze their teaching, reflective teachers will ask a follow-up question for each of the questions listed above, such as, How do I know that? or Why do I think that happened? or What is my evidence? These additional questions will help you examine your students' learning and your performance in greater depth.

Student-Centered Rationales for Curricular and Instructional Decisions

Professionals in every field need to be able to explain the rationales behind their decisions. In addition, professionals must be able to explain their decisions to a variety of people. For example, a surgeon would explain the nature of a surgical procedure in one way to a young patient's parents, but the vocabulary, level of detail, and manner would change significantly when explaining the same procedure to the child. As the doctor describes the procedure or specific technique to colleagues on the surgical team, the vocabulary, manner, and level of detail would be technical and much more sophisticated.

Teachers need to be able to explain their curricular and instructional choices to multiple audiences: parents, students, fellow teachers, administrators, and the general public. However, they may also have to defend their choices to other professionals and to parents who may disagree with those decisions. Therefore, an integral part of curriculum development at both the lesson level and the unit level is the ability to articulate your vision. Be ready to explain why each of your choices is appropriate on the basis of learning theory and student development, the state standards or benchmarks you are addressing, the specific demands of the content you are teaching, and your knowledge of individual students; and be ready to explain those choices to a variety of audiences. This brings us back to reflection and deliberation. When you have thought carefully about your goals in the classroom and have made decisions with specific purposes in mind, you will carry the professional rationale for your decisions with you into every teaching moment. To other knowledgeable and experienced educators, your choices will be evident in everything you say and do in your classroom.

Modifying Curriculum

Once you have developed an original unit and taught it to your students, you need to reflect on whether to **modify the curriculum** itself. Even if you will not be teaching the unit again for another year, it is wise to consider which aspects of the unit worked well, which you would modify next time and why, what needs to be added, and what needs to be discarded altogether. You must review the curriculum in the light of your students' success. You will have made notes throughout the unit addressing these questions. It is wise to review these notes once again after you have evaluated your students' final achievements in each unit.

Here are some of the questions you might ask yourself at this point:

1. Was the level of difficulty of each in-class task or project appropriate?

2. Should more or less time be spent on specific topics, lessons, or projects?

3. Would the students benefit from more hands-on time with any lessons?

4. Should the objectives in this unit be sequenced differently?

5. Were the assessments appropriate? Were they sufficiently engaging? Did they provide the kind of information needed to assess student learning?

6. Was there anything that should have been assessed but wasn't?

7. Were any lessons or experiences unnecessary or unhelpful?

You will find that some difficulties arise during a unit that can be attributed to the design of the unit itself, and that is to be expected. It takes some time to polish an instructional unit. After you have taught a unit for the very first time, you will most likely make several significant changes. After that, you will probably continue to refine instructional units for as long as you teach them. You will find much satisfaction designing and redesigning the units you develop on your own. Over time, this process of continual revision will improve your initial efforts in developing original curriculum.

Summary

Curriculum and instruction concerns are a primary focus of our work as teachers. We must continually balance our students' needs, the content standards and benchmarks we must address, and the many instructional choices we make to ensure our students' understanding. As we consider how to accomplish all this, we are developing curriculum. If the curriculum we are required to teach is not completely original, we tailor it as much as we can to fit the students in our classrooms. Once we know the scope of the curriculum in each subject in our grade level, we need to make decisions as to what learning experiences will be best for our students. Our instruction can be organized in single-subject or interdisciplinary units. The lessons we develop may be teacher-directed or student-centered, small group or full group, traditionally conceived or discovery-based.

Long-term and daily lesson objectives provide an itinerary for each unit. Strong and precise verbs structure each lesson and indicate how student achievement will be assessed. In addition to strong verbs, well-written objectives state the conditions under which the objective will be met and the criteria for acceptable student performance.

As teachers, one of our most important tasks is to provide a professional, relevant, and clear rationale for each of the curricular and instructional decisions we make in our classrooms. Our students and their parents, our administrators, and our fellow teachers need to see the wisdom in the choices we make in our classrooms.

We must ask a significant number of reflective questions as we prepare to teach an instructional unit, after we have taught each lesson, and after the unit has been completed. These questions will become internalized the more we work as curriculum developers and teachers. Our first consideration will always be the success of each student. If students did not fare as well as we would have liked, we need to determine how we could have improved the curriculum, changed our instruction, and designed our assessment. If students have done uniformly well, we need to analyze which factors we believe contributed to their success.

While curriculum development is demanding for novice and seasoned teachers alike, the process is also rewarding. Working in collaboration with a team of teachers can both lighten the load and enliven the process. Relying on one another's strengths and learning from one another provide daily professional development for every teacher.

Student Study Site

The Companion Web site for *Models of Teaching: Connecting Student Learning With Standards*

www.sagepub.com/dellioliostudy

Visit the Web-based student study site to enhance your understanding of the book content and discover additional resources that will take your learning one step further. You can enhance your understanding by using the comprehensive Study Guide, which includes chapter learning objectives, flash cards, practice tests, and more. You'll find special features, such as the links to standards from U.S. States and associated activities, Learning from Journal Articles, Field Experience worksheets, Learning from Case Studies, and PRAXIS resources.

References

Alleman, J., & Brophy, J. (1991). A caveat: Curriculum integration isn't always a good idea. *Educational Leadership, 49*(2), 66.

Bloom, B. (1956). *The taxonomy of educational objectives, handbook 1: The cognitive domain.* New York: Addison Wesley.

Bruner, J. (2004). *Toward a theory of instruction.* Cambridge, MA: Harvard University Press.

Campbell, D. S., & Caswell, H. L. (1935). *Curriculum development.* New York: American Book.

Ellis, A., & Fouts, J. (1996). *Research on educational innovations.* Princeton Junction, NJ: Eye on Education.

Gardner, H. (1999). *The disciplined mind.* New York: Simon & Schuster.

Good, C. V. (1973). *Dictionary of education* (3rd ed.). New York: McGraw-Hill.

Guskey, T. (2000). *Evaluating professional development.* Thousand Oaks, CA: Corwin.

Harrow, A. (1972). *A taxonomy of the psychomotor domain: A guide for developing behavioral objectives.* White Plains, NY: Longman.

Hayes-Jacobs, H. (1989). *Interdisciplinary curriculum: Design and implementation.* Reston, VA: Association for Supervision and Curriculum Development.

International Reading Association. (2003). *Standards for reading professionals 2003: A reference for the preparation of educators in the U.S.* (Rev. ed.). Newark, DE: International Reading Association.

Krathwohl, D., Bloom, B. S., & Masia, B. B. (1964). *A taxonomy of educational objectives: The classification of educational goals: handbook 2: Affective domain.* White Plains, NY: Longman.

Lortie, D. (1975). *Schoolteacher: A sociological study with a new preface.* Chicago: University of Chicago Press.

Michigan Department of Education. (1996). *Michigan curriculum framework.* Lansing: Author.

Merriam-Webster OnLine. (2005). *Merriam-Webster's words of the year 2005.* Retrieved September 6, 2006, from http://www.merriam-webster.com/info/05words.htm

National Council of Teachers of Mathematics. (2003). *Principles and standards for school mathematics* (3rd ed.). Reston, VA: Author.

O'Neil, J. (2005). *Curriculum: A comprehensive introduction.* New York: Harper Collins.

Passow, H. Class notes, fall 1987, Teachers College, Columbia University. Modified by J. M. Dell'Olio, fall 1995.

Popham, J. (2001). *The truth about testing*. Alexandria, VA: Association for Supervision and Curriculum Development.

Rowling, J. K. (1998). *Harry Potter and the sorcerer's stone*. New York: Arthur A. Levine Books.

Rowling, J. K. (1999a). *Harry Potter and the chamber of secrets*. New York: Arthur A. Levine Books.

Rowling, J. K. (1999b). *Harry Potter and the prisoner of Azkaban*. New York: Arthur A. Levine Books.

Rowling, J. K. (2000). *Harry Potter and the goblet of fire*. New York: Arthur A. Levine Books.

Smith, J., Smith, L., & DeLisi, R. (2001). *Natural classroom assessment: Designing seamless instruction and assessment*. Thousand Oaks, CA: Corwin.

Taba, H. (1962). *Curriculum development: Theory and practice*. New York: Harcourt Brace.

Tanner, D., & Tanner, L. (2006). *Curriculum development: Theory into practice* (4th ed.). New York: Prentice Hall.

Tyler, R. (1949). *Principles of curriculum and instruction*. Chicago: University of Chicago Press.

Wiggins, G., & McTighe, J. (1998). *Understanding by design*. Alexandria, VA: Association for Supervision and Curriculum Development.

Appendix:
Purposes of Inquiry-Based Learning

Inquiry-Based Learning experiences can be categorized as having a number of purposes in the classroom. In their extensive discussions of inquiry in science, Carin, Bass, and Contant (2004) characterize the inquiry model as providing students with opportunities to describe, classify, and explain what they have learned about the world. In every state curriculum document, you will find that students are asked to describe, classify, and explain in most areas of the curriculum—including the visual and performing arts and physical education. Sustained investigations that continue over time may include inquiry questions from each of these categories. These inquiry experiences may or may not be structured using the scientific method.

Descriptive Learning Experiences

Descriptive inquiries ask students to observe and record properties of a subject under investigation and then describe those properties in objective terms. For example, in many curriculum documents, high school students are asked to describe the physical characteristics of different kinds of cells based on observations with microscopes. Middle school students are asked to describe common physical characteristics of materials when they are affected by evaporation, condensation, thermal expansion, and contraction. Early elementary students are asked to describe physical properties of butterflies at different stages of their life cycles. These lessons focus on the inquiry processes of observation and description in addition to their specific content (cell characteristics, reactions of matter, and stages of a life cycle). Each of these inquiry tasks provides students with the opportunity to observe and record important information, some of which may be needed for subsequent inquiry. Descriptive inquiry tasks generally require students to work at the knowledge level of Bloom's taxonomy.

These are the kinds of questions that structure descriptive inquiries:

How do these things look?

How do these things feel?

How do these things move?

How do these things respond to _____?

Classificatory Inquiry-Based Experiences

When we ask students to categorize items, materials, actions, or events, we are moving them beyond descriptive and into classificatory inquiry. **Classificatory inquiry** requires students to separate items into groups that share the same characteristics, the same critical attributes. This ability to categorize is one of the main

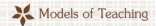

indicators of intelligence in humans. Classrooms provide many opportunities for students to sort items into groups, then name the attributes they share. Like descriptive inquiry experiences, classificatory inquiry is possible in most areas of the curriculum and in every grade level. During classificatory inquiries, students may be working at the application, analysis, or evaluation levels of Bloom's taxonomy.

Classificatory inquiry can be divided into two main categories. Activities in the first category require students to categorize something unfamiliar according to specific criteria set beforehand. Specific criteria will be given directly by the teacher. For example, students may be asked to categorize unidentified single cells as either plant or animal cells after having studied the characteristics of both types of cell. Or students may be asked to categorize unfamiliar foods as either fruits or vegetables based on the characteristics of each. This kind of classifying is a convergent activity, which means that the inquiry has correct answers, and the teacher knows them beforehand.

The second kind of classificatory inquiry is asking students to not only categorize but also develop their own criteria for the categorization. One familiar early-childhood example is asking students to sort a large number of buttons in any way they choose and to state the criteria for their sorting. Teachers sometimes ask their students to sort the buttons a second time, this time according to new criteria. Younger students may limit their sorting to color, size, shape, or personal preference ("These are the ones I like, and these are the ones I don't"). Asked to complete the same categorization task, older students might add specific design features, such as the presence of ridges on the edge of the button; number of button holes; materials the buttons are made from; function, such as buttons for indoor or outdoor clothing; or plain and fancy buttons. Unlike the majority of younger students, older students are able to develop multiple criteria for each button—buttons that are small, not round, and have only two holes, for example. When they perform an open-ended inquiry task such as this, students are engaging in divergent thinking, and they can respond with many different answers.

These are the kinds of questions that structure classificatory inquiries:

In what ways are these items the same?

In what ways are these items different?

What attributes do they have in common?

In what categories might you place the 25 items you have at your tables?

Explanatory Inquiry-Based Learning Experiences

The point of explanatory Inquiry-Based Learning experiences is to explain a phenomenon, a concept, or a process. Other explanatory inquiries may result in solving problems or analyzing cause-and-effect relationships. In state and district curriculum documents, you will find benchmarks in every content area that ask students to explain, organize and analyze, conduct an investigation, explore, or gather and analyze, among others. Most of these benchmarks are Inquiry-Based Learning experiences by their very nature. Explanatory inquiry tasks will also provide students with opportunities to work at Bloom's application, analysis, and evaluation levels.

Explanatory inquiries can be hands-on experimentation or inquiries that are dependent on traditional or electronic research skills. Either way, if your primary goal is to reinforce students' abilities to think systematically when they encounter problems, then using the scientific method to structure students' explanatory inquiry experiences will be as important as the specific content they will learn. In the second case study in Chapter 11, explanatory inquiry was structured and illustrated around the question, Why do cities in different parts of the world have similar temperatures? As a result of their inquiry experiences, Mrs. Munoa's students were able to answer that question.

These are the kinds of questions that structure explanatory inquiries:

What materials did you use?

What happened when _____?

When you tried a second time, what were your results?

What are the relationships between _____?

What will you try next and why?

Alternative Designs for Inquiry-Based Learning Experiences

The Inquiry-Based Learning model comprises a wide variety of specific instructional designs that teachers must consider: closed, open, guided, and unguided.

Closed Inquiry

Closed inquiries usually take only one or two class periods to complete. In a **closed inquiry**, teachers provide all the research materials and information required for the students to be successful. The reason is that the teacher already knows the outcome of a closed inquiry. One purpose of closed inquiries is for students to discover or develop certain concepts and not others. Another purpose of a closed inquiry is to provide focused practice of specific intellectual skills. Closed inquiries are most successful when the problem or situation that is the centerpiece of the inquiry is of intrinsic value or interest to students. Mr. Zwart's science lesson in Case Study 11.1 is an example of each of these attributes of closed inquiry. He has set up all the materials his students need for the experiment, he wants the students to discover properties of density they have not yet explored, and he wants to provide them another opportunity to experience each stage of the scientific method. The soda can experiment sparked the students' interest in his lesson.

Open Inquiry

The content of open inquiries may be chosen by the student or by the teacher. As with closed inquiries, students respond best in open inquiries when they are investigating a meaningful problem. In an open inquiry, students design their own investigations and find their own research materials. The students' design of their investigations and search for appropriate information and materials are seen as integral parts of the inquiry experience. Because students need to find their own sources of data and other information, open inquiries generally last for an extended time. Open inquiries are appropriate across the curriculum, but they are especially effective in math, science, and social studies. A common example of open inquiry is a science fair project.

Guided Inquiry

The difference between guided and unguided inquiry focuses on the role of questioning throughout the course of the inquiry. As in closed inquiries, the teacher sets the agenda for guided inquiries by asking a specific question at the beginning of the experience. At various stages of the guided inquiry, teachers will introduce follow-up questions, prepared in advance, to respond to students' successive discoveries. The teacher guides students through the experience directly by means of specifically stated and sequenced questions. In guided inquiry, the teacher remains in control of the concepts discovered by the students. Students are not encouraged to ask their own questions arising from their thoughts and experiences during a guided inquiry. Mr. Zwart's experiment is also an example of guided inquiry. After his students' initial exploration and discussion, he raises the question of adding corn oil to the water in the aquarium. He asks them whether, under these new circumstances, they think the two different cans of soda will behave differently when they are immersed in the aquarium. He had already chosen the next stage of the experiment.

Unguided Inquiry

Unguided inquiries begin very much like guided inquiries. In unguided experiences, teachers are responsible for asking the first question, providing materials for students to find their own answers, and organizing the initial processes in the inquiry. However, in unguided inquiry, the role of the teacher is to encourage students to formulate their own questions on the basis of their initial experiences. Students are free to choose the direction of their inquiry, decide what additional materials they may need, and design their subsequent investigations. At a later stage of an unguided inquiry, individual students or small groups may have moved in different directions as a result of their unique ways of approaching the same problem. For example, a series of student-directed pendulum experiments incorporating different variables may result from an initially unguided inquiry experience. The overall processes of unguided inquiry can make for an exciting, diversified experience for teachers, as well as for their students. The scientific method is always embedded in unguided inquiry, and it resembles the way scientists themselves work in their laboratories.

Reference

Carin, A. A., Bass, J., & Contant, T. L. (2004). *Teaching science as inquiry*. New York: Prentice Hall.

Glossary

Academic rationalism: Philosophy of curriculum and instruction that states that the purpose of schooling is to transmit the major concepts, truths, and values of a society to students. The academic rationalist curriculum consists of the classical canon found in the Great Books. Traditional teacher-centered instruction and the Socratic method are associated with academic rationalism.

Active teaching: Traditional instruction characterized by continual teacher-student interaction throughout a lesson.

Adequate yearly progress (AYP): A required annual publication by each state, detailing the academic achievement of its K–12 students. This requirement is part of the No Child Left Behind Act. Schools that do not achieve AYP can be sanctioned in a variety of ways.

Advance Organizer: Model that provides a scaffold that allows students to develop an understanding of the structure behind a subject or content area—the hierarchy. It is not an outline or a summary but rather introduces students to this structure at a level of abstraction, generality, and inclusiveness that frames the subject—as noted by David Ausubel, who developed it. It is a versatile model for helping students understand and recall information by seeing how it fits into the larger structure of the subject.

Affective domain: Students' feelings, beliefs, attitudes, personal value systems, and levels of self-esteem.

Automatic level: Level of learning at which one can perform a task without the need to think through the process.

Back-to-basics: Description of a curriculum or school that focuses on basic skills in literacy, numeracy, and traditional organization of the natural sciences and social studies. Traditional instruction is generally associated with back-to-basics curriculum or schools.

Baseline skill: One of the skills necessary for students to be successful in a lesson or unit. Baseline skills are similar to entry-level skills.

Behavioral objective: Instructional objective written using strong and specific verbs to describe what can be seen when a student attains it. Behavioral objectives are easily assessed.

Behaviorist learning theory: Theory that states learning is a behavioral change that occurs as a result of external events.

Benchmark: "A specific statement of what all students should know and be able to do at a specified time in their schooling. Benchmarks are used to measure a student's

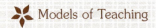
progress toward meeting the standard" (Yates, 2004, p. 13; see Chapter 1 References). In some curriculum frameworks, these are referred to as indicators, performance standards (a term we use differently in this text), and learning expectations.

Block scheduling: Secondary school extended instructional periods with fewer classes each day.

Canon: Collection of great works of literature in the arts, humanities, natural sciences, and social sciences.

Categorization: To place objects or ideas in like sets according to their common attributes or characteristics.

Child Study Team: Team comprising teachers, special education staff, counselors, administrators, and parents that meets to discuss the instructional challenges or behavior issues of a child. Teachers need to provide significant documentation describing the student's particular difficulties and what measures teachers have taken to address those difficulties in the classroom.

Clarifying: A central process of Reciprocal Teaching that involves pausing while reading to create understanding of a range of topics and issues, from checking a word or phrase that doesn't make sense to attempting to make sense of missing information in a passage. Teachers and students work together to develop and employ helpful strategies.

Classificatory inquiry: Students separate items into groups that share the same characteristics. Classificatory inquiry may require categorizing something unfamiliar into categories with criteria specifically determined beforehand or may require categorizing something according to self-determined criteria.

Closed inquiry: Inquiry whose outcome is known beforehand by the teacher. In a closed inquiry, the teacher provides all necessary materials.

Closure: Final step in the Direct Instruction model; briefly summarizes the content of the lesson and brings the lesson to a close. Students should take an active part in this step.

Cognitive domain: The range of intellectual components of human experience, from lower-level skills (recall and comprehension) to higher-level skills (application, analysis, synthesis, and evaluation).

Cognitive processing: Philosophy of curriculum and instruction that states that the purpose of schooling is to develop students' higher-order critical thinking and problem-solving skills. Inquiry-based instructional strategies are associated with the cognitive processing philosophy.

Comparative advance organizer: Advance organizer used when the subject to be learned is relatively familiar to the learners. It allows the learner to distinguish between two familiar concepts or subjects.

Competency-based teacher education: Teacher education movement in the 1970s and 1980s that focused on mastery of specific teaching skills.

Compressed conflict: A description using two words that appear to be in opposition to each other (e.g., working poor); part of the Synectics model of teaching.

Concept Attainment: Lessons promote students' cognitive skills in naming a concept based on the attributes and characteristics of a set.

Conceptual distance: The mental space between an individual and a subject that allows the individual to look at something in a new way. Its creation is an important element of the Synectics model.

Conditions: Circumstances under which students will demonstrate mastery of an instructional objective (e.g., *Given the coordinates of ten major U.S. cities,* the learner will identify each city" or *While listening to a tape-recorded lecture,* the learner will take notes using the formal outline structure").

Content standard: Describes "what students should know and/or be able to do within a particular discipline" (Kendall, Ryan, & Richardson, 2005, p. 1; see Chapter 1 References). Content standards provide general statements that divide the subject into manageable parts. In some curriculum frameworks, content standards are referred to as expectations, goals, or learning results.

Contextual knowledge: Knowledge that is dependent on context. For example, knowing how to cut and paste paper involves procedural knowledge in the use of a pair of scissors and application of glue, but doing so to create a mosaic requires understanding of the context.

Continuum: A list of daily lesson objectives, sequenced from the least difficult to the long-term objective.

Cooperative learning: An alternative to independent learning or competition in classrooms. In cooperative learning groups, students work together to attain a shared goal. In cooperative learning, the contribution of each member is essential to the success of the group.

Cooperative learning structures: Specific lesson or activity designs that have students working in pairs or small groups. Cooperative learning structures can be categorized for different purposes: class building, team building, concept development, concept mastery, or communication. Some cooperative learning structures, such as Jigsaw, are multidimensional and serve several purposes.

Criteria: Statement of quantity or quality that students must meet for a task to be successfully completed (e.g., "The learner will multiply any two 4-digit numbers with 90% accuracy" or "The learner will sequence five events as they appeared in a newspaper article").

Criterion-referenced test: Type of test that does not compare test takers to a norm; used to determine how well an individual performs in specified skills or understanding of a particular content. Theoretically, all test takers can receive a perfect score on the test. Many teacher-constructed exams would fit this definition.

Critical attributes: Characteristics that distinguish one thing from another.

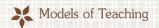

Cross-categorize: To place objects or ideas in more than one category. or ideas in more than one category.

Culminating event: Hands-on experience or activity used to bring closure to an instructional unit.

Cultural literacy: Knowledge about the shared culture of a nation; historical and contemporary national and world events; and primary concepts in the arts, humanities, and natural and social sciences.

Curriculum: The content taught in any educational institution.

Curriculum articulation: The connection of the grade-level curriculum from one year to the next.

Curriculum as technology: Philosophy of curriculum and instruction that espouses the organization of content in increments leading to a long-term objective. This philosophy advocates traditional teaching methodology, such as Direct Instruction.

Curriculum framework: Document designed to help local school districts and schools as they align their own curriculums and assessments with state mandates. It contains content standards and benchmarks for each area of the school curriculum. State-mandated annual assessments are based on the contents of these documents.

Curriculum map: Document that outlines what instructional units will be taught in each grade level and when they will be taught.

Daily lesson objective: What students will know or be able to do at the end of an instructional period.

Declarative knowledge: Information someone needs in order to understand a particular subject. For example, in a high school anatomy course, students may need to know the names of bones in the human body.

Descriptive inquiry: Inquiry learning in which students observe and record properties of a subject and describe it in objective terms.

Developmentally appropriate: Tasks or activities at a level at which the learner can successfully accomplish them with some assistance from a teacher or other adult.

Differentiated instruction: Instruction in a lesson or unit that is adjusted to meet the needs of particular students. Differentiation may include adjustments in pacing, level of difficulty, attention to learning styles, or student interests.

Direct analogy: In the Synectics model, the comparison of two unlike things.

Direct Instruction: Model of a traditional teacher-directed lesson structured as a series of sequenced steps.

Discovery learning: Term coined by Jerome Bruner to describe learning experiences in which students discover principles rather than being taught those principles directly.

Distributed practice: Practice spaced over time to retain students' skill abilities and content knowledge at the mastery level.

Diversity: Describes how students may be different from one another. Students represent different genders; cultures or ethnicities; religions; learning styles; intelligences; interests; academic strengths or needs; and special needs that are cognitive, emotional, or physical.

Document analysis: Activity in which students analyze the meaning and significance of primary sources such as letters, speeches, newspaper articles, or government documents.

Educational priorities: Carl Rogers's list of conditions that provide an optimum classroom climate for learning. Rogers's educational priorities focus on the emotional well-being of students, their individuality, and their natural interests in learning.

Elementary and Secondary Education Act: See *No Child Left Behind Act.*

Entry-level skill: One of the skills that students have mastered when they begin an instructional unit. Students' learning can be measured from their entry-level skill to the last objective they have mastered on a continuum of skills.

Essential questions: Questions developed for an instructional unit that provide direction for the unit, motivate the students, and serve as its conceptual structure.

Exemplars: Examples of things belonging in particular category.

Expert groups: One of two groups used in a Jigsaw lesson. Expert-group members work with one another to master content or skills and then teach the content or skills to their home-group members.

Explanatory inquiry: Part of Inquiry-Based Learning in which students explain a phenomenon, concept, or process or analyze a cause-and-effect relationship.

Explicit teaching: Alternate term for *Direct Instruction.*

Expository advance organizer: Type of Advance Organizer used when the subject to be learned is relatively unfamiliar to the learners.

Face-to-face interaction: One of David and Roger Johnson's elements of cooperative learning. Face-to-face interaction means that students work directly with one another on their shared task.

Focus activity: Beginning step in a Direct Instruction lesson. Focus activities catch students' attention and help them make the transition from the previous lesson or activity into the new lesson.

Formal formative assessment: Assessment such as weekly quizzes and an observation checklist; used for gathering information about student learning during instruction.

Formative assessment: Assessment integrated with instruction to provide a feedback loop that allows teaching and learning experiences to be modified as needed. In short, they guide instruction as it is occurring. Frequent quizzes, observation checklists, and questioning are common tools of formative assessment.

Generalization: Statements that describe a relationship between or among two or more concepts. Generalizations provide us with information about the world or human experiences in the world that are generally said to be true. "Violence and war are not effective solutions to human problems" and "People carry cultural traditions from their old country when they immigrate to a new country" are examples of generalization.

Generating questions: Process in the Reciprocal Teaching model in which the teacher or students read a section of text and then form questions to be answered by group members. When developing the questions, learners rely on background information or the information in the text itself.

Grade-level indicators: Often attached to benchmarks, these guides state when students should reach various standards. In some documents they are grade specific (K, 1, 2, etc.), while in others they consist of a range (K–3, 4–6, etc.).

Group processing: One of David and Roger Johnson's elements of cooperative learning. Group processing is what occurs when teachers provide time for cooperative learning groups to discuss with one another how effectively they functioned as a group. Groups are asked to identify how they worked well together and what they can improve next time.

Guided inquiry: Process in which teachers guide students through an inquiry experience by asking a specific question and predetermined follow-up questions. As in closed inquiries, the outcome of a guided inquiry is known by the teacher in advance.

Guided practice: Stage of the Direct Instruction model in which teachers can assess individual students' mastery of the content or skill of the lesson. Guided practice is done alone and not with partners or in small groups. Teachers will check students' guided practice before allowing them to continue to the independent practice stage.

Heterogeneous grouping: Composing groups of students with different genders, cultures, ethnicities, ability levels, and other aspects of diversity.

Hierarchy of needs: Abraham Maslow's pyramid of human needs. Deficit needs are those that concern safety, belonging, and self-esteem; being needs are those that promote an individual's self-actualization. Maslow believed that deficit needs must be met for being needs to thrive.

Home groups: One of two groups used in a Jigsaw lesson. Home groups comprise students from each expert group. During home-group time, students teach one another what they have learned in their expert group.

Independent practice: Stage of the Direct Instruction model in which students have demonstrated mastery of the content or skill to be learned and work without teacher supervision.

Individual accountability: One of David and Roger Johnson's elements of cooperative learning. Individual accountability means that students in cooperative groups will be assessed or evaluated on what they have learned from one another.

Individualized Education Program (IEP): Individualized program revised each year for special needs students that states annual academic or behavioral goals or both. IEPs are developed each year by special education teachers, general education teachers, support staff, and parents.

Inductive teaching models: Models of teaching in which students observe, analyze, and evaluate data to arrive at conclusions. Examples of inductive models of teaching include Concept Attainment (Jerome Bruner), the basic Inductive Model (Hilda Taba), and inquiry approaches to learning.

Inductive thinking: Students' thinking when they are involved in inquiry experiences and discovery learning. Inductive thinking is required when students are asked to hypothesize, perform an experiment, observe, record data, and then communicate their data. Working from their specific experimental outcomes, students are asked to make generalizations about the meaning and applicability of their results.

Informal formative assessment: Assessment such as asking students questions when discussing a story or topic or carefully observing student behaviors and responses to set tasks. Attentive teachers use these opportunities to analyze and adjust their teaching, as well as other factors in the learning environment, to facilitate student understanding.

Information processing theory: A theoretical perspective in which learning and memory can be thought of metaphorically as a computer. Among its most prominent contributions are models of human memory. In such models, all information begins in short-term memory. Some of it moves into working memory, and very small amounts are then moved into long-term memory through a variety of processes.

Initiating event: Lesson or learning experience that begins an instructional unit. Initiating events should motivate students and provide a preview of the content of the unit.

Inquiry-Based Learning: Learning experiences characterized by a question to be answered through experimentation and analysis.

Instruction: The way teachers present lesson content. Instruction may be teacher-directed, inquiry-based, full-group, small-group, individualized, or provided through print media, technology, or other means.

Instructional objective: Statement of the teacher's goal for students' achievement by the end of the lesson.

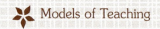

Instructional unit: Long-term series of sequenced lessons about one topic. Units may be single subject or interdisciplinary.

Instructivist teaching: Model of a traditional teacher-directed lesson structured as a series of sequenced steps; same as Direct Instruction.

Interactive teaching: Alternate term for *Direct Instruction*.

Interdisciplinary unit: Instructional unit that integrates two or more subjects.

Interpersonal intelligence: Students' ability to interact well with others in social and work settings.

Intrapersonal intelligence: Students' ability to understand themselves, their own motivations, and personal values.

Jigsaw: In a heterogeneous group, each student contributes a unique component of the task at hand.

Intrapersonal intelligence: Students' ability to understand themselves, their own motivations, and personal values.

Lifelong-learning standard: Skills and processes used in a variety of subject areas. For example, being a critical thinker is important in many school subjects, such as math, history, reading, and science.

Locus of control expectancy: Students' belief that they are in a position to influence what happens to them in a positive way.

Long-term memory: Memory that holds one's permanent store of knowledge.

Long-term objective: Statement that describes what students will know or be able to do at the end of an instructional unit or other extended time.

Maieutic teaching: The Socratic method. Maieutic teaching consists of asking students a series of questions to elicit understanding, as opposed to directly instructing them.

Manipulative: A hands-on item that can be used as students are building concepts. Manipulatives are typically used in math class at the elementary level, although their value extends across the curriculum, as well as the grade levels.

Mass practice: Many opportunities for practice in a short amount of time. Mass practice is given after independent practice in a Direct Instruction lesson to ensure students' mastery and overlearning of content knowledge and skills.

Mastery learning: Instructional approach that requires students to master one performance objective before moving on to the next objective in a continuum.

Media specialists: Teachers at school sites in charge of computer labs and other forms of technology centers.

Metacognition: The ability to think about our own thinking processes.

Metacognitive skills: The skills involved in thinking about one's own thinking as one reads and processes information. These skills might include realizing that a sentence does not make sense and rereading it for understanding, recognizing that a word is unknown and actively using context clues to define it, and so on.

Modeling: Teacher action in a Direct Instruction lesson that demonstrates skills and explains procedures to students in a variety of ways.

Modify curriculum: Change the content or content organization to better meet student need.

Modify instruction: Change the style, design, pacing, or other aspects of instruction to better meet student need.

Moral dilemmas: Situations that require action but in which no choice is unambiguously right. Lawrence Kohlberg used moral dilemmas to evaluate moral reasoning according to stages of moral development.

No Child Left Behind Act of 2001: Common name given to the reauthorization of the Elementary and Secondary Education Act. This act requires each state to set standards for what children should know and learn in school and to measure their achievement on an annual basis. For more information, visit www.ed.gov/nclb.

Nonexemplars: In the Concept Attainment model, examples of things that do not belong in a particular category.

Norm-referenced test: Type of test that allows for comparisons between the test taker and a sample of students—the "norm." Individual student scores can be compared to those of others who took the test, and scores can be reported as percentiles. For example, a percentile score of 90 means that a student scored better than 90% of those in the sampling group. The higher the percentile score, the better the student performed against the norm.

Open classroom: Classrooms where student interest generates curriculums. Open classrooms typically employ small-group and individualized instruction. Open classrooms are arranged to provide and promote movement and frequently are organized into learning centers.

Open inquiry: Inquiry in which the content may be chosen by the teacher or by the students. Students will design their own experiments, identify their own materials, and identify sources of data and information. Open inquiries generally take place over an extended time. One example of an open inquiry is a science fair project.

Overlearning: Describes students' ability to perform a task beyond the point of forgetting the skill. Overlearning can help in the transfer of skills from one context to another.

Paideia: Education to promote cultural development. Mortimer Adler's Paideia Program curriculum centers on the Great Books. Instruction in Paideia schools is primarily didactic (traditional) and maieutic (through questioning).

Performance indicators: Specific long-term behavioral objectives that describe what students will demonstrate as they meet each standard of the National Educational Technology Standards for Students.

Performance objective: Statement that describes what students will know or be able to do at the end of a lesson. Performance objectives are sometimes referred to as behavioral objectives.

Performance standard: "Describes the levels of student performance in respect to the knowledge or skill described in a single benchmark or a set of closely related benchmarks" (Kendall, 2001, p. 3; see Chapter 1 References).

Performance verbs: Strong verbs that state clearly what students will be doing in a lesson to demonstrate understanding of lesson or unit content.

Personal analogy: Identification with an object at an emotional or empathic level; developed as part of the Synectics model of teaching.

Positive interdependence: One of David and Roger Johnson's elements of cooperative learning. Positive interdependence means that each student's contribution is important to the success of the group. To ensure interdependence, teachers sometimes assign each group member a specific role, such as recorder, timekeeper, reader, encourager, or summarizer.

Positive reinforcement: Praise for correct answers or appropriate behavior. Positive reinforcement strengthens students' behavior that precedes it and makes that positive behavior more likely to occur again.

Posttest: Test given at the end of an instructional unit and used to assess learning. Posttests are written in tandem with pretests so that student achievement from the beginning of the unit to the end of the unit can be assessed accurately.

Potpourri effect: Possible result of a poorly designed interdisciplinary unit. Connections among disciplines are weak when the unit is developed; there is little conceptual coherence in the content organization; and as a result, student learning is haphazard.

Practice schedule: Regular practice so that students can master and retain content and skills. Guided and independent practices are placed after checking for understanding in Direct Instruction lessons to help students achieve instructional objectives. Mass and distributed practice help ensure mastery and retention of knowledge.

Presenting content: Step in the Direct Instruction model that refers to the material being taught in the lesson. Content is the "what" that students will be learning during the lesson.

Pretest: Test given prior to the beginning of an instructional unit to assess what students know and can do. Pretests are written in tandem with posttests so that student achievement at the end of the unit can be assessed accurately.

Problem-based learning: Learning experience that centers on an authentic problem to be solved. Problem-based learning can take place across the curriculum.

Procedural knowledge: Describes the "skills and processes important to a given content area" (Kendall & Marzano, 2000, p. 11; see Chapter 1 References). For example, in mathematics a student would have to know how to use a protractor to measure angles.

Progressive education: Movement in U.S. education beginning in the late 19th century that centered on child development, teaching the ideals of democratic citizenship, self-directed learning, and problem solving.

Providing the rationale: Third step in a Direct Instruction lesson, when teachers tell students the importance of the content or skill they will be learning. Rationale statements should describe the relevance of the material for students. Stating the objective and the rationale are often done at the same time in a Direct Instruction lesson, generally after the focus activity.

Psychomotor domain: Fine or gross motor abilities or skills.

Question-Answer Relationship (QAR): Model of teaching developed by Taffy Raphael. This model can be used for content area reading or narrative text. It is useful for helping students find the relationship between questions and answers, as well as giving them the language to describe the relationships.

Reciprocal Teaching: Model for improving reading comprehension and for helping learners develop comprehension-monitoring skills. In Reciprocal Teaching, students and teachers ultimately exchange roles as they generate questions, clarify information, make predictions, and summarize. It was developed by Annemarie Palincsar and Ann Brown.

Rehearsal: Opportunities in a Direct Instruction lesson for students to work with material in a variety of ways. Content rehearsal takes place publicly during checking for understanding, with the teacher's supervision during guided practice, and without teacher supervision during independent practice.

Role Playing: Students act out various possible solutions to social problems.

Scaffolding: A central process of the constructivist view of learning. It may be thought of metaphorically as the scaffold that surrounds and supports a building under construction. As the structure becomes capable of supporting itself, the scaffolding is carefully removed. Similarly, as learners engage with a new concept, teachers provide support and then remove the support as it is no longer needed.

Scientific method: An inductive process in which students state a question; generate a hypothesis; observe, record, and analyze data; and then communicate the significance of their findings to others.

Self-actualization: Abraham Maslow's term for fulfilling one's human potential.

Short-term memory: Memory that holds a limited amount of information for 20 to 30 seconds.

Signaling: The variety of ways in a Direct Instruction lesson that students can show their answers to a problem. Signals can be given through gestures, signs, or actions.

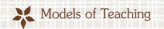

Single-subject unit: Instructional unit that focuses on one content area (e.g., language arts, math, or science).

Smart Board: Electronic interactive white board with specialized software and on-line applications.

Social reconstructionism: Philosophy of curriculum and instruction that espouses education to promote social change. Social reconstructionists view the teacher as a social change agent. One goal of social reconstructionism is to raise students' awareness of social problems.

Social skills: One of David and Roger Johnson's elements of cooperative learning. Students must possess social skills to be effective members in cooperative learning groups. Cooperative tasks may require specific social skills for the groups to work effectively. Social skills range from foundational, such as calling group members by name, to more sophisticated, such as critiquing ideas but not individuals. Typically, social skills must be taught directly before they will be used in a small-group task.

Standardized test: Type of test that has a specified procedure. Typically, teachers or other test administrators have a manual or other guide that stipulates exactly how the test must be administered, including timing, directions to be read, which materials can be used, and how the testing situation must be organized. Common examples of this type of test would include the SAT and the ACT. Nearly all state-mandated tests are standardized. This ensures that all test takers receive the same directions and testing conditions.

Standards-based reform movement: An educational reform that began with the publication in 1983 of *A Nation at Risk*, which criticized the state of education in the United States and called for changes. The goal of standards-based reform is to raise standards and accountability in the K–12 system of schools. It is supported by the state-by-state call for standards, benchmarks, and annual testing in the No Child Left Behind Act.

Stating the objective: Second step in a Direct Instruction lesson; teachers tell their students what they will know or be able to do at the end of the lesson.

Strand: A subtopic used to organize a subject. It comes between a standard and benchmarks. For example, the language arts may be divided into several strands, such as reading, writing, listening, speaking, viewing, and visually representing. In some documents, strands are referred to as topics.

Stretching exercises: Part of the Synectics model of teaching; may be used to provide students unfamiliar with working with analogies or metaphors an opportunity to practice them before beginning the stages of Synectics. Analogies are drawn in isolation.

Study print: Large photographs related to instructional units. Although study prints are typically used in social studies, they may be used across the curriculum as appropriate.

Summarizing: Reciprocal Teaching process in which readers might engage in tasks such as sequencing ideas, making inferences, or synthesizing information as they read texts. These summaries are then provided to other group members.

Summative assessment: An assessment typically used at the end of a unit of instruction; often includes such tools as unit tests, portfolios of student work, final projects, and state-mandated assessment instruments. These tools are traditionally used to determine grades or report summary information.

Synectics: Model formulated by William Gordon for developing creative thinking capacity. Individuals work with metaphors and analogies as they create, invent, or solve problems.

Task analysis: Breaking down a long-term objective into sequential daily lesson objectives. Task analysis is also used to describe the process of breaking down the steps needed to teach a single skill or lesson objective and then sequencing each step to support student mastery.

Taxonomy: A way of categorizing mental tasks. These can be hierarchical (Bloom's taxonomy) or organized by levels of control (Marzano's taxonomy).

Teacher-proof curriculum: Pejorative characterization of curriculum and teaching materials, such as teacher's manuals, that prescribe what teachers will say and do during lessons.

Text-based advance organizer: Type of advance organizer that conveys information primarily through the use of text. This text could be a written passage designed specifically for the occasion or one selected from sources such as newspapers, magazines, or books.

Think aloud: A modeling process in which teachers literally tell students what they are thinking as they engage in a task. Think alouds in Direct Instruction lessons are modeled by the teacher or by capable students.

Topic: A subdivision used to organize a subject. It comes between a standard and benchmarks. For example, the language arts may be divided into several topics, such as reading, writing, listening, speaking, viewing, and visually representing. In some documents, topics are referred to as strands.

Transmission models of teaching: Traditional models of teaching, such as lecture or Direct Instruction, in which knowledge is imparted explicitly to students.

Unguided inquiry: Form of the Inquiry-Based Learning model in which teachers ask the initial question, provide materials, and organize the initial processes. Teachers then ask the students to design their own subsequent investigations and choose their own materials.

Unit topic: Content focus of a unit.

V-A-K-T presentation of content: Presenting lesson content through a visual (V), auditory (A), kinesthetic (K), or tactile (T) approach or some combination. Individual students may be visual, auditory, kinesthetic, or tactile learners. Teachers should model lesson content in as many of these ways as appropriate during lessons.

Visual advance organizer: Type of advance organizer that conveys information primarily through photographs, charts, or other visual modes.

Wait time: Time that teachers give students to process questions and to think about their answers. Wait time increases the likelihood that more students will participate in a lesson. Teachers will generally wait until many hands are up before asking for a choral response or calling on individual students.

Whole child: Applied to education that addresses the cognitive, affective, and psycho-motor needs of students.

Index

About the Authors

Jeanine M. Dell'Olio is Professor of Education at Hope College in Holland, Michigan. She teaches courses in curriculum and methods and foundations of education. She was a classroom teacher for 11 years in Los Angeles and New York City, working with students from kindergarten through ninth grade in both general education and special education classrooms. Prior to working as a teacher educator at the college level, she served as a teacher specialist for the New York City Teacher Centers Consortium. She has presented papers and published on such topics as reflective practice, preservice and inservice supervision, and professional development. Her most recent publications were in *Finding Our Way: Reforming Teacher Education in the Liberal Arts Setting* (Mezeske & Mezeske, 2004). In 1998, she received the H.O.P.E. (Hope Outstanding Professor Educator) Award for excellence in teaching.

Tony Donk is Professor of Education at Hope College in Holland, Michigan. He teaches courses in educational psychology and literacy. Previously he was a classroom teacher for 17 years, working with students from first grade through middle school. He has presented widely at local, state, national, and international conferences. His research interests are teacher decision making and the teaching of writing. He has also worked extensively with classroom teachers engaged in professional development activities related to literacy learning and teaching. His most recent publication was a chapter in *Finding Our Way: Reforming Teacher Education in the Liberal Arts Setting* (Mezeske & Mezeske, 2004).